The Experience of Old Age

The Experience of Old Age

Stress, Coping, and Survival

Morton A. Lieberman
Sheldon S. Tobin

Basic Books, Inc., Publishers　　　　　　　New York

51836   #9281048

HQ
1064
U5
L54
1983

Library of Congress Cataloging in Publication Data

Lieberman, Morton A., 1931-
    The experience of old age.

    Bibliography: p. 420
    Includes index.
    1.   Aged—United States—Psychology.
2.   Stress (Psychology).   3.   Relocation (Housing)—
United States.   4.   Death—Psychological aspects.
5.   Adaptability (Psychology).   I.   Tobin, Sheldon S.
II.   Title.   [DNLM: 1.   Aged—Psychology.   2.   Stress,
Psychological—In old age.   3.   Adaptation,
Psychological—In old age.   WT 150 L716e]
HQ1064.U5L54   1983   305.2′6   82-72401
ISBN 0-465-02170-0

To our wives,

Mariann and Maureen,

with whom we look forward

to sharing the enriching experiences

of our own old age

Contents

List of Tables and Figures

x

List of Tables and Figures

Acknowledgments

The four studies that make up the basis of this book could not have existed without the numerous and important contributions of many students and colleagues. We would like to thank Roberta Marlowe, who served as the project director for the Death of an Institution study and who contributed to developing the methods required to study that particular population. We would also like to acknowledge the help of Darrell Slover, project director of the Deinstitutionalized Elites study, and that of David Miller, who performed a similar role for the Unwilling Old Ladies study. A large number of students worked with us over the years in developing measures and concepts, and to them we owe a debt that goes beyond the usual faculty-student relationship. Gratitude is due to all of them: David Chiriboga, Annie Coplan, Gloria Edelhart, Elizabeth Etigson, Jacqueline Falk, James Gorney, Herbert Haberland, Joseph Kuypers, Alan Pincus, Valencia Prock, Virginia Revere, Arthur Rosner, Diana Slaughter, Barbara Turner, and Leonard Untenberger.

Our efforts were made possible by grants from the National Institute of Child Health and Human Development, the Department of Mental Health of the State of Illinois, and the Department of Mental Health of the State of California. A USPHS Research Career Development Award, and subsequently a Research Scientist Award to Morton A. Lieberman, made it possible for the senior author to devote the necessary time and effort to these studies. During much of the work, our students were supported by a training grant from the National Institute of Child Health and Human Development and later the National Institute on Aging to the Committee on Human Development at the University of Chicago.

Ann Erickson is to be thanked for her perseverance and skill in translating illegible script into understandable text through countless revisions. And finally we would like to thank Powell Lawton and Rudolph Moos, who provided perceptive feedback on chapter 5, and Bernice Neugarten, who performed a similar function for chapter 13.

Part 1

PROBLEMS AND METHODS

1

Stress in the Aged: Concepts and Issues

Overview

ONE YEAR after 639 elderly people changed their living arrangements, one-half were dead, physically impaired, or psychologically deteriorated. Using life as a laboratory, this book seeks to determine why relocation constitutes such a profound crisis in the lives of the elderly—and why some are able to adapt successfully whereas others fail in the face of circumstances that clearly pose a stress for all. Our search for the sources of individual differences in adaptation provides new insights on development in the later years as well as new ways of understanding adaptation to stress regardless of age.

The psychology of old age is often synonymous with the study of crises that alter the elderly's social world and psychological milieu. Retirement, economic changes, widowhood, alterations in family constellation, numerous signals that the body and the mind are not functioning as well as they previously did, frank physical illness, and the increasing sense of personal finitude have all been considered within a stress perspective. These conditions have become the benchmarks of the last decade or two of life; they are the filters through which investigators examine what it means to grow old, as well as what is necessary to age successfully. We examine in this book the effects of three specific age-associated crises: adaptational chal-

3

lenges generated by life-space changes due to relocation, losses, and the increasing certainty that life is terminating.

Under what conditions and for whom are changes in life space, loss, and impending death experienced as crises? What kinds of circumstances determine maladaptive consequences? Are all aged people equally affected by such ubiquitous life events, or, if not, can we identify particular characteristics of people that affect their ability to handle stress? Everyday observations suggest that we can always point to some individuals who flourish and grow under a given stress, others who appear to stay sufficiently "on top of" a situation that they are not seriously affected, and still others who cannot cope and who deteriorate psychologically and physically. What characteristics of people and of their social surrounds enable some people to overcome the trials and tribulations of overwhelming life crises? Why, in short, do some old people make it while others do not?

Our goal, then, is to examine psychological and social conditions that may explain individual differences among the elderly in adaptation to stress. Basic to much of our work is the view that a reasonable understanding of stress adaptation among the elderly can be achieved only through an understanding of what we might call a "life stage–specific" psychology. We believe the models used to understand the psychology of the elderly, and particularly their adaptive processes, have all too frequently relied only on schemata developed in studying the young. Our approach, therefore, not only incorporates elements from the large body of previous work on adaptation to stress among younger people but also focuses on issues uniquely characteristic of later life. Through this admixture, we hope, as this book unfolds, to demonstrate that to adequately understand the psychology of the elderly, new theoretical constructs are necessary. In turn, these constructs can shed light on the general phenomenon of adaptation to stress.

Four relocation studies form the empirical basis of our inquiry. Over an eight-year period we conducted a series of studies of elderly people undergoing major environmental changes and found that a significant proportion were adversely affected by such relocations. In two of the four studies, the relocated elderly were mentally and physically comparable to samples of aged residing in the community; in the other two, the subjects of our research were or had been mentally ill. The range of physical and psychological characteristics among the elderly in the four studies was considerable, as it was for the relocation conditions.

In the initial investigation, the "Unwilling Old Ladies" study, 45 physically healthy and psychologically intact elderly women were forced to move from a single small institution to a large, rather impersonal institu-

4

tion for the aged. In the second, the "Home for Life" study, 85 community-dwelling older people voluntarily entered homes for the aged, partly for physical and partly for social needs. In a third study, of "Deinstitutionalized Elites," a group of 82 geriatric mental hospital patients were discharged from a highly selective geriatric unit to a variety of community-based institutional and semi-institutional settings. In the final investigation, the "Death of an Institution" study, a population of 427 geriatric patients was relocated from a state mental hospital to a variety of other institutional settings after an administrative decision was made to close the hospital. The third and fourth studies differed from each other in that, although both involved mental hospital patients, the former group were all selected, physically healthy "therapeutic discharges," while the patients in the latter study consisted of the total population of a state mental hospital, including individuals who were both physically and mentally deteriorated as well as patients who could have been discharged (for therapeutic purposes) to community residency.

All four studies shared a common design. Predictors of adaptation were assessed before relocation, and the effects of stress were assessed afterward. This common design provides an opportunity to replicate the prediction of the consequences of stress across studies. To the extent that the same pre-relocation characteristics predict post-relocation adaptation, strong support emerges for their critical role in adaptation. A common predictor framework was thus developed for relocation in general and was equally applicable to all four studies. Before discussing the framework, we offer some comments on the organization of this book.

The report of our findings is divided into four main parts. Part 1 covers the common conceptual framework, the research design, and the settings and people involved in the studies. Part 2 examines the sources of stress; Part 3, the predictors of adaptation to stress, drawing on psychological and social characteristics that are common to persons of all ages. Part 4 develops a psychology of the aging, wherein predictors of adaptation are specific to the last decade or two of life.

Following the three introductory chapters, chapter 4 considers threat and loss as sources of stress; and chapter 5 focuses on adaptational challenges caused by environmental change. The three chapters that follow directly examine predictors of success and failure in adaptation. Chapter 6 considers strategies to cope with threat and loss; chapter 7, personal resources and ego functions; and chapter 8, personality dispositions. The wide diversity of factors studied is for us a distinctive feature of our investigation: Rather than seeking to prove that a particular dimension predicts adaptation, we, for the most part, inquire about the relative importance of different predictors. Chapter 9 focuses on a crisis unique to the elderly: approaching death. Then, in chapters 10, 11, and 12, we propose and explore a predictive framework for crisis adaptation based on a psychology of the elderly. In chapter 10 the task of maintaining self-consistency and identity is examined; in chapter 11, the relationship of oneself to one's personal past (reminiscence); and in chapter 12, the projection of the self into the future (hope).

After completing the twelve chapters we step back from our findings and from our interpretations of them in the preceding chapters and provide, in the final chapter (chapter 13), integrative speculations on the nature of stress and of old age.

A Conceptual Framework

We have organized our thinking about people under stress into a series of interrelated questions which provide a framework for examining characteristics of people and situations relevant to predicting differences in adaptation to crises. What will be portrayed in this framework is a series of interrelated and overlapping "templates" for examining individual differences. Figure 1–1 provides a schematic overview of the predictive framework used throughout this book.

As shown in figure 1–1, nine areas of predictions are represented by the nine chapters (chapters 4 through 12) that contain the findings of the investigation. Dimensions representing each area are examined for their linkage to stress reactions and long-term outcomes (mortality, morbidity, and psychological disability). The major predictive relationships examined are shown in the diagram by arrows. For example, Threat and Loss are hypothesized to predict outcomes through the major mediation of management strategies; in contrast, Adaptational Challenges are thought to directly affect outcome. Likewise, approaching death is linked to age-specific issues.

STUDYING THE SOURCES OF STRESS

As indicated in the left-hand side of figure 1–1, we begin by assessing the sources, as well as the intensity, of the stress to which the elderly in our studies were exposed in the course of relocation. We have set as a goal the determination of sources of stress, recognizing that although stressor

FIGURE 1–1

Predictor Framework

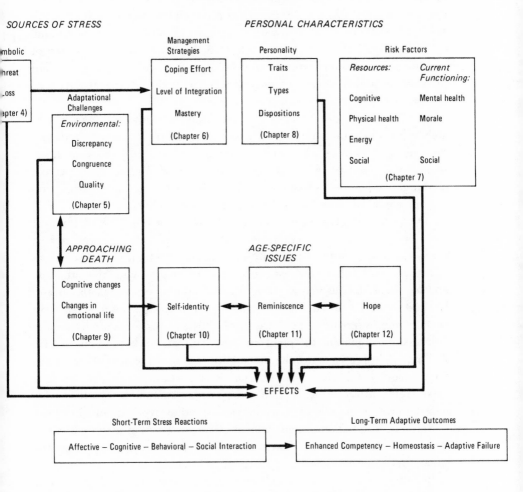

SOURCES OF STRESS

mbolic

reat

.oss

pter 4)

PERSONAL CHARACTERISTICS

Management Strategies

Personality

Risk Factors

Adaptational Challenges

Environmental:

Discrepancy

Congruence

Quality

(Chapter 5)

Coping Effort

Level of Integration

Mastery

(Chapter 6)

Traits

Types

Dispositions

(Chapter 8)

Resources: *Current Functioning:*

Cognitive   Mental health

Physical health   Morale

Energy

Social   Social

(Chapter 7)

APPROACHING DEATH

Cognitive changes

Changes in emotional life

(Chapter 9)

AGE-SPECIFIC ISSUES

Self-identity

(Chapter 10)

Reminiscence

(Chapter 11)

Hope

(Chapter 12)

EFFECTS

Short-Term Stress Reactions

Affective – Cognitive – Behavioral – Social Interaction

Long-Term Adaptive Outcomes

Enhanced Competency – Homeostasis – Adaptive Failure

and stress response are theoretically distinct, it is often empirically impossible to distinguish the two. We will look at the stress occasioned by relocation in terms of both its symbolic properties (chapter 4) and the adaptive challenges it poses (chapter 5). These represent two distinct models for explaining why certain conditions are stressful.

Although the course of human life can be conceived as a series of events or situations that require adaptive effort, and almost every type of event and situation has been examined for its potential stress, little consensus exists regarding the most appropriate model for understanding the nature of stress. Confusion reigns, in large part, because the term *stress* has been used alternatively to refer to an event or situation that causes disequilibrium; to the processes involved in coping with the disequilibrium; and, finally, to the reactions to the disequilibrium and the long-range outcomes. Although many investigators have examined stressors, coping, and adaptation, it is not easy to delineate the boundaries of this area of inquiry. Stress, in contemporary psychology, is so broadly conceived and so variously studied that it is difficult to conceptualize it as a distinct area of inquiry.

Such conceptual differences in approaching the study of stress immediately raise the question whether existing empirical studies, considering their massive number and variety, have in fact examined the same questions. Is the investigator who is interested in how well a person adapts to a seemingly benign new situation—be it the Peace Corps, kindergarten, college, or a new job—exploring the same issues as one who studies people in unanticipated circumstances, such as the parents of fatally ill children or the victims of natural disasters or early widowhood? Some researchers focus exclusively on the situation itself, referring to their investigations as "stress studies"; others address the process of dealing with the situation, and see themselves as investigating, for example, appraisals of threat and loss and strategies for coping with them; a third group examines reactions or outcomes, referring to "culture shock" to "survival in captivity," or to "successful adaptation to spinal cord injury." Still others, such as Erik Erikson (1959), refer to developmental crises in terms of resolutions: Thus, the developmental crisis of adolescence is viewed as the crisis of "identity versus role diffusion." An emphasis on one or another of the three elements, however, is invariably accompanied, either explicitly or implicitly, by references to the other two elements. The consensus of investigations in the field is that the study of stress or crisis must encompass all three: the situation, coping processes, and adaptational outcomes.

Investigators differ in their classifications of events and situations that are stressful. Coehlo, Hamburg, and Adams (1974) distinguish between situational stresses and developmental crises; however, a third kind of stress—chronic stress—can be inferred from their compilations of studies.

Furthermore, there is a basic division between theorists who focus on the symbolic meaning of a potentially stressful situation or event and those who consider the amount of adaptive challenge—the "life change" per se—as the source of stress. Even among those who rely on meaning as the primary issue in stress research there is wide diversity in the specific theoretical framework applied. Lazarus (1966) focuses on appraisals of threat as a proximate cause of stress; in contrast, Janis (1958) emphasizes

8

the unconscious meanings of stressful events or situations as well as transference relationships emanating from early development.

INVESTIGATIONAL ISSUES

We are studying adaptive processes under conditions of high stress rather than in response to the pressures of everyday life. One advantage of this strategy is that it limits the response repertoire to be observed. Crises are events that elicit in the person subjective experiences of loss and the absence of control, and demand that one adjust his or her behavior to a new set of circumstances. The advantages of studying high-stress circumstances are obvious; not so apparent may be the conceptual dilemmas they pose. Is it reasonable to assume that the ability to adapt to the stresses and strains of everyday life is related to the ability to adapt to extreme situations? Does the individual who is able to adapt successfully to the exigencies of combat, for example, use the same processes with relatively the same degree of success to cope with more common transitional crises, such as parenthood? In other words, are the same traits and qualities of equivalent value in all stressful situations?

Most of those events considered crises are of two major types: (1) events involving loss—a subjective experience associated with a break in previous attachments to persons, places, or things; and (2) situations that disrupt the customary modes of behavior of the people concerned, that alter both their circumstances and their plans and impose a need for strenuous psychological work. Both kinds of events present the individual with the obligation (and the opportunity) to abandon many assumptions and to replace them with others, thereby constituting a challenge. Although analytically distinct, in real life they are usually inextricably intertwined. Perhaps the best example of their interdependence can be found in studies of reaction to widowhood.

In any bereavement, it is seldom clear what exactly is lost. The loss of a husband, for instance, may or may not mean the loss of the sexual partner, companion, accountant, gardener, baby minder, audience, bedwarmer, and so on, depending on particular roles normally being performed by the husband. Moreover, one loss often brings other secondary losses in its train. The loss of a husband is usually accompanied by a considerable drop in income, and this often means that the widow must sell her house, give up her job, and move to a strange environment. The need to learn new roles without the support of the person upon whom one has come to rely, at a time when others in the family, especially children, are themselves bereaved and needing support, can place a major burden on a woman over and above the fact of bereavement itself.

Apart from grief, two other facts that always play a part in determining the overall reaction to bereavement are stigma and deprivation. By stigma is meant the change in attitude that takes place in the society when a person dies. Every widow discovers that people who were previously friendly and approachable become embarrassed and estranged in their presence. Expressions of sympathy often have a hollow ring and offers of help are not followed up. It often happens that only those who share the grief or have themselves suffered a major loss remain at hand. It is as if the widow has become painted with death in much the same way as the funeral director (Parkes 1972).

Deprivation refers to the absence of the necessary person or thing, as opposed to the loss of that person or thing (including, for example, the absence of those essential supplies that were previously provided by the lost person). A bereaved person reacts to both loss and deprivation. Even in such a clear situation as bereavement, then, the nature of the stress or crisis is complex and involves not only the loss of a significant other, but also numerous other sources of stress or strain requiring adaptive behavior.

MEASURING THE LEVEL OF STRESS

Most human stress studies outside of the laboratory do not confront the issue of *stress intensity* directly. Intensity has been looked at on the basis of a "life change index," which assumes that the amount of stress a person experiences is related to the number of life change units within a particular period of time. But more often than not, investigators assume that they have chosen an event, situation, or condition that is of sufficiently high stress that all those who encounter it can be considered exposed to a potential stressor; individual differences in adaptation are seen as a function of the characteristics of the person or the situation.

It is easy to understand why most human stress studies do not address the intensity of the stressor (except in laboratory conditions, where experimental manipulation of intensity is possible). The measurement problems of independently assessing stress intensity without recourse to appraisal of intensity or to the consequences of the stressor on behavior or on psychological or physiological states are difficult. Furthermore, the impact of a stress is sometimes more a function of the appraisal of the stress (or of its intensity) than of the characteristics of the stress. Thus, although some investigations have examined environmental stressors such as noise level and population density as potential independent variables in accounting for stress response, a recent review by Cohen (1980) suggests that cognitive or perceptual conditions rather than the objective intensity of the noise or population density is much more relevant in predicting responses to such stress.

One approach is to assume that intensity of experienced stress depends upon the degree to which an individual is required to make new adaptations associated with environmental change. We explore three strategies for measuring the intensity of stress engendered by adaptational challenges: (1) environmental discrepancy, the degree of difference between the initial and subsequent environments; (2) environmental congruence, the "fit" between the demands of a particular environment and the person's characteristic modes of behaving; and (3) environmental quality, inherent aspects of the environment considered without regard to the person or the previous setting. High stress is associated with large discrepancies between pre- and post-relocation environments; low correspondence between a person's characteristic behavior and the new demands of the relocation environment; and "poor-quality" environments.

Although the conception of stress as proportional to the amount of adaptive challenge present lends itself to a more adequate appraisal of stress levels, we did attempt to "independently" assess the stress levels engendered by the threat that relocation posed for our respondents.

The degree of anticipated as well as experienced threat and loss was assessed through direct questions about the impending relocation, through indirect measures of the degree to which the person was embedded in a meaningful social network (we assumed that a high degree of embeddedness implied high loss), and through projective measures of early memory themes. Threat themes were also assessed through a discrepancy measure based upon cognitive performance in response to two sets of TAT (Thematic Apperception Test) cards, the standard Murray set and a specially constructed TAT depicting older people in situations associated with moving to an institution, or with aspects of the new environment assumed to be problematic. The respondent's cognitive ability to deal with the Institutional TAT cards was compared with his ability to deal with the Murray series of TAT cards; poor performance in the former was interpreted to indicate high threat. Finally, groups of elderly not in the hypothesized threatening situation were contrasted on measures of cognitive, social, and emotional functions with respondents hypothesized to be in threatening circumstances.

THREAT AND LOSS MANAGEMENT STRATEGIES

Threat and loss management strategies represent specific personal characteristics that directly index what someone does in response to a potentially harmful event that will occur in the future. Our interest in examining such strategies is of course linked to one of the two major perspectives explored on the source of stress, the symbolic meanings associated with relocation.

In studying strategies, our attempt is to separate the processes the person brought to bear in managing threat from the intensity of the threat itself. Although obviously intertwined, analytic methods were developed that could, in part, distinguish the coping procedures from the intensity of the threat and loss.

In looking at specific threat and loss management strategies, we asked a series of questions: To what degree does the individual attempt to master the threat? To what degree has he or she succumbed to the threat? What coping or defense strategies did the person bring to bear in managing the threat situation? Did the individual, for example, deny or shut out of awareness the impending event, as contrasted with what has been called a "working-through process"? Some, but not complete overlap exists among management strategies and general personality dispositions—between, for example, the tendency to use denial as a way of handling most problems that might be anticipated. The difference is, of course, that general personality dispositions are unrelated to particular events, whereas management of a threat is specifically tied to the person's attempts to handle a particular anticipated crisis and the attendant current psychological state subsumed under the word *threat*.

PERSONALITY

How does a person typically cope with crises? Personality dispositions represent generalized characteristics of people based on past behavior in contrast to threat and loss management, strategies that represent responses linked to a specific situation. Individuals differ widely in their preferred coping modes. These differences among people suggest that predictions of adaptation must take into account variations in the personal process or styles which people bring into play under crisis conditions. We inquire about how the individual deploys his or her resources and acts upon himself or herself and the surrounding world when accommodations to crisis conditions must be made.

The underlying assumption is that previous behavior is a valid indicator of the strategies a person is likely to apply in meeting a future crisis. In general, a person's relevant past responses tend to be the best predictors of future behavior in similar situations. Such a perspective, of course, implies that reasonable continuity of personality exists, so that future crises are likely to elicit the same response pattern a person has used in the past.

More generally, we have studied a variety of personality traits—generalized dispositions to behave in particular ways—as well as several personality characteristics hypothesized to be crucial in crisis management. Among the traits assessed were dominance, submissiveness, and narcissism. These generalized dispositions are predictions about what resources and what process a person might activate in managing a crisis situation; they do not provide information on how the person will manage a specific crisis.

RESOURCES

Our framework shares many common elements with investigators who have considered stress, stress appraisal, coping and adaptation. Like them, our attempt to understand individual differences requires an examination of the kind and level of resources that individuals can bring to bear in a crisis or stress situation. Individuals differ in their psychological and biological resources; when confronted with situations that require major adaptative effort, differences in success may depend upon the resources available to the person. Usable resources available to a person set limits on the processes the person can employ for coping. This orientation implies, therefore, that there is no point in examining a process such as threat appraisal without examining whether the person has the cognitive resources required to appraise the situation. The inability of a person to differentiate among environmental stimuli limits his or her ability to assess the possible constraints and opportunities within the environment, thus limiting the range of coping strategies he or she is likely to develop. Or, to cite another example, before asking about various consequences of different coping or defense strategies, we would need to know something about the capacity of the person to mobilize energy.

The linkage between capacities and adaptation to stress is usually described by two interrelated concepts: ego strength and impulse control. Ego strength is used as an indicator of capacity for perceiving external reality. It reflects the ability to integrate internal needs and external reality so that the executive capacities of the ego are freed for coping with demanding events. Conceptually related to ego strength is impulse control, which has been used to characterize the level of coping ability. It is usually assumed that those individuals who have arrived at higher levels of cognitive development as assessed by impulse control capacity have more resources for coping with stressors in the environment. Our approach has been to fractionate these two rather broad concepts into more specific functions that serve as underpinnings of ego strength. We studied four basic variables: cognitive capacity, physical health, available energy, and social supports available to the individual.

The ability to take in, process, organize, store, and recall complex information; to orient oneself in time and place; and to accomplish cognitive shifts are probably all abilities that are required to appraise threat accurately and realistically so that coping strategies can be organized and carried out. In this sense, the level of cognitive functioning probably sets a floor or lower limit on coping. Poor cognitive functioning should be related to inability to adapt to stress; adequate cognitive functioning would not, on the other hand, ensure adequate coping. Age decrements in the rate of processing information, however, suggest that for old people cognitive capacity would become central in the ability to adapt to stress.

Health status is not ordinarily considered in most human stress studies. Those who have considered psychological functioning in response to stress adaptation have viewed adaptation in relation to specific psychological mechanisms, or they have examined adaptation relative to differences in physiological types. How the physical status of the individual affects or is affected by psychological processes is still, after so many years, an open question. In the area of aging, however, one can hardly ignore the question of physical capacity. The ability to maintain physical integrity is rapidly exhausted as the organism ages. Although we may not understand the processes, it seems reasonable to assume that the physical capacities of the aged set limits on their ability to adapt. Previous findings, such as those of Birren et al. (1963), suggest that although psychological and social functions are largely unrelated to somatic functioning in relatively healthy aged people, they do make a difference when some critical limiting level of physical capacity is reached. Like cognitive functioning, physical capacity is seen in our framework as a limiting condition. For the older person who is relatively adequate in physical capacity, the question of predicting the effects of stress must be considered in terms of other, more complex variables. At the lower limits, physical capacity for older people may be the most important and perhaps the only salient predictor of adaptive failure.

Popular conceptions of the aging process assume diminished energy during the last phase of life. Such a simple observation may, of course, relate to several perhaps more discrete aspects of the aging process: It may reflect, for example, actual decrease in physical energy or the increase in depressive affect that so often accompanies aging. As a psychological concept, energy has been primarily employed in psychoanalytic theory. The concept of psychological energy has been varyingly fashionable in psychology, possibly because it has been peculiarly unresponsive to measurement. Despite the serious limitations in appropriate technology, measures have been developed to assess this potentially important aspect of human functioning in relation to stress adaptation.

Increasingly, investigators interested in stress and adaptation have turned their attention to the role of social resources or supports in mitigating the occurrence of stressful circumstances, as well as the effect of stress on maladaptive consequences (Cobb 1976; Gore 1978; Heller 1978; Kaplan, Cassel, and Gore 1977; Lin et al. 1979; Pinneau 1976). We assessed respondents' perception of meaningful others' availability and their willingness to offer emotional as well as task-relevant support.

In our model, all four of these functions are assumed to have negative rather than positive predictive value. Thus, limitation in any one of these capacities would, we expect, be associated with unsuccessful adaptation, but sufficient capacity would not necessarily predict success.

ASSESSING CURRENT FUNCTIONING

Predictions about ability to cope with future stress are facilitated by knowledge of how well an individual functions in the absence of extreme stress, since such information affords additional clues about resources possessed. The assessment of how well someone ordinarily functions in turn requires information about whether his or her current environment is basically harmonious or stressful. The contextual issue becomes clearer if we look at the various forms that responses to the question of how well a person is functioning may take.

The concept of psychological health offers one general framework in which to evaluate overall functioning. In order to make such an assessment of our elderly respondents, individual differences in psychological health and maladjustment were assessed using the Block Q-Sort (1961). This measure is akin in many ways to the concept of ego strength, which has been found by many investigators to be a proven predictor of stress coping capacity. The items in the Q-Sort represent a wide range of feelings, attitudes, interpersonal characteristics, symptoms, and moods. Underlying these various behavioral variables are the essential ingredients of a concept of psychological health which involves impulse control, flexibility, the ability to form meaningful relationships to other human beings, a positive view of oneself and others, and the absence of incapacitating symptoms. Several other indices were used to obtain an assessment of the individual's mental health. Measures of anxiety and of depression have been shown by several investigators to be relatively precise indicators of current functioning as well as predictors of future adaptation to crisis. Behavioral indices of pathology offered yet another perspective on mental health.

No matter how broadly the concept of mental health is defined, it certainly does not offer the only possible perspective for assessing how well people are doing. Many investigators contend that the most reasonable way of assessing how well a person is functioning at any given time is to ask him or her. The concepts of gratification or satisfaction and the related concepts of happiness and positive self-view were, therefore, also operationalized in our assessment procedures.

A third approach to examining how well an individual is functioning is to look at the extent, range, and quality of his or her interpersonal relationships. It should be emphasized that both the nature of the person's interpersonal relationships and the level of happiness and self-esteem are in general ways included in the more comprehensive concept of psychological health. Thus one would expect overlap but not identity among these different assessment perspectives.

A Life-Stage Perspective on Processes of Adaptation

DISTANCE FROM DEATH

We begin the exploration of a developmental perspective on stress adaptation by looking at one potential stressor: nearness to death. The increasing certainty in the seventh and eighth decades of life that one is approaching the end of life was an event common to all the elderly we studied. To what extent approaching death constituted a crisis and to what degree it functioned as an organizing concern in the minds of those affected were, for us, the key issues. A strategy, based on psychological changes associated with death, was developed. Using this strategy, we raise a series of questions concerning the interaction of distance from death with external stressors as well as psychological reorganization, involving self-identity, reminiscence, and hope.

The framework we have so far presented for examining those personal characteristics, resources, and strategies that permit some individuals to respond to stress successfully while others fail is, for the most part, age-irrelevant. As the results of our study unfold throughout this book, it will become clear that some of the characteristics associated with such a framework must of necessity take the age of our respondents into account. Where appropriate, in the chapters that follow, such considerations will, or course, be underscored. However, such observations do not by themselves constitute a developmental perspective on the adaptation process. There exists another tradition within the field of aging that places at the center of the investigator's interest aspects of the psychology of those individuals in the last two decades of life and ask questions that are specific to such a psychological perspective. As investigators, part of our effort was illuminated by such thinking, and we gave attention to specific psychological issues confronting the elderly that we thought would be relevant to the adaptational process.

THE SELF—PRESENT, PAST, AND FUTURE

We see the elderly as confronting several critical issues during the last decade or two of life, issues that are inherent in the aging process. The first involves how one maintains a sense of self-consistency despite the obvious, externally induced changes that are part and parcel of being old in our society. The maintenance of a consistent self-concept is a task that engages all elderly people. It is a task that some meet successfully and others do not; that engages some in useful, life-enhancing strategies, while others invoke potentially self-destructive mechanisms. We believe that how one maintains and whether one does maintain self-consistency is at the center of understanding how well a person can confront any stress condition in the late stages of life.

Another task at this stage of life, one that has been described by novelists as well as social scientists, concerns relationships to one's past life. The unique perspective on the past characteristic of aging, presumably elicited by the addressing of personal mortality, has for many theoreticians made the definition of a person's relationship to personal past a core or central task of late life. As with our concern with self-consistency, we believe that how individuals address their historical self—how well it is integrated into current life—is a useful indication of how well they can respond to any and all crises or stresses in their life; for crisis situations confront the self with psychological work to be done. Being able to address these issues, then, is critical for adaptation. In fact, it may in some sense be taken as synonymous with the capacity for successful adaptation.

The last life-stage issue that we we wish to address here, which in some sense may simply be the converse of the "reminiscence" question, is the extension of the self into the future, which again seems particularly relevant to the last decade or two of life. It has been expressed in a number of theoretical terms; we have chosen the construct "hope" to explore this issue. Because of the particular position the elderly occupy in our society and because their time is increasingly limited, it would seem that facing the future—realistically and positively—is a crucial task.

Measuring the Effects of Stress

If the sources of stress represent "inputs," at the other end are the consequences of stress—that is, the degree of success or failure in adaptation. Just as stress itself and the sources of stress are conceived and defined differently by different investigators, so are there variations in the conceptualization, classification, and measurement of responses to stressors. Two major approaches are apparent.

Some investigators assess adaptive processes using such concepts as mastery and competence. People respond to the demands created by an event or situation by meeting them at a level above that which they had heretofore achieved. A study of children entering school for the first time illustrates this approach. Successful adaptation is viewed in terms of the child's ability to meet the demands of the situation by employing behaviors that may not have been in his or her repertoire before. Thus, children entering school must "learn" new mechanisms to cope with a more complex social system—to relate to larger groups of people, to deal with peers and unfamiliar adults, and so forth. Competence implies more than the ability not to break down (regress, withdraw, be emotionally upset). Investigation emphasizes the identification of behaviors that were not previously in the individual's repertoire.

In the second major approach, adaptation is assessed by measuring the absence of breakdown. Are the demands of the new condition met without showing signs of psychological distress or functional inability (such as regression, withdrawal, or emotional upset)? The person is considered to adapt if he or she deals with a new set of demands by maintaining a homeostatic level.

This difference in perspective is particularly important to those interested in adult development, for it raises the question whether it is possible to develop unified concepts which allow fruitful investigation of adaptation over the life span. If adaptation has thus far been so diversely defined, can successful adaptation at different stages of life be compared? Can general criteria of coping adequacy be determined that allow different stages of life to be studied in a uniform way?

The approach that we employed in assessing effects is based on a homeostatic model, wherein departures or changes from baseline defined adaptive failures, and stability implied success. With respect to both short-term reactions and long-term adaptation, changes from before relocation to afterward were assessed in the areas of affect, cognitive functioning, and social interaction—that is, according to the criteria typically used to assess reactions to stress.

2

The Study Design

OUR INVESTIGATIONS of the elderly were based on the following assumptions:

1. That radical changes in living arrangements confront the vast majority of those aged who undergo the change with a stress of sufficient severity to seriously affect a significant portion of the sample.
2. That is was possible to study respondents prior to the stress—an important consideration, inasmuch as in many studies of "predictors of stress adaptation," individuals are examined only subsequent to the stress event, making it impossible to disentangle stress reactions from pre-stress characteristics.
3. That changes in life space contain the crucial elements involved in all stress situations, including both symbolic meanings, defined here in terms of threat and loss, and adaptational challenges.

The basic design in all four studies was similar. Respondents (and in two studies, matched controls) were initially examined up to a year prior to being relocated, providing baseline information for levels of adaptation as well as predictor information, and then were examined again within one year after environmental change. Although the techniques of measuring successful or unsuccessful adaptation to the crisis varied from study to study, all were directed toward answering the same question: To what extent, subsequent to being moved, did the person depart in major ways from his or her prior physiological, behavioral, and psychological status?

The analyses to be presented are derived from four major studies of elderly people who underwent radical changes in their life space. One of these studies included an examination of healthy elderly moving into top-quality institutional facilities; another involved sick, highly debilitated individuals moving into circumstances that would delight a muckraker. Two of the four studies examined aged people who were mentally and physically comparable to elderly samples living in the community; two involved populations of aged who had formerly been or were still mentally ill.

The range of psychological and physical resources among the 639 elderly who made up the four populations was considerable, as were the conditions under which the environmental changes occurred. In the initial study, the Unwilling Old Ladies, 45 physically healthy and psychologically robust women were studied when they were forced to move from a small, "hotel-like" institution to a larger, "quasi-military" institution for the aged. In the Home for Life study, 85 community-dwelling aged were studied as they voluntarily entered homes for the aged in order to meet their physical or social needs. In the Deinstitutionalized Elites study, a selected group of 82 geriatric patients was studied as they were prepared for discharge from a mental hospital to a variety of community-based institutional and semi-institutional settings. In the Death of an Institution study, we examined 427 geriatric patients who were relocated from a state mental hospital to a variety of other institutional settings. Although the last two studies both involved mental hospital patients, in the first case respondents were all physically healthy "therapeutic discharges," whereas the final study involved the total population of a state mental hospital, including both physically and mentally deteriorated individuals as well as others who were to be therapeutically discharged to community residences. Table 2–1 summarizes the features and findings of each study.

The Four Studies

THE UNWILLING OLD LADIES

A newspaper report of the planned closing of a home for the widows of veterans came to our attention. Inquiry led eventually to launching the Unwilling Old Ladies study. We focused in this initial study of 45 resi-

TABLE 2–1
The Four Studies

Study	Sample	Environments	Environmentally Related Assessments	Reaction to Relocation (not mutually exclusive)	Outcomes (mutually exclusive)
Unwilling Old Ladies	45 women: 42 widows, 3 never married; mean age = 78.1, range = 61–91; relocated when a soldiers' widows' home closed. Interviewed for 2–3 hours plus staff assessments 2 weeks prior to relocation. Follow-up: 6 weeks after relocation for reactions and 9 months for outcomes.	*Pre*-relocation: Small, self-contained, flexibly situated, and highly centralized facility. *Post*-relocation: Large, highly structured, complex, decentralized facility broken up into four living arrangements, splitting friendship groups.	No systematic assessments.	(6 weeks post-relocation) 27% physical change 14% cognitive change 38% interactive change 55% affective change	(9 months post-relocation) 23 (52%) deteriorated (including 4, 9%, deaths) 21 (46%) unchanged 1 (2%) improved
Home for Life	85 elderly (mean age = 80, range = 68–93) who voluntarily applied for admission to homes for the aged. Interviewed 12–16 hours in 4 to 6 sessions on the average about 4 months prior to relocation. Follow-up: 2 months after relocation for reactions and 1 year for outcomes. Control samples interviewed twice over a 1-year interval. (Community Control Sample: n = 35; Institutional Control Sample: n = 37.)	*Pre*-relocation: Of those on waiting list, 68 living had been living independently and 17 transitionally, in nursing homes. *Post*-relocation: 3 sectarian homes for the aged.	The three homes were assessed on 4 dimensions: public/private space; structured/unstructured social control; resource-sparse/resource-rich; isolated from/integrated with larger community. Also, "old-timers" used to identify characteristics presumed congruent with adaptive demands.	(2 months post-relocation) 32% physical change 26% cognitive change 14% interactive change 11% affective change	(1 year post-relocation) 41 (48%) deteriorated (including 15, 18%, deaths) 39 (46%) unchanged 5 (6%) improved

Deinstitutionalized Elites	82 elderly state mental hospital patients (mean age = 69.5, range 66–91) selected for discharge because of therapeutic potential. Interviewed for 2–3 hours plus staff assessments 2½ weeks prior to relocation. Follow-up: 15 weeks after relocation for reactions and 1 year for outcomes. Control sample, $n = 26$ interviewed twice before discharge over a 2½-month interval.	*Pre*-relocation: Therapeutic unit in state mental hospital. *Post*-relocation: 26 boarding houses and nursing homes.	Relocation environments assessed on 10 psychosocial aspects and ranking after observations and interviews (½-day), using 221 structured items. Also assessment of individuals on 7 needs related to the environmental aspects.	(15 weeks post-relocation) 9% physical change 18% cognitive change 31% interactive change 18% affective change	(1 year post-relocation) 40 (49%) deteriorated (including 2, 2%, deaths) 25 (30%) unchanged 17 (21%) improved
Death of an Institution	427 state mental hospital patients (mean age = 78, range 65–98) all relocated when hospital closed. Interview of 1 hour plus staff assessments 1 month pre-location. Follow-up: 1 year for outcome. Control sample $n = 100$ interviewed and then followed 1 year for outcome.	*Pre*-relocation: Units in state mental hospital. *Post*-relocation: 142 boarding houses and nursing homes.	Assessment of pre- and post-relocation environments using scales developed for previous study. Discrepancy between environment at Time 1 and Time 2.	Not done.	(1 year post-relocation) 237 (56%) deteriorated (including 78, 18%, deaths) 103 (24%) unchanged 87 (20%) improved

dents (mean age = 78.1, range = 61–91) on a few salient adaptational predictors, such as cognitive functioning, coping styles, and affective state. The major details are summarized in table 2–1. Data provided by the staff of the pre-relocation home were used to supplement respondent interviews. (Appendix A provides measurement details on this and other study samples.) Systematic assessments of environments were not made. Six weeks after relocation, reactions to relocation information were studied. Nine months after relocation, information used to assess outcomes was gathered.

HOME FOR LIFE

The cooperation of three sectarian homes for the aged in the Chicago area made it possible to launch an in-depth study of prospective residents while they were awaiting admission. (The Unwilling Old Ladies study served as a pre-test for this investigation.) Pre-relocation interviews ranged from twelve to sixteen hours, usually conducted in four to six separate sessions. Follow-up interviews and assessments of the eighty-five elderly (mean age = 80, range = 63–93) were conducted at two months (for reactions) and again at one year (for outcomes) after relocation. Two control samples were developed, one composed of thirty-seven selected residents who had been living in the three homes for one to three years and the other, of thirty-five community elderly who would apply to these homes if they needed institutional care. Both samples were followed over a one-year interval. Criteria for control samples, composition and demographic comparisons appear in appendix A.

DEINSTITUTIONALIZED ELITES

A newly developed therapeutic discharge program for elderly patients at a state mental hospital was the setting for the third study. This program afforded us the opportunity to investigate an important phenomenon in its own right: namely, the relocation of geriatric mental patients through selection, preparation, and careful placement. Our theoretical interest focused on the opportunity to more fully explore environmental change, fit, and quality as important sources of effects on adaptation—a line of inquiry initiated in the Home for Life study. The three relocation environments examined in the earlier study were quite similar (Pincus 1968); in contrast, in the Deinstitutionalized Elites study, the eighty-two patients were relocated to twenty-six distinct environmental settings. The Deinstitutionalized Elites study, involving 82 elderly (mean age = 69.5, range =

66–91), decidedly different from those in the previous two studies, permitted us to broaden the population base for testing our predictors of adaptation. We also studied controls for the effects of environmental change, using a delayed treatment design: Twenty-six patients who were delayed relocatees were interviewed twice over a two-and-one-half-month interval before their discharge into the community. All but six of the twenty-six became part of the study sample.

THE DEATH OF AN INSTITUTION

The impending phasing out of a state mental hospital in California was the setting for our fourth and final study, comprising 427 patients (mean age = 76, range = 65–98) who were relocated to 142 nursing homes and boarding houses. In this investigation we were able to apply both our predictor model as well as our hypotheses of environmental discrepancy, congruence, and quality in a sample of mental hospital patients who had not been selected for discharge because of their therapeutic potential. Assessments were made of pre- and post-relocation environments using the scales developed for the previous study of therapeutic discharges. A matched control sample of 100 state mental hospital elderly was developed from among patients in a different but comparable California state mental hospital and was followed over the corresponding one-year interval. (See appendix A for comparison of controls and relocatees.)

Comparisons Among the Studies

DESIGN COMMONALITIES

The four studies share characteristics beyond the relocation of elderly persons from one environment to another. In general, the transition was to nonindependent living, although the post-relocation setting was not always more "institutional" than the initial environment. Obviously, the selection of a nonindependent environment reflects a salient aspect of this population. Someone judged each of these elderly to need, or to function better in, such a setting. The soldiers' widows in the first study themselves chose a collective environment, most often to be with others and to have medical care readily accessible. Pre-location assessments pointed to psychological and self-care functioning comparable to that of elderly who live independently in the community and suggested that for these elderly, the home for soldiers' widows was similar to a retirement community rather than a more traditional institution. The old age homes in the Home for Life study were perceived by professionals as institutions from which care is sought only if necessitated by the inability to maintain independent living. However, many of the eighty-five elderly in this study sought care because of lack of social supports—they wanted to be with people, both for activities and for security—and today, with the development of alternatives to institutional care, would probably be less likely to seek admission to these kinds of sectarian facilities. The mental patients in the third and fourth studies were judged at some time in their life to be mentally incompetent to live independently.

In all four studies, information was collected directly from the elderly person in a face-to-face interview that included multiple response items, open-ended queries, and psychological tests, some of which were designed to assess manifest functions, attitudes, and stress, while others included projective tests used to assess latent levels of psychological functioning. Some respondents, however, particularly in the Death of an Institution study, were unable to respond to all but the simplest of mental status items and then only enough to permit us to assess their lack of orientation in time and place. Controlled time sampling observations provided the major data source in this study. Information about respondents was also gathered from staff members of pre- and post-relocation facilities in three of the four studies. (The Home for Life study respondents did not live, prior to relocation, in a communal environment.)

In each study, there was at least one follow-up assessment of outcome status after relocation. In the first study, externally imposed constraints required that post-relocation information be gathered nine months after relocation, whereas in the other studies the follow-up for outcome was conducted one year after relocation. Short-term reactions to relocation were assessed in all but the fourth study. In the Unwilling Old Ladies study, data to assess reactions to relocation were assessed six weeks after relocation; in the Home for Life study, two months afterward; and in the Deinstitutionalized Elites study, fifteen weeks afterward. For the assessment of reactions as well as outcomes, changes in four areas were measured: physical functioning, cognitive functioning, social interaction, and affective state.

COMMONALITIES IN RELOCATION AS A STRESS

The reader may wonder whether we are justified in bringing a common conceptual framework and a common set of questions to bear on such diverse settings. Is it reasonable to compare elderly Jews voluntarily entering homes for the aged, often for social reasons, with rural women being torn out of a comfortable environment and placed in a semimilitary setting? Is it reasonable to compare such populations with debilitated psychiatric patients, many of whom have spent their entire adult lives in the confines of back wards? How useful is our assumption that we can compare a highly select sample in a sophisticated geriatric community placement program with the total population of a mental hospital? In large part, the responses to these questions lie in the remainder of this book. However, before we move on, it may be useful to place the four relocation circumstances in a comparative context.

Marked changes in life space may occur for a variety of reasons and may be viewed by those undergoing such changes with a mixture of positive and negative feelings. Any real attempt to understand the processes involved in relocation and the effects such changes may have on those who undergo them must take into account the attitudes and expectations of the relocatees. Most of the respondents we studied had in common that they did not welcome their move; by and large, they were forced either by external circumstances or by self-perceived physical or other changes that signaled future problems. We have not addressed life space changes resulting, for example, from decisions to migrate to retirement communities—changes often seen as status gains by the people who initiate them. Thus, the four studies, despite their acknowledged diversity, do not represent the possible spectrum of relocations. Our studies address, rather, a limited range of possible relocations.

In general, studies of the relocation of the elderly focus on variations in attitudes and expectations that may account for the observed empirical differences in relocation effects. Investigators usually emphasize the critical role of the degree of perceived control in affecting outcomes of relocation. Thus our concern is with the similarities and differences among the four studies in the amount of perceived control and the degree to which the elderly viewed the impending move as positive or negative, welcome or painful. We must exclude the Death of an Institution study from this exploration; that study relied primarily on observational means for gathering information, and we did not have the interview data required to rate expectations. For the remaining three studies, the interview data were rated on a series of scales examining perceived control over relocation and expectations regarding the move to the new environment.

Two of the studies involved situations in which individuals were forced to move by circumstances totally beyond their control—the closing of an institution. In the other two studies, the reasons for relocation were more ambiguous. For the elderly who moved from community living to homes for the aged, it was the stated policy that only those who made affirmative decisions to enter would be admitted. In the elite sample of hospital patients selected from some 2,500 elderly, patients were given the opportunity to decline. In interviews with these three populations, the modal response expressed by the Home for Life sample was that they felt that they had had the major responsibility for the decision, although they might have been influenced by others or believed that they were required to consider the needs and opinions of others in making this decision. A fairly frequent response was that the person saw the decision as being made equally by themselves and by others. He or she "got together with the family" and decided that a move was necessary and desirable. Whatever the various sources of influence, the elderly respondent felt that he or she had made an important contribution to the decision.

In contrast, among the Unwilling Old Ladies sample the modal response was for the elderly woman to feel that she had neither control nor influence over the decision to be relocated. Some felt helpless ("I'll just have to do whatever they decide"); others were passive and accepting ("I'll do whatever they think is best").

Among the Deinstitutionalized Elites, the most frequent perception was that they influenced the decision in some small way: that either they were consulted or they had their interests taken into account. They believed that strong feelings on their part may have influenced the decision made.

Numerically, 12 percent of the Deinstitutionalized Elites felt that they had some real influence in the decision making; not one person in the Unwilling Old Ladies sample believed that she had real influence; and 79 percent of the Home for Life sample believed that they had importantly influenced the decision. We used a six-point scale to code the interviews with respect to perceived control, as follows: 1, where the person did not know that he or she was leaving; 2, where control was not perceived; 3, where influence was perceived to be minimal; 4, where decision making was shared equally; 5, where the person felt he or she had major responsibility for the decision; and 6, where the person felt total responsibility for the decision. We found that the mean response for the Deinstitutionalized Elites was 2.4; for the Unwilling Old Ladies, 2.02; and for the Home for Life sample, 4.57. These mean scores were significantly different one from another beyond $p < .05$.

We examined another aspect of decision making by assessing the sense of participation in or control over the decision regarding *where* the person was to be moved. The modal response in the Home for Life sample indicates that the person believed he or she had a choice. In contrast, the Unwilling Old Ladies, although reporting that they had influenced the choice of alternatives in some small way, primarily saw themselves as giving in to external forces. The typical response among the Deinstitution-alized Elites was to report neither control nor influence over the alterna-tive living site being considered. In general, they did not perceive alterna-tives, or if they did they could only describe them in the most vague and remote terms. The Home for Life respondents again clearly perceived themselves as being intimately involved in the decision making (about 75 percent felt that way), compared with 18 percent for the Unwilling Old Ladies and only 8 percent for the Deinstitutionalized Elite respondents. Mean response scores, calculated along a scale similar to that described above, were as follows: Deinstitutionalized Elites, 2.32; Unwilling Old La-dies, 2.58; and Home for Life, 4.7. The first two mean scores were not significantly different from each other; both, however, were significantly lower ($p < .05$) when compared with the Home for Life sample.

These findings suggest that the Home for Life respondents differed markedly from the other studies on a critical dimension, the sense of mas-tery over relocation conditions. Such findings may call into question our plans to consider the four relocation settings in similar conceptual terms. Further analysis, however, suggests that the mastery responses elicited may be more apparent than real.

A special Thematic Apperception Test (TAT) depicting critical issues around institutionalization was administered to all Home for Life respon-dents. (The series of cards is discussed more fully in chapter 4.) The first TAT card in the series depicts an aged person packing a suitcase as sever-al younger adults and children stand in the foreground and background. The latent stimulus demand elicited separation and rejection concerns from the respondents. The TAT cards were given to the elderly respon-dents prior to their relocation and then again six weeks after they were relocated. The prototypical story elicited prior to relocation showed that the elderly saw entering the home as a self-generated act. A typical story was the following:

This is Grandma fixing to go away. That is her son and grandson. The rest of the family is in the other room. She is going to the Old Folks home. See all these things she is packing. Here's her knitting, or something, I'm not sure. There are two handkerchiefs. Here is a small grip that her grandson has. The people in the back—her daughter, 2 daughters, and her son-in-law. One of them looks invalid. This is the living room. See the lamp, couch, table with cups on it, pictures. There's a teapot. She's very happy about it. She is smiling.

This daughter is an invalid. She is sitting in a chair. Her son is waiting to help her when she is ready. There is a lamp, couch, table, grip with clothes, kitchen table with coffeepot and cups to one side. Grandma is very happy to go where she is going. The toys belong to her grandson.

In contrast, when the series was readministered after institutionalization, entering the home was seen by the same people as an act imposed by others. This is the story from the same individual after relocation:

This woman is packing things for her son and grandson. No—uh-uh! She's going to leave her son and grandson. People in that far room are saying good-bye—her daughter-in-law, other members of her family. She is distressed to think she has to leave, particularly her son and grandson. She's taking something of her grandson's with her—maybe as a keepsake. Handkerchiefs, I think. Maybe she's going to a Home for the Aged.

Ratings based upon a scheme developed by Lieberman and Lakin (1963) indicate several statistically significant differences between the same person's response to this story pre- and post-relocation. Prior to relocation, all of the respondents perceived action as originating in themselves; six weeks after entering the institution, only half saw the action that way. Half the respondents at Time 1 (pre-relocation) selected independence as the motivation attributed to the TAT figure chosen as the hero, while only 17 percent did so at Time 2 (after moving into the institution).

These projective test findings call into question the distinctiveness of the Home for Life sample's response on the issue of control and suggest that in this area, the respondents in all of the studies are probably more alike than different. The sense of mastery in the sample entering institutions may well result from the defensive need to maintain integrity. Once inside the institution it is much more difficult to maintain the myth of the institution's social desirability, and this alters TAT responses in the direction of a lessened sense of control or mastery.

We also conducted analyses of the respondents' expectations with respect to relocation, including their anticipated feelings of loss and gain, their anticipated satisfactions, and their feelings about leaving. Rating scales based on pre-location interviews were constructed in a manner similar to the method for assessing locus of control. The pattern of our results was similar. The Home for Life respondents showed significantly higher positive expectations about the move, perceived lower levels of loss, and anticipated greater satisfactions when compared with both the Deinstitutionalized Elites and the Unwilling Old Ladies samples. (Scale details and tables showing this information are presented in chapter 4.)

Differences among the studies in expectations were again called into question by an analysis of the Home for Life sample's projective data. In this case, a scale assessing loss based on early memories was constructed. Separation, mutilation, and death were typical themes expressed by those waiting to enter institutions. (Details of the analysis of early memories are given in chapter 4 and will not be presented here.) Sixty-one percent of the respondents waiting to enter institutions exhibited such themes, compared with only 39 percent of a matched control group not about to enter the institution. This finding of loss themes stands in sharp contrast to the level of positive anticipation expressed and mirrors the previous findings presented on locus of control. It suggests that our samples were more similar on relocation expectations than the attitude scales would suggest.

In summary, despite variations in why and how people move (including how voluntarily), the relocations in our studies may represent a single kind of radical life change. We believe that this change almost always makes for a time of great stress in the lives of those involved, and that, at a symbolic level, the actual move entails a similar psychological task for all the elderly people we studied. It is the psychological dilemma represented by life space changes engendered by relocation that constitutes the potential stressor. Why it is a stressor, and how we can account for individual differences in adaptation, are central issues addressed in this book.

Assessing the Effects of Stress

Both short-term reactions and long-term adaptation were assessed by measuring changes in pre- and post-relocation functioning. Systematic assessments were made for changes in physical health, cognition, interpersonal relationships, and affects.

Determination of changes in physical functioning is a particularly important area among the elderly, as morbidity and mortality have been found to be sequelae to severe life crises. For example, physical deterioration and then death following the loss of a spouse in advanced old age has been cited by many investigators (see reviews by Jacobs and Ostfeld 1977; Rowland 1977). Cognitive decline, constriction, and disorientation are also not unlikely reactions to crisis, and reports of maladaptive changes in social functioning—including constriction in interpersonal repertoires or social roles, withdrawal from others, and inappropriate and occasionally bizarre interpersonal behavior—are widespread in the literature. Finally, the most commonly encountered reactions to stress are affect reactions, encompassing a range of emotional states including anxiety and depression, lessened feelings of well-being, and diminished self-esteem. (Details of the assessment of short-term reactions and long-term adaptation are included in appendix B.) These four dimensions of stress response (physiological responses, cognitive changes, relationship changes, and dysphoric affect) correspond to categories employed by other investigators in their assessments of responses to stress (Lazarus 1966). For most investigators, the absence of responses in our four areas is indicative of the absence of stress.

REACTIONS

For three of our studies we chose a time for assessing short-term reactions (six weeks after relocation in the Unwilling Old Ladies study, two months after in the Home for Life study, and fifteen weeks after in the Deinstitutionalized Elites study) that would allow for a transitional period and discount the worst of the initial impact. During the first month or so, elderly who are relocated may demonstrate confusion or even behaviors resembling psychosis; however, most soon appear more like themselves as they adjust to relocation. (Post-relocation information in the Death of an Institution study was gathered at only one time—one year after relocation.)

Deteriorative change—physical, cognitive, interactive, and affective—was, in each of our samples, not highly intercorrelated. The reasons behind the absence of a stronger association are unclear; more understandable are the associations between the type of reaction and the relocation situation. Thus, in the Unwilling Old Ladies study, more than half of the subjects (56 percent) manifested an adverse affective reaction, whereas less than one in six (13 percent) showed deteriorative cognitive reactions. In the Home for Life study, on the other hand, close to one-third (27 percent) showed negative cognitive reactions and declines in physical functioning (32 percent). The Deinstitutionalized Elites showed most change on social interactive measures. The area of maximum stress reactions, as will be more fully discussed in the chapters that follow, is a function of the relocation situation and the specific characteristics of the sample.

OUTCOMES

In each study, respondents were categorized on the basis of idiographic (using each person as their unique control) changes into one of four outcome groups: dead, extremely deteriorated, unchanged, and improved. Except for those who died, assessments of change were made in the four areas noted earlier. Changes in these areas between pre-relocation and outcome-measurement periods, in contrast to changes assessed for short-term reactions, were highly intercorrelated (with correlations of about .9). Since placement into an outcome category was based on change in status rather than on absolute status, it was necessary to separate out pre-relocation-level functioning from the effects of relocation.

The contrast between a man with Parkinson's disease who subsequent to entering one of the homes for the aged showed extreme deteriorative change and a woman who showed signs of deterioration prior to institutionalization illustrates the relativity of our ratings. Prior to relocation the man had lived by himself in a furnished apartment, and although experiencing some difficulty in walking and some discomfort associated with his Parkinson's disease, he walked around the neighborhood, visited friends, and dined in restaurants. He took care of himself, was very well oriented in time and place, and was of a pleasant, cheerful disposition. One year after institutionalization, however, he was confined to a wheel chair, required care for all his physical needs, was very disoriented, and spoke in a whisper; indeed, he often could not make any intelligible sounds. He was, furthermore, deeply depressed and would not cooperate in any therapy efforts.

The woman, on the other hand, who showed many signs of deterioration in the initial interview was also rated as in marked decline one year after admission, but the "distance traveled" appeared less than in the man just described. This woman was suffering from hypertension, which made it difficult for her to walk and to see, and needed considerable physical care. She was clinically depressed and reported feelings of hopelessness. One year after admission, she had been hospitalized several times for severe hypertension. She felt weak and did not participate in any of the home's activities; she felt persecuted, was constantly complaining and very depressed, and described herself as "the most unhappy person who ever lived." While she had deteriorated markedly, she did not exhibit the same degree of change as the man with Parkinson's disease. Recognizing such variability among respondents showing deterioration does not detract, however, from the fact that all categorized as extremely deteriorated demonstrated a striking change for the worse.

The relativity of our classifications is perhaps best illustrated among those who died subsequent to relocation. For one thing, the "distance traveled" by some residents who died within the first year after relocation appeared to be less than that of other respondents who showed extreme deterioration but had not yet died. Among the dead respondents themselves, the "distance traveled" to death sometimes differed markedly. To illustrate, a man from the Home for Life study with Parkinson's disease was, before relocation, in rather poor physical health and suffered acutely from the disease, exhibiting a marked tremor and impaired speech. He was further weakened by having had four operations in an eight-week period about five months earlier. He required help in washing, bathing, and dressing and was placed in the "urgent" category by the institution when on the waiting list. In contrast, another respondent from the same study who also died was living in a walk-up apartment and was cooking, shopping, and cleaning for herself and her husband at baseline. Just before this interview she had been to two family parties, and she complained only of some fatigue; she had been placed by the home on the "nonurgent" waiting list. Clearly, in terms of observable level of functioning she was not deteriorated to the same extent as the first respondent; yet she also died after moving into the institution.

The "stressfulness" of changes in living arrangements is clearly shown in table 2–1. In each study about one out of two elderly who were relocated either deteriorated or died (52 percent of the respondents in the Unwilling Old Ladies, 48 percent in the Home for Life studies, 47 percent in the Deinstitutionalized Elites study, and 56 percent in the Death of an Institution study). Percentages of elderly who showed improvement after the move, on the other hand, are much smaller: only 2 percent in the first study, 6 percent in the second, and 20 percent in the third and fourth studies. Although adverse changes are apparently associated with the relocation, it is impossible to determine precisely the extent to which such changes are a function of relocation stress. In the absence of stress, some of the elderly we studied would have deteriorated or died anyway in the time interval between the pre-relocation interview and the post-relocation assessment of outcome.

Control Samples. Control groups generated by random assignment to relocation and nonrelocation groups obviously are not possible in real-life situations such as the ones we studied. Several ways of obtaining control information were possible, however, by using both the deterioration rates available for comparable samples as well as contrast samples. In the Death of an Institution study mortality rates for institutionalized elderly in the same institutions for the previous three years (12.7 percent, 9.8 percent, and 9.6 percent; average = 10.7 percent) were considerably less than the death rate associated with the relocation year, 18.2 percent. Better estimates of mortality, however, are available from the matched sample of 100 drawn from a comparable California state mental hospital. Only 5 (5

34

percent) of the 100 died in the same time period. (The match of this contrast sample with the study sample is shown in table A–1, appendix A.) The increased death rate associated with the transfer of mental patients, as compared with the rate for those patients who did not relocate and remained in the state mental hospital, is presumptive evidence for the effects of relocation. The quality of comparative evidence in the other studies is less compelling.

In the Unwilling Old Ladies study, deaths were infrequent (only 4 of the 45, or 9 percent, had died at the time of our second follow-up). Negative outcomes in the study consist primarily of deterioration rather than death: 19 (or 42 percent) of the sample deteriorated by our criteria because so many deteriorated, whereas only 1 (2 percent) improve during the four-and-one-half-month follow-up interval, it is reasonable to infer that it was the relocation that "caused" such widespread deterioration.

In the Home for Life study, we contrasted the distribution of outcomes in the study sample with that of two contrast samples. The outcome distribution during the follow-up year for the contrast sample who had already been institutionalized from one to three years is almost the same as for the study sample. Nearly half of this sample (18 of 37, or 47 percent) had markedly deteriorated or died. The community sample, however, had far fewer negative outcomes. Less than one-fifth of the community sample showed marked deterioration or death (6 of the 35, or 18 percent; 2 refused to be interviewed). These findings are difficult to interpret. It can be argued that the difference between the entire study sample and the community sample reflects the "excess" deterioration and death associated with institutionalization. This argument would be valid if the samples were "randomly assigned" to either community living or institutional life. If so, then one out of three (that is, the approximate difference between the 52 percent rate of deterioration and death for the study sample and the 18 percent rate for the community sample) of those older people who deteriorated or died after becoming institutionalized could be said to have done so because they entered and lived in homes for the aged. On the other hand, the similarity in percentages between the sample undergoing institutionalization and respondents who had been institutionalized for one to three years suggests that no excess morbidity and mortality was associated with the process of becoming institutionalized.

The intact—that is, unchanged or improved—relocatees did not differ systematically from the nonintact (deteriorated or dead) in age or sex: The average age of the intact survivors was 77.8 years old and of the nonintact, 79 years old; of the 44 intact, 12 (27 percent) were males, and of the 41 nonintact, 13 (32 percent) were males. There was a difference, however, in the living arrangements prior to admission. Of the 85 respondents, 17 had lived in nursing homes while on the waiting list, and 65 had lived alone or with others in community dwellings. Of the 17 admitted from nursing homes, 13 (77 percent) were in the nonintact groups, as opposed to only 4, or 23 percent in the intact group ($\chi^2 = 17.70$, p<.001).

This finding was somewhat surprising, because residents who were admitted from nursing homes were similar on most measures to those admitted from community dwellings. Living in a nursing home, for example, was not associated with degree of functional adequacy, nor with the severity or number of events leading to the decision to seek institutional care. Possibly the difference between the groups before admission to the homes was a combination of deteriorative processes not isolated by standardized measures and the nature of the family decision-making process. This process included, for some but not most respondents, residing in a nursing home while awaiting admission to the home for the aged. Although respondents admitted from nursing homes may indeed have been more deteriorated, none of the eighty-five was considered terminal at admission. If the residents who were admitted from nursing homes were more deteriorated than those admitted from community dwellings, it is also possible that this deterioration resulted from earlier relocation; they had had to adapt to two relocations in a rather brief time interval. This double relocation may explain the few differences that were found between those elderly who lived transitionally in a nursing home and those who did not. Indeed, the elderly admitted from nursing homes tended to have those psychological characteristics that were associated with negative outcomes, characteristics that will be discussed in later chapters.

Another kind of contrast (Lieberman 1961) consisted of comparing death rates for applicants who remained on the waiting list for one year to rates over a comparable interval for those who went from the waiting list into the home. The death rate for the relocated sample was 24.7 percent as compared with only 10.4 percent for those who remained on the waiting list, which is less than half the rate for the first year of institutionalization.

Although at the time of Lieberman's study, in the late 1950s, residents were taken into the home in the order of application, occasionally a more needy person would be taken in sooner and a less needy person later. Thus there is a small but unknown bias toward a greater death rate among the relocation sample when using this method of comparison. The Home for Life study illustrates above all else the problems of obtaining an adequate control sample when people's well-being is at stake and when services must be used appropriately and not be denied to those with the most immediate need.

In the Deinstitutionalized Elites study, the death rate was negligible, as expected, because of the nature of the select sample. Demonstrating the adverse effects of this relocation from the evidence at hand rests partially on the contrast between the percentage of patients that deteriorated after relocation (49 percent) and those who improved (21 percent): More than twice as many deteriorated as improved. The delay-control sample is of only limited value for establishing effects one year after relocation, because this sample consisted of twenty-six individuals who were interviewed twice over a short, twelve-week interval (that is fourteen weeks and then again two weeks before therapeutic relocation). When it is compared with the study sample, however—who were interviewed over a seventeen-week interval to assess short-term reactions (that is, two weeks pre-relocation and fifteen weeks afterward)—the contrast is dramatic. Whereas none in the delay-control sample declined in physical functioning, seven of the eighty-two (or 9 percent) in the study sample had declined in physical functioning. Cognitive decline for the relocatees was 18 percent, for the delay-control sample, only 4 percent. Whereas only 12 percent of the delay-control sample (one of twenty-six) declined in interaction behavioral functioning, 31 percent (twenty-eight of eighty-two) did in the experimental sample; and, similarly, only 4 percent of the delay-control sample (one of twenty-six) manifested deteriorative changes in affect, while 18 percent (thirteen of eighty-two) did in the study sample. These contrasts strongly suggest the effects of relocation as a stressor in this study. Moreover, because short-term changes in affect were, to some extent, associated with long-term outcomes in the study sample, the impressive difference in deteriorative changes in affect must also be considered presumptive evidence of adverse long-term outcomes.

SHORT-TERM REACTIONS AND LONG-TERM OUTCOMES

Associations between short-term reactions and long-term outcomes were weaker than had been anticipated. In the Unwilling Old Ladies and the Home for Life studies, only short-term changes in physical functioning were associated, beyond a 0.05 level of significance, with long-term outcome; while in the Deinstitutionalized Elites study, there was a statistically significant relationship between affective change and long-term outcome. These associations largely reflect the type of long-range outcome characteristic of each study. In the first two studies, those in the negative outcome group tended to show primarily deteriorative changes in physical functioning; such decline apparently begins soon after relocation and is an early indicator of a more serious subsequent downward course. In the Deinstitutionalized Elites study, long-term negative outcome tended to primarily take the form of deterioration in affect states; it is understandable that earlier adverse affective changes may persist or further deepen from shortly after impact through one year after relocation.

Outcome Comparisons with Other Studies. Some of the ambiguities in our data are echoed in the literature on the effects of relocation. Numerous investigators, as well as many reviewers, have attempted to either verify or disprove an association between relocation in the elderly and adverse sequelae. To single out only one of the most recent reviews: Coffman (1981) reanalyzed the data from twenty relocation studies of the elderly and concluded that "increased mortality is not a typical or usual finding in the geriatric mass relocation literature" (p. 494). But this reviewer (who is not alone in this respect) focused explicitly on death as the sole "relocation effect" of interest; other kinds of criteria are rarely examined in the literature. As our findings show, only in the Death of an Institution study was mortality a prominent outcome. In all our studies, however, sufficient deteriorative changes occurred among those who survived to strongly support an association between relocation and adverse effects. Our findings certainly support the assumption that many respondents who deteriorated subsequent to relocation did so because of the stressful nature of such an event.

We cannot, however, identify specific individuals who would have deteriorated or died had they not been relocated. Not everybody we have studied is "at risk." Indeed, if they were, we would not have a study! Fortunately, as was shown earlier in this chapter, outcomes vary less among the four studies than they do within each; it is this variability that we set out to explain.

3

Settings and People

The Unwilling Old Ladies

THIS initial study of the drastic consequences suffered by forty-five elderly women who were moved, much to their displeasure, from one institution to another demonstrates that radical environmental change can constitute a severe stress even for a group of elderly who are physically and psychologically healthy.

The State of Illinois made an administrative decision, in the interest of economy, to close a state-maintained home for the aged and relocate the residents in another state institution. Both institutions accepted elderly who were veterans or family members of veterans. The institution from which the residents were moved was located near a small rural Midwestern community. It accommodated forty-five women in a single building, with a central dining room and an adjoining infirmary. Residents had their own rooms, furnished with personal belongings, and they usually assumed responsibility for minor housekeeping tasks in their rooms. Most activities were self-initiated, and their daily life was strikingly independent; the only organized activities were weekly religious services and occasional parties.

The atmosphere was protective, genteel, homelike, and permissive—more like that of a residential hotel than of an institution. The staff seemed eager to satisfy the whims of individual residents, and a high resident-staff ratio permitted personalized attention. Most residents referred to staff members as "the girls," while staff spoke of the residents as "our ladies."

The staff, most of whom had worked in the home for a number of years, were very tolerant about listening sympathetically to complaints and arbitrating differences that arose among residents. Each person was afforded considerable flexibility and latitude in behavior. Many residents readily admitted to having been "pampered" or "spoiled" by the staff; some voiced the opinion that they could not imagine receiving better care.

The institution to which the women were transferred, although located in an adjacent rural area, contrasted markedly with the first institution. One of the largest homes for veterans in the state, it consists of some seventy-five buildings spread over more than 200 acres. It is operated in a modified military fashion and houses approximately one thousand residents, primarily men. A large variety of personal, recreational, and medical services are available on the grounds.

Residents of this institution are termed "members" and are admitted, not committed, to the home. They are not confined to the buildings or grounds during residency, except for disciplinary reasons, and may leave the grounds during the day without restriction or question. They may be granted a leave of absence or furlough if they wish to be absent for a longer period of time. Groups of members residing in the various cottages are termed "companies" and are supervised by another member, called the "sergeant," who is appointed by the superintendent. He or she is responsible for the maintenance of the building and the conduct of the members assigned to that company, and makes the daily morning reports on that company to the adjutant's office. Regular army bugle calls are sounded for reveille, mess call, sick call, pay call, call to quarters, and lights out, and also at the raising and lowering of the flag each day.

THE MOVE

Several weeks prior to the actual relocation, a team of social workers from the State Department of Mental Health interviewed residents who were going to be relocated. Their job was to answer residents' questions and familiarize them with what they could expect when they were moved. Movies of the new institution were shown as part of this preparatory phase. In general, an attempt was made to help "work through" some of the residents' anxieties about the pending relocation.

The forty-five women were settled into four different kinds of living accommodations, depending on the desires of the residents, the recommendations of both the social worker and the attending physician, and, of course, the availability of space. Eighteen were given their own rooms in one cottage, nineteen shared rooms in another cottage, three were placed in the hospital, and five were placed in the infirmary. All were limited in the amount of personal belongings that they could transfer.

THE SAMPLE

The women in the sample ranged from age sixty-one to age ninety-one, and all were born or raised in the Midwest. The sample included forty-two widows and three women who had never married. The widows had at least one living child. These women had lived in the institution for from three months to fifteen years; eight had lived in the home for eleven years or more. Their mean educational level was eight years. Using the husband's major lifetime occupation as an index of social class, 95 percent were lower middle class.

All were ambulatory. As a group they were physically and psychologically healthier than most institutionalized populations previously reported on in the literature, and on the measure of ego pathology (Dana 1955), the group compared favorably with noninstitutionalized aged. Only three women showed any test indications of brain impairment. In short, these forty-five women are typical of residents of residential institutions who enter such settings for psychosocial reasons rather than because of incapacity.

A Case Illustration. Mrs. S., a seventy-eight-year-old widow of five years, provides a typical illustration both of the way in which the women managed their lives prior to relocation and of their reactions to the relocation. She had lived at the institution for two and one-half years; conflicts with her daughter-in-law, in whose home she had formerly lived, had precipitated her move there. Four years before her admission, she had broken her hip and given up working in a factory. On measures of cognitive functioning, Mrs. S. scored at about the mean for the group, suggesting no difficulty in this area.

One staff member described Mrs. S. as a very nice woman, with a pleasant disposition: well behaved, socially active and participating in everything going on, able to take adversity in her stride, never getting ruffled, and with many social ties within the institution and outside. Another described her as pleasant and friendly, intelligent, asking for very little, and well liked by everyone. A third staff member spoke of her as being able to use quasi-therapeutic and friendship relationships with the staff to deal with her worries about her family.

When interviewed about her feelings and her reactions to the move, Mrs. S. responded:

I said I didn't want to go, but if I have to I would go. I just felt terrible, like all the rest did about moving. I don't want to go so far away from home; I'm a hundred miles from my children now. I just don't want to go, I don't think the home is going to be a home, either. That is an institution, that's no home. This has been a home. The superintendent has been more than wonderful. I don't know what I can do about it, but I did write five letters to Springfield. [She took active steps in trying to influence political policy with regard to closing the home.] At this point I'm going to try it, but if I don't like it, I'll go back to my boys.

Mrs. S.'s initial reactions to the move were typical for our sample— anger, frustration, and a strong desire not to leave, but a philosophical resignation to "give it a try."

Somewhat later in the interview, in discussing her daily pattern of living, Mrs. S. complained that time now hangs heavy on her hands, and then launched into a more direct expression of her feelings about leaving. "I feel this since the change has come; before that I was feeling very content, until they upset the applecart. I am very much provoked at them, I really am, because I don't think it was necessary. All these years this home has been here, dear."

In response to a question about what were some of the best things about her current home, she stated:

Well, I think this way it's wonderful, to have a room of your own where you can be by yourself. I think everybody is very nice. Living in your own room is much better, much better. With two in a room, when you old, ain't what it's cracked up to be. That bothers me; who's going to be in with you and who's going to do what. One will want the window up and one will want it shut, one will want to go to bed and the other one won't, it's not going to work. I think about the move pretty much of the time. I've had a horror against that institution ever since I heard my dad tell me about it. Of course, he was never there.

When asked if there were any things that she thought might be better at the new institution, Mrs. S. responded: "Oh, there might be, every day somebody tells how wonderful it is on the outside, but I tell them we are not going to live on the outside, we are going to live on the inside." She expressed concern that "there would be an awful lot of walking down there, when I can't walk. I'll have to go to a different building for everything. Here, we've got it all right here."

In response to the question "Tell me how you feel about the years to come," Mrs. S. responded: "Well, you wonder, you wonder, don't you.

Well, I surely hope they are not any worse than what I've been through. That's sure. I've had a pretty rough time, but I've come out on top so far." (She was talking about her husband's alcoholism, which required her to work and raise their children on her own.)

> I wonder about the future—I just wonder how you'll be took care of. I hope I won't be sick long, I hope I won't last too long. It makes me wonder, it surely does, just what's going to become of you. And that's why I've said all the time, I don't want to die down there, I surely don't. I surely didn't want to go down there to die.

The interviewer then asked, "What is it about [the new institution], that you don't want to die there?" Mrs. S. explained:

> I look at the people they took down there, there is sixty-one, they are all in one room, and I know how terribly bad some of these were over here. No, I took good care of my father and mother, and I don't want to have to go down there that way. I just don't want to go down there that way. I just don't want to go down there, that's all there is to it. It may be all right and all that, but I've got really a horror of going down there.

In discussing her depressed feelings, Mrs. S. said,

> I don't feel that way too often. I don't feel bad too often, but I've felt more [that perhaps it was no use to go on living] since we've heard that we're going down there than I've every thought about it before. It does upset me, and I know it's an institution and its so-so, but the superintendent here is different, we know that we've got to mind her and you know that if you do what's right, everything is going to be all right.

Clearly for Mrs. S., the symbol surrounding the relocation was that of a death institution and her reactions were a resigned horror to the forthcoming move. She also believed that the new setting would place in jeopardy her previously successful strategies for controlling the environment.

That Mrs. S. was a strong, stable, tough, independent individual is perhaps best expressed by her responses to questions about medical care. "Oh, it's been all okay here. I couldn't ask to be taken care of any better than I am here." The interviewer asked her how often she felt sick and what she did about it. "Oh, I take a couple of aspirin tablets, I take lots of aspirins, my legs gets to aching so terribly." She was asked if she saw the doctor often.

> No, I know it can't be any better, it aches too hard. I don't like this going to the doctor, he doesn't know any more about me than I do myself. I've been over to him I think twice. I was over here once in the hospital. I had virus pneumonia,

and I couldn't eat. I take care of myself usually. I think I'm pretty good (physically) for a woman as old as I am. If it weren't for my leg I would still be trying to work, I'm telling you. If they would have me.

A sense of Mrs. S.'s self-image can be gathered from the following: "Well, I don't know, I've had to do for myself for so many years that I guess I've been my own boss. I get along, I have to. I've had to earn my own way all the time. Ever since my youngest boy was eight years old, I've paid for myself." She communicates a sense of pride and a belief in her own ability, and the theme of independence recurs frequently in her reminiscences. She mentioned it in talking about her decision to enter the institution several years ago.

I think sometimes you can get advice that will help you, but I came down here because I thought I was doing better. Of course, maybe I would have been better off to stay home, I don't think I missed it coming down here. I made up my mind myself. I stayed with this decision until they kicked the bucket over [referring to the closing of the institution].

Another view of Mrs. S.'s character may be gleaned from the way in which she had mastered her current environment.

During an average day I always have plenty of sewing for different ladies to do; listen to the television, there are three stories I like to listen to. Oh, I sewed and fussed and fiddled for different ones, it passed my time away. I would earn a little money by the sewing, and I had done this for nothing for some that couldn't afford to give me. I like to have something to do. I don't mind I ache so terrible from my arthritis all the time that, if you've got something to do, your mind is on that instead of your own troubles.

"Well, I think that you've got to learn to pick your crowd," Mrs. S. continued, "learn to pick the people that you want to learn to associate with. There's been six of us that's kind of chummed together at first." She was referring to a group known in the institution as the "coffee klatch," a group of six residents who had associated with one another for the past several years. When they were moved to the new institution, they were separated. Most of the "coffee klatch" suffered major deterioration, perhaps in part because of the breakdown of these important social ties.

Mrs. S. also expressed herself socially in correspondence. "I write on Sunday mornings, generally six, maybe seven or eight letters. I've got lots of nice friends, I really have, I surely have. I never talk on the telephone, I just can't hear good enough." When asked who visited her, she stated, "Oh, the _____ from my hometown and other friends, and my kids come from another town. Otherwise, I don't have anyone from away

44

come. When they come we usually crowd up the room, borrow a few chairs. They never stay too long. When the friends come we always just go uptown for dinner." She was asked if she ever asked her children to visit her when she was lonely. "Oh yes, I do, but when they are working, you know, they can't always come. Yes, my children have been good to me. . . ."

When asked what she did when she felt troubled about something, Mrs. S. responded, "Oh, just sit and think it over and over, I guess. And I wonder why things are as they are. At times I talk it over with the lady upstairs—she's the closest person in that home to me. I don't go to talk it over with the ladies that work here, excepting the superintendent occasionally."

For many of the respondents, the superintendent was a central individual who could be approached for quasi-therapeutic help. Compared with many of the other respondents, Mrs. S. did not make frequent use of this person. Clearly, Mrs. S. had not only a network of friends and children, but also a close confidant within the institution who could be used for such purposes.

She had also worked out the feelings of rejection so common in elderly people who have living children and enter an institution. Mrs. S. was asked about her earliest memory of this home.

> Well, I know when I came, my boy felt terrible. I just took it in my stride and let it go because I had worked here and there, even before I worked in the shop, I took care of sick people. It didn't bother me to be away from home, so it didn't bother me to come down here. . . . No, he [her son] didn't like it, but I thought it was best I did come. I felt that way then. They have their family to take care of, and I thought, well, if I come down here and I have a home, it was better.

Although some signs of depressive affect in Mrs. S. are clear, so are the numerous strategies which suggest that she is up to the task of coping with these conditions and staving off overwhelming depression. She perseveres.

An examination of Mrs. S.'s pattern of living in the institution suggested a highly organized individual who made use of a wide variety of resources. These included a highly structured pattern of television watching (for approximately six hours a day); a work schedule of sewing, both for pay and as a volunteer to those who could not afford it; a small social group (the coffee klatch, which had patterned activities during meals and a weekly social gathering); a special confidant with whom she could discuss her troubles and thoughts, particularly her worries about her children; a "volunteer" activity of visiting those in the home who were ill

(Saturdays); and a set time (Sunday mornings) for writing letters to a larger social group outside the home. Mrs. S., therefore, had organized a life pattern, involving concrete activities at specific times, that maintained her as an active individual and satisfied her help-giving needs as well. Additionally, she had succeeded in coping with a large institution by having a small number of intimate friends. Her world was under her control and provided numerous levels of gratification and activity. Her relationship to the staff showed a similar degree of differentiation. With the kitchen staff and cleaning help she had a vague, distant relationship; in contrast, she maintained a relatively close, if not frequent, relationship with the superintendent to discuss troubles. In many ways, then, the new setting clearly put in jeopardy Mrs. S.'s heretofore successful strategies for controlling her environment.

After the move, Mrs. S. showed more signs of depression, experienced considerably more difficulty in mobility, and had a marked increase in blood pressure and increased physical disability. Although she did not disintegrate as much as some of the women studied, her physical problems and her increased depression were enough to place her in the negative outcome group. The specific issues leading to the change in her condition involved primarily those aspects of life in the first institution that made up the very fabric of her social world—the coffee klatch, the confidant, the availability of the superintendent to discuss problems—and that were no longer available to her. (The members of the coffee klatch group, for example, were spread throughout the institution, making social interaction difficult, if not impossible.) Sharing a room and being forced to leave some of her personal belongings behind also seemed to be blows for Mrs. S. She appeared unable to recapture her previous independence and sense of mastery.

Perhaps the feelings that she attached to the new institution as a "death institution" played a role in her increased feelings of depression and hopelessness. She appeared stymied in using her considerable energy to make her new world into a predictable and controllable setting.

Home for Life

We began this study by interviewing applicants to three sectarian homes for the aged. They were initially processed by the staff of a central family service screening agency. If the screening agency assessed the person as unable to maintain himself or, most likely, herself, in the community, application to one of the homes was recommended. The applicant was free to choose among the three homes, which were widely scattered within the city. The applicant then visited the home of his or her choice and was interviewed by an intake caseworker, a consultant psychiatrist, and medical personnel. Staff approval was usually related to the absence of psychosis or terminal illness, and the appropriateness of custodial care for the applicant. The average period from application to admission was seven months; the range, however, was rather large—from less than one month to over two years. Those applicants who needed immediate custodial care usually entered a nursing home until space was available in the home they had selected. The applicant had the option to defer admission until a later date. Most applicants, however, preferred immediate admission.

Although the applicants entered three different sectarian homes, confirmation of the similarities among the three homes was offered by Pincus (1968), who attempted to highlight the differences among the homes by adapting a framework originally developed by Kleemier (1961). Only minor differences on the four dimensions of public/private, structured/unstructured, resource-sparse/resource-rich, and integrated/isolated were observed. The similarities among the homes allowed us to treat them as if they constituted one institution—a voluntary sectarian home for the aged.

The three homes were located in a large Midwestern city and were operated by the same sectarian social agency. The smallest of the three had a maximum capacity of 120 residents and the largest, 286. The homes were similar in mean age of residents, percentage of females, percentage of residents on old age assistance, and general level of health of the residents.

The homes were also similar in their facilities. The majority of the residents shared a room with another person; there were no large dormitories or wards. Residents were allowed to keep personal possessions in their rooms. They were free to leave the building.

Each home had a large central dining room and one or more dining rooms for residents who needed special help in eating. Each institution had a large auditorium, several day rooms, a sheltered workshop, occupational and physical therapy facilities, and up-to-date medical facilities. Each also had an infirmary, and while the residents may at times have been temporarily transferred to a hospital for special care, only very rarely did they have to be transferred to a state mental hospital because of uncontrollable disruptive behavior. Very few residents were discharged to the community, so these homes were generally their homes for the rest of their lives.

All three homes met the high professional and legal standards required for accreditation and licensing. All had a full complement of medical and paramedical staff, including full-time social workers and consulting psychologists and psychiatrists. Each also had a recreational director who ran a wide range of programs, from mass activities to small interest groups. Each maintained a resident organization and a synagogue. Opportunities were made available for residents to perform small jobs around the home.

THE SAMPLE

The one hundred persons (eighty-five of whom actually entered one of the three institutions) who constituted the study sample were first interviewed while on a waiting list to enter one of the homes. All interviews were conducted during a two-and-one-half-year period. The study sample does not include all the aged persons admitted to the three homes during that period; rather, it represents a selected sample. Of the total potential respondents, 22 percent refused to take part in the study after the initial contact, saying, "I don't want to talk about myself" or "I don't want to be bothered." An additional 30 percent of the individuals were excluded because they were too physically ill to be interviewed or had serious limitations in vision, hearing, or communication. In another 9 percent a relative, usually a daughter, intervened, stating that the respondent was "too confused" or "too nervous" or "too sick" to be interviewed.

Most respondents had grown up in Eastern Europe and emigrated to America in early adulthood; only twenty were born in the United States. The average educational level was less than five years of formal school, and the typical occupations for the men or the husbands of the women had been small shopkeepers or unskilled tradesmen. While most had reared a rather successful generation of children, they themselves suffered both the hardships that necessitated emigration in the first place, and the stresses of adapting to the melting pot of American society with little education or financial security.

The eighty-five aged persons who actually entered one of the homes averaged eighty years of age; the youngest was sixty-eight and the oldest, ninety-three. (Of the fifteen who did not enter during the four years of the study six withdrew their applications, five preferred to delay admission, and four died while on the waiting list.) Congruent with the sex distribution among the general population of the very old, sixty of the study group (71 percent) were women. Of the seventy-four who had married (86 percent), fifteen had a living spouse at the time the study began;

most of the remaining sixty-two had been widowed in recent years, although a few had been divorced or separated many years before.

About one in three respondents did not have any living children, whereas most had two or more living children. About one in three did not have any living siblings. About one in three were living alone when first interviewed; about half were living with others, either with another unrelated older person, with one or more family members other than a spouse, or with their spouse. One in five were living in a nursing home while awaiting admission.

A Case Illustration. Mrs. A. was interviewed twice as a respondent in our community (control) sample at six-month intervals. At the time of the follow-up interview she was still living independently in the community and had not reached a decision to seek institutional care. She was aware, however, of the likelihood of her being accepted into the home if an application was made and was familiar with the homes, having visited friends or relatives who had been residents. This case is particularly appropriate for exploring feelings about separation from family members and attitudes toward the institutional home, because Mrs. A. had family members with whom she was in frequent contact and who felt a responsibility for her well-being. Mrs. A. applied for admission after her second interview and was accepted and placed on the waiting list.

When first interviewed a year before application to a home, Mrs. A. was seventy-seven years old. She was about five feet three inches tall and somewhat heavy, with a dark olive complexion. Having just recovered from an illness, her face was somewhat pallid. She spoke rather rapidly and with a slight accent, and she expressed her feelings strongly and seriously while maintaining her emotional control.

Her physical capacity and appearance were marked by the aftereffects of a right hemisphere stroke six years earlier, which had left her left hand and foot minimally functional. Her left foot was slightly turned and she dragged it along the ground, and she had to walk with a cane. She still could grasp with her left hand, but her grasp was weak. In addition, she had had rectal surgery a year prior to the first interview, and her condition had worsened since surgery; her doctor had suggested further surgery. She questioned surgery because of her age, commenting, "Thank God I'm able to take care of myself." She watched her diet and took Orinase to abate a tendency toward diabetes. She also reported some trouble with her eyesight: "The doctor said I'm getting a cataract." Yet she felt her health was about average.

Her daily schedule was to get up about 8:00 A.M., eat breakfast, and do her daily chores, such as shopping, washing, and ironing. Watching television was a prominent activity in her day, especially watching the news. In the afternoon she often rested, but she was quick to add: "I'm a busy lady; I belong to three clubs. Two have weekly meetings, one meets monthly." She commented that she always had something to do: talking with friends on the telephone, spending weekends with her sister, and visiting her son every Friday night. She received quite a bit of mail and wrote many letters in return.

Her relationship with all of her four children seemed very close. Despite her closeness to her daughter, neither wanted to live with the other: "My love for her is great, and I want it to remain that way." Mrs. A. was financially independent and able to maintain this independent living arrangement because she had made good investments. She displayed many pictures of her children, grandchildren, and great-grandchildren and kept close tabs on what was happening in each of their lives. Her children were very attentive, and she was quite satisfied with how they had turned out and with her relationship with them. She said that she always consulted with her children. She indicated that she "lives to enjoy their marriages and graduations." Because these occasions were very important to her, she was making plans to attend family events even in faraway states. In her own words: "The most important thing in my life is to see my children happy."

Two events occurred that were to change this picture. Her sister, with whom she was very close, died. Although her sister was only five years older than Mrs. A., "She was like a mother to me. I always used to talk things over with her. She used to advise me." Although Mrs. A. said she felt that "nothing really mattered" after the loss of her sister, she continued to have a warm and continual relationship with her family. She had visited her daughter in a distant state for a few months during the past year, and was planning to return there for her grandson's graduation the following year. Shortly after the death of her sister, she had undergone surgery again, which further increased her feeling that "nothing really matters." The surgery went remarkably well in spite of her being in mourning, and she recovered her physical health quickly.

Because she was depressed while recuperating from the surgery, the family suggested that she apply to an old-age home, and that in the interim she stay in a convalescent home. Mrs. A. chose to go back to her apartment, however, and indicated that she was rather pleased with her decision. Finally, however, at the insistence of the children, she applied to the home and went to the convalescent home while awaiting admission. When interviewed at the convalescent home, she indicated that she now stayed indoors most of the time, because with her "poor eyesight" she was uncomfortable walking outside alone. She now spent more time watching television, listening to the radio, and trying to do some reading. Since her eyesight had become worse, she said that she was unable to write letters and did not get as many in return. Despite her inability to move around and her need to be in the home, it was clear that she was still reasonably mobile and active. Her personal assessment: "Compared to some, I'm a giant. I'm not in pain. It's just that I'm a little weary, but that's my age. Just like a car wears out, people do." She looked forward to going to the old age home, both for the activities and for the people, and "to be settled."

On the other hand, adverse changes were noted. While Mrs. A. remained lucid and oriented in time and place, she was beginning to have problems with her memory for recent events. In the second interview she was less able than in the first to remember at what ages she went to various places, or even to recall the dates of her more recent trips.

Most dramatic was a marked increase in anxiety and depression (assessed by means of a thirty-two-item sentence completion test), apparently related to her feelings of abandonment. Mrs. A. suffered a protracted period of mourning that began with the loss of her husband two years prior to her application and was exacerbated by the death of her sister. In those two years she lost the two most important persons in her life, both of whom had helped sustain her independence for so long. Her children had not become replacements for her husband and sister, although she could depend upon them for emotional support. With impending institutionalization, the form this support would take was now in doubt, and she was apprehensive about what her relationship with them would be after she entered the home.

Deinstitutionalized Elites

The setting for this study was a large state hospital in the Midwest housing approximately 5,000 patients, nearly half of whom were aged sixty and over. This facility was built in the 1920s and was several miles from a major metropolitan area. It consisted primarily of one-story brick wards, each housing about 120 patients on several acres of attractive, well-kept grounds.

In 1967, an administrative reorganization took place which resulted in the creation of a geriatrics program with its own administrative structure and staff. The geriatrics program encompassed approximately 2,500 patients over sixty years of age. Patients in the geriatric unit were housed in four types of wards:

1. A large, one-story infirmary, consisting of several wings, for medically indigent elderly patients.
2. A number of large custodial wards, each housing over 100 patients.
3. A resocialization ward, housing approximately thirty patients, which was an experimental, intensive, short-term, milieu therapy program designed to rehabilitate the long-term elderly patient and prepare him or her for possible discharge into the community. The program of the resocialization ward was geared to reestablishing interpersonal relationships, increasing personal autonomy, and improving self-care capabilities, including such skills as managing one's own finances, taking part in maintaining one's quarters, preparing food, and the like.
4. A temporary discharge ward, created by the geriatric unit during the course of the research project (approximately one year). Many of the patients who were scheduled for discharge were transferred to this ward while awaiting an appropriate placement. The discharge wards emphasized resocialization and improving self-care capabilities.

The geriatric staff used four criteria to select elderly patients for discharge: An eligible patient had to be judged as (1) not dangerous to self or others, (2) unlikely to benefit from further hospital treatment, (3) suitable for custodial care available in the community, and (4) not constituting a serious psychiatric management problem. Patients who met these criteria were moved to the resocialization ward and/or the temporary "discharge" ward.

A discharge recommendation from the staff initiated a screening process involving several members of the staff and one or more physicians. Once a patient had been judged suitable for a community placement, the hospital staff would examine the possibilities available in the community and would attempt to find a placement best suited to the level of the patient's medical and psychosocial needs. In most cases the various types of placements would be discussed with the patient and his or her preferences explored. Some patients were taken into the community to visit potential facilities in order to help determine their preferred placements.

Most were relocated to facilities within a seventy-mile radius of the hospital. The most frequently used institutions were sheltered-care settings, usually old hotels that had been renovated and converted to sheltered-care use. They offered lodging, meals, some supervision, and, in most cases, a part-time program of recreational and occupational therapy.

Other placements included domiciliary facilities, nursing homes, extended-care institutions, and small foster-care homes. In all, twenty-six settings were used.

THE SAMPLE

The patients for the study were selected by the staff of the hospital and, therefore, did not represent a random sample of the elderly patients in the hospital. During the year's study, the research project staff was notified by the hospital geriatric unit whenever a patient aged sixty or over was scheduled for discharge. All such patients were studied except, (a) short-term patients who had resided in the hospital less than two years; (b) patients who were discharged on very short notice, so that the research staff could not schedule an interview prior to their discharge; and (c) patients who were discharged to their families. Despite these exclusions, the resulting sample encompassed nearly the total universe of long-term geriatric patients scheduled for discharge from this facility during a one-year interval.

Eighty-two people having a mean age of 69.5 years and a mean length of stay in the hospital of 13.7 years (ranging from two to forty-three years) were followed from pre- to post-relocation. The sample was 66 percent female and 89 percent white; 19 percent married, 32 percent single, 17 percent divorced or separated, and 32 percent widowed. These eighty-two patients were obviously not representative of the total population of approximately 2,500 geriatric patients in the hospital; they tended, rather, to be the most manageable patients.

Unfortunately, we do not have good psychological data on the characteristics of the total population from which this relocation sample was drawn. Status measures indicated that approximately 20 percent of our sample showed physical functioning scores indicative of high needs for physical care; one-third showed relatively high degrees of cognitive disorientation. Thus, despite the homogeneity created by the discharge process, these eighty-two older men and women varied considerably in physical status and cognitive functioning. At the time of discharge, using the Block Q-Sort measure of mental health status (Block 1961), 40 percent were clearly mentally ill, 28 percent were "marginal," and 32 percent showed no evidence of major mental illness. Forty-nine percent of the sample were recorded as having affective disorders, 8 percent were alcoholics, and 40 percent had a primary diagnosis of brain disorder. In each case, staff members who knew particular patients best were asked to judge the consequences of discharge; in only 5 percent of the cases did the staff feel that the person could not successfully leave the hospital, and in only 3 percent of the cases was a judgment made that they could not maintain at least a status quo in their new environment.

CASE ILLUSTRATIONS: SOME BRIEF VIGNETTES

Mr. K. was an unmarried white male aged sixty-nine, who was born in the Midwest and had a sixth-grade education. He was tall and somewhat stout, with thinning gray hair. This was his first admission to a mental hospital, but he had been in the same facility for the last fourteen years. His diagnosis at the time of admission was involutional psychosis, and he was currently in the infirmary. Although he suffered from diabetes, his mobility was average for his age and he was capable of many self-care activities. He had no physical handicaps except the absence of teeth. He generally wore a bland expression but often responded cheerfully to questions, although he had a serious speech impediment, which made him difficult to understand. Mr. K. indicated that he was anxious to go home from the hospital and relax after having been "so busy in the ward for such a long time."

Mr. K.'s interpersonal contacts were very limited. He could not answer eight of the ten Mental Status Questionnaire items, indicating substantial amounts of disorientation or memory loss. He did seem to enjoy talking with the interviewer, and his narrative was frequently interspersed with jokes and laughter. His description of a typical day in the ward included helping the staff with a variety of activities, such as changing sheets, helping other patients, and carrying the laundry. He indicated that he read very little and seldom left the ward. He felt that the ward was all right, but that he was ready to go home now.

Mrs. T. was a white married female, aged seventy-one, who was born in Hungary and had a high school education. She had recently been transferred to the resocialization therapy ward (the intensive, milieu treatment section with a small number of patients). She had had a mastectomy, but currently her health was fair, her mobility was good, and she was capable of taking care of herself. She did not appear handicapped in any way except for a lack of teeth; she had gray hair worn quite short. Her facial expression rarely changed during conversations, and her speech was somewhat difficult to follow because of her lack of teeth and some remaining traces of a Hungarian accent. She spoke spontaneously and frequently offered a good deal of information beyond that sought by the interviewer.

Although Mrs. T. indicated a desire to leave the hospital, her demeanor during the interview was that of a submissive, depressed, anxious, and apathetic person, fearful of the future. She talked about her children and grandchildren a good deal, but indicated that she "didn't want to see them because she didn't want to hurt them." There were strong indications of feelings of worthlessness and apathy as well as the possibility of some delusions. Mrs. T.'s memory and cognitive orientation were fair— she made only four errors on the ten items of the Mental Status Questionnaire. She had few interpersonal relationships and remained relatively inactive, although she indicated that she would like to have closer relationships with those around her.

Death of an Institution

The state hospital was located in the farming area of a Western state. This hospital was completely phased out over an eight-month period, and its resident population of 1,100 was either transferred to other state hospitals, placed in community-based institutional facilities, or released to their families. The relocation of every patient, regardless of physical, psychiatric, or cognitive condition that was to take place providing a unique research opportunity.

Our study sample was composed of all patients sixty-five years of age or older. This group constituted a highly diverse population: fragile patients needing total care along with completely self-sustaining ones; highly confused people and others who were quite mentally alert; actively psychotic as well as seemingly "normal" individuals. They were moved to 142 different nursing homes, board and care homes, and state hospital units throughout the state.

The state hospital was housed in buildings constructed in 1942 for use as a United States Army general hospital. Its physical plant consisted of long rows of wooden, single-story barracks which were connected by literally miles of covered corridors. Throughout its existence, the hospital was known as a "transfer facility," indicating that the majority of its residents had been transferred to the hospital from another hospital in the state system. Indeed, half of our study group was part of a group of patients transferred during its first six years in operation (1947–53), and a third had arrived during 1948 alone.

At its peak in 1957, the hospital contained over 3,000 patients, including not only the large transfer group but also patients admitted directly from within the four-county "catchment area" that it served. Thereafter, however, the hospital steadily declined in population, reflecting the situation prevailing in most state hospitals during this time period. The advent of psychotropic drugs and behavior modification techniques; the emergence of specialized caretaking institutions in the community; the allocation of federal money to support community-based mental health programs; and the development of a welfare system that could sustain the disabled in non-hospital settings all resulted in a rapidly declining resident population in the state hospital system.

This hospital had been designed as a temporary measure, and its closing had been considered many times over the years. Its physical plant was now inadequate, and the small units (twenty to twenty-five patients) required an uneconomical staff-patient ratio.

THE INSTITUTION

The hospital was divided into four administrative divisions. The eleven-unit Acute Division contained the new admissions, the adolescents, the alcoholics, and groups of the more or less actively psychotic younger patients. Three of the hospital's seven physicians were assigned to this division. The nine-unit Rehabilitation Division contained those patients who were considered to be in good physical and cognitive condition. This division was responsible for preparing long-term patients for their release. The Geriatric Division comprised thirteen units and contained primarily those undergoing long-term hospitalization or who were too confused to function without assistance in normal daily activities. Finally, the Medical Division contained eleven units: an acute medical and a surgical "hospital" unit, four postmedical or surgical care units, and five units of total care, "crib" patients who required twenty-four-hour nursing services.

Most of the elderly in our study group came from the Geriatric and Medical divisions, but forty-three were from the Acute Division and seventy-two were from the Rehabilitation Division.

The typical day of the elderly in this hospital was simple: They got up at 5:00 A.M., ate at 7:00, 12:00, and 5:00, and retired between 7:00 and 9:00 P.M. In between they were pretty much on their own. Some patients had job assignments in their own or other units. They cleaned, sorted laundry, made beds, or helped with patients; others worked in the kitchens, on the grounds in the garbage detail, or with maintenance personnel. Patients of sufficient capability could visit the library, craft rooms, or recreation center, and many spent their day in the canteen or wandering around the grounds. Movies, dances, and parties were featured on weekends, and some of the elderly attended these regularly. For the most part, however, the geriatric patients in our study spent their days in their units, and most of their time was spent just sitting. Some units played a record player or radio occasionally, but most relied on the ubiquitous television set, which was on from early morning until late at night. Patients sat in neat rows facing this machine—or, in a surprising number of units, they could sit only along the walls, where they had to lean forward to see it. Very few patients talked to each other, and most would respond monosyllabically, if at all, to questions from the staff. Little in the way of reading or recreational material was available, and few patients made use of what was provided. At infrequent intervals—between bathing, cleaning, feeding, charting, and other routine chores—some staff members would come into the lounge area to play cards or checkers with the men, to set the women's hair, to take a group into the yard for a game of catch, or, less frequently, just to talk to the patients. For the most part, patients just sat, as presumably they had done for twenty years, and ignored the routine events that went on around them.

THE RELOCATION: STAFF REACTIONS

Since, according to the staff, threats to close the hospital had been made frequently in the past—"about every other year"—their first reaction to printed notices announcing the closing was to disbelieve, and therefore to ignore, the announcement. Even when our research staff arrived for the specific purpose of studying the closing, many of the staff were not convinced that the hospital would really close.

When this fact could no longer be avoided, the mood of the staff changed, and plans were made to thwart the closing scheme through legislative and popular appeals. Interviews were given to the news media, meetings were held by employees' groups, and the State Employees Association was particularly active in urging state personnel to write state legislators and the governor urging them to abandon the plan. During this phase, one could not go into a hospital unit without being told of the marvelous things that were being done for the patients there and of the dire consequences of relocation for the patients' physical and mental wellbeing.

Finally, when these appeals were ignored and definite plans for the movement of both patients and staff were formulated, much of this unity disintegrated and was replaced by griping, infighting, and angry but grudging acceptance. Many staff members quit before any patients were moved; others withdrew into an "I don't give a damn" attitude and provided only the bare essentials of patient care. Most grumbled but went about their jobs much as usual, and a few redoubled their efforts to provide the best possible care for their patients in the time remaining.

THE RELOCATION PROCESS

In order to facilitate the movement of the entire resident population within a ten-month period, the hospital was mandated to relocate at least ninety patients per month. The formula that finally evolved consisted of placing as many of the ninety as could be managed in outside facilities and filling the rest of the quota with transfers to other state hospitals. Relocation criteria and priorities were established, stipulating that the patients should be located in a situation which (1) met their medical needs, (2) placed them as close as possible to interested relatives, and (3) returned them to their county of origin.

The steps involved in the basic decision-making process for each patient were the following:

1. Letters were sent to the families of the patients, advising them of the closing, asking for their cooperation, and requesting information on the family's wishes in relocating the patient.
2. Staff members were asked to fill out a preliminary questionnaire on each patient. These data, which pertained to the patient's level of functioning, activity range, and special problems and needs, were used only in the development of a rough patient typology to serve as a basic guideline. Another part of the questionnaire dealt with the staff's estimation of the degree of detriment each patient would experience as a result of relocation. Overall, they estimated that 64 percent of the total hospital population would suffer "minimal" or "no" detrimental effects from the move.
3. The hospital's team of psychiatric social workers, in conferences with unit-charge-nurses, reviewed the records of each patient and categorized patients as "good," "doubtful," or "poor" candidates for discharge to community facilities. These lists were then submitted to the unit physician for review, and disagreements were resolved through a multidisciplinary conference. Generally, a patient was considered a "poor" placement risk if he or she (a) was critically ill, (b) was totally bedridden, (c) had a history of violent episodes or a criminal commitment, or (d) manifested assorted antisocial behaviors that were considered to be too extreme for acceptance in community facilities.
4. Each patient was given a physical examination, a psychiatric evaluation, and a behavioral-functional assessment. The results of these evaluations be-

came part of the patient's records and went with him or her to the receiving institution, whether it was a state hospital or a community facility. In addition, patients who were to be placed received a complete social-behavioral assessment by the social worker assigned to his or her case.

5. In the case of patients over sixty-five, an "outside" physician, not employed by the state, had to review the records of these patients and/or reexamine them and concur with the recommendations of the staff before they could be moved.

6. The community facilities in which the patients were to be placed were selected by the local offices of an agency of the state's Department of Social Welfare. The department reviewed the patient's "social service packet"—including physical, psychiatric, social behavioral, and financial assessments—and selected an appropriate facility from among those available in the area.

THE SAMPLE

At the start of the study, the geriatric population was composed of 461 patients (aged sixty-five and over) who were not new admissions (that is, had been there more than three months). Of these, 23 died before leaving the state hospital, 5 were transferred (in acute medical emergency) to other hospitals before the study began, and 6 were transferred before data could be collected on them. This left 427 patients for study. They had been in state hospitals for an average of twenty-nine years; 72 percent had been hospitalized for more than twenty years. Most of these were continuous hospitalizations. The earliest admission date from our group was 1900, and 30 percent of our patients had been admitted before 1930. When these patients were admitted, the youngest was fourteen and the oldest was eighty-eight, with the majority (81 percent) having been admitted prior to age sixty-five. Most of the sample studied were people who simply grew old in the hospital.

Females outnumbered males by nearly two to one (64 percent female, 36 percent male) in this population. Together they had a mean age of seventy-eight with a range between sixty-five and ninety-eight. Similar distributions of males and females were found within each age group. About 48 percent of our sample were between ages sixty-five and seventy-four, 36 percent were between seventy-five and eighty-four, and 15 percent were eighty-five or older. Sixty percent had not progressed beyond grammar school; 31 percent had never married. Eighty-nine percent were Caucasian; 32 percent were foreign-born.

Thirty-five percent of these patients carried the label "organic brain syndrome," whether from senility, cerebral arteriosclerosis, or other organic brain disorders, while 23 percent were diagnosed as chronic schizophrenics, 20 percent as paranoid schizophrenics, and the remainder as having other functional disorders.

Our population was best characterized as singularly debilitated. The pervasiveness and severity of apathetic withdrawal, which is classically associated with long hospitalization, cannot be overemphasized. The most prevalent "activity" engaged in by our patients was sitting. Fifty percent of our group spent all their time just sitting. They did not engage in any other activity, arising from their chairs only for meals and trips to the bathroom. This 50 percent figure becomes an even more meaningful indicator of debilitation if one notes that these people did not even engage in such behavior as pacing, hallucinating, or talking to themselves. Whether or not these people were lost in their own internal thoughts is moot; they most certainly did not attend to their surroundings. In fact, 66 percent never, or only on rare occasions, actively observed events and activities occurring around them; only 34 percent anticipated routine events or responded to or manifested any curiosity about environmental phenomena that were not directly related to the fulfillment of their basic needs.

For those patients able to function within the ward routine, their behavior had a mechanically conditioned quality. When the staff turned on the light the patient automatically got out of bed and quickly dressed; when the staff announced bath time, the patient stripped at his or her bed, walked nude into the shower room, and passively waited in line for his or her turn; when the staff announced a meal, the patient docilely trudged along with the others to the dining room, hurried through the meal with downcast eyes, and totally ignored the existence of other patients sharing the table. After the evening meal, the patients retired almost immediately. For the "nonsitters," participation in activities outside the regular ward was minimal. Only 25 percent ever watched television; only 29 percent performed chores of any description, no matter how minimal; and a mere 8 percent involved themselves in card playing, sewing, craftwork, or similar occupations. While 30 percent did visit the canteen occasionally, only 15 percent attended church services, 9 percent frequented the movies or dances, and 4 percent made use of the library. As for socializing, 38 percent of the group were either completely nonverbal or made only monosyllabic utterances, while another 24 percent had never been heard to speak more than a short sentence. It is not surprising that 72 percent of the sample were judged to be totally unrelated to other persons. Some interaction did occur, but it tended to be directed more toward the staff than toward other patients: 20 percent of the group sought out interactions with the staff, while only 13 percent sought similar diversion from fellow patients.

Direct contact with the outside world was minimal. What family and friends the patients had prior to hospitalization had long since disappeared, died, or simply lost all interest in them. Family members who bothered to write, visit, or otherwise inquire about the patients' welfare were decided exceptions: 72 percent of our patients never received visits, 68 percent never received mail, and 89 percent never wrote letters themselves. Only 3 percent of the patients had left the hospital for short daytime visits with family or friends, and only 1 percent had left on a "definite leave" for more than a day.

Many were also physically debilitated. Twenty-four percent of the group were bedridden, confined to a wheelchair, or able to walk only with physical or mechanical assistance. Although the remaining 76 percent could ambulate unaided, the majority of our patients did not care for themselves. On a self-care measure, only 22 percent were able to care for themselves without supervision, while another 58 percent needed physical assistance or considerable individual prompting. The remaining 20 percent required total physical care in all areas of daily living, except perhaps for feeding themselves. The majority were neither sensorially deprived (5 percent were blind, 4 percent deaf) nor the victims of major, serious somatic illness. When the ambulatory patients were rated on a "degree of severity of illness" scale, 36 percent had no major physical illness and another 43 percent had one serious, usually chronic, problem.

Out of twenty-five psychiatric symptoms that we measured—such as hallucinations, delusions, talking to oneself, and pacing—the sample had a mean score of five such symptoms, with only 13 percent displaying none at all. The most frequently found symptoms were those relating to confusion or withdrawal: being unable to keep to a time schedule, forgetting to do important things, or appearing to be confused or dazed most of the time. Between 20 and 30 percent engaged in repetitive motor activity, repeated meaningless words, "heard" messages, or said things that were "untrue." On the other hand, when eight indices of violent or aggressive behavior were measured, 42 percent of the study group showed none and 35 percent displayed only one or two, giving a median score of one such behavior per patient. As this list of indices included such relatively mild behaviors as arguing with others, being verbally abusive, and threatening others—along with actual physical violence—we may conclude that our population was primarily pacific.

Thus far, we have attempted to convey an image of the study group as a whole. We do not mean to imply, however, that there was complete homogeneity among the patients we studied. On the contrary, there was a range of patient behavior and functional capacity, and despite the pervasive effects of institutionalization, diversity in patient types and personalities was evident.

THE RANGE OF PATIENT TYPES

To give some idea of the range of these patients, we will describe the extremes of functional capacity. In terms of four broad dimensions of functioning—physical, cognitive, psychiatric, and social-behavioral—there seemed to be a consistency among dimensions at the extremes of the population, but every imaginable combination away from the extremes.

At one end were the "crib" patients, constituting 16 percent of the total population. This is an appropriate designation for these patients, since they lay in high hospital beds with side rails, completely dependent on skilled nursing care for life maintenance. Physically, these patients were extremely incapacitated, having lost all bowel and bladder control and the motor coordination and strength necessary for even such simple tasks as feeding themselves. In addition to general physical feebleness, almost all of them were plagued by a variety of specific somatic ailments, such as heart dysfunction, urinary infections, and pneumonia. The majority were so cognitively debilitated that their only responses were to open their mouths when fed. Because these patients were too enfeebled or regressed to behave in any fashion, they generally lacked any psychiatric symptomatology.

Yet there was some, albeit minimal, variety even among the crib patients. They ranged from those who were kept alive only by intravenous or bottle feeding to those whose bodies were decrepit but whose sensorium and mental functioning still seemed to be intact. Among those on the latter end of the scale were patients who were reasonably alert to their environments, who conversed with the staff or observers, and who sometimes possessed a delightful sense of humor. A few read and wrote letters. One man, for example, kept on his bed a box of "goodies" containing such things as fruit, magazines, a pencil, and writing paper. He spent much of his time going through his possessions, arranging, and rearranging them, nibbling on his food treats, reading, or writing a letter. Several of the crib patients actively hallucinated or presented bizarre delusional material. Since the crib patients were maintained together in several wards, those who were alert and sociable or who presented personally distinguishing behaviors like hallucinations tended to become staff pets because they were such welcome exceptions to the norm.

At the other extreme of the study population were those patients who seemed reasonably "normal" for this age group. Constituting about 17 percent of the population, these individuals were physically healthy and appeared youthful and robust. They were active, alert to their surroundings, and interested in what went on around them. The majority worked. For example, one man worked on the hospital garbage truck, taking advantage of his position to scavenge whiskey bottles along the way and drain whatever they might still contain. An avid sports fan, particularly of college football, this man followed his hobby by watching television and reading the newspaper. He also occupied his time by writing letters. While the research team was in his ward, he was extremely cordial, serving coffee and chatting. These patients generally kept the wards clean by mopping, buffing, and dusting. They assumed responsibility for the ward laundry, helped care for the less functioning patients, served and cleaned up after meals, and generally operated in a useful capacity to lighten the work load of the staff and occasionally even take over for them. They typically exhibited some response to the research team, often approaching us socially but sometimes expressing resentment about our intrusion into their ward. Without assistance or reminders from the staff, they consistently and independently took care of themselves and their possessions. Few manifested psychiatric symptoms.

A variation of this "normal" group could be seen among those whom we called the "ward bosses" or the "elite." This group, making up 11 percent of the patients, was distinguishable from the "normal" group on the basis of psychiatric status. By and large, this group was actively paranoid and exhibited a number of antisocial behaviors. In addition to the work they performed in the wards, these patients assumed an authoritarian attitude toward the other patients, ordering them about in a dictatorial, loud, and often abusive fashion or, alternatively, watching over them in a compulsive, mother-hen fashion. In general, they held themselves aloof from the other patients and identified with the staff. These patients were usually accorded a good deal of status and a number of special privileges by the staff, and their idiosyncratic habits and psychiatric symptoms were tolerantly ignored. For example, every Sunday afternoon, one lady literally scalded her feet in almost boiling water to "keep bad spirits away." Although this behavior understandably created dermatological problems, the staff made no attempt to stop her. Privileges granted these patients included some measure of privacy. They could seclude themselves in the unit's work rooms and even take their meals there if they wanted. Showers could be taken privately instead of during the assembly-line process of bathing undergone by other patients. They had much greater access to staff offices and were often spoken to in an almost employee-to-employee fashion by the staff, who trusted them as sources of information and frequently apprised them of ward affairs or explained changes in the ward routine. For instance, one of the staff explained to a ward boss, "I'm pushing these two beds closer together so that Mrs. E. doesn't fall out of bed again." Even though the patient sarcastically retorted, "Well, what do you think I care?" the staff member continued, "I just wanted you to know why I did it, that's all." These patients had essentially carved high-status niches for themselves which received the support of the staff.

THE RELOCATION-PATIENTS' REACTION

The participation of the patients in their pre-placement planning was minimal, and assistance with emotional preparation for the move was negligible. The research staff's attempt to obtain an assessment of the patient's reactions to the imminent relocation encountered numerous difficulties. Many of the patients were simply nonverbal, and others were unresponsive to our attempts to interview them. Some were suspicious to our questions and appeared to be hesitant to discuss their feelings candidly with virtual strangers. Still others lacked any clear understanding of the nature of the move. At the same time, the staff were also less than desirable as informants, as they did not probe more than superficially for patient responses. Despite these limitations, we were able to detect a response in a quarter of the patients. Anxiety, fear about what would happen in a new place, depression, and regression were present in 12 percent of the group. Seven percent either denied that the hospital was closing or that they would have to leave, or acknowledged the closing and reacted with anger that they were evicted from their home. Only 6 percent seemed to be at all happy about the move, genuinely eager to leave the hospital and enthusiastic about or at least interested in living in new surroundings. As for the remaining patients, 28 percent were aware of the impending move but seemed nonreactive and indifferent to it, accepting it as inevitable.

Part 2

ON THE NATURE OF STRESS

4

The Impact of
Threat and Loss

THE ABILITY to anticipate future events, to experience feelings about such events, and to form attachments—to other people, to places, and to things—are fundamental human characteristics. Because of such attachments, losses as well as potential losses can critically affect psychological functioning. Indeed, it is only when other people or things are valued that one can be threatened by their possible loss. Because of the increasing likelihood that valued extensions of self will be lost with advancing age, threat and loss models are prevalent for explaining wellbeing and adjustment among the elderly. Although loss has at one time or another throughout history been associated with the vast diversity of the physical as well as psychological ills that befall mankind, loss models are particularly relevant to the second half of life. Death of others becomes ubiquitous among the elderly; decreasing physical capacities and chronic impairments must be confronted; and loss of work and family functions results in the roleless role of the elderly.

This chapter examines threat and loss to determine their contribution to the deleterious effects of relocation. Threat and loss as explanations, in contrast to environmental change hypotheses, which will be examined in the next chapter, assume that the individual reacts to the symbolic impli-cations—ranging from death of self to abandonment, when separations are perceived as both permanent and caused by others—that he or she attributes to relocation. People, however, not only react to meanings after the fact; they also respond to anticipation, to the threat of loss, prior to its actual occurrence.

Although threat and loss can be readily understood as theoretical con-structs, measurements of these variables are problematic. Observable re-sponses are a mixture of threat and loss reactions evoked by the situation, along with coping responses directed both toward the situation and toward the noxious affects aroused. We shall endeavor to distinguish among these behaviors, albeit aware of the difficulty in isolating and sep-arating them empirically. To do this, independent assessments of threat and loss intensity are critical, particularly if we do not wish to make the more common a priori assumption that the conditions studied—namely, environmental upheavals—necessarily cause such states. We have already demonstrated that changes in the elderly's living conditions are associated with frequent maladaptive consequences, but our goal here is to examine such situations analytically to determine the source of stress. To accom-plish this, we must examine the relative degree of threat and loss across each of the studies as well as individual differences in levels of threat and loss within each sample. Finally, we must determine whether variations in threat and loss intensity are systematically associated with both short-term responses to stress and long-term outcomes.

We will begin by discussing the reported assessments of threat among the respondents prior to relocation. Such reports encompass personal feel-ings and attitudes and perceptions of specific elements of the impending event. We will then focus—in this instance, in the Home for Life study only—on several less direct ways of assessing threat. First, we shall report on attitudes toward entering and living in the home among members of the community sample, a group composed of elderly people who have not applied for admission. Then, by using a special series of institutional TAT cards (Lieberman and Lakin 1963), we shall report on how threat disrupts perceptual processes. Next, we shall estimate the degree of threat by studying its effects, through contrasts among the community sample, those awaiting entrance to institutions, and elderly who have re-sided in the homes for one to three years. These contrasts assume that both the elderly in the community and the institutionalized residents are "nonthreatened" samples; to the extent that the "threatened" study sam-ple on the waiting list manifests worse psychological functioning than these other samples, threat intensity can be inferred. Finally, we will examine evidence indicative of the experience of loss subsequent to relocation.

Threat

ON THE NATURE OF THREAT

Respondents in all four studies were aware of their impending relocation before the actual physical move. Each person either had been selected, had chosen, or had been forced by a set of circumstances beyond his or her control to relocate. Whatever the reason for the relocation, the aged person is faced with an impending event to which he or she is likely to ascribe fearful attributes, in response to which he or she will presumably engage in some adjustive behavior.

For an event to be threatening according to Lazarus (1966), it must be appraised at some level of consciousness as likely to cause harm. Only when a future event is experienced as potentially dangerous can threat be considered as present. In turn, the appraisal and experience of threat leads to mechanisms for warding off the affect attendant on the meanings of the event and for reestablishing an internal equilibrium that may be viewed, from an external perspective, as adaptive or maladaptive. It is common to speak of threat as being denied or as being worked through, and of an individual in a threatening situation as showing signs of disorganization or incapacitating anxiety. To determine whether changes in life space pose a threat for the aged, the meaning of the impending move for those affected must be examined, along with those anticipatory behaviors directed toward warding off the event or mastering it, and the management of the affective states aroused by the impending event. A full demonstration that the condition or event can induce threat requires an examination of respondents who are potentially threatened for signs of disorganization and unmanaged affect attributable to the impending event.

RESPONDENTS' PERCEPTIONS OF RELOCATION

Beginning at the simplest level, we asked how those aged people about to be relocated perceived the move. Relevant data were gathered in three of the four studies; respondents from the Death of an Institution study were not included because the primary data were observations and not the phenomenologically based information required to assess conscious perceptions of threat. In the three remaining studies, interviews prior to relocation provided information for constructing scales to measure the following:

1. Feelings about leaving the environment in which they currently reside (rated on a five-point scale, ranging from +2, in which the respondent welcomes the environmental change, to −2, where there is opposition to and strong negative feelings about the move).
2. Expected losses associated with leaving the current environment (assessed as the extent to which individuals feel they must dissolve attachments or leave behind things that later will be missed, with a score of 1 referring to significant losses, while a score of 5 signified things people were "happy to lose").
3. Anticipated satisfactions in the new environment (with a scale ranging from −2, where the move is seen as totally devoid of any gratification potential, to +2, where positive expectations outweighed negative attributes). (See technical note 1 at the end of the chapter for illustrations of the rating scales.)

Both the Deinstitutionalized Elite respondents and the Home for Life respondents had favorable feelings about leaving their current environments (89 percent positive and 87 percent positive, respectively scored +1 or +2) whereas the Unwilling Old Ladies sample did not (only 12 percent positive), preferring to remain where they were. Most of them were opposed to the move, as vividly expressed in their comments. ("That would be too cruel, for me to be moved." "This has been my home for many years—I have nowhere else to go." "I'd like to stay here—it would kill me if they sent me out of here.")

A similar pattern emerges on the measure of expected losses. The Home for Life and Deinstitutionalized Elites samples are similar, with the most common rating being the anticipation of some moderate loss or a mixture of some meaningful loss tempered by "good feelings about things I'm happy to leave behind." Only 30 percent of the discharged mental hospital patients anticipated experiencing any loss (and, of these, only 4 percent expected a major loss); for the Home For Life sample, the corresponding figures were 25 percent and 6 percent. In contrast, the modal response of the Unwilling Old Ladies sample suggests a greater expectation of loss: 67 percent expected loss, and one-half of them, a major loss.

On the scale of anticipated satisfactions, the standard response among the Home for Life respondents was to perceive a net gain in satisfactions from the new environment, such as an increase in activities, people, and care, or the alleviation of problems and hardships: "I'll be cared for. Be kept busy. There are things going on all the time, I hear. It should be pleasant. People go there that need caring for. Someone to look after them. But it's not a prison. You can come and go as you like. I'll still be able to see my friends on the outside. I think I'll be able to keep busy there." In contrast, the typical response among respondents in the Unwilling Old Ladies study emphasized loss of status or some difficulties in the new situation. The typical response of the Deinstitutionalized Elites fell somewhere in between the two samples; they were generally more vague and most did not have definite opinions.

Differences among the three samples, as shown in table 4–1, suggest that the Home for Life sample was minimally threatened; the Deinstitutionalized Elites only moderately threatened, and the Unwilling Old Ladies respondents greatly threatened. The Unwilling Old Ladies sample had the most negative feelings about leaving, expected the most losses, and anticipated the least amount of satisfaction. The Home for Life sample, although comparable to the Deinstitutionalized Elites in feelings about leaving, expected the fewest losses while anticipating the highest satisfaction. These rankings become intelligible when the facts about the three relocations described in chapter 3 are considered. The elderly who moved into institutions in the Home for Life study were provided by the intake staff of their new homes with explanations concerning what they would gain from the move: care, security, activities, and people with whom to relate. Prospective residents and their families were encouraged to welcome the move because of these benefits. Moreover, because these homes only accepted "voluntary" admissions (no matter what the situation that occasioned application), the residents-to-be were encouraged to view the move as voluntary rather than as a necessity that was forced

TABLE 4–1

Conscious Appraisals of Threat and Loss in Three Studies (mean responses)

	Studies		
Appraisals	*Unwilling Old Ladies* (N=45)	*Home for Life* (N=85)	*Deinstitutionalized Elites* (N=82)
Feelings about leaving	−1.00	1.29	1.21
Expected losses	2.13	3.24	3.03
Anticipated satisfactions	−0.11	1.31	0.44

NOTE: Data not available for the Death of an Institution study, because systematic interview data were not collected.

upon them. Appraisals that suggest threat, therefore, became tempered by incentives to become a voluntary resident in a home that can provide care, security, activity, and people. If both the future residents of the home and their families can organize their perceptions so as to perceive the situation in this way, the painful affects associated with threat might be contained.

The Unwilling Old Ladies sample, on the other hand, were not provided with such rationalizations—which constitute an important cognitive strategy for coping with threat. Before relocation, these respondents— along with family and friends and the old institution's staff—all believed that it would be a painful move. Indeed, the intake staff of the relocation facility also recognized and communicated to their new charges that the relocation would be quite difficult for them. Externally supported ways of coping with the experience of threat were, therefore, not available.

The Deinstitutionalized Elites, in turn, had little clear understanding of how the relocation environment would be different, but were encouraged to accept the professional judgment that life would be as good, if not better, after the move. Perhaps because these respondents were compliant long-term patients, many tended to accept the professional judgment— but some apprehension remained.

In all three studies, however, many elderly did not report the event as threatening. Does this suggest that, despite evidence showing that significant portions of the populations undergoing environmental changes suffered grievously, threat is not a central component of relocation? Such an interpretation would be premature. Responses to queries eliciting feelings about leaving, expected losses, and anticipated gratifications may reflect less the underlying experience of threat and more the coping strategies for minimizing dysphoric affect. Respondents' reports of anticipated gratification, for example, may reflect attempts to convince themselves that a very threatening situation will not be harmful. The potentially threatening meaning becomes cognitively restructured so that apprehensions, fear, and anxiety are contained or reduced. In making these measurements, then, we cannot easily disentangle the experience of threat from the coping strategies employed to contain the painful and frightening affects generated by anticipations of harm.

APPRAISALS OF THREAT AND FUTURE ADAPTATION

Although our measures of consciously reported threat suggest that the majority of respondents did not perceive the impending move as threaten-

The Impact of Threat and Loss

ing, there clearly were individual differences—so that in each study, some elderly responded in ways suggesting that threat was experienced. Did those who experienced threat adapt less well to the relocation than those who had not provided responses that would suggest an experience of threat? Two approaches, described in chapter 2, were used to assess (a) short-term reactions—changes, from before the relocation until shortly after the move, in the physical, cognitive, social, and emotional spheres; and (b) long-term outcomes—the maintenance of biological and psychological integrity one year after the move.

The rather sizable variations in short-term reactions among the three studies make correlational analysis the most appropriate statistic; whereas for the long-term outcomes, analyses of variance procedures were appropriate. Because of age differences, analysis of covariance was used with age. As shown in table 4–2, the only consistent finding was an association between measures of threat appraisal and negative emotional reactions subsequent to the move. Associations with other reactive measures (physical, cognitive, and social interaction changes) are rare across studies, as is any association between threat appraisal and long-term outcomes.

Although most elderly did not appraise the impending moves as representing a threat, those who did view the event with feelings of loss and dissatisfaction became more depressed. Overall, our analysis of the relationship between consciously reported threat and both long- and short-term assessment of reactions is equivocal. That dysphoric affect increases in those who anticipate the move in threatening terms jibes with theoretical expectations about the nature of threat and threat reactions. When coping strategies are not useful in limiting painful affects associated with threat, our measures index experience threat. Or to state it another way, the measures of manifest threat reflect the capacity to contain painful feelings associated with threat. When these negative emotions are not contained prior to relocation, there is a likelihood that there will be an increase in subsequent dysphoria. Despite this linkage, evidence that the ability to contain threat effects long-term outcomes was not found.

We thus turned to other measurement strategies in order to more fully appraise the conceptual utility of threat and anticipatory loss as sources of stress in relocation. In large part we took this step because appraisal of threat can theoretically indicate several contradictory hypotheses. Thus, let us consider what it means to consciously report that painful affects are associated with an impending event. Such reports may occur when intense fear exists, and their direct expression may indicate inadequacy in coping.

73

TABLE 4-2
Correlations (of ± .20 or Greater) Between Conscious Appraisals of Threat and Loss and Short-Term Reactions

| | Short-Term Reactions | | | | | | | | | | | |
| | Physical | | | Cognitive | | | Affective | | | Social Interaction | | |
Measure	Old Ladies	Home/Life	Elites	Old Ladies	Home/Life	Elites	Old Ladies	Home/Life	Elites	Old Ladies	Home/Life	Elites
Feelings about leaving							.35	.26	.39			−.22
Expected losses							.29	.22	.29			
Anticipated satisfactions						−.20	.45	.30	.30			

On the other hand, since intense affect expression is appropriate to the threatening situation, reports of negative affect may signify sound coping, and those who permit themselves to experience painful affects may thus be the most active copers rather than the most inadequate.

The absence of threat appraisals, in turn, can be explained by conflicting hypotheses. The absence of negative appraisals may reflect the reality that a situation is not threatening, as was apparently the case in the Deinstitutionalized Elites study. On the other hand, if a potential threat truly exists, then the absence of such reports might reflect inadequate coping. The experience of threat and concomitant negative affects may exist for a brief time, idiosyncratic for each individual. A poignant moment of overwhelming threat may have existed but have been quickly contained by coping strategies. Thus, at the time of our interview, the absence of such reports may reflect such containment. Such complexities may represent the true state of affairs, and our failure to link threat to long-term outcomes may be a function of time of measurement as well as of the measurement itself. Some support for the view that the consciously reported attitudes held by those awaiting institutionalization represent, in large part, defensive containment can be found in other studies of institutionalization, as well as in the interviews with our control group of community-dwelling elderly.

It is common wisdom, supported by findings from several studies, that the elderly view entering institutions with dread. Kleemeier (1961b), for example, suggests that older people exhibited a generalized negative feeling toward all special settings for the elderly. Montgomery (1965), who studied rural elderly, found a consistent desire to remain in their present residence and equated this with a highly valued independence. Shanas (1961) found that older people associated moving to institutions with loss of independence and saw rejection by their children as a prelude to death. Elderly people in their late seventies and eighties can be expected to have considered the possibility of seeking institutional care if required by circumstances.

Open-ended interviews with community-dwelling aged revealed some of the following images of institutionalization: "Entering the institution would be giving up everything." "It is a place to die." One respondent said, "I'd have to give up everything. It's a new life. If, God forbid, I became helpless, that would be my only reason. And I hope and pray that day will never come." For another respondent, the home is "an institution" and "an institution means a place where people are sent—a home, a hospital, it could even be a jail!" Still another respondent said:

Most of them go there because they have to. Their children don't want them. They have no money. They're weaker. Their mates are dead. They have no choice. They play cards, look at TV, sit and look out of the window; read newspapers; listen to sermons, lectures, debates; they have entertainment. I know everything's regimented. You have to be up at a certain time. You have to have a bath at a certain time. Meals are at a certain time. Then there are times when you are free and can go to the sun parlors and talk or laugh with your friends. I wouldn't like it; if I have to, because of deterioration, I would make up my mind that that's my fate. I think it's a place to die.

The attitudes expressed by elderly living in the community who had no plans to enter institutions contrast sharply with the attitudes found among those waiting to enter institutions. It is thus likely that conscious reports of apprehension among those who have already made such a decision reflect their attempts to adjust to the impending event more than they reflect their feelings about such an event. To circumvent the problem posed by direct queries, an indirect strategy for measuring personal symbols each respondent attached to relocation was developed.

MEASURING THE IMPACT OF THREAT ON PERCEPTUAL PROCESSES—THE TAT CARDS

A series of TAT cards was constructed to represent issues and conflicts thought to be critical for elderly people anticipating entrance into homes for the aged (Lieberman and Lakin 1963). This "Institutional TAT" was designed to elicit responses of separation, dependency, and potentially conflictful issues of institutional life, such as intimacy with peers and interaction with staff. Two identical series of cards were constructed, with the sex of the central person changed for men and for women. The series consisted of the following cards:

Card 1. Rejection—Packing: An aged person packing a suitcase and several people, both younger adults and children, standing in the foreground and background.

Card 2. Separation—Entering: An aged person walking down the path into a building clearly identified as an old-age institution.

Card 3. Intimacy—Roommates: Two aged persons of the same sex in a setting drawn to represent a typical room in an institution.

Card 4. Authority/Dependence—Director Scene: An aged person about to enter a room clearly designated as the office of an institutional director, who is drawn as a middle-aged man.

Card 5. Isolation/Integration—Group Scene: Four elderly persons seated in the foreground; a man with his hands raised as if gesturing is apparently talking to another man and two women; in the background, facing away from the group, an elderly person with his head resting on his hands.

Both the standard Murray TAT series (Cards 1, 2, 6BM, 7BM, and 17) and the Institutional TAT series were shown to the respondents. The standard Murray TAT instructions were used, with the addition of the demonstration method of instructions. A Murray TAT card, not one used in the aforementioned series, was shown to each respondent and he or she was told that "we are going to show you a series of such cards, for which we would like you to tell a story." The interviewer then read a prepared story, told the respondent that different stories are equally appropriate, and then read a second prepared story. Reading of prepared stories doubled the length of stories told when compared with story lengths using the standard Murray instructions. Our instructions also made it clear that there were no right or wrong stories, which is particularly important for the elderly, who appear to view such tests as measures of their intelligence or memory and assume that there is a "right" answer.

Given the issues evoked by the Institutional TAT cards, it was assumed that apprehension or anxiety regarding the meaning of these stimuli would cause distortion in the stories told to the cards. The Dana (1955) scoring system that has been developed for the Murray TAT series was adapted for the Institutional TAT series. (See technical note 2.)

Results.   Did those waiting to enter the institution—individuals under assumed threat—perform more poorly on the Institutional TAT than on the standard Murray TAT? Table 4–3 shows the proportion of people in two control groups as well as among those waiting to enter the institution who showed discrepancies between their results on the Murray and Institutional TAT series. (See technical note 3.) When compared with the control groups, almost three times as many of those waiting to enter institutions performed better on the Murray TAT than on the institutional TAT, which suggests that the latent content of the Institutional TAT cards is

TABLE 4–3
*Threat as Measured by TAT Discrepancy
in the Home for Life Study*

	Discrepancy (percentage)		
Sample	*Murray TAT Better than Institutional TAT*	*Murray TAT Same as Institutional TAT*	*Murray TAT Worse than Institutional TAT*
Study Sample—while on Waiting List	49	6	44
Control Samples			
Institutional	16	6	78
Community	20	10	70

disruptive to an appreciable number of elderly awaiting institutionaliza- tion. Although this contrast is rather dramatic, only about one-half the sample under threat revealed perceptual distortions.

Because this measure of the disruption of preceptual processes does not have the obvious validity of conscious appraisals of threat, correlations between the TAT discrepancy scores and other measures assessed at the same time, while respondents were awaiting admission to the homes, were used to determine the score's significance. The TAT discrepancy measure was found not to be associated with general affect states, such as anxiety or depression, which may have disrupted performance. Nor was the mea- sure associated with general mental health or with most personality char- acteristics measured in this study. The only appreciable associations of high discrepancy (that is, greater distortion on the Institutional TAT) were with less adequate social functioning, less ability to extend beyond the present into the future, greater use of evidence from the past rather than from present social interaction for maintaining stability of the self, and passivity. This configuration suggests that those who demonstrate ap- prehension associated with the Institutional TAT have a general tendency to restrict their vision, not only in telling TAT stories but also in coping with the future; they show a propensity to rely on the past and adopt a passive stance toward the world.

Perceptual discrepancy was not, however, associated with subsequent short-term reactions or long-term adaptations. Thus, although it was possi- ble to determine that an appreciable minority of elderly awaiting institu- tionalization manifest perceptual distortion indicative of threat, neither its presence nor its magnitude is associated with subsequent short- or long- term outcomes. The absence of a relationship between level of threat, as measured by its effects on perceptual processes, and relocation effects led us to explore yet another strategy for testing the hypothesis that relocation constitutes a stress for the elderly because it symbolizes a dreaded and potentially harmful event.

THE CONSEQUENCES OF THREAT

In the previous section, those elderly awaiting admission to homes for the aged were compared with the community and institutional control samples. Differences between the waiting list sample and the other two samples on discrepancies in perceptions of TAT cards were interpreted to be a function of experienced threat. This comparative design was expanded.

78

The Impact of Threat and Loss

Most threat studies examine situations in which the investigators assume that the impending event is of sufficient negative valence that measurable consequences are likely. Assessed in such designs are consequences; the intensity of threat is inferred, not directly measured. Consistent with this approach, our "threat group"—elderly people awaiting entrance into the home—was compared with the two demographically matched control groups. One group was composed of community-dwelling elderly; the other, of individuals already living in a home, who were assumed to have gone through the upheavals of admission and initial impact and were now "stabilized." The reason for using these two control groups for contrasts is obvious; a much more powerful case for threat can be made if it can be shown that those awaiting entrance to the institution, those in the "threat condition," show signs of threat response when compared with a matched group already living in the institution. The samples were compared on indices assessing functioning hypothesized to be "threat"-sensitive, including levels of psychological functioning as well as signs of mobilization in response to threat. Our measures included a variety of assessments of individuals' cognitive functioning, affective responsivity, emotional states, and self-perception.

The findings, as portrayed in table 4–4, indicate that the "threatened" respondents showed the following characteristics (when compared to both control groups):

1. Cognitive constriction, encompassing some disorientation in time and space and a moderate degree of cognitive disorganization. The overall pattern is more suggestive of constriction in response to the external environment than of disorientation or disorganization.
2. Constriction in affective responsivity. The evidence points to intensely felt affects that are strongly contained.
3. Diminished feeling of potency in interpersonal relationships.

The analysis, however, failed to demonstrate the expected increase in anxiety and depression; although individuals under threat were significantly more anxious than the elderly in the community, they were not more depressed or anxious than elderly already living in institutions. These differences among closely matched groups of elderly people suggest that those waiting to enter the institutions showed some behaviors commensurate with what is known from other studies about the effects of threat on psychological functioning.

Threat, of course, is not an enduring condition. We would expect that those psychological characteristics affected by threat would be altered in

TABLE 4-4

Comparisons among the Study (under Threat) Sample and Control Samples in the Home for Life Study

Area of Psychological Functioning	Mean			Cross-Sectional Comparisons Contrast				Change for the Study Sample (N = 78)			
	Community (N=35)	Waiting List (N=100)	Institution-alized (N=37)	Community vs. Waiting List		Waiting List vs. Institutionalized		While on Waiting List	Two Months after Admission	t	p
				F	p	F	p				
Cognitive functioning											
Orientation (Mental Status Questionnaire)	.7	1.3	1.7	.44	N.S.	1.29	N.S.	1.3	2.2	5.00	.001
Time estimate	23.2	21.8	26.4	.84	N.S.	7.57	.007	21.7	23.6	.93	N.S.
Retention (paired word learning)	7.6	12.6	16.2	30.63	.0001	23.14	.0001	11.5	10.8	.53	N.S.
Organization (Bender-Gestalt Figures)	27.3	34.5	35.2	3.79	.05	.02	N.S.	36.2	32.4	2.80	.01
Perceptual accuracy (TAT)	27.9	21.8	21.1	20.11	.0001	.21	N.S.	21.7	21.9	.29	N.S.
Originality (Reitman Stick Figure Test)	10.2	9.4	9.9	10.82	.0007	3.68	.05	9.7	10.5	1.67	N.S.
Signs of cognitive inadequacy	.5	1.4	1.0	5.12	.02	4.42	.04	1.4	1.2	.21	N.S.
Affective responsiveness											
Range of affects	5.8	4.3	5.2	21.54	.0001	6.03	.01	4.5	4.3	.68	N.S.
Willingness to introspect	3.4	2.1	1.8	35.26	.0001	.03	N.S.	2.1	1.9	1.61	N.S.
Emotional States											
Well-being	19.2	15.8	16.8	15.86	.0002	.36	N.S.	15.9	16.3	1.01	N.S.
Hope	.7	-.9	-.4	15.37	.0002	1.89	N.S.	0	-.2	2.41	.02
Anxiety	15.3	19.8	16.2	6.16	.01	1.22	N.S.	19.7	18.3	1.59	N.S.
Depression	7.6	13.9	12.3	17.01	.0001	.39	N.S.	13.5	13.5	.16	N.S.
Self-perception											
Perception of self-care inadequacy	.8	2.3	2.7	.86	N.S.	.05	N.S.	2.5	3.7	2.80	.01
Self-esteem	23.2	19.2	18.3	15.82	.0002	2.31	N.S.	20.3	19.7	.79	N.S.
Adequacy	3.9	-.83	1.8	8.50	.004	5.89	.02	-.86	-.74	.18	N.S.
Dominance	.34	-.21	.31	3.75	.05	4.72	.03	-.04	-.18	1.00	N.S.
Affiliation	.08	.16	.09	.21	N.S.	2.43	N.S.	.27	.02	2.41	.02

a positive direction once the threat condition was lifted. The elderly waiting to enter the home were assessed on the same measures approximately two months after institutionalization, a time at which the disruptive effects of entry could safely be assumed to have passed. Very little change in the direction of improvement occurred, however, as shown in table 4-4. Only one measure—cognitive integration, as measured by the Bender-Gestalt test—showed significant improvement. This improvement is probably an artifact influenced by practice effects.

Our expectation that the measurable effects attributed to threat would dissipate once the threat condition no longer existed was not borne out by the findings. Several explanations for this lack of amelioration once the threat dissipated suggest themselves. The overall research strategy and attendant analytic procedure look at crises through an examination of specific issues: threat, loss, and new adaptive demands. In our longitudinal design, these issues are confronted at different points in time; we can talk of individuals waiting to enter the institution facing threat and can describe changes in the environment that require new patterns of behavior as taking place once the individual has entered the institution. Despite this sequencing, our ability to isolate specific consequences uniquely associated with different sources of stress is, to say the least, imprecise. To link cognitive disorganization uniquely to threat and increased depression to loss may be beyond current theoretical and especially measurement capabilities. Perhaps the elderly respondents failed to show a recovery from the assumed effects of threat because of other influences associated with life in the institution. We did find, for example, as described in the section that follows, that loss is most intense several months subsequent to institutionalization, and perhaps psychological functioning, initially depressed by threat, is similarly affected by loss. Equally possible is that in reporting population means, we have obscured individual differences and have obscured differences in reaction to threat when it is no longer present. This issue will be dealt with at the end of this chapter.

At this point in our presentation, the best we can say is that the evidence for threat as an explanation of the effects of relocation is ambiguous—despite the evidence that the functioning of the elderly people in a threat situation was negatively affected compared with that of elderly people not under threat and the modest positive correlations, replicated across studies, between threat appraisal and subsequent depressive affect. The findings of a stable pattern of malfunctioning subsequent to threat cast doubt on explaining the all too real level of malfunctioning subsequent to relocation on the basis of a simple anticipatory framework.

Loss

MEASURING ANTICIPATED LOSS

Studies of loss ordinarily examine the effects of life events such as the loss of functions or roles. Such investigations focus on the processes used to cope after an actual loss. In our study, the specifications of what is lost are less clear; what was lost varied from individual to individual. In the move from one institutional setting to another—the Unwilling Old Ladies study—the respondents described the impending loss of significant relationships with particular staff members or particular friends within the institution. The Death of an Institution participants frequently experienced loss in terms of a particular role within the institution which seemed to serve as a major source of status and differentiation; some talked about particular relationships with a staff member or with another patient. In the Home for Life study, losses were often described by those about to enter an institution in terms of losing independence or self-respect, or losing personal objects that had been part and parcel of their lives for many years; others focused on the loss of a place in which to entertain children and grandchildren; for still others, it was moving away from one or more friends or family members that was most upsetting. Thus, in contrast, for example, to studies of widowhood, which have a specific focus of loss, relocation is a much more ambiguous loss stimulus.

Bereavement studies examine individuals who have experienced a loss that for them appears irreplaceable. Such studies are psychological examinations of the inner states of people subsequent to an event; in contrast, we are studying loss in an anticipatory framework. We looked at an event that had not occurred and asked whether they associated this imminent event with loss.

This ambiguity of loss stimulus necessitated a distinct investigative strategy. We could not assume—as we were able to do in the analysis of threat based on TAT discrepancy scores, for example,—that threat-induced anxiety interferes with performance when the respondent is confronted with specific stimuli representing relocation. Since we could not specify the stimulus conditions, we relied on measures assessing the individual's feelings of loss without being able to ascribe the loss directly to relocation. Loss intensity scores were based on the respondent's earliest memory.

The Impact of Threat and Loss

THE MEASUREMENT OF LOSS

The respondent's earliest memory was selected as the source of data to assess loss intensity because older people are quite willing and able to talk about their personal past. The contemporary view in psychology is that earliest memories reflect the incorporation of a meaningful early event into a current environmental context; the early memory is a vehicle through which the person expresses current concerns. For example, Schachtel (1947, p. 3) has succinctly stated that "memory as a function of the living personality can be understood only as a capacity for the organization and reconstruction of past experience in the service of present needs, fears and interests." This process of organizing the earliest memory in the service of current adaptation is indeed a complex one, which necessitates mechanisms for translating unconscious or latent content to a manifest level. Two primary models exist for understanding the mechanism of translation: Freud focused on the concealing properties of the reconstruction of early memory, while Adler focused on its revealing properties. For Freud (1938), earliest memories were like screen memories, masking recollection of the true event, because of "their banal and often meaningless" content; concealment has occurred through repression of persistent dynamic content. For Adler (1937), on the other hand, the manifest content of the earliest memory provided a direct clue to understanding an individual's persistent style of life.

Scales were developed to classify intensity of loss expressed in the earliest memory. A five-point ordinal scale was constructed in which the low end represented the least expression of loss and the high end, the highest expression of loss. (See technical note 4.)

The following themes in the respondents' memories were noted:

Level 1. Nonloss: For example, "I used to have another fellow. We used to go out for good times. We used to go to a concert, listen to music. We used to play ball. You know how kids are." Or, "It's been so long ago. There were seven children, and I was the only daughter. As soon as I could walk I helped my mother in the house. I'd wash the dishes. There was a house full of children. And mother was also cooking. I was about ten years old."

Level 2. Nonloss; implied loss that is defended from awareness. A Level 2 rating was given to themes in which the respondent is the recipient of direct and primitive gratification and where overt loss is not introduced. "I remember I was in a dream—and father being in the army and coming home on furlough. He was good-looking, tall and dark and handsome. He used to bring us presents when he came. I was about four or five."

Level 3. Interpersonal loss: Losses at Level 3 include separation and loneliness. For example, "My mother and father going on a shopping trip for a place of business. Though we had supervision, I felt very lonely."

Level 4. Injury or mutilation: For example, "When I was two I had scarlet fever. . . . I just remember that I had it, no detail." Or, "I was ten years old. A rabid dog bit me on the leg. The doctor was not there . . . in the alley. Doctor came . . . gave father a prescription for some medicine. Two men came in and tried to burn it out. . . . Five marks of teeth. For six months doctor came and scraped off skin. Doctor and two men had to hold me. Very painful. Scars are there yet."

Level 5. Death: For example, "When my mother was sick in bed, as she passed away I cried. I was about five or six. I try not to think about it."

Early memory material was collected from respondents in two of the four studies—the Home for Life study and the Deinstitutionalized Elites study. Table 4–5 shows the proportion of individuals from these studies showing nonloss themes (Levels 1 and 2), separation themes (Level 3), and mutilation and death themes (Levels 4 and 5).

As shown in table 4–5, the awaiting institutionalization group in the Home for Life study introduced more themes of loss than did the matched community sample not awaiting entrance into institutions. Themes of separation are the single most important indicator of differences between the waiting list and community samples ($p < .05$). In contrast, comparisons between the waiting list and institutionalized samples show differences, although not statistically significant ones, in mutilation and death themes.

An analysis of information on life events that was available for the waiting list and community samples suggests that the significant difference

TABLE 4–5
Loss Expressed in Respondents' Earliest Memory

		Expression of Loss					
		Nonloss (Levels 1 and 2)		Separation (Level 3)		Mutilation or Death (Levels 4 and 5)	
Study	N*	N	%	N	%	N	%
Home for Life study							
Study sample—while on waiting list	68	27	40	19	28	22	32
Institutional sample	30	11	37	5	17	14	47
Community sample	28	17	61	3	11	8	28
Deinstitutionalized Elites							
Study sample pre-discharge	73	44	60	9	12	27	37

* Nearly 20 percent of the respondents refused to complete this task.

between these samples in loss (as measured by the early memory scales) is not a product of actual losses prior to the time of measurement. Rather, themes in the early memories of those awaiting admission are related to the meanings they ascribe to relocation. (See technical note 5 for details.)

The finding that those facing institutionalization interpret its meaning in terms of loss was not replicated in the study of the Deinstitutionalized Elites. Why this should be so is not immediately clear. In table 4–1, when the studies were compared on conscious attitude toward relocation, they were similar. Yet the two samples produced dramatically different early memories: The typical early memories among the Home for Life respondents prior to their move were of childhood, whereas the early memories of the psychiatric patients from the Deinstitutionalized Elites study prior to relocation ranged from childhood to adulthood. Perhaps the task of providing an early memory is a qualitatively different experience for a psychiatric population than it is for an elderly person living in the community who is not psychiatrically impaired. On the other hand, for the Deinstitutionalized Elites, the relocation situation was not "objectively" as threatening because their relocation may have symbolized a status increase, in moving from a mental institution to community-based halfway houses, boarding homes, or similar facilities.

An analysis, similar to the previous examination of the relationship between threat and outcome, indicated that anticipated loss was not associated with either short-term reactions or long-term outcomes. Thus, despite our observations that impending environmental change is experienced by many elderly people as both threatening and portending loss, only weak support was developed to the effect that relocation affects subsequent behavior because of the meaning it has for the elderly.

RELOCATION AS A LOSS

Although we have been able to demonstrate that relocation for those awaiting entrance into old-age homes is anticipated and symbolized as a loss, no association was found between such psychological states and subsequent reactions and outcomes. To pursue the psychology of loss one step further, we changed our focus from the anticipation of loss to the loss experienced after respondents had actually encountered relocation. This analysis is analogous to the classical studies of loss, in which the interest is in examining psychological states after the occurrence of bereavement.

To explore the loss associated with relocation itself, earliest memories were examined for changes between pre- and post-relocation periods. Changes in earliest memories from before to after entering and living in the homes in the Home for Life study, along with similar changes from before to after discharge to a variety of environments among those in the Deinstitutionalized Elites study, were compared with changes over one year for elderly in the community and for elderly who had already been institutionalized in homes for at least one year.

We found that the elderly entering homes for the aged manifested a significantly greater shift toward the increased introduction of loss themes in their earliest memories than those in the control groups. As reported in detail by Tobin and Etigson (1968), 51 percent (or 23 out of 45) of the repeat memories of those becoming institutionalized manifested such shifts in introduction of loss, as contrasted with only 20 percent (or 14 out of 70) of all other repeat earliest memories. This represents a significant difference of 31 percent (t=4.8, p<.001).

In contrast to the shift among those individuals entering institutions, the changes in intensity of loss found among the Deinstitutionalized Elite respondents were in an opposite direction. Early memory loss themes were manifested by 47 percent of the sample prior to discharge and 39 percent subsequent to discharge. The mean level of intensity at Time 1 was 2.6 and at Time 2, 2.2. Again, our findings suggest that in the Home for Life study of individuals moving into institutional settings, loss is a characteristic emotional experience. In contrast, for a highly selected psychiatric population residing in mental hospitals before being discharged to community facilities, the intensity of loss is, on the average, initially lower, and it changes in a direction suggesting that the experience is not one of intense loss.

Our analysis, then, using a projective technique to assess loss intensity, suggests that in one of the studies, the Home for Life study, a significant portion of the population experiences more intense loss following relocation. As with our findings on anticipated loss, however, intensity of loss subsequent to relocation was not predictive of long-term outcome. Thus, although a significant proportion of the elderly respondents experienced relocation as a loss, its intensity is not appreciably associated with subsequent adaptation.

Implications

Our goal in the present chapter and the one that follows is to determine what aspects of relocation constitute a stress for the elderly. Evidence on outcomes provided by the four studies in which elderly were interviewed prior to relocation is stark testimony to the stressful nature of such moves. The present chapter explored the thesis that such situations pose a crisis in the lives of the elderly because of the personal meaning that they signify for them. We were able, in three of the four relocation studies, to examine, through a variety of strategies, the hypothesis that the symbolic meanings associated with relocation are the source of stress. Our findings support the view that threat and loss constitute the psychological realities of relocation for a substantial number of respondents studied. We found both individual differences and differences in the number of individuals across studies who exhibited high levels of threat and loss. Such differences are consistent with the differences in the relocation circumstances described in chapter 3.

The clearest evidence that threat and loss are psychological realities in the relocation situation was found in the Home for Life study. Both the design of this study and detailed data permitted us to examine a variety of evidence about threat and loss associated with relocation. The finding that cognitive performance on the Institutional TAT series was different for those who were waiting to enter institutions provided support for the view that threat has negative psychological consequences. Of greater import were the comparisons among comparable samples differing only in their status vis-à-vis institutionalization: community-dwelling elderly, the already institutionalized, and those awaiting entry into institutions. Measurable psychological effects of a deleterious nature were found to occur prior to relocation, an occurrence that is reasonably attributable to threat and anticipatory loss. Thus, the case for viewing radical changes in the life space of the elderly (such as relocation) as engendering threat and loss—and for holding that such states do have effects on psychological functioning—was supported.

When, however, we turn to the relationship of threat and anticipated loss to subsequent effects, our findings are less clear. Measures of anticipated loss were not associated with subsequent short-term reactions or long-term outcomes (increased morbidity, mortality, and psychological disability). Although measures of threat were linked to increased depression, they were not predictive of long-term adaptation. The association between intensity of threat and increased depressive affect shortly after relocation (but not long-term adaptation) is puzzling, particularly so because we have evidence that changes in level of depression from pre- to post-institutionalization are predictive of long-term outcomes. We believe that the absence of a strong linkage between both threat and anticipated loss and subsequent adaptation is, in part, a result of measurement problems. Although they are theoretically distinct, it is well-nigh impossible to empirically disentangle intensity of threat or loss from the simultaneous defense and coping strategies used to ward off the fact of the event itself, along with its emotional impact. We shall see in chapter 6, when we turn our attention away from measures directly assessing anticipatory states and examine threat management strategies, that the linkage between threat and subsequent adaptations becomes more comprehensible. It is not the intensity of threat or anticipated loss that is critical as much as the strategies that the elderly develop to cope with such feelings.

Although threat and loss are psychological realities in these situations, and although they have a measurable impact on the functioning of the elderly, the magnitude of relationships to outcomes is certainly not large. The fact that the situations of relocation differed markedly in the level of threat and loss despite similarities in outcome rates across studies does, however, suggest that the source of stress associated with radical changes in life space must lie in factors beyond the symbolic properties of the relocation. In the chapter that follows, we address once again the issue of what it is about these circumstances that constitutes a crisis and examine an alternative hypothesis, which we call the "magnitude of challenge."

Technical Notes

1. *Examples of Expectation Rating Scales.* Some examples of feelings about leaving: (+2) "Leaving here would be the best thing in the world for me. Everything will be all right once I get out of here"; (+1) Less importance is placed on the event or it is qualified, for example, "I'd like to leave but . . ." or, "It's nice to be here, too, because you don't have to worry about where your meals are coming from . . ."; (−1) "It might be nice to have my freedom, but . . ."; (−2) "That would be too cruel, for me to be moved," or, "This has been my home for _____ years; I've nowhere else to go," or, "God wants me to stay here so I'll do what He says," or, "It would kill me if they sent me out of here."

Some examples of expected losses: Ratings of 1 were given to individuals who listed a large number of losses as well as those who indicated only one particular loss associated with intense dysphoric affect. One respondent who was rated 1 said: "Moving means I have to give up everything." A rating of 2, "some loss," was given to those who experienced losses but appeared not to be as strongly disturbed by them. A 2 rating was also used for those expecting some losses, but feeling that these losses were to some extent balanced by gratifying "losses," negative things that they were happy to leave. At the other end of the five-point continuum were respondents who talked about losses entirely in terms of those things that they were "happy to lose"—such as conflictual interpersonal relationships and noxious environments.

The following are some examples of anticipated satisfactions: Those receiving a score of -2 were respondents who viewed the new situation as an insult with no redeeming features. For example: "You're nobody in the home—nobody anymore—and you can't do things for people. My life is doing things for people. What could I possibly do for others in the home?" Or, "I haven't told a soul that I'm going to the old people's home. They think it's terrible there; it's so depressing—there are so many sick people sitting around." At the other end of the scale were those individuals who could describe concrete aspects of the new situation that they considered positive. These individuals did not necessarily completely avoid mentioning negative aspects, but the general quality of the person's expectations was positive and negative features of the new environment were deemphasized.

2. The Dana system evaluates adequacy of performance through two major components: perceptual organization (PO) and perceptual range (PR). The perceptual organization component, which reflects the person's ability to follow standard directions in telling a story, consists of evaluation of seven categories: (1) description; inclusion of (2) present, (3) past, and (4) future events; (5) attribution of feelings; (6) thoughts to the person represented in the TAT; (7) an outcome of the story. Perceptual range, in turn, is focused on whether the story contains the content usually found in stories told by others, that is, the elements in the stories of 90 percent of a normative population. For the Murray TAT, the norms established by Dana were used; for the Institutional TAT, the norms were established by analyzing the stories told by the elderly living in the community. By this procedure, the criteria of adequate perceptual range in stories told to Card No. 1 of the Institutional TAT series, the Packing Scene, included: (1) identification of the scene as a family scene, (2) a specific reference to a packing activity, (3) the concept of transience, and (4) a description of the emotional state of the person packing.

The interrater reliability for the scoring of the Murray TAT using two independent judges on ten cases was a rank-order (rho) correlation of .65 for the PO scores and .75 for the PR scores; and for the institutional TAT on ten cases, the rho for PO was .95, and for PR, .90.

3. It will be noted from table 4–3 that approximately three-quarters of each of the two control groups—both those already living in the institu-

tion and those from the community—exhibited better performances on the institutional TAT cards than on the Murray. Despite our attempts to create equivalent scoring procedures for both sets of cards, it appears that the norm for an aged population that is not threatened by institutionalization is slightly better on the institutional set of TAT cards. Perhaps—and we can bring no direct evidence to bear on this hypothesis—this difference can be explained by the greater ambiguity of the Murray cards. The institutional TAT cards may be easier for the elderly, thus producing a skewed distribution showing less adequate performance on the Murray than on the institutional TAT.

4. Interjudge reliability was established by having three independent judges rate a sample of 120 earliest memories on a five-point scale. For 57 percent of the memories there was exact agreement by the three judges, and on the remaining 43 percent of the memories, two out of the three agreed.

5. The assumption that loss themes expressed in early memories are associated with the actuality of entering and living in the relocation environment rather than with idiosyncratic losses in the elderly's personal lives is based on data from notes about actual life events during the three years preceding the waiting list interviews. These events included physical illness and economic changes as well as a variety of social changes in the lives of the individuals (changes in living arrangements and relationship and losses of significant others through moves and death). The aged in the community control sample had in the past several years been through events that were similar to events experienced by those becoming institutionalized, particularly in terms of loss. We further examined such events by constructing an accumulation score. When the waiting list sample was compared with the community sample, there were differences in the accumulation of events (p<.001 using the Kolmogoroff-Smirnoff tests). Whereas 12 percent of the community sample (five out of forty) did not change in any of the four areas, only 2 percent in the waiting list sample did not change. The major differences between the two samples lay not in the actual events, such as death of others or increased physical separation from others, but in changes in relationships, which were reflected in perceptions of the event by the person rather than in the actual occurrence of a specified event. Our analysis, therefore, of actual life events that occurred to the individuals in the control sample and to those awaiting institutionalization suggests that events directly associated with loss are not significantly greater for one than for the other group—despite our findings that loss measured by a projective test clearly distinguishes these two groups.

90

5

The Crisis of
Environmental Change

THE MOVE from one environment to another constitutes a severe stress, wreaking havoc among a large proportion of the elderly people we have studied. How are we to understand such findings? In the preceding chapter we interpreted the stress associated with changes in social contexts from the perspective of the symbolic meaning of the relocations in terms of psychological threat and loss. Here we will examine an alternative hypothesis: that life space changes constitute a crisis because of demands on individuals for new adaptive efforts in their reconstituted social surrounds. Relocation constitutes a stress to the degree that it disrupts customary modes of behavior and imposes a need for strenuous psychological work. From this perspective, crises present the individual with the need to abandon many assumptions about the everyday world and the challenge of replacing them with others. This may involve new mechanisms for relating to and fulfilling needs in their social world that either are not in their current repertoire or require considerable effort to accomplish. This view of stress, then, is one of overload of capacities required to meet the new demands—a perspective especially relevant to the elderly, whose weakened biological capacity places them at high risk.

Environmental discontinuity can take many forms. Consider the following case vignette: Mrs. B. was an eighty-four-year-old widow who had been living a fiercely independent life since her husband's death fifteen years earlier. Although her children, who lived in the same city, were her primary source of instrumental and affective resources, she maintained her own apartment and life-style. A prime characteristic of Mrs. B.'s life-style, one particularly relevant to environmental change, was her "internal time clock." Her use of time was highly flexible and varied from day to day. She arose in the morning when she "felt like getting out of bed," ate when she felt hungry, and so forth. To the casual observer, this may have seemed like a disorganized life pattern, but in actuality it was not. Because Mrs. B. had few normative constraints or demands on her, she could indulge herself in many ways, including scheduling her daily use of time. Her self-indulgence should not be interpreted as isolation. She had meaningful relationships with kin and neighbors, but they were conducted within her flexible schedule. Failing health impelled Mrs. B. to enter a home for the aged. Although she looked forward to becoming a resident in the institution, the month after Mrs. B. entered she was a troubled woman perceived by the staff as having "difficult adjustment problems." In large part, these problems resulted from the incongruity between her previous flexible scheduling pattern and the requirements of the institutional life, with its highly structured time schedules. Major readjustments were required for Mrs. B. if she were to live comfortably in the institutional setting.

This brief example illustrates one kind of incongruity between individuals and their relocation environments. While not all elderly people experience the difficulty Mrs. B. did with respect to the structuring of time, her story does illustrate how a previous life-style, with its particular idiosyncratic relationship to a prior environment, can create adaptive problems in a new environment.

SOURCES OF ENVIRONMENTAL STRESS

In studying relocation, stress overload—and the adaptive crisis it entails—can be reduced to three environmental sources. Most straightforward is the quality of the relocation environment. A noxious environment is one that impedes adaptation and limits the use of previously successful coping mechanisms. Although there is no absolute definition of a noxious environment, nor would we propose that a given environment will be noxious for everyone, we do accept the view that investigators can specify environmental conditions that are likely to restrict the possibilities for successful adaptation. As will be described later in this chapter, we operationally defined noxious environments using social-psychological characteristics that have been related empirically to the elderly's adaptation to institutional life.

A second source of overload is the congruence or fit between the individual's personality or life-style and the adaptive demands of a particular environment. Here our emphasis is on individual style and environmental opportunities. A simple example would be that environments that reward competitiveness would not be favorable for individuals who shy away from competition.

A third source of environmentally generated stress overload is the lack of congruence between the environment in which a person is accustomed to existing and the new or relocation environment. The larger the dissimilarity or discontinuity between environments, the more numerous are the personal changes required to reestablish homeostasis. The now classic example of the effects of environmental discontinuity is culture shock among Peace Corps volunteers. The impact of the quality of the environment in underdeveloped countries cannot be minimized, nor can the effects of the discrepancy between the volunteers' previous adaptive styles, which had been developed in advanced Western societies, and the demands of their new foreign environments. Still, the sheer magnitude of difference between the home and new environments, and the accompanying perceptual disorganization, suggests that environmental discontinuity per se can be implicated in causing disorientation and other untoward reactions. We recognize, however, that although these three environmental perspectives can be conceptualized as distinct, obviously when we look at relocation in real life they are not.

PLAN FOR STUDYING ENVIRONMENTAL STRESS

Investigating environmental changes as a source of stress requires the study of individuals at two points in time and in two distinct environments. Before we can attribute stress to environmental discontinuity or noncongruence, we must also entertain the alternative hypothesis that stress is contingent on the quality of the environment into which the elderly person moves. Thus, it is not sufficient to know that maladaptive reactions were associated with living in a new environment. Rather, the design requires an examination of the effects of both the quality of the person's social surround and the changes in environments on subsequent adaptation.

Our conceptual framework, as well as the methodological strategies we used to explore environmental hypotheses, emerged during the eight years in which the studies were conducted. Each study reflects an increasing specificity about environments. In all, three conceptual frameworks and several methodological strategies were used.

The Home for Life study explored the congruence model by applying an assessment framework of person-environment fit. Well-adjusted "old-timers" who were already living in the institution were used to establish the characteristics of adapted persons, after which we assessed these dimensions in individuals who had not yet been admitted. In the second study, Deinstitutionalized Elites, the hypothesis was more fully examined by assessing the need system of the person about to be relocated, along with the capacity of the new environment to meet these needs. Since the respondents were relocated into twenty-six different and distinct environments, the study also provided us with an opportunity to explore the effects of environmental quality on adaptation. In the final study, Death of an Institution, assessments were made by measuring the social-psychological characteristics of both the pre-relocation and post-relocation environments and generating discrepancy scores for each individual. Recall that this was the only study among the four in which both pre-relocation and post-relocation settings varied. Because the methods used to make environmental assessments were identical at both points in time, a direct test of the environmental discontinuity hypothesis was possible. Moreover, the even larger number of post-relocation environments (142) than in the study of Deinstitutionalized Elites permitted a more refined test of environmental quality.

Conceptualizations of Environments. What do we mean by *environment?* Probably no more complex and conceptually muddled area can be found in the social sciences. To some investigators, environment implies physical attributes: size, pathways for mobility, and complexity. To the social geographer, it may imply accessibility to transportation and community resources. For social psychologists, the relevant environment may consist of the significant personal networks that surround an individual or the formal and informal rules, regulations, and obligations of social interaction—the normative rules of behavior and contingencies for reward and nonreward. To sociologists, environments may reflect the basic structural aspects of society and, particularly when the focus is on the elderly, the ability of the environment to maintain role behavior. The range of perspectives on what constitutes the relevant aspects of environments thus covers much of the substance of the social sciences.

Moos (1974) identified six typologies according to which investigators have sought to relate characteristics of environments to adaptation: (1) ecological dimensions, which include both geographic, meterologic, and architectural-physical design variables; (2) behavioral settings—units that possess ecological and behavioral properties; (3) dimensions of organizational structure, such as size, staffing ratios, and average salary levels; (4) dimensions identifying the collective, personal, and/or behavioral characteristics of the milieu inhabitants; (5) dimensions relating to psychosocial characteristics and organizational climates and emotional tones; and (6) variables relevant to the functional or reinforcement analysis (reward patterns) of environments.

The work to be reported in this chapter emphasizes the study of psychosocial characteristics and the psychological climates of environments.

Successful Old-Timers: A Matching Procedure

CONCEPTS AND METHODS

We began our investigation of environmental change as a source of stress by focusing on the congruence between personality or life-style and environmental demands in the Home for Life study. Those most stressed by the transition to institutional life might, we reasoned, be elderly whose previous adaptational styles were least congruent with the demands of the homes for the aged to which they were relocated.

The environmental dimensions chosen for study were dictated by some of the most obvious characteristics of institutional life that stand in marked contrast to life in the community. Institutions are specialized social structures containing their own patterns of reward and punishment, unique status hierarchies, and norms that regulate, in important ways, the interaction both among residents and between the staff and residents. Two central issues were hypothesized to be of particular importance: the degree to which institutional norms regulated intimacy or distance among residents and between staff and residents, and the institutional pathways for maintaining self-esteem.

We reasoned that individuals differ in the ease with which their pre-institutional life-style fits into the particular demands of a specific institution. For some the fit is relatively easy; for others, it requires major reorganization. Stress is thus defined as the degree to which the individual is required to reorganize his or her pattern of behavior to fit into the particular demands of a given social setting.

What are the adaptive demands of a particular institution, and how is it best to study them? We chose to approach the problem through an assessment methodology and reasoned that if we were to study individuals who had been living in the institutions for from three to five years, we would be able to develop an empirical definition of the characteristics of those elderly who had met the adaptive demands of the institutions. They were the ones who best weathered the disruptive impact of institutionalization and who had apparently retained a level of functioning similar to the one they had prior to their admission. In other words, we assumed that these "successful old-timers" were successful partly because they had fit well into the life of the institution.

Thirty-seven successful old-timers were intensively studied in order to determine their common behavioral and personality characteristics. Each had lived in the institution for at least three years and functioned at a level that would make them admissible to the institution if they were now community residents. In our inductive search for relevant characteristics we asked, "How did a particular behavioral characteristic manifest itself in the institutional environment?" Specifically, we attempted to characterize the reward system that the institutions emphasized and asked, "How do these behavioral traits match the institutional reward system?" and "What are the dominant, normative regulatory principles of the institution, particularly with regard to resident-resident interaction, staff-resident interaction, and the institutional pathways for maintenance of an integrated self-image?" These successful old-timers were also used as informants. We were interested in their advice to new residents: "How does one make it in the institution?" Many recommended, for example, that new residents avoid interaction with other residents, because such interaction would only prove unrewarding and lead to interpersonal conflict. Finally, in determining relevant personality characteristics, we reviewed previous literature on institutionalization (Goffman 1961; Martin 1955; Sommer and Osmond 1961; Townsend 1962) to determine other dimensions that might be important for adaptation.

Nine Dimensions. We isolated nine dimensions that appeared to characterize the thirty-seven successful old-timers relevant to a social-psychological analysis of the reward, punishment, and norm structure of the institution. These nine dimensions, along with the direction we think will be congruent with adaptive demands, are as follows:

1. Activity-Passivity: *High Activity,* because the institutional staff rewards residents who are active participants in institutional functions and penalizes more passive, withdrawn residents.
2. Aggression: *High Aggression,* because in a setting in which many residents are to varying degrees physically and/or mentally incapacitated, an aggres-

sive resident is best able to meet personal needs through assertively reaching out for himself or herself.

3. Narcissistic Body Image: *High Narcissism*, because sick, physically unattractive residents tend to be avoided by other residents, and projecting an attractive appearance is rewarded by overtures and admiration from other residents. This tangible differentiation of the self from unattractive residents enhances self-esteem.

4. Authoritarianism: *Authoritarianism rather than egalitarianism*, because an orientation of dominance facilitates differentiation of the self from debilitated residents. Even "helping" other residents confers a dominant position. Identification with strength and scorn for weakness—an egocentric focus— may be helpful in obtaining one's share of available resources.

5. Status Drive: *High Status Drive*, because an orientation of identification with staff rather than patients is encouraged by staff-resident status differentiation, by the hierarchy within the staff, and by explicit efforts on the part of staff to develop and reward resident "leaders."

6. Distrust of Others: *High Distrust of Others*, because distrust may be functional for institutional living, where the debilitation of many residents decreases their ability to respond to interpersonal overtures. If one does not soon learn to distrust others, disappointments come from not receiving "appropriate" responses to friendly overtures. Old-timers suggest that most residents should be avoided, because interpersonal contacts are likely to be conflictual. Distrust of others may thus reduce interpersonal conflict and diminish unrealistic expectations of pleasant and rewarding interaction.

7. Empathy: *Low Empathy*, because lack of interest in and disregard for the viewpoint of others is enhanced by efforts to avoid identification with illness and debilitation.

8. Extrapunitiveness: *High Extrapunitiveness*, because a tendency to blame others increases engagement and focuses staff attention on the self.

9. Intrapunitiveness: *Low Intrapunitiveness*, because high self-blame further diminishes self-esteem within the institutional setting and causes a reduction in the type of outer-directed interpersonal activity that is rewarded by other residents and institutional staff.

Five-point scales were developed for each of the nine characteristics, using different sections of the interview for each of the nine assessments. Total congruence scores ranged from 9 to 45, the higher score reflecting greater congruence. (See technical note 1.)

THE RELATIONSHIP OF CONGRUENCE TO ADAPTATION ONE YEAR AFTER INSTITUTIONALIZATION

As previously described in chapter 2, forty-four of the eighty-five Home for Life respondents who entered the institutions successfully adapted to institutional life, whereas forty-one showed marked deteriorative changes or had died one year afterward. The intact survivors had a mean congruence score of 30.1 (s.d.=4.7), while those who died or deteriorated had a mean congruence score of 25.6 (s.d.=5.0), (t = 4.32, p< .01). Thus those who were more congruent were more likely to adapt successfully to the new environment. Personality styles, then, that are consistent with the style rewarded in the new environment may cause the relocation to be less of a radical psychological change.

It is important to note that possessing traits associated with low "congruence" did not predict subsequent deterioration and death for the community control sample. This lack of predictability of outcome for the sample not undergoing stress associated with environmental change suggests that it is congruence, the relationship between people and their particular environments, that is the predictor rather than the specific personality traits indexed by the measure. Further support for this view emerges from correlations between congruence scores and a number of psychological measures prior to relocation. The correlational evidence suggests that the congruence measure was not assessing other personal characteristics. The correlation with cognitive functioning, for example, was −.09—and, indeed, congruence was, as expected, inversely correlated with mental health measured by the Block Q-Sort technique (−.32), and with life satisfaction (−.21). These correlations suggest that congruence does not, in any simple way, reflect well-being or adequacy of functioning. The particular characteristics used to construct the congruence measure as well as the inverse correlations with mental health and life satisfaction suggest that environmental congruency in the setting we have studied does not reflect adequacy in functioning; rather, it reflects quite the opposite. Those elderly in the sample who were most congruent with the demands of institutional life were on the basis of measures of mental health and life satisfaction, least well-adjusted to community life.

The finding (see technical note 1) that all but one of the personality traits contributed to the overall congruence score suggests that it is not a single characteristic that accounts for the successful prediction of outcome. The role of personality in stress adaptation will be considered in chapter 8.

Although empirically successful, the strategy of assessing environmental congruence using personality characteristics has limited generalizability, because the assessment model for measuring congruence is highly specific to particular institutions and specific conditions. There is no reason to assume that these particular personal qualities would, under other conditions, predict similar outcomes. These findings do, however, support the hypothesis that the stresses and strains associated with radical changes in the elderly's life space are, in part, contingent upon the degree to which the individual fits or does not fit into the new environment. By implication, it is reasonable to assume that those people whose adaptive styles are congruent with a new environment are not required to make as many adaptive changes as those who are incongruent with their new environment. Because of this limited generalizability of personality fit, however, our pursuit of the congruence hypothesis shifted in the subsequent study to those characteristics of environments that offered the likelihood of greater generalizability across settings.

The Fit Between Needs and Environments

CONCEPTS AND METHODS

In the Deinstitutionalized Elites Study, we examined a sample of highly selected state hospital patients who moved into twenty-six community-based settings. The settings provided a wider range of environmental conditions than the three homes for the aged studied in the first investigation. The elderly involved were moved from a single "total institution" to a range of settings that varied from residential hotels and homes for the aged to nursing homes. We speculated that the important differences between the Time 1 and Time 2 environments for this sample would be environmental characteristics indicative of institutional "totality." It is likely that the state hospital from which all the patients came represented one extreme in institutional totality, while the twenty-six community-based institutions provided variation in this variable. Dimensions that we considered important in characterizing the totality of an institution included similarity in the treatment of a mass of people; sharp boundaries between classes of individuals, such as patients and staff; and nonpermeable boundaries between the institution and the external world.

Our environmental framework owes much to the pioneering work of Kleemeier (1961b) and Hall (1966). Kleemeier used three basic dimensions—congregate, control, and segregate—to examine institutional settings. The *congregate* dimension refers to the group aspects of the setting: group size, closeness of individuals to each other, and the degree of privacy. *Control* refers to the degree to which individuals must adjust their life-style to imposed rules, discipline, and the various means of social control utilized by administrators, by medical and other personnel, and by residents or patients themselves in order to bring about desired behavioral patterns. The *segregate* dimension refers to the degree to which the setting provides an opportunity for interaction with all age groups in the community.

These ideas were tested by developing four reliable dimensions in assessing the three old age homes examined in the Home for Life study: (1) public-private, the degree to which the environment allows the resident to establish and maintain a personal domain that is not open to public view or use and into which the institution will not transgress; (2) structured-unstructured, the degree to which the resident does not have to adjust his or her life to imposed rules, discipline, and the various means of social control exercised in the institution; (3) resource-sparse–resource-rich, the degree to which the environment provides opportunities to engage in a variety of work and leisure activities and to participate in social interaction with other residents and staff in a range of social roles and statuses; and, finally, (4) isolated-integrated, the degree to which the institution affords opportunities for communication and interaction with the larger heterogeneous community (or people and places) within which it is located. (The pilot results are reported in a Ph.D. dissertation by Alan Pincus [1968].)

These concepts and associated methods provided the initial tools for examining the twenty-six environments in the Deinstitutionalized Elites study. Hall was the other major influence on our developing framework. He suggested a basis for the systematic study of proxemics with the publication in 1966 of "A System for the Notation of Proxemic Behavior." Hall delineated the sensory bases underlying the perception and use of space. Although his primary emphasis was on interpersonal transactions, Hall's ideas were adapted by us to study transactions between people and the environment as well.

Our primary focus was on the demand characteristics of the new environment. In particular, we studied the degree to which environments encourage achievement and affiliation, supply recognition to individuals, and foster dependency. Such psychosocial aspects of the environment were likely to make for variations in ways that would have an impact on the behavior of residents and provide a meaningful contrast to their Time 1 environment. Other aspects of the environment that interested us and appeared to be salient in identifying differences among environments were the extent to which an environment was capable of accommodating or accepting various forms of behavior (tolerance for deviancy); the degree of stimulation it provided; and, some of its physical characteristics, such as the pathways it provided for interaction, the impact its structure had on the degree of privacy provided, and its physical attractiveness. A total of ten psychosocial scales were developed to assess environmental characteristics; an eleventh scale was added measuring the capacity of an environment to provide for the physical care of the elderly.

A skilled judge who was trained as both an anthropologist and a psychologist of environmental design spent half a day in each of the twenty-six relocation environments, where he made 216 ratings using structural scales. Of the 216 ratings, 110 were based on his observations and 106 on interview data gathered from an administrator. The 216 scales were grouped so as to form ten dimensions; for the eleventh variable—health care adequacy—all available data were used. (See appendix D for the interview and observation schedule.) The eleven dimensions were as follows:

1. Achievement Fostering: The extent to which the environment provides opportunities for and encourages residents to achieve meaningful tasks or engage in goal-directed activities, and rewards them for doing so.
2. Individuation: The extent to which residents of the environment are perceived and treated as individuals in being allowed and encouraged to express individuality.
3. Dependency Fostering: The extent to which residents are provided for, "coddled," and protected in ways that discourage or prevent the development of self-sufficiency and autonomy.
4. Warmth: The warmth and humanity of the staff in its attitudes toward or relations with residents. Also, the extent to which these same qualities are expressed in the residents' attitudes toward and relations with each other.
5. Affiliation Fostering: The extent to which social interaction occurs in, and is encouraged by, the environment.
6. Recognition: The extent to which the environment recognizes, responds to, and rewards both the activities and the accomplishments of residents.
7. Stimulation: The extent to which the environment provides a variety of sights, sounds, and activity, and other stimuli to perceive and interact with.
8. Physical Attractiveness: The attractiveness or aesthetic appeal of the physical plant, including interior, exterior, and immediate surroundings.
9. Cue Richness: The extent to which the environment functions to differentiate or provide cues for perceptual orientation, such as signs, distinctive colors, odors, textures, sounds, varied furnishings, clutter, and so on.
10. Tolerance for Deviancy: The extent to which the staff tolerate "deviant" behaviors on the part of residents, such as aggression, drinking, wandering, complaining, and incontinence.
11. Health Care Adequacy: The extent to which the environment is equipped and staffed to provide health care, in the form of physical examinations, physical therapy, nursing, doctor's care, and drugs, and handle medical emergencies. (The environments were rank ordered by the observer.)

The framework developed for assessing environment can usefully be compared to the work of Moos (1974), who established three basic dimensions that discriminate among different subunits within institutional environments as well as between different institutional environments, such as mental hospitals and prisons. Moos's *relationship* dimension, which determines the extent to which individuals are involved in the environment and provide one another with support and help, is assessed by indices of involvement, support, and expressiveness. The *personal development* dimension refers to whether personal growth and self-enhancement tend to occur in a particular environment. In psychiatric and correctional programs, this dimension focuses on treatment goals (indices of autonomy; the extent to which people are encouraged to be self-sufficient and independent) and indexes both practical orientation (the extent to which the program prepares an individual for job training, looking to the future, setting concrete goals and working toward them) and personal problem orientation (the extent to which individuals are encouraged to be concerned with their feelings and problems and to seek to understand themselves). Because we studied institutions that are not primarily treatment-oriented, and particularly because they are rarely seen as temporary institutions but rather as "homes for life," the relevance of such goal-oriented environmental dimensions is diminished. Moos's third general dimension, *systems maintenance and systems change*, is indexed in terms of order and organization, clarity of expectation, and control.

Our framework thus shares some important similarities with Moos's work, although some significant differences must also be noted. Our concern with the personal development dimension is associated with the enhancement of functioning rather than, as noted previously, with treatment goals. System maintenance and change, or the control system in the environment, is certainly underscored in a number of dimensions. However, our emphasis on stimulus demands of the environment is not reflected in Moos's work. Finally, our concern with the relationship of the particular environment to the external world has not been emphasized by Moos, perhaps because he studied systems primarily seen as transitory rather than permanent. The most important distinction between Moos's pioneering work and our study may be in the method of measurement. Moos relied on assessments by participants in the environment. His environmental dimensions are based upon the collective perceptions of the residents themselves; ours are based upon the work of trained external observers. In part, methodological differences reflect the environmental dimensions of interest to each investigator. Perhaps most critical in influencing method were the differences in populations studied. Many of the elderly we studied were cognitively unable to respond to complex information and would not be in a position to make judgments such as the ones that are required in Moos's scales.

Measurement of environmental fit. Whereas in the first investigation congruence was operationally defined as the fit between pre-relocation adaptational styles and the style of the "old-timers" who had successfully adapted to the relocation environment, in this investigation the psychosocial aspects of the environment were assessed directly. To measure fit between person and environment, respondents were rated on eight psychosocial needs, as adapted from the work of Murray (1938). Prior to the move, two judges rated each respondent on five-point scales for his or her need for stimulation, achievement, affiliation, autonomy, counteraction, physical maintenance, recognition, and succorance. Thus congruence was here defined in terms of match between the eight needs as assessed prior to the move (Time 1) and the environmental ratings made after the move (Time 2).

FINDINGS

The Contribution of Environmental Characteristics to Adaption.
The review of relocation studies cited in chapter 1 indicates that the effect of environmental conditions on adaptation to relocation has often been reduced to an all too simple cliché: "the better the quality, the better the outcome." As previously suggested, although we see this as an oversimplified hypothesis, it requires examination prior to a full exploration of both the congruence and discrepancy hypotheses. The Deinstitutionalized Elites study, with its elderly who were moved from a single environment to twenty-six different institutions, provided a suitable context for examining the effect of environmental quality on adaptation.

Of the eighty-two patients moved from the state hospital to community facilities, forty showed behavioral, physical, or social changes of sufficient magnitude, a year after the move, to be rated as decliners, whereas the remaining forty-two showed only minor adverse changes, remained stable, or even showed modest improvement (see chapter 2). The institutional environments in which the forty decliners resided were compared with the environments of the forty-two nondecliners (the Intact). Using a multivariate analysis of variance, the eleven environmental dimensions discriminated between the decliners and those who remained stable at an overall p of less than .07 (see table 5–1, first column). Four of the eleven dimensions contributed appreciably to the differences between the two groups. Associated with decline were environments that were less foster-

TABLE 5-1
Environmental Characteristics and Adaptation:
The Deinstitutionalized Elites Study

Environmental Predictor	Total Sample			Group with "Aging Characteristics"			Group without "Aging Characteristics"		
	Means		univariate	Means		univariate	Means		univariate
	Intact	Decline	p	Intact	Decline	p	Intact	Decline	p
1. Achievement fostering	.57	-8.29	.06	-7.47	-10.33	.48	8.27	-.79	.03
2. Individuation	6.93	6.62	.58	6.36	6.24	.85	7.47	7.01	.57
3. Dependency fostering	6.87	8.61	.02	8.04	9.56	.16	5.73	7.66	.05
4. Warmth	30.62	29.96	.07	23.94	23.05	.82	37.19	28.86	.004
5. Affiliation fostering	21.90	26.58	.23	19.98	19.32	.68	23.88	21.90	.16
6. Recognition	13.99	12.50	.18	12.66	12.33	.87	15.38	12.61	.06
7. Stimulation	95.42	94.24	.35	92.91	92.03	.81	100.74	96.45	.30
8. Physical attractiveness	31.29	32.75	.77	25.71	34.69	.25	36.89	30.81	.35
9. Cue richness	14.15	13.22	.24	12.04	12.65	.76	16.31	13.83	.01
10. Tolerance for deviancy	14.33	13.27	.15	14.48	12.52	.10	14.14	13.99	.87
11. Health care adequacy	11.17	9.51	.05	9.64	8.36	.27	12.74	10.65	.07
Degrees of freedom (Univariate analyses)	df = 1 and 82			df = 1 and 40			df = 1 and 40		
Degrees of freedom and p value (Multivariate analysis)	df = 11 and 72 p<.07			df = 11 and 30 p<.50			df = 11 and 30 p<.10		

ing of achievement, less fostering of dependency, less warm, and less adequate in health care facilities. Two other environmental dimensions also contributed to the overall statistical differences: less individual recognition and lower tolerance for deviancy.

The role of environmental quality in adaptation can best be understood by analyses which compare the association between quality and adaptation with the relationship between personal characteristics, assessed prior to the move, and outcome. Seven predictor areas, fully discussed in chapters 6, 7, and 8, were assessed. These included: demographic characteristics of the respondents; their resources, including cognitive functioning and physical health; their level of current functioning, in terms of mental health and life satisfaction; the adequacy of their social functioning; and coping strategies for threat and loss management associated with the impending move. In all, forty-two specific indices were measured. These were grouped into seven areas: demographic characteristics, adaptive capacity, interpersonal behavior, emotional life, personality traits, expectations, and psychosocial needs. Multivariate analysis of variance, in which overall p levels were calculated for each of these seven areas, indicated that the overall p was .34 for the demographic characteristics, .12 for adaptive capacity, .15 for interpersonal behavior, .47 for expectations, .31 for psychosocial needs, .14 for personality traits, and .31 for affects.

Although individual indices representing some of these dimensions reached conventional levels of statistical significance, the overall p level provides a basis for comparisons among the various areas. Because environmental characteristics reached a p level of .07, environmental characteristics were more potent overall predictors of adaptation than were any of the demographic, behavioral, or psychological characteristics considered.

A further exploration using linear discriminant analysis, which maximizes the probability of distinguishing among groups or categories, provides additional proof for the effect of environment on adaptation. For this analysis, scales assessing the seven areas previously described as well as environmental dimensions were selected, using as the criterion of selection their importance in distinguishing unsuccessful from successful adapters. Of the twelve measures that contributed to discriminating among the decliners and nondecliners, eight were either environmental dimensions or measures of environmental fit: (1) environment dependency fostering (57 percent correct "placement"); (2) amount of interpersonal contact (increased to 61 percent); (3) need recognition (65 percent); (4) environment stimulation (66 percent); (5) environment individuation (67 percent); (6) environment warmth (72 percent); (7) environment-health care adequacy (77 percent); (8) environmental fit-stimulation (78 percent); (9) need stimulation (79 percent); (10) environmental fit-recognition (80 percent); (11) amount of role activity (82 percent); and (12) environment-achievement fostering (85 percent). A linear combination of these twelve variables, therefore, placed 85 percent of the cases in their appropriate outcome categories. A single variable—that of environment characteristic of dependency fostering—contributed to this correct placement 57 percent of the time. This analysis underscores the finding that environmental characteristics are critical in their effect on adaptation.

The Contribution of Person-Environment Fit to Adaptation. Comparable analyses to determine the role of congruence unfortunately could not be carried out as planned, because few "mismatched" persons were found. Congruence scores, as measured by correlations among the eight psychosocial needs corresponding to eight specific environmental qualities, were uniformly high. A chi-square analysis of fit yielded similar highly significant findings. The dimensions of need and environment that were most closely matched were achievement, stimulation, and physical care. The high degree of match reflects the context of the Deinstitutionalized Elites study. The patients in this study were the recipients both of considerable care in preparing them for the move into the new environments and of a careful selection of appropriate settings. Although the special geriatric staff at the hospital had neither an awareness of our hypothesis nor access to our data prior to relocation, the greater-than-chance matching which our data revealed suggests that some of the same considerations expressed in our matching hypothesis were taken into account by the relocation staff of the geriatric unit.

To examine the congruence hypothesis within the limitations imposed by the successful matching, a different strategy of analysis was explored. Required was a means of subdividing the original sample into theoretically relevant subgroups so that the interrelationship between environment and person could be examined in detail.

The thinking in the field of gerontology, most articulately expressed by Lawton (1980a) as the environmental docility hypothesis, offered a productive lead in inquiring into person-environment relationships. The environmental docility hypothesis suggests that the infirm elderly are more dependent on environmental properties for their well-being than are the less infirm and the young. Of course, since all of those transferred in our study were over 60, they were subdivided into groups based upon those who showed characteristics commonly associated with aging processes and those whose current behavior was not so marked by "aging" characteristics. We were limited, however, by the measures we had already generated in developing this post hoc hypothesis.

A review of the literature on changes in aging suggested agreement on a limited number of changes. The best-documented kind of age change is cognitive. The aged are clearly unable to process information at the same rate as their younger counterparts. On a psychological level, the disengagement hypothesis (Cummings and Henry 1961) posits that an increased "interiority" best describes the psychological characteristics associated with aging. In the social psychological realm, role attrition, caused by personal characteristics or social contingencies, is a well-documented characteristic of the aged. Four dimensions were chosen from the available data to reflect these characteristics of the aging process: cognitive performance, role behavior, involvement with others, and need stimulation. (See technical note 2.)

Sum scores of "aging" based on the median of the population were used to define two groups as more and less "aged." As expected, many differences were found when we compared these two groups on the other psychological variables. Most important, however, is that the groups were similar on all demographic characteristics, physicians' health ratings, and mental health. There were no outcome differences; for each group, twenty-two nondecliners and twenty decliners were found. Although differing on "degree of aging," they did not show different reactions to relocation.

We next sought to determine the role of environment in predicting outcomes. Statistical analyses were identical to those used previously for the entire sample. The results, as shown in the second and third columns of table 5–1, clearly indicate large differences between the subgroups. Environmental characteristics did not contribute to success or failure in adaptation among the subgroup identified as showing more aging characteristics. For the "less aged" subgroup, however, a number of environmental characteristics significantly distinguished between the intact and the decliners. Several important consequences follow from this finding. Although we could not directly study environmental docility across age groups, those individuals who show more of the cognitive and personality changes commonly associated with aging are least responsive to environmental contingencies; conversely, those that show less "aged" behavioral patterns are most responsive to environmental qualities. The psychosocial environmental variables crucial to well-being for the "nondocile" subgroup include warmth and recognition but not dependency fostering. The implications of these findings will be explored in the final section of this chapter.

Although the Deinstitutionalized Elites study does not allow us to directly test the environment-person match hypothesis, the preceding analysis does suggest that environmental contingencies are crucial to adaptation for certain types of elderly people. Those elderly who show less of the debilitating psychological and social changes associated with aging were more affected by environmental contingencies than those whose behavioral patterns show typical age-related decrements. Placements into the relocation environments by the geriatric staff of the state hospital made it impossible to directly test the hypothesis that the degree of stress associated with environmental change is associated with the degree to which the individual needs to reorganize his or her behavior in order to adapt to the environment. Overall, however, the findings underscore the central role that environment plays in the adaptation of some elderly people.

A Direct Test of Environmental Discontinuity

The Death of an Institution study, involving the relocation of the total population of a state hospital into a large number (142) of different facilities, provided the most extensive opportunity we had to test the effects of both environmental discontinuity and environmental quality on adaptation.

Unlike the previous study, in which environmental stress was based on person-environment congruence (tested by fitting need at Time 1 to environmental characteristics at Time 2), in this study environmental discontinuity as a stress was tested directly by using independent assessments of environments measured both before and after relocation. The discontinuity approach was not appropriate in the previous investigation, because the pre-relocation environment in the Deinstitutionalized Elites study was a single experimental geriatric ward. In contrast, the environments in which the patients lived prior to relocation in the Death of an Institution study comprised a large number of wards within one state hospital. These were environments which could be reliably discriminated from one another on environmental measures. The environmental discontinuity hypothesis was tested by assessing the degree to which each patient's pre-relocation environment matched the post-relocation environment on ten environmental dimensions previously described. (The dimensions assessed were similar, but the scale items differed slightly in wording and composition from those used in the previous investigation.)

The Effects of Environmental Quality on Adaptation. One year after relocation of the 427 patients studied, 78 were dead, 159 had shown marked deterioration, 87 improved, and 103 showed no substantial change from baseline (prior to relocation). The large sample permitted more precise categories of adaptation than was heretofore possible. In the previous three studies, the sample size permitted analysis only of individuals categorized as either those who maintained the status quo or those who deteriorated. In the Death of an Institution study, four outcome groups were identified: dead, deteriorated, unchanged, and improved. Table 5–2 shows mean scores on the ten environmental dimensions for these four outcome groups.

Several statistical procedures were used to evaluate the effects of environmental quality on outcome. A simple univariate analysis of variance, as shown in the first part of table 5–2, indicated that all of the environmental scales discriminated among the four outcome groups at better than .05 level of significance. Such an analysis, however, ignores the extent of correlation among the various environmental dimensions. A step-down multivariate analysis of variance was used to correct for such correlation. This analysis revealed that six of the dimensions—achievement fostering, warmth, recognition, activity, stimulation, cue richness, and tolerance for deviance—were statistically significant beyond the .05 level. The overall probability level, which provides a measure of the relative power of this group of environmental variables in discriminating among the four outcome classifications, was .0001, providing substantial support for the role that environmental characteristics play in affecting the adaptation or maladaptation of the aged in their new environments.

These analyses, however, neither isolate differences between individual outcome groups nor factor out the effect of having relocated elderly who were initially very different from each other into radically different environments. To address these issues, further analyses were performed by comparing those who died with those who did not die. As shown in the second column of table 5–2, only four of the environmental dimensions (individuation, warmth, recognition, and tolerance for deviation) were statistically significant. The overall probability of $p = .16$ (generated by multivariate analysis of variance) for the ten environmental characteristics suggests that these characteristics are less important in discriminating between those who died subsequent to the move and those who did not. Indeed, further analyses on the three other groups of survivors (deteriorated, unchanged and improved), as shown in the last column of table 5–2,

TABLE 5–2

Environmental Characteristics and Adaptation: The Death of an Institution Study

	Four Outcome Groups					Alive vs. Dead			Among Survivors F=Ratios	
	Dead (N=78)	Deteriorated (N=159)	Unchanged (N=103)	Improved (N=87)	$F=$ Ratio	Dead (N=78)	Alive (N=349)	$F=$ Ratio	Unchanged vs. Deteriorated	Unchanged vs. Improved
1. Achievement fostering	61.3	61.7	61.7	78.7	21.52[b]	61.3	66.0	3.32	0.00	32.95[b]
2. Individuation	28.8	29.4	30.4	33.8	8.59[b]	28.8	30.8	4.16[a]	1.12	8.79[b]
3. Dependency fostering	49.0	47.2	48.6	44.2	6.49[b]	49.0	46.8	3.79	1.76	12.52[b]
4. Warmth	31.7	36.7	33.3	41.9	8.08[b]	31.7	37.0	7.87[b]	3.37	16.47[b]
5. Affiliation fostering	6.9	7.4	6.6	8.1	5.00[b]	6.9	7.3	1.05	3.86	10.15[b]
6. Recognition	15.6	18.4	14.5	19.1	9.77[b]	15.6	17.4	3.03	14.48[b]	15.37[b]
7. Stimulation	2.3	3.1	2.4	14.7	9.27[b]	2.3	3.3	8.60[b]	6.89[b]	18.07[b]
8. Physical attractiveness	41.5	42.4	40.2	43.4	3.04[a]	41.5	42.0	0.18	3.82[b]	5.64[b]
9. Cue richness	32.3	32.4	27.7	30.4	4.39[b]	32.3	30.5	1.22	8.82[b]	2.11
10. Tolerance for deviancy	82.0	81.0	80.2	74.2	12.20[b]	82.0	79.1	4.84[b]	0.30	15.55[b]

[a] $p < .05$

[b] $p < .01$

revealed more differences between the unchanged and improved groups than between the unchanged and deteriorated. All but one dimension (cue richness) significantly differentiated the unchanged from the improved, whereas four dimensions (recognition, stimulation, physical attractiveness, and cue richness) significantly differentiated the unchanged from the deteriorated. For both of these contrasts, overall p levels generated by multivariate analyses of variance indicate that the set of ten environmental dimensions was highly predictive. The overall p in the comparison of the unchanged and deteriorated was .003, and in the comparison of the unchanged and improved, .001. Also evident in table 5–2 is that those who died and those who showed no change went to similar environments, while those who improved and those who deteriorated went to vastly different environments.

Prior to examining specific environmental characteristics and their role in adaptation, we will briefly review other factors affecting outcome. The role of factors other than environmental characteristics in affecting differences in outcome is clearest when those who died are considered. Analysis of the association between personal characteristics and outcome revealed that those who died were initially the most physically and cognitively deteriorated patients. In a linear discriminant analysis, these two characteristics correctly sorted out those patients who were alive one year after relocation from those who were dead with an accuracy of over 80 percent. Environmental characteristics did not contribute to this predictive equation.

The findings, however, are quite different for comparisons among those who did not die. Comparisons were made among the stable, deteriorated, and improved groups on psychological, physical, and behavioral measures assessed at Time 1 (pre-relocation). Forty-five indices encompassing demographic characteristics, psychiatric status, physical health ratings, cognitive dimensions, social behavior, activity patterns, and staff ratings of reactions to relocation were included in this analysis. Only three measures distinguished the improved from the deteriorated patients (although a considerably larger number distinguished these two groups from those who did not change). In brief, the deteriorated and improved respondents were identical in almost every respect and differed from both those who died and those who were unchanged after relocation. These findings of similarity prior to relocation between those who improved and those who deteriorated afterward reinforces the importance of environmental qualities. Of all those relocated, the respondents who deteriorated or improved were the most physically healthy, cognitively intact, and socially integrated patients prior to relocation, differing primarily in the environmental characteristics of the relocation setting.

The Effects of Environmental Discontinuity on Adaptation. Environmental discontinuity was assessed by comparing pre-relocation and post-relocation environments for each person. Discrepancy scores were computed using four scores based on environmental characteristics identified by factor analyses rather than the ten scales. Independent factor analyses of Time 1 and Time 2 environmental data revealed identical factors at both points in time. The four environmental factors identified were independence (comprising the dimensions of personalization and low dependency-fostering), achievement fostering, individuation relationship (referring to warmth and affiliation); activity (meaning stimulation and cue richness); and, finally, physical attractiveness. Four discrepancy scores were generated by summing the scores on the characteristics within each factor for each person at two points in time, and subtracting the Time 1 scores from the Time 2 scores. Table 5–3 shows the discrepancy scores for each of the outcome groups, as well as an overall summed total environmental discrepancy score. As shown, the pre-relocation settings were less independence-fostering, lower on relational characteristics, less activity-fostering, and less physically attractive than were the relocation environments. Environmental discrepancy, then, could only be indexed relatively, since all discrepancy scores were unidirectional.

Given this salient restraint in interpreting our data, the findings as displayed in table 5–3 would suggest that respondents who remained unchanged were more likely to reside after relocation in settings more like their original environment. Stated the other way, patients who changed, as contrasted with those who did not change, moved into more discrepant environments. Among those who changed, the improved went to the most discrepant environments. Specific environmental elements that contributed to differences in discrepancy scores between those who improved and

TABLE 5–3
Environmental Discrepancy and Adaptation:
The Death of an Institution Study

| Factor | Environmental Discrepancy Score | | | F=Ratios | |
	Deteriorated (N=159)	Unchanged (N=103)	Improved (N=87)	Unchanged vs. Deteriorated	Unchanged vs. Improved
Overall	480.90	462.9	502.9	5.37[a]	20.14[b]
Independence	134.5	134.0	153.4	0.01	19.45[b]
Relationship	108.30	103.2	111.7	3.97[a]	8.23[b]
Activity	118.8	109.5	116.2	12.17[b]	4.79[a]
Physical attractiveness	119.3	116.2	121.6	3.70[a]	8.61[b]

[a]$p<.05$ [b]$p<.01$

112

those who deteriorated suggest that those who improved resided in environments that were more encouraging of relationships, made more activities available, and were more physically attractive. The major difference between the environments of the improved and those of the deteriorated patients was in the degree of independence in the new and old environments: Those who improved, as contrasted with those who deteriorated, resided in facilities which allowed for more independence.

These findings suggest some important alterations in our environmental discrepancy hypothesis. Support for the hypothesis was found in the results which indicated that elderly who moved into environments similar to those whence they came are likely to maintain stability, and that large environmental discrepancies do produce instability. This instability, however, when coupled with certain environmental characteristics, more often than not led to improvement; similar levels of environmental discrepancy, in the context of nonfacilitating environments, led to deterioration. This observation may in part be a product of the relative uniformity of the pre-relocation environments; all were lower on independence, relationship, activity, and physical attractiveness dimensions than the post-relocation environments. The uniformly poor quality of the original state hospital environments limited adequate testing of the environmental discrepancy hypothesis. The evidence available does support the general hypothesis that discrepant environments cause more strain and, thereby, require new coping behavior, readjustment, and adaptation. Whether the strains lead to overload or recovery, however, depends more on the particular qualities of the environment than on the extent of discrepancy.

Summary and Implications

ENVIRONMENT AND ENVIRONMENTAL
CHANGE AS A SOURCE OF STRESS

As in the previous chapter on Threat and Loss, we asked in this chapter: What is it about relocation that constitutes a crisis for the elderly? Here, however, we viewed challenges that result from environmental change as the source of stress. Environmental change is seen as requiring adaptive efforts in order to maintain homeostasis. Despite the variety of contexts examined, populations involved, and methods used to assess environments, the findings from the three studies provide impressive support for the effect of environment on adaptation. Radical life space changes are stressful for the elderly, who are faced with settings that require life-styles incompatible with their typical patterns or with environments that are radically dissimilar to their accustomed settings. Comparisons of the predictive power of both person-environment congruence and environmental quality with the predictive power of threat and loss measures supports the greater importance of adaptational challenge in explaining relocation effects.

The first investigation, "Successful Old-Timers: A Matching Procedure," examined congruence in order to study environmental change as a stressor. Examined were particular stylistic characteristics of individuals which match the demands of specific environments. Those elderly who possessed personality characteristics that matched their new environments would, it was assumed, not experience a crisis to the same extent as those without this match and would hence be less likely to show departures from homeostasis. That is, there would be less of a requirement to make new adaptive efforts. The findings, based on our study of Home for Life respondents, supported this hypothesis. Moreover, they were strengthened by subsequent analysis, which showed that congruence was not associated with optimal or even better initial functioning. Indeed, congruent people were more likely to initially have poorer mental health and lowered feelings of well-being.

The second investigation, "The Fit: Needs and Environments," based on the Deinstitutionalized Elites respondents, affirmed the impact of environmental quality on adaptation, and although the congruence approach could not be fully tested, the study revealed that those showing the most "aging characteristics" were least affected by environmental conditions. Further support for the critical role of environment in affecting adaptation was found in the contrasts between environmental and personal characteristics as predictors of outcome. Among the Deinstitutionalized Elites, environmental characteristics provided considerably better predictions of outcome than did personal characteristics.

The final investigation, "A Direct Test of Environmental Discontinuity," based on the Death of an Institution respondents, underlined, once again, the critical role of environment in affecting adaptation. As in the study based on the Deinstitutionalized Elites, among the less vulnerable elderly, environmental characteristics were more important than personal characteristics for predicting adaptation. Although we did find support in this direct test of discontinuity for the hypothesis that environmental change was a key source of stress, such an adaptational challenge proved to be as much a precursor of improvement as it was of debilitation. The environmental continuity hypothesis, then, requires revision. Discontinuity is a source of disequilibrium, but depending on the quality of the new setting, homeostasis at a level higher than before may be quickly established.

Some important parallels to both the effects of congruence between person and environment and the challenge posed by discrepancy or amount of environmental change are apparent in a diverse research literature.

Some investigators have expended their efforts on specifying the particular conditions of environments when examining the fit between the individual and the environment as a source of strain. Others have looked at the movement of individuals from one cultural setting to another and assumed that discontinuity between cultures has dramatic effects on individuals. In this case, specific differences in environmental conditions are assumed rather than investigated, and the phrase "culture shock" is applied to the subjective experience of the individual who makes such moves. Usually in such research, the assumption is made not that one is moving from a "good" to a "bad" environment, but rather that there is discrepancy between the two. Festinger (1957), in developing dissonance theory, looked at the issue from the individual point of view in terms of the person's needs in relationship to environmental stimuli.

Maddi (1968), in his consistency model of personality, notes that discrepancies between the individual and the environment produce discomfort, anxiety, or a motivation to act in a way that will mitigate this discrepancy. At a more concrete level, congruence has been studied in various treatment settings. For example, Fleisher and Kulare (1972) studied the relationship between compatibility and stability in eight foster-home-care groups. They found that more men dropped out from groups incompatible in the psychological dimension of control. In the psychotherapy area, Tuma and Gustaad (1957) reported a positive relationship between client-counselor personality similarity and client learning in counseling sessions. Studies by Carson and Heine (1962) reflect similar findings.

Studies investigating the effects of need and personality complementarity on mate selection and the stability of marriages echo a similar theme. A review by Hicks and Platt (1970) suggests that there are positive relationships between marital happiness and husband-wife congruence. Congruence in significant dyadic or group relationships, be they psychotherapeutic or marital, offer evidence for the effects of characteristics and social stimuli on adjustment.

This fit between person and situation has also been noted in several studies of extreme settings. Wolf and Ripley (1947), in a report on adaptation to concentration camp internment, suggested that a predisposition toward psychopathological ruthlessness (evidenced especially by former criminals who became inmates) maximized the chances for survival. Gunderson (1964) found that a predisposition toward task orientation facilitated adaptation in Antarctic isolation, whereas orientations toward social interaction and physical activity were maladaptive. In a discussion of types of prison inmates, Jackson (1966) suggested that chronic convicts whose criminal and noncriminal careers outside of prison were marked by persistent failure often find prison to be the only place where they can settle in some comfort.

Possibly the most extensive research on macroenvironments, in the context of the relationship between discontinuity and stress, is found in the study of the environmental settings of college students. For example, Decoster (1966) constituted groups with high and low concentrations of high-ability students and found that the groups in which ability was matched to a greater extent produced greater comfort. Stern (1970) found that twenty-eight of thirty correlations between scores on an index of preferred type of activities and the characteristics of the college students were positive. Stern's interpretation was that students who have specific needs select out those that match their needs, as defined by types of preferred activities. Feldman and Newcomb (1965) concluded that their evidence revealed a tendency for students incongruent with the specific college to be more dissatisfied with their experience at college and to be more likely to consider leaving and actually to leave. These illustrative findings, utilizing a variety of settings and diverse methods, generally support the view, developed in our own work, that the congruence between personal and environmental characteristics is a major determinant of adaptation.

THE SPECIAL ROLE OF ENVIRONMENT IN AFFECTING THE ELDERLY'S ADAPTATION

The finding that respondents low on "aging characteristics" are more affected by their environment than those high on "aging characteristics" runs counter to the assumption that the many adverse changes associated with age make the elderly more dependent on and, therefore, more affected by their environment than younger people. Lawton (1980a), in an effort to add precision to this conventional wisdom, has developed the environmental docility hypothesis, which posits that aging and frailty are associated with increased behavior control by environmental contingencies. Lawton based this hypothesis on the frequently noted reactions of the vulnerable aged to environmental change. Such evidence does not, in our view, support the environmental docility hypothesis. The intensity of reaction and the frequency with which the reaction occurs may imply only that the elderly are more vulnerable and have lessened ability to deal with stress, rather than that they are stressed more by environmental contingencies.

There are no comparative analyses across the life span that would permit an answer to the question of whether or not there is a more direct relationship between age and the increasing contingency of behavior upon the external environment. Analogous situations of younger individuals relocating certainly do not lead to a clear-cut conclusion suggesting increased environmental docility over the life span. The numerous reports on the reactions of children to hospitalization would belie a linear increase across the life span. Studies of environmental change among the adult population—young adults entering college, household moves, and migration—do not support the unique role of environmental change in the lives of the aged. Although the magnitude of maladaptive reactions is not as great in younger populations, there is no reason to think that such reactions are not as frequent. The difference may be only in the intensity of the reaction: Old people react with increased rates of death and morbidity to environmental change, whereas younger adult populations react by increased discomfort, signs of depression, and less adequate role performance in occupation, parenting, and marriage.

Does current knowledge regarding psychological changes associated with aging shed light on environmental dependency? With increasing age there is a greater dependency on others for social support and a lessened capacity to influence the external world. Thus, for example, a shift in the locus of control, from inner to outer sources, has been noted. To be less in control of one's own fate, however, is not identical with becoming more influenced by the environment. Possibly of greater relevance to the increasing effects of environment on behavior are the cognitive deficits associated with aging. The elderly are less able than the young to process complex environmental stimuli. Although diminished capacity to process information quickly and efficiently suggests that a simplified environment is more conducive to adaptation, it does not necessarily suggest that behavior is more regulated by the environment.

Other age-associated phenomena suggest *less* dependency on the environment. For example, the greater intra-individual variability among the elderly on psychological measures may reflect less external, as opposed to internal, influence. Moreover, the elderly increasingly manifest idiosyncratic behaviors that are independent of environmental influences. This observation reflects what some (see, for example, Neugarten, Moore, and

Lowe 1965) have referred to as a decreased normative control over behavior in the aging. Underlying this freeing from normative control may,
in turn, be a need to maintain the self when inner and outer changes
occur that undermine the sense of self, an issue addressed in chapter 10.

Given the current state of knowledge, therefore, there is no reason to
conclude that the elderly are either more or less dependent on environmental contingencies than people of other ages. Indeed, demonstrating
that environmental change is a crisis for the elderly does not provide support for or against the environmental docility hypothesis.

Technical Notes

1. Each scale was rated separately, and each was constructed to distribute
the sample evenly among the five points. For example, ratings of "activity-passivity" used open-ended questions on health and the daily rounds
and on interviewers' comments, whereas ratings for "distrust of others"
were made using responses to the questions on respondents' anticipations
of institutionalization, interpersonal relations, and the Self-Sort Instrument
(forty-eight items respondents use to describe themselves). Appendix C
shows the scale points and data base for the nine characteristics. Interjudge reliability on twenty cases ranged from .78 to .90 across the nine
characteristics. To verify an earlier assumption that "old-timers" fell on
the high end of each scale, nine respondents from the institutional sample
of thirty-seven were rated by a scorer who was not aware of the assumption that these respondents were hypothesized to be high on congruence.
None of the nine "old-timers" received ratings of 1, the least congruent
rating possible. Indeed, on five of the nine characteristics there were no
ratings of 2, on three characteristics only two of the nine received ratings
of 2, and on the last, only one did. In all, out of eighty-one ratings, fifty-
six (or 70 percent) were ratings of 4 or 5. The distribution of these ratings
suggests the appropriateness of the earlier assumption. Moreover, among
the study sample before institutionalization, only 318 of 765 ratings (or 42
percent) were rated 4 or 5, and 264 (or 35 percent) received ratings of 1
or 2 (and of these 264, only 111, or 15 percent of the total sample, received a rating of 1).

Intercorrelations among the nine traits ranged from −.28 to .54. The
correlation of each scale with the total congruence score revealed that
only nonintrapunitiveness failed to be appreciably associated with total

congruence. The congruence score was thus considered to assess the level of general fit between preadmission adaptational style and the style most congruent with post-admission environmental demands.

2. Cognitive performance was measured using responses to two sets of TAT cards. A modified version of the Dana scoring system (interrater reliability of .93, stability coefficient of .70) provided a measure of the adequacy of processing complex stimuli. Maintenance of role behavior was assessed by an activity index which estimated the amount of time spent in each of seven levels of activity. This is a score based on the summation of interviewers' judgments of the number of hours that each person spent in each of the seven levels of activity multiplied by constants representing amount of behavioral output; interrater reliability for this measure was .76, with a stability coefficient of .66. Interpersonal contact was judged by raters from patient interviews about activities and relationships. Amount of involvement with others was rated on a four-point scale (interrater reliability was .68, with stability of .67). Need stimulation was judged using the entire focused interview on a five-point scale (interrater reliability, 45 percent exact agreement, 92 percent within one point; stability was .65). Individuals who scored low on all four of these indices were hypothesized to show more of the changes associated with aging. In brief, what is being indexed is a general dimension of responsiveness/involvement/activity.

Part 3

ADAPTATION TO STRESS

6

The Management of Threat and Loss

IN the previous two chapters our focus was on examining the sources of stress engendered by relocation. We explored two general hypotheses regarding stress: the symbolic meaning of the situation and challenges associated with environmental changes. This chapter initiates a shift in focus, moving from an examination of the nature of crises in the lives of elderly to the psychologist's more traditional concern with individual differences. Here, and in the two chapters that follow, our concern is the following: Given a major stress—relocation—in the lives of our respondents and the deleterious effects of this stress found in close to half of all those studied, how and why do some succeed despite the external pressure, while others falter under the same "objective" circumstances?

Although the previous two chapters did address differences among respondents in success of adaptation, variations were accounted for by differences in level of stress—some respondents experienced neither intense threat and loss nor discontinuity in their environment. Theoretically, they were not stressed and hence were not expected to manifest maladaptive reactions to relocation.

In contrast, the explicit focus in this chapter is on individual differences, on how people vary in their management of the threat and loss

123

associated with relocation. Our interest in the management of threat, however, extends beyond an understanding of variability. We want to examine whether some strategies for coping with threat are more successful than others. To do this, in turn, we will ask whether, across relocation studies, particular management strategies consistently predict successful outcome.

We must mention one caveat. Although they are theoretically distinguishable, it is almost impossible in real life to disentangle relocation's symbolic meanings from management strategies. The meanings of a situation to the individual always reflect the way he or she copes with it and, likewise, a person's strategies for coping with a situation always include the affective experience emanating from the situation's meanings. An in-depth analysis of meanings and management always reveals that each person forms a unique synthesis. In our studies, each person we studied had his or her own story to tell. Some exhibited a philosophical resignation to events they clearly saw as less desirable; others could barely bring themselves to discuss their feelings and thoughts about the impending event; and still others maintained an air of rosy optimism, seeing all for the best and telling stories that took on the character of a badly written soap opera. Some raged against their fate, at times directing their anger impersonally toward the powers that be, while still others blamed those in close proximity.

Our goal, however, is not to reflect on the poignancy of each story, but rather to examine them, guided by meaningful abstractions, for the purpose of addressing our primary concern: how different strategies for managing threat affect adaptational success or failure. Achieving this goal, of course, will likewise reduce the stories that are characteristic of each respondent to a dry set of abstractions. Therefore, we shall begin our discussion of these issues by first portraying one of our respondents in all her human complexity as she faced the threat and losses associated with relocation.

The Case of Mrs. A.

A SUCCESSFUL AGENDA FOR CONTAINING THREAT AND LOSS

Mrs. A.'s story is eloquent testimony to the ability of the elderly to utilize strategies for containing the intense feelings of abandonment and loss we believe are at issue for many who experience relocation. Mrs. A. was introduced in chapter 3 to represent the Home for Life Study. We will return to her at various times throughout this volume to illustrate other psychological processes addressed in the chapters that follow.

Our initial contact with Mrs. A. was after she had moved from California to Chicago to be near her sister and children. At that time she was part of the community control sample. Mrs. A. informed us in the first interview that she had considered the possibility of moving into a home for the aged because she did not want to live with any members of her family, fearing she would be a burden on them and disturb her excellent relationships with them. Although she set up an apartment for herself near her sister, she was aware of the difficulty in maintaining her independence because of the residual incapacity from her stroke. Yet she felt that she could manage by herself and that she would not be lonely. She thought that relying on her family and a local community center would provide sufficient support and a way to remain active. She did suggest to her family, however—more for reassurance we believe than for an affirmative answer—that it might be better for her to live in a home for the aged where she could obtain care for her physical ailments and also people with whom to relate. They counseled strongly against it but said that ultimately this was her decision.

Mrs. A.'s ambivalence and concern about living independently were reflected in the stories she told to the parent-child Murray TAT cards (Card 6 depicting a mother and an adult son and Card 7 depicting a father and son). In her story in response to Card 6 she attributed the following to the female figure: "She cannot make up her mind because it is very disturbing to her." About Card 7, she said: "They cannot make up their minds what to do. Just weighing what to do or what not to do."

Moving into an institution was not the desired alternative, but she was appropriately apprehensive about managing alone and about the availability of others with whom she could interact on a daily basis. Consideration of entering the home was, to a large extent, prodded by the strength of her desire to always be among others. When asked, for example, if there were ever times she would prefer privacy she responded: "I'd always rather prefer to be with people than to be alone." The extreme dread that some community-dwelling elderly displayed, however, when mentioning the possibility of living in an institution was not characteristic of Mrs. A.

Several months later, after her sister died and following her own successful surgery, Mrs. A. applied to the home and was accepted for admission. At that point she was reinterviewed. Now separation was uppermost in her thoughts. Mourning the death of her sister became fused with the protracted mourning for the much earlier death of her husband. Her children, as noted in the previous comments on Mrs. A., were not replacements for her husband and sister and although she could depend upon them for emotional support, she was apprehensive about what her relationship with them would be after she entered the home. This concern was reflected in her preoccupation with her eyesight. Although there was no apparent change in her eyesight—as previously, she did not wear glasses but used a magnifying glass to read—she said, "I can't write now. That's the trouble. I used to write three or four letters a week. Now I don't write and people don't answer. If you don't knock on someone's door they don't let you in."

Some signs of her psychological state are hinted at in the response to a simple projective test, the Reitman Stick Figures, in which one figure is in a position of praying: "This one is praying. After he achieved all those things, he's asking for forgiveness [laughs]. People can't think of God when they are happy. Just when they got a little pain they turn to God. It's just like children and a mother. When they're grown, they don't think of her unless they got troubles. Then they come to her." All existing data suggested, however, that Mrs. A.'s children thought of her often and were very attentive. Apparently, the move's rapid approach awakened a concern with their continued attentiveness. Because Mrs. A. was admitted to the home before the final interview session, the Institutional TAT was not administered, and these data are not available to confirm this interpretation. Since we found no themes of separation or abandonment in her earliest memory, it is likely that Mrs. A.'s defenses were successful in containing the painful emotions associated with perceptions of loss.

Suppressing painful thoughts of impending separation, Mrs. A. began to focus on how much she needed institutional care. Her poor eyesight, as noted above, becomes a major reason for her need for care: "I would say the main handicap I have now is my eyes." "I'd like to go more places, but I don't account of my eyes." "I'd like to write letters and be able to shop for myself. I'm trying to prevent I shouldn't fall." She also introduced complaints about arthritis of her arm: "My arm pains me so. The arthritis is so bad. I got pills to kill the pain but who cares if you got arthritis if it don't hurt." She made no mention of her lame leg and other arm, which was virtually useless from the aftermath of her stroke of seven years before; nor did she mention her more recent surgery. Rather, she selected failing eyesight and arthritis for assurance that seeking institutional care had become appropriate for her. Why she chose these two ailments and not others is unclear, but their use is indeed clear: If you can't see and if you can't move your arms you certainly can't take care of yourself and must have institutional care!

Her conscious appraisals of relocation were indeed positive. She stated succinctly and affirmatively: "Physically I'm not fit to be alone!" and "The _____ Home has a wonderful reputation." She expected no losses from the move and, correspondingly, she enumerated almost all the kinds of satisfactions that anyone could expect from the relocation into the home: "I hope when I get there I can paint"; "I know they have a workshop"; and "I will make ceramics." Despite her previous references to her impaired arms, manual activities became a future source of gratification. But her primary gain would be her renewed friendship with residents that she had known for several years.

Mrs. A.'s sense of being in control underscored that it was her choice: "I decided all by myself two or three months ago because I'm not able to keep an apartment for myself anymore. I'm not strong enough. . . . The hospitals are for sick people. When you go to a home it's because you can't keep house for yourself." Had she thought of alternatives? "No, I never wanted to live with relatives. That's why I want to go to the home. I don't want to go to the children. I'm too independent. Why should they have excess baggage?" Shortly thereafter she added: "There they have doctors and people to help you if you need it." And then, "What I hear from other people it shouldn't be difficult. I adjust very easily to everything. I can tell you, I won't be a problem." For all her justifications and positive expectations, her comments on "excess baggage" when referring to living with her children probably reflected feelings of abandonment, and "I won't be a problem" referred to lingering apprehensions regarding living the rest of her years in a total institution.

Mrs. A.'s success in containing the potentially debilitating effects of threat and loss is perhaps most eloquently portrayed in the reconstructions of her earliest memory. Feelings of abandonment were not introduced into the earliest memory. A year before applying to the home Mrs. A. reported her earliest memory as follows:

> I remember one thing that happened when I was only about two years old. My mother nursed me until I was that age. She was afraid to have another baby. I guess eighteen was enough for her. I remember I was walking. There were some chicks in our yard. I put my hand out to them. A chicken flew on my head. I was very scared. I ran to my mother. Who else does a child run to? Later my mother told me that I was only two at the time.

Here concern is expressed with being one of many children as well as with issues of birth, being nursed, and the possibility of personal injury.

Over a year later, when on the waiting list for the home, Mrs. A. reported a very similar memory:

> When I was very little, two years old, I went out to the yard. A little chicken had just been hatched and I didn't know. I picked him up and the mother hen flew on my head. My mother told me she was still nursing me because she didn't want to get pregnant again. After all, I was the eighteenth child.

Essentially, the memory has the same content as before.

As with many of the elderly in the Home for Life study (see chapter 4), for Mrs. A., strategies that successfully contained the painful feelings stimulated by the impending relocation appeared not to work as well after she moved into the institution. After admission, she described her earliest memory as follows:

> One thing I remember very distinctly. My mother said I was two years old and still nursing. I remember I saw a chicken was hatching an egg. I went out and squeezed the egg. The chicken flew out of my hand. My mother said I was two. I was still nursing. You know why I was still nursing? Because my mother said if she were nursing, she wouldn't get pregnant. I was the eighteenth child. Of course, they didn't all live. They had epidemics in those days. No medicine like today.

While this third version describes the same incident, it contains a reference to epidemics and death. The introduction of death is a new element that also appeared in a comment Mrs. A. made to the interviewer after admission, that she would now welcome death. It is evident that after admission, elements of hopelessness surfaced. How did Mrs. A. cope with such feeling engendered by the symbols surrounding relocation?

Overall, Mrs. A.'s strategies were remarkably stable over the nearly three years after her relocation, during which she was studied at four points. Regarding the reality of her assessments, when asked after admission what she would advise the interviewer if the interviewer were a prospective resident, she said: "I would advise you to come and if you should come with the idea that you will do as the Romans do and abide by the rules then okay. . . . Take everything in stride. Look at things the right way not the wrong way. I don't think there's another home like this." To the question "What ways did you have to change in order to adjust to the home?" she answered: "Didn't have to change at all. When I made up my mind to come here, I made up my mind to follow the rules. Like the food. If they cook something I don't like, I don't complain. I just don't eat any of it." She continued to see the relocation as her choice: "Had several people here that I knew so that I knew it was a good place. I felt I couldn't keep up my apartment." When asked if relatives or friends played any part in the decision, she answered: "To tell you the truth, they all left the decision to me. I had to make my own decision." This comment suggests that while it was indeed her choice, some ambivalence is reflected in her use of the phrase, "I had to." For all her protestations, at some preconscious level, she very well may have preferred to be "excess baggage" and live with a son. Still Mrs. A. did maintain a feeling of control over her destiny; she was the one who made the decision and she continued to perceive the home as congruent with her needs for people, for care, and for security. Her positive feelings about the home persist.

Mrs. A. thus coped very well with threatened loss as well as with the real losses associated with becoming institutionalized; and her style of coping with these losses boded well for her subsequent adaptation. She combined a sense of control with the capacity to make the situation congruent with her wishes, while not distorting the realities inherent in the situation. As the pre-admission interviewer commented when asked to predict Mrs. A.'s future adaptation to the home: "She will do okay in the home. She knows the score!" Indeed it was knowing the score, accepting reality, and actively coping with that reality, that contributed to Mrs. A.'s subsequent fine adaptation.

Concepts and Measures

Our thinking about threat and loss management owes a heavy debt to the work of Janis (1958, 1969) and Lazarus (1966). Lazarus's model of cognitive appraisal, and Janis's view on the role of information is reflected in many of our analytic units, although our goal was not to replicate their sophisticated models nor to test a model of our own. Rather, we wished to capture the variability within and across our studies. The categories assessing threat and loss coping styles represent a combination of borrowed theory and the realities, as we saw them in listening to the stories of the elderly. Our desire was to describe how the elderly experienced and contained their reactions to threat and loss; not to develop descriptions assessing generalized coping strategies. Such general coping will be explored in subsequent chapters. In this chapter we are interested in what a person does in attempting to master feelings engendered by threat and loss associated with environmental change.

Although studies of coping among people facing stress have examined a range of strategies, including avoidance of the danger, overcoming it by attack, as well as alloplastic defense activities, in the circumstances of our studies only the latter strategy was realistically a possibility. The elderly could not avoid the relocation; they could do precious little to change circumstances; they could and did, however, attempt to manage the loss and threat posed by the events through a variety of strategies directed toward the meaning of the circumstances surrounding relocation.

In developing ways to examine these strategies, we soon found that the context of our investigation influenced the framework we could utilize. Ours was neither a situation in which people were unprepared for the event nor a setting in which ambiguity and lack of information existed for the respondents. Quite the contrary, in the three studies in which systematic interview data were collected from respondents and, therefore, assessments of management strategies were possible, respondents possessed considerable prior knowledge about the relocation environments. Obviously, management strategies are influenced by preparation provided by others. In the past two decades, there has been an increasing focus on preparing the elderly for relocation. Although preparation has always been good social work practice, the current emphasis has been influenced by the research literature on the negative sequelae associated with relocation.

Respondents in the three studies who were assessed on management strategies had been informed before relocation about their new environment in one or more face-to-face conversations with a professional. Some were also shown a movie of the new environment or even visited their new residence. As discussed in the descriptions of "Settings and People" in chapter 3, respondents in the Unwilling Old Ladies study had group meetings that included a movie of the new environment in addition to face-to-face discussions. In the Home for Life study, the prospective resident visited the home at the time of application and discussed the home with the intake worker. More often than not, the prospective resident had heard about the home through friends who had lived in the home or were currently living there. Some had even visited friends there or participated in a day care program at the home. In the Deinstitutionalized Elites study, the discharge planner discussed the relocation residence, and many prospective residents visited the relocation nursing home or boarding house before the actual move. Because respondents in all the three studies were reasonably aware of the nature of their relocation environment, the assumption underlying our measures of coping strategies was that an inability to discuss the new environment reflected an unwillingness to do so, that is, a purposeful avoidance or even a denial of a previously communicated or perceived reality.

The Management of Threat and Loss

Several assumptions underlie the categories of management strategies we chose to represent this area in our research; (1) coping efforts to alter, change, or undo the threatening event were not a viable alternative for the elderly respondents in our investigations and thus the major coping issue for study was the strategies the elderly used in altering or changing the *meaning* of relocation to diminish and contain threat and loss; (2) large amounts of usable information about the potentially threatening event were available for all respondents; (3) relocation and the attendant symbols surrounding such relocation represented a central and important issue for all the elderly respondents, that is, it was a psychologically salient issue; (4) actively addressing, working with, and integrating a threat into more encompassing cognitive structures represents better management strategies (leads to better subsequent adaptation as well as lowered noxious reactions) than do strategies that are marked by avoidance, compartmentalization, and psychological isolation.

Within this informational context, three coping issues were addressed: *degree of coping*, indexed by three scales that collectively measured the level of activation characteristic of a respondent in addressing the problems faced by the threat and loss stimulated by relocation; *level of integration*, assessed by two scales that focused on the cognitive restructuring used to diminish the threat and loss; and *degree of mastery*, assessed by two scales that looked at the modifications directed toward the self-image endangered by the symbolic meanings associated with relocation. All these strategies have as their goal containing and channeling the affective dangers associated with threat and loss; they address the meanings of and emotional reactions to the impending relocation rather than attempt to alter the circumstances themselves.

SCALES MEASURING DEGREE OF COPING

Information Absorbed. The amount of relocation information available to the respondents was considerable. The amount of information "absorbed" by the respondents was rated on a four-point scale. A score of four indicated that the person had an accurate and extensive knowledge of the new environment. At the opposite end, a rating of one was given when the respondent literally did not know that he or she was about to move or had no idea where he or she was going; he or she exhibited a total inability either to describe the new environment or to engage in conversations about it with the interviewer.

Working Through. The concept of working through represents the willingness to discuss the move. In the Unwilling Old Ladies and Deinstitutionalized Elites studies we relied on the length of responses to five queries on the impending relocation to measure this factor. In the Home for Life study we developed a more subtle measure by assessing the respondents' introduction of the topic of the home when discussing the past and the present, eliminating responses to direct questions about the move itself. Forty sections of the pre-relocation interview (which was conducted in four to six sessions, for a total of twelve to sixteen hours) were selected and coded for the number of spontaneous references to the home. In the other two studies, the extent of verbal output was assessed by counting the number of words used to respond to the five direct questions on the move. Word counts ranged from a low of four words to a high of eighty-three words. Counts were then corrected for the general level of verbal output in the interview as a whole. Those who answered with terse answers— some with only a word or two or even a nod—were assumed to be avoiding coping with their relocation, whereas lengthy answers were assumed to reflect a working through of the impending relocation. Although this scale could be interpreted as an index of "preoccupation," measuring the breaking through of defenses that contain feelings about threat and loss, its correlations with other coping measures suggests that it primarily reflects the degree of coping.

Active Coping versus Denial. The last measure indexing degree of coping was based on the extent to which the defense mechanism of denial was employed. Here the focus was on the classical interpretation of denial—the exclusion of the event itself from consciousness—rather than on the exclusion of the meaning of the event. This assessment was made only in the Home for Life study because these respondents were shown the special set of Institutional TAT cards (Lieberman and Lakin 1963). As already described in chapter 4, the details of the cards were closely patterned after physical elements of the actual relocation settings. The five cards depicted a range of situations associated with the transition into the home, such as packing, entering the building, talking with the director, talking with a roommate and being among other residents in the home. Figures were drawn to suggest ambiguous attitudes, although the age differences were clear. Ratings of denial were based on a marked departure from the manifest, as well as latent, stimulus meaning of the scene depicted. Each card was scored on a three-point scale, with 0 representing absence of denial, 1 some denial, and 2 high denial, and the five scores were summed. Interjudge reliability coefficients on the five cards ranged from .86 to .90.

SCALES MEASURING LEVEL OF INTEGRATION

Extent of Accurate Appraisal. This scale reflected awareness of several aspects related to the relocation including accurate knowledge of the relocation environment, evidence of having examined the advantages and disadvantages of the move, an awareness of both emotions and reactions to the impending move, and the expression of relevant feelings about the move. High ratings on the five-point scale were given when several of these elements were in evidence, suggesting a differentiation of appraisal. At the other extreme, a rating of 1 was made where the respondent was clearly and extensively distorting both the nature of the relocation site and their feelings. For example, in discussing the impending move, one elderly man described the new environment as something completely different than it was in actuality, seeing the move as returning to his family rather than as moving to another institution.

Balanced Appraisals. This scale was only developed for the Home for Life Study. In this study, Pincus (1968) had identified five specific issues associated with institutionalization of the elderly. Three of the five represent gains associated with the institutionalization—care and security, people and companionship, and social activities. The other two represent possible losses—losses of freedom and privacy. The more of these five issues a respondent spontaneously addressed, the greater the differentiation and balance of appraisal. Low scores indicated that the respondent was not directing his or her efforts toward an affectively relevant integration of the impending relocation.

SCALES MEASURING DEGREE OF MASTERY

Perceived Control. The general challenge to the elderly is to maintain a sense of self-respect and self-effectiveness in the face of changing circumstances in their real world. The loss of roles and the failures of the body are intrinsically associated with becoming very old, and in most Western societies, requisite compensations are not readily available. Locus of control, as a psychological dimension relevant to aging, has become a prime focus for investigation in the past ten years or so. Particularly among the institutionalized, perceptions of control over one's own destiny have become a major analytic explanation for differences in outcomes of a variety of relocation circumstances (see, for example, Lawton 1980b).

The respondents in the relocation studies that compose the empirical base for this present book varied considerably in their modal perceptions of control, as described in chapter 3. In the Home for Life study, respondents felt they had the major responsibility for their decision to relocate. In the Unwilling Old Ladies study, respondents felt they had neither control nor influence over the decision to be relocated, expressing either helplessness ("I'll just have to do whatever they decide") or passive acceptance ("I'll do whatever they think best"). In the Deinstitutionalized Elites study, respondents felt that they had influenced the decision in some small way, often commenting that others had consulted them. Thus, there were rather large differences in perceived control among the samples, as well as considerable variability within each sample.

Prior to describing the scales developed to assess perceived control, we would like to briefly address the issue of voluntary relocation. We believe, as previously noted in chapter 2, that voluntary relocation is often a myth shared by the social agency, the older person, and frequently the family. The scales we developed to assess perceived control in relocation situations, as well as similar scales developed by others, measure a coping strategy based upon the individual's requirements and supported by significant others around them, which serves to maintain a sense of personal integrity. It is not necessarily an objective condition of the relocation. When we examined responses of elderly in the Home for Life study to the Institutional TAT prior to relocation (see Lieberman and Lakin 1963), we found that their stories portrayed the elderly people as making voluntary decisions to relocate, and as being in control of their lives. Yet the same TAT administered two months after entering the institutions elicited stories in which the elderly were portrayed as victims of their fate and not in control of the relocation situation. Apparently, when no longer under the threat of relocation, the former need to justify the move as a voluntary one diminishes. The need no longer exists to ward off threat and loss meanings associated with relocation. By and large we are not addressing a set of circumstances that have objective reality, and we do not believe that reasonable objective distinctions about control can be made among the four studies. What is important is that individuals do develop perceptions of the degree of control they have over their lives and of specific situations.

Two scales were developed to measure perceived control: *control of relocation* and *control of alternatives*. The first reflects the respondents' perception of their participation or control in decisions about relocation. A score of 1 on a six-point scale indicated a lack of knowledge about the relocation, a 2 indicated the absence of any perceived control over the decision to relocate; at the other end of the scale, a 6 indicated a perception of total responsibility for the decision. The second scale, control alter-

natives, assessed the extent to which the respondent felt a sense of participation in or control over the decision about where they should move once
the decision to move had been made. Again, a six-point scale was developed, ranging from a low of 1 for respondents who did not know whether
or where they would move and were waiting to be told, to a high of 6 for
respondents who felt they had a total responsibility for deciding where
they would move. As might be expected, the correlations between these
two scales were moderate to high, ranging from a low of .28 in the Unwilling Old Ladies study to a high of .95 in the Home for Life sample.

Degree of Congruence. This scale indexed the congruence between
adjustments respondents made in their self-perceived needs and the actual
potential for meeting these needs in the new environment. Operationally,
the measure was based on the extent to which respondents' preferences
regarding where they would like to move agreed with where they were
actually going. We elicited respondents' views of their preferred setting
and compared their perceptions to the actual characteristics of the new
environment. A score of 6 was given when there was a very close match
between the person's ideal, preferred environment and the setting into
which they were moving. A rating of 1 indicated a total mismatch. Here,
as with the measure of perceived control, it was assumed that any respondent could modify his or her perceptions, in this case to increasingly perceive the relocation environment as a preferred environment, or, in the
case of perceived control, to increasingly perceive himself or herself in
control of the situation.

Findings: The Effects of Threat Management Strategies

PREVIOUS FINDINGS

Before discussing the findings on the effects of threat management
strategies relevant results on threat and loss previously reported in chapter
4 will be summarized.

1. No relationship was found between the level of threat intensity and long-
   term adaptation.
2. There was a significant replicated relationship between the level of threat
   intensity assessed through conscious reports and short-term reactions: The
   higher the threat measured prior to relocation, the higher the level of depression subsequent to relocation.
3. There was a replicated relationship between increases in depression assessed

soon after the respondent entered the new environment and long-term adaptation. The finding of a linkage between short-term reactions and long-term adaptation suggests that level of threat may be indirectly associated with long-term adaptation.

4. The relationship between the intensity of threat and threat management strategies is in some instances substantial; in others cases it is inconsequential. Threat intensity as well as threat management strategies were, of course, measured at the same point in time; and as we have indicated, although theoretically distinguishable, responses in practice are an admixture of distressed affect reflecting threat and management attempts at mitigating such feelings. Appendix F shows the intercorrelation between the measures of direct threat and each of the threat management strategies (see also chapter 4). In all three studies, the most substantial association was between threat intensity and congruence between characteristics of the preferred and actual relocation settings. The next strongest association was between threat intensity and perceived control. Degree of coping and level of integration were, however, not appreciably associated with intensity. Although measures of threat management and measures of threat itself were associated, as one might expect, the levels of the associations were not impressive; and, as will be seen, there is substantial evidence that the two sets of measures are, in fact, empirically distinct.

Figure 6–1 provides a schematic summary of findings on the effects of threat management strategies on short-term reactions and long-term outcomes, which are discussed in the following sections.

EFFECTS OF THREAT MANAGEMENT ON DEPRESSIVE REACTIONS

We found moderately strong associations between some strategies and short-term affective reactions in the expected direction. For degree of coping, only one of the three measures applied across studies affected depression; Respondents who absorbed more information reacted to the subsequent relocation with less depression. A strong relationship was found only in the Unwilling Old Ladies study, which probably reflected the finding described in chapter 4 that they experienced the most intense threat. The linkage between degree of coping effects and the level of threat is supported by the finding that working through somewhat lowered depression among the Unwilling Old Ladies.

Integration appeared much more effective in containing depressive reactions. Respondents who showed evidence that they were able to address and connect affects with appraisal in some balanced and realistic mix were less likely to react to relocation with depression. Mastery proved to be the strongest predictor; those who perceived themselves in control of

FIGURE 6–1

Effects of Threat/Loss and Threat/Loss Management Strategies on Outcomes

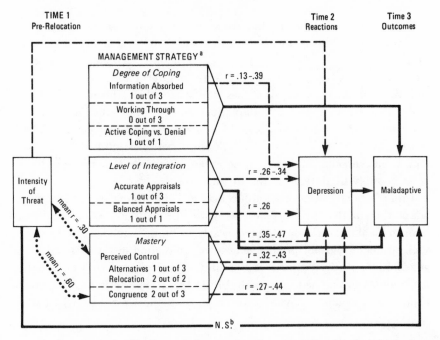

[a] Figures indicate the number of studies in which statistical significance was achieved at the .10 level or better, as shown in table 6–1. Two of the measures were not available in all studies.

[b] N.S. = not significant.

NOTE: Correlations below .20 not shown in diagram.
————— = outcome
— — — — = reaction

the circumstances and who had adapted their self-perceived need to the actual opportunities to be found in the new settings were more able to avoid depressive reactions.

All in all (particularly among the Unwilling Old Ladies study respondents, who showed the highest level of threat), there were moderate associations between threat management strategies and short-term reactions. The level of relationship (.30 on average) is the same level found between threat intensity measures themselves and short-term reactions. Because of the general and similar sets of associations between our measurement of perceived threat, our measurement of reactions to the threat in terms of depression, and our measurement of coping strategies, the "net" effect of threat management strategies in mitigating threat would be difficult to demonstrate statistically by applying causal statistical models.

137

THREAT MANAGEMENT STRATEGIES AND
LONG-TERM ADAPTATION

Despite the statistical limitations, when we examined the relationship between threat management strategies and long-term adaptation, some insights on causal relationships can be developed. Threat management strategies are significantly associated with long-term adaptation; generally the more of the mastery strategies, the more likely the individual will make an adequate long-term adaptation or at least not suffer maladaptive consequences, as manifested by physical, social, and behavioral decline. Recall that we did not find a relationship between level of threat and long-term outcome. Rather it is the coping strategies that make a difference, possibly by mitigating the threat.

Table 6–1 shows the relationship between the strategies and long-term adaptation in the three studies. As with our findings in linking threat management strategies to affective reactions immediately after relocation, such strategies did not predict long-term adaptation in the Deinstitution-alized Elites study. We believe this finding is explained by the fact that respondents in that setting reported little threat and anticipatory anxiety about the upcoming move. However, in both the Unwilling Old Ladies

TABLE 6–1

Association Between Threat/Loss Management Strategies
and Long-Term Adaptation (level of significance)[a]

| | Study[b] | | |
| | Unwilling Old Ladies (N=45) | Home for Life (N=85) | Deinstitu-tionalized Elites (N=82) |
Measure			
Degree of coping			
Information absorbed	.04	N.S.	N.S.
Working through	N.S.	N.S.	N.S.
Active coping	—	.04	—
Level of integration			
Accurate appraisals	N.S.	.04	N.S.
Balanced appraisals	—	.04	—
Mastery			
Perceived control: alternatives	.10	N.S.	N.S.
relocation	—	.02	.10
Congruence	.02	.03	N.S.

[a]The .10 level of significance for two-tailed tests was used, as reflecting presumptive evidence of prediction of outcome.
[b]N.S. = not significant at the .10 level; a dash indicates that the measure of management strategy was not carried out for this study.

and the Home for Life studies, in which threat, anticipatory anxiety, and feelings of loss were more common, the strategies individuals used significantly predicted long-term adaptation up to two years prior to the outcome assessment.

In the Unwilling Old Ladies study we found a significant linkage for information absorbed: The more information absorbed, the less likely it was that maladaptive outcomes would occur. Also, the higher the mastery, measured by both perceived control and congruence, the less maladaptation.

In the Home for Life study, we found that active coping significantly predicted outcome. Cognitive integration measured both by accurate appraisals and balanced appraisals significantly predicted adaptation. We also find a highly significant association between perceiving oneself in control of the situation and successful outcomes.

Some Final Thoughts on Threat and Coping Strategies

The relationship between threat management and threat intensity is a dynamic one. An initial, often instantaneous experience of being threatened is rapidly followed by an active searching process directed toward minimizing the threat. Among the many theorists, Lazarus (see, for example, 1966) postulates that the initial threat experience reflects cognitive processes. For him, the initial experience, the primary appraisal of threat, is determined by two issues. The first, phrased in terms of the question that person asks himself or herself is "How much danger am I in from the situation?" The second is "How much am I in danger from anything I do about the threat?" Independent of whether the initial experience is considered to necessitate such an inner dialogue, the immediate confrontation with threat is followed by processes addressed to coping with such threat.

In our own work, respondents were assessed on the measures of both threat intensity and coping processes at a point where they were immersed in this interactive dynamic process of reacting and acting. Based on the findings we have presented in this chapter and chapter 4 on threat and loss, it is perhaps most reasonable to assume that the level of threat assessed reflects the success of the management strategies. Thus, if we inspect figure 6–1 again, we see that there are few correlations beyond .2 between threat intensity and degree of coping or between threat intensity and level of integration. We did, however, find substantial correlations between threat intensity and mastery. The greater the perceived control, the greater the congruence between the preferred and the actual environment, the less the level of experienced threat. The strongest relationships between threat management, and both reactions and adaptation again were found for the mastery measures. These sets of observations suggest that alterations in the self in relationship to an event that symbolizes apprehension, loss, and the very destruction of the self is the key to understanding the major mechanism for reducing the level of experienced threat and loss. In turn, this implies that subsequent reactions will be less severe and long-term outcome will be more positive. We believe the state of affairs is as follows: Mastery leads to lower threat and loss, which leads to lower depression, which leads to more successful adaptation.

It appears to matter less how active the coping efforts are or how realistic and integrated the appraisal processes. What matters is the capacity to perceive the situation as being in one's control when all indicators suggest otherwise. Turning a noxious situation into a palatable one—both by seeing the self as essential to the action and by altering one's needs to be consistent with the actual circumstances—is essential to adaptation.

The findings we have presented are consistent with such a view, although we recognize that portraying them in this fashion ignores some other linkages that are apparent in our data. The perspective developed here may seem to ignore the general thrust of previous studies that have explored similar coping strategies. After all, the effective use of information, efforts to work through anticipated noxious events, utilization of active coping efforts rather than avoidance or denial, and the ability to integrate and balance appraisals are all strategies that ordinarily connote effective coping. In fact, our emphasis on mastery, with its reliance on perceptions of the self as the perpetrator of destiny, may reflect the creation of mythology among respondents. As we have indicated elsewhere, their sense of control or perception of control was greater than any external view of the situation. In this sense, the indices we have described in the chapter that represent degree of coping and level of integration appear, from the perspective of models of mental health, to mirror such concepts more than do the characteristics we have described under mastery. This issue will be revisited many times in this book in more general terms, beginning in the next chapter where we examine traditional models of mental health and their role in mitigating risk, as well as later where we look at the functions of reminiscence. We will have ample opportunity to examine characteristics of myth making and its possible adaptive function among the elderly.

7

Risk Factors:
Prediction of Adaptation

COMMONSENSE VIEWS on why people differ in their ability to endure adversity often center on notions of strength—biological, moral, mental, and social. Scientific views of individual differences in adaptation to stress frequently represent measurable elaborations of these common-sense views. We describe people as possessing poorer constitutions, lower ego strength, less flexibility, unavailable social networks, poor mental health, and so forth. Risk factors are characteristic of individuals and their surroundings that increase the susceptibility to disease. Smoking and obesity increase the likelihood of cardiovascular disease; air pollution, the likelihood of respiratory disease; and fatigue, the likelihood of accidents and infectious diseases. Risk factors that predispose individuals to disease have a counterpart in behavioral variables that decrease the capacity to cope with stress. We have divided such risk factors into two general kinds: resources that can be utilized when coping with stress and current functioning that reflects general adaptive capacity.

Our goal in this chapter is to examine a variety of individual character-istics—risk factors—found by other investigators to meaningfully predict failure of adaptation in response to stress. These objectives are consonant with a wide-ranging field of inquiry, which may best be labeled stress and illness research. Numerous personal characteristics have, over the years, been examined for their potential as explanations of successes and failures in dealing with stress. In a recent monograph, Antonosky (1979) catalogues "generalized resistance resources." Included are physical, biochemical, cognitive, emotional, valuative-attitudinal, interpersonal-relational, and social-cultural characteristics. The desire to explain why some individuals manage successfully when reacting to stress while others suffer untoward consequences is an ancient one. Our intent, however, is not to review either the history or the current status of the variety of speculations and investigations but rather to provide the reader with an orienting framework in which to place the specific questions we will ask.

We begin with the assumption that people differ in their psychological, biological, and social resources and that when confronted with situations that require major adaptive efforts, differences in success will depend upon the resources available to the person in the face of the situational demands. The resources available to a person set limits on the processes the person can use for coping. Four simple conditions underlying adaptive capacity will be discussed: physical, cognitive, and energy potentials, and social resources.

Beyond such resources, predictions about ability to cope with future stress are facilitated by knowledge of how well an individual functions in the absence of extreme stress, since such information affords some clues on how the person will function when confronted with crises. Psychological health offers one general perspective for calibrating overall functioning. No matter how broadly the concept of mental health is defined, it certainly does not offer the only perspective for assessing how well people are doing. Many investigators contend that the most reasonable way of assessing how well a person is functioning at any given time is to ask him or her. Level of gratification or satisfaction and the related concepts of happiness and positive self-view were also operationalized in our assessment procedures. A third approach to examining how well an individual is functioning is to look at the extent, range, and quality of his or her interpersonal relationships.

Thus, this chapter focuses on the risk factors that were reflected in the resources and functioning of the respondents in our studies, as they were assessed prior to relocation for their saliency in predicting long-term adaptation within one year or so after the move. Given the current state of knowledge regarding risk factors, the task we have set for ourselves in this chapter is indeed a difficult one. We seek to determine characteristics of people that place them at risk when they encounter major challenges and by such inquiry to develop a framework that can be replicated across the four studies. By now the reader is familiar with the obvious fact that the populations examined shared little besides their chronological age. The study samples differed in innumerable ways. Respondents varied from highly debilitated, uncommunicative elderly people who had spent their entire adult lives in mental hospitals to articulate, physically healthy women who would be at home in most rural communities. Some respondents were sick and decrepit; others were psychologically beyond repair; still others were close to death. Their life experiences, their religious affiliation and ethnic origins, varied widely. Beyond such personal variability, the findings presented in chapters 4 and 5 speak to the diversity of adaptive challenges among the studies even though all four were of elderly people undergoing relocation. The available evidence suggests that the Unwilling Old Ladies underwent the highest stress, whereas the least stress was found among the Deinstitutionalized Elites because they were the least threatened and they experienced the least environmental challenge. Those in the Home for Life study who moved from the community to institutions, as well as respondents in the Death of an Institution study, occupy the midpoint on this continuum of stress.

Such diversity, both in populations and in presumed stress levels, places a heavy burden on the attempt to uncover meaningful generalizations about risk factors. The research design, however, does provide a powerful context for examining such questions. The base rate of maladaptation was high among the elderly who were relocated. Such failure rates (about 50 percent) are not characteristic of most studies of stress or illness. (Correlational studies of life changes usually find that the majority of respondents demonstrate high life changes and low symptoms. They rarely produce correlations between events and adaptive failures greater than .30.) In addition to the problem of base rates of maladaptation, our research design provided partial antidotes to some of the typical dilemmas that researchers on stress or illness have faced. As we have indicated in the previous chapters, respondents' knowledge of the impending relocation was to some extent stressful, and coping strategies were initiated to address such distress; however, respondents were studied prior to the point of maximum stress, prior to the relocation itself. Our investigations were predictive unlike the more usual retrospective strategies of stress and illness studies. We also believe that our studies, by using idiographic change measures based on functioning, have successfully negotiated the dilemma of adequate outcome measures posed by failures to distinguish between illness and illness behavior (Cohen 1979). That is, linkages reported in the literature between stress and illness may most often be parsimoniously described as associations between stress and illness behavior, for example, between stress and increased sensitivity to symptoms, increased report of symptoms, increased seeking of medical treatment, and so forth.

The major analytic framework adopted to study the influence of available resources and adequate current functioning on later adaptation is based on the assumption that respondents within each sample were equally stressed. The reader will obviously understand that this assumption is just that—an operational convenience rather than an accurate portrayal of reality. The findings presented in chapter 4 indicate that not all respondents perceived the relocation circumstances as entailing threat or symbolizing loss. The analyses of environments and environmental discrepancy as a source of stress described in chapter 5 indicated that not all who were studied found themselves in either negative or discrepant environments. When we subsequently examined environment-person interactions, we began to recognize empirically that the same "objective" set of circumstances had different stress potentials for different people, which in turn were contingent on the "reactivity" of each respondent.

Our assumption, then, that all respondents studied were stressed is a convenience rather than an empirical reality. Such a working assumption places our study in a similar framework to investigators who have examined such events as widowhood, job loss, and other major life stresses as well as to those who examine catastrophic circumstances—situations that may present very high levels of stress for most people.

Two general categories of risk factors—resources and current psychological and social functioning—were assessed in all four studies prior to the actual physical move. The next section describes the measures and findings on resources and the following section presents those on current functioning.

Resources

Theories as well as empirical studies of human stress suggest that individuals with better psychological, social, and biological resources are better able to confront stressful situations successfully. Individual differences in successful adaptation or maladaptation are associated with variations in the resources people can command to cope with stress-producing events. Those who approach human stress studies from this perspective must, of course, ask what resources are critical to the specific circumstances challenging adaptation. Does it make a difference whether the condition studied is incarceration, combat, a school examination, migration, loss of a significant other, or one of a multitude of other events that are usually assumed to induce relatively high levels of stress for most individuals? Does the culture, life stage, or gender of those studied lead researchers to examine the role of particular and perhaps different types of resources in adaptation to stress?

The framework we used to define the personal characteristics that are necessary to confront high stress-producing situations differs in some ways from the usual constructs other investigators have used in studying human stress, such as ego strength and impulse control. Our attention was directed to characteristics such as cognitive functioning, physical functioning, ego energy, and social resources, which have been shown to decrease with advancing age. Many elderly people are at the lower limits of these functions, and therefore individual differences in these resources may radically affect their ability to withstand stress. The selection of resources for assessment was also influenced by assumptions regarding the particular stress-inducing events studied—that they entailed radical changes in life space. Although such radical changes imply the appraisal of threat and the experience of loss, environmental change and the consequent adaptational challenges requires the use of specific resources if pre-stress levels of functioning are to be reestablished in the new environment.

MEASURES OF RESOURCES

Cognitive Resources. Cognitive resources, operationalized as cognitive abilities, represent a critical component of ego strength. The ability to orient oneself in time and place; to take in, process, store, and recall information; to organize complex information; and to shift perceptions are all skills required to accurately and realistically appraise threat. Because appraisals are so fundamental to organizing and executing coping strategies, the level of cognitive functioning establishes the lower limit for coping with stress. Although inadequate cognitive capacities are hypothesized to be related to the inability to adapt to stress, adequate cognitive functioning does not necessarily assure adequate coping. Yet the decrements in these capacities associated with aging suggest that as the decrease in functioning becomes more evident among the elderly, these capacities become more central in adapting to stress.

In three of the studies, test data to assess such cognitive abilities were available. (See technical note 1 for a description of tests and measures.) The test instruments were inappropriate for many respondents in the

Death of an Institution study of long-term hospitalized mental patients, however, and cognitive ability scores for this group were based on ratings developed from time sampling observations. (See technical note 2 for a description of these observations.)

Physical Health Resources. Physical capacity is not usually considered as a predictor of outcome in most studies of human stress. Those investigators who have examined the relationship of physiological functioning to adaptation to stress have either focused on specific physiological mechanisms or have focused on genetically determined physiological typologies. Our own studies did not share either of these theoretical perspectives, nor was information generated to explore physiological mechanisms. Despite the intentional bias in three of the four studies toward the physically healthy portion of the population, however, we could hardly ignore the simple question of physical disease. (See technical note 3.) The aged are physically more vulnerable, and their ability to maintain physical homeostasis can be rapidly exhausted. The efforts of researchers to disentangle "normal aging" from processes of disease have met with only modest success, however. It is perhaps most appropriate in our studies to think of the physical capacities of the aged person as setting limits on adaptation, a view consonant with that of other investigators (Birren et al. 1963).

Assessments of physical functioning or health status were based on self-reports; on physicians' ratings, using either medical records or medical examinations; and on reports of nonmedical staff who were familiar with the health functioning of the elderly respondents before their relocation. In addition, health status was also assessed in the Death of an Institution study by the number of serious illnesses in the near past, and the number of hospitalizations and other changes found in the medical records over the past year.

Energy. Popular conceptions of aging often note the diminished energy experienced during the last decades of life. This observation may, of course, reflect a variety of processes characteristic of the elderly, including the depressive mood that so often accompanies aging. Theoretical conceptions of psychological energy have been a primary concern of psychoanalysis, particularly in the constructs of ego psychology (Hartmann 1950). Empirically, the concept of psychological energy has not fared well in the history of psychology, despite its emphasis in classical psychoanalytic thinking and subsequent development in ego psychology. Perhaps the most thoroughgoing examination of this area, including measurement issues, can be found in the work of Cattell (1962).

Energy, in the aging, with rare exception, has been discussed from a self-report perspective, including strategies for the "conservation of energy" and self-reports on amounts of energy individuals possessed. Rosen and Neugarten (1960), using an ego psychology framework, developed a strategy for assessing ego energy based on responses to TAT cards. (See technical note 4.) We adapted their method for assessing energy. In a pilot study of persons with an average age of eighty-four, however, we determined that the cognitive abilities required to perform on the TAT limited the generalizability of the ego energy score, since at the low end of the continuum, ego energy and cognitive skills were confounded (Slaughter 1964). To bolster our measure of ego energy, we devised indices that reflected overall "output" levels, measuring the amount of effort expended in response to the open-ended interviews, structured questionnaires, and projective tests. Word counts provide a crude measure of output.

Social Resources. Although the intellectual roots of social support extend back to the very beginning of sociology, recent empirical investigations have highlighted the conditions under which a person's social world will be functionally related to mental health and health issues (Cobb 1976; Gore 1978; Heller 1978; Kaplan, Cassel, and Gore 1977; Lin et al. 1979; Pinneau 1976). Investigations have been undertaken, for example, to examine the role of social supports in reducing the number of complications of pregnancy, recovering from surgery and from illness, protecting against clinical depression in the face of adverse events, reducing psychological distress and physiological symptomatology following job loss, mitigating the effects of bereavement, and protecting against emotional problems associated with aging. These and other human conditions in which social support has been seen as a protective coating have been recently reviewed by Hamburg and Killea (1979). It might be supposed that such a vigorous outpouring of empirical research would suggest a line of inquiry that exhibits coherence. Unfortunately, such is not the case. In a recent series of studies, Lieberman (1982) suggests that stress mitigation or the protective function of social resources is an empirical reality only in highly limited circumstances.

Conceptual clarity is diminished further when social resources are investigated among the elderly. Although numerous investigators have noted that with advancing age there is a decline in the number of social roles and that the elderly are embedded in fewer networks, there is controversy regarding how the elderly change in their amount of interaction across the variety of social contexts (Riley and Foner 1968), as well as the meaning and the relevance of such data for adaptation (Cumming and Henry 1961; Havighurst and Albrecht 1953; Maddox 1964, 1965; Neugarten and Havighurst 1969; Tobin and Neugarten 1961). At times, diminished social interaction and the lessened availability of social supports are interpreted as normative developments in late life, whereas at other times they are seen as a consequence of highly specific social structures that are associated, in turn, with specific adaptational or personality styles in late life. (For a review of these issues, see Lowenthal and Robinson, 1976).

Despite these serious questions concerning both conceptual and measurement problems, the stress mitigating effects of social resources remain an attractive hypothesis for stress researchers. We thus asked: To what extent did the elderly people we studied perceive their social world as containing others who could be counted on to provide both tangible and emotional resources: An eleven-item Personal Resource Questionnaire was developed requiring respondents to indicate who they could call in each of the following situations:

1. Whom do you like to be with when you feel happy?
2. Whom would you ask when you needed someone to go shopping for you?
3. Whom would you call for help when sick?
4. Whom would you like to see when feeling down in the dumps?
5. Whom would you ask for a charitable contribution?
6. Whom would you go with if you won a trip for two to Florida?
7. Whom would you like to see if you felt lonely?
8. Whom would you ask if you were short of money and needed to borrow five dollars for two days?
9. Whom would you ask if you wanted company on a walk?
10. Whom would you ask if you needed help in filling out income taxes?
11. Whom would you see if you felt like having company of the opposite sex?

Scores were computed by counting the number of different people mentioned by name and the number of items for which no one was named.

THE EFFECTS OF RESOURCES ON ADAPTATION

Our general hypothesis regarding resources was that those elderly people with the least cognitive abilities, physical capacities, ego energy, and social resources would be at risk. Overall, we found an association between inadequate cognitive and physical resources before relocation and maladaptation after relocation. The nature of the findings led us to conclude that health and cognitive resources best fit a *pathognomonic sign model* because, when above a minimal level, they are not risk factors. Findings for each study will be reviewed in turn.

Among the Unwilling Old Ladies sample, consisting of well-functioning women, neither general cognitive abilities nor ego energy (the only other resources measured in this study), were linked to subsequent adaptation. We did, however, find that respondents manifesting cognitive dysfunction

on one measure of cognitive resources were likely to have negative outcomes; those with high scores on the Mental Status Questionnaire (four
errors or more, a standard cut-off point for diagnosing cognitive deficit)
experienced adverse reactions following relocation.

The large array of resource assessments that were available in the
Home for Life study provided a more adequate test of the hypothesis.
Respondents who showed cognitive malfunctioning, physical incapacities,
and low levels of ego energy were significantly more likely to show maladaptive responses to becoming institutionalized. As shown in table 7–1,
however, there was no evidence that social resources were associated with
subsequent adaptation. The role of cognition, health, and energy in predicting subsequent adaptation was also examined for respondents in the
two control samples developed for this study. Controls who initially
showed poorer cognitive functioning and physical capacities were at
greater risk, being more likely to have deteriorated or died during the
ensuing year. Although, as shown in table 7–1, the level of significance is

TABLE 7–1

Resources and Current Functioning as Predictors of Adaptation:
The Home for Life Study (mean scores)

Measure	Home for Life Subjects			Controls		
	Intact (N=44)	Declined (N=41)	p	Intact (N=48)	Declined (N=24)	p
Resources						
Sum of cognitive tests	.84	2.02	.02	.77	1.39	.10
Physical health	1.25	3.12	.01	1.53	2.06	.05
Energy	65.30	56.20	.05	63.80	58.20	N.S.[a]
Social	4.16	4.13	N.S.	—	—	—
Current Functioning						
Mental Health						
Block Q-Sort	.17	.17	N.S.	—	—	—
Anxiety	19.80	19.40	N.S.	14.80	18.00	.10
Depression	13.40	14.20	N.S.	11.10	12.80	N.S.
Well-being						
Life satisfaction rating	15.70	16.10	N.S.	17.40	16.30	N.S.
Self-esteem	20.40	18.60	N.S.	19.60	17.40	N.S.
Social Functioning						
Role functioning	9.52	8.56	N.S.	10.30	8.70	N.S.
Quality of interaction	4.16	4.13	N.S.	—	—	—
Amount of interaction	11.20	11.20	N.S.	10.36	8.81	.05

[a]N.S. = not significant; a dash indicates that the measure was not carried out for that population.

lower for these respondents than for those undergoing relocation, in both samples cognitive, physical, and, to some extent, energy resources do make a difference. Such resources do not appear to play a unique role under stress, but rather their relative absence portends a lowered ability in general among the aged to maintain homeostasis. Although elderly people who have low resources will not adapt well to stress, deterioration is likely to occur even without stress. Such individuals apparently are on the road to decline regardless of the level of situational stress in their lives. Of course, the control samples were not exempt from the ordinary stresses found among people their age; indeed, as discussed in chapter 4, respondents in the community control sample had experienced these age-associated stressful events (assessed by inquiring in the initial interview about life changes that occurred during the previous year).

The findings from the Deinstitutionalized Elites study—the relocation situation with the lowest stress—partially supported the resources hypothesis but also provided some surprises. Respondents who were in poorer physical health prior to the move did, as expected, show subsequently more maladaptive reactions, as shown in table 7-2. Cognitive abilities, however, were not generally predictive. Only one of the four measures of cognitive abilities, perceptual adequacy, had a meaningful association to outcome, but the direction of the association was opposite to the expected one. Respondents manifesting better cognitive functioning on this measure were more likely to decline subsequent to relocation. In isolation this observation may appear to be of little relevance. However, findings from the Death of an Institution study, and current functioning, were also in the opposite direction from that expected in predicting maladaptation.

The Death of an Institution study, with its larger sample, its nonselectivity of respondents, and broader range of outcomes, permitted more complex analyses of the effects of resources on adaptation. Recall that the sample size made it possible to analyze four patterns of adaptation among the residents: those who remained stable; those who declined socially, psychologically and/or physically; an appreciable group of people who died; and respondents who showed social, psychological, or cognitive improvement subsequent to relocation. As shown in table 7-3, when those who subsequently died were compared to the remainder of the sample, the results were unambiguous. Respondents who died after relocation had significantly poorer health resources, as reflected in all four measures. Similarly, those who died after relocation were significantly more cognitively impaired, as reflected in verbal comprehension, verbal ability, awareness, and responsiveness. Here, all differences were significant at least at the .0002 level.

TABLE 7–2
Resources and Current Functioning
as Predictors of Adaptation:
The Deinstitutionalized Elites Study (z=scores)

	Deinstitutionalized Elites		
Measure	Intact (N=42)	Declined (N=40)	p
Resources			
Cognitive			
Face-Hand Test	.00	−.01	N.S.[a]
Visual organization	−.06	.07	N.S.
Perceptual adequacy	−.19	.21	.04
Mental states	−.04	.14	N.S.
Physical health			
Physician rating	.19	−.28	.03
Staff rating	.06	−.11	N.S.
Current Functioning			
Mental health			
Block Q-Sort	−.20	.14	.09
Deviant behavior	.08	.01	N.S.
Anxiety	.07	−.13	N.S.
Well-being			
Life satisfaction rating	−.14	.10	N.S.
Social functioning			
Activity/passivity	−.06	.01	N.S.
Amount of activity	.02	−.11	N.S.
Staff rating	−.08	.09	N.S.
Role activity	−.10	.08	N.S.
Interpersonal contact	−.18	.20	.04

[a]N.S. = not significant.

In this study, energy and social resources were less adequately measured, and only one index proved to be suitable for assessing social resources—number of close friends. This measure of social resources was, as in the Home for Life study, not predictive of subsequent outcome. This lack of association between social resources and subsequent adaptation contrasts with the importance of cognitive and health resources in predicting maladaptation for individuals undergoing stress. Moreover, the role found for cognitive and health resources replicates some of the findings from the previous studies.

As also shown in table 7–3, among residents who survived, those who deteriorated or improved generally had similar mean scores, whereas those who remained unchanged had lower mean scores than the other two groups. These lower mean scores reflect a trend toward having less re-

TABLE 7-3
Resources and Current Functioning as Predictors of Adaptation: The Death of an Institution Study

Measures	Means Dead (N=78)	Means Alive (N=349)	p	Means Deteriorated (N=159)	Means Unchanged (N=103)	Means Improved (N=87)	Contrasts (p levels) Deteriorated vs. Unchanged	Contrasts (p levels) Improved vs. Unchanged
Resources								
Cognitive								
Verbal comprehension	2.5	3.0	.0001	3.2	2.7	3.1	.001	.01
Verbal ability	3.4	3.9	.0002	4.3	3.5	3.8	.0001	N.S.
Awareness	2.1	2.6	.0002	2.7	2.3	2.8	N.S.	.006
Responsiveness	3.0	4.0	.0001	4.2	3.4	4.2	.003	.000
Physical health								
Total illness	20.7	13.5	.0001	13.6	13.2	13.6	N.S.	N.S.
Serious illness	2.1	1.4	.0001	1.5	1.2	1.3	N.S.	N.S.
Physician rating	2.8	3.2	.0001	3.2	3.1	3.2	N.S.	N.S.
Declining medical condition	2.1	2.6	.0001	2.5	2.7	2.8	.01	N.S.
Social								
Close friends	1.1	1.1	N.S.	1.2	1.1	1.1	N.S.	N.S.
Current Functioning								
Mental health								
Psychiatric symptoms	5.2	6.1	.05	5.9	6.4	6.3	N.S.	N.S.
Social functioning								
Sociability	37.6	39.4	N.S.	42.3	36.2	37.9	.0001	N.S.
Interaction—staff	9.0	9.6	N.S.	10.2	8.8	9.3	.0001	N.S.
Roles functioning	13.7	16.9	.0001	17.8	14.9	17.6	.01	.000
Relatedness	.78	1.21	.06	1.49	.92	1.04	.0001	N.S.

sources in the unchanged group than in the other two groups. When each of the changed groups was compared to the no-change group, statistically significant differences were found in initial levels of cognitive resources but not for the initial level for the health measures. Thus those who died clearly possessed more impoverished cognitive and health resources than these who did not, but the picture becomes more complex when more specific levels of adaptation are examined for the survivors: Those who changed, either negatively or positively, possessed significantly better cognitive resources than those who remained stable.

We believe these puzzling findings can only be interpreted by examining the source of stress experienced by these elderly people in their relocation. On the measure of environmental discrepancy (assessed by the difference between pre- and post-relocation environments as discussed in chapter 5), the scores of those who died did not differ from scores of those who remained alive. Among the survivors, however, those who deteriorated and those who improved were significantly different from the no-change group in environmental discrepancy (both differences were significant beyond the p < .01 level). Those who died and those who remained unchanged were less different in their pre- and post-relocation environments than both the deteriorated and improved groups; that is, they were apparently less "stressed." Despite being under less stress, however, those who subsequently died were apparently so precariously balanced, as reflected in the paucity of their cognitive and health resources, that perhaps even a modest level of strain destroyed their fragile homeostasis. Although those who remained unchanged had levels of stress apparently comparable to those who subsequently died, they also had greater cognitive resources.

In contrast, whereas the deteriorated and the improved groups may have experienced greater stress, they also possessed considerably higher resources. But what accounts for the different outcomes in these two groups? The specific characteristics of the new environments provide part of the answer. Although the characteristics of the post-relocation environments of those who died were not significantly different than the environments of those who remained unchanged, the environments of the unchanged group were decidedly different from the environments of those who deteriorated (p < .05) and from the environments of those who improved (p < .01). Of greater importance than the overall comparisons, however, were the specific qualities of the environments. The improved group moved into environments that fostered autonomy, were somewhat more personalized, were warmer, were more socially affiliative, were less encouraging of dependency, and did not tolerate deviant behavior but expected adult behavior from their charges. The subjects who improved, in short, were relocated to settings that emphasized independence and normalization of behavior, which, as we have indicated previously, are environments that encourage competency. Again, as discussed in chapter 5, environmental change necessitates a more complex explanatory model than simply the amount of challenge or the requirement for new adaptation. Although the adaptive challenges of relocation constitute a stress, such challenges can also produce enhanced rather than maladaptive behavior. The outcome is, in part, determined by characteristics of the person—his or her capacities and resources—and in part by specific psychosocial qualities of the new environments. Whereas both the improved and the deteriorated groups found themselves in environments that were discrepant with their previous settings, and both had some of the resources and capacities needed to adjust to a new environment, those who deteriorated were relocated to less enhancing environments, while those who improved went to more enhancing environments. We cannot, unfortunately, completely rule out the relative contribution of crucial health resources. Those who deteriorated had less health resources than those who improved, but they were identical on all other resources and as will soon become apparent, they were also identical in functional status.

An adequate framework for prediction based on personal resources obviously must take into account not only the level of challenge or stress but also the context. Such a framework must also consider resources to be discontinuous, in the sense that minimal levels must be reached if adaptation is to be assured. We believe that below a certain level of resource, neither degree of stress nor quality of context is relevant. Thus, those who died were so markedly precarious and had so few resources, that other characteristics—whether of person or of context—were irrelevant. This view is consonant with the earlier discussion of "environmental responders" in the Deinstitutionalized Elites study. We reported in chapter 5 that the environmental dimensions made a difference among those respondents most responsive to their environment, defined as those who did not possess qualities of "aging."

Unfortunately, our measures are rarely scaled in such a manner that categorical groups can be demarcated with any degree of certainty. We cannot tell with certainty, for example, the boundary line above which cognitive resources no longer contribute to adaptational outcomes. Nor can we demonstrate with precision that resources function as assymetrical predictors so that their absence implies potential disaster, whereas their presence does not necessarily imply successful adaptation.

Added support for our revised view about the role of resources can be found in the parallel analysis we conducted on the control sample for the Death of an Institution study, the one hundred elderly people who were residing in a similar state hospital that was not being closed down. Although they were comparable to the Death of an Institution population (see table A–4, appendix A), the death rate was five out of one hundred, only one-third that observed in the relocation sample. Because of the small number who died, comparisons were made only between the unchanged, deteriorated, and improved groups in the control population. Comparisons on measures of resources between the deteriorated and the no-change groups, as well as between the no-change and improved groups, revealed a relative lack of predictive power. On the two of the six cognitive measures for which differences were found, the improved residents had the best cognitive resources, followed by the unchanged group and then the deteriorated group, who had the lowest level.

Stated another way, although the observation of the association between cognitive resources and subsequent adaptation is unfortunately based on too few significant differences, those who did best in a relatively stable environment were those who started off best, whereas those who did worst started off worse. This association was expected for the group undergoing the stress of relocation, but obviously this kind of association was modified by the nature of the post-relocation environments.

From another perspective, personal resources' relative lack of power to predict outcomes in nonstress conditions may suggest that such characteristics become more salient in crisis situations. However, resources were found to be modestly associated with subsequent adaptation for respondents in the control samples in the Home for Life study who were not undergoing the stress of relocation. Thus, a more complex model is necessary to adequately explain the association between resources and adaptation in which the level of challenge and the nature of the environmental context must be considered. Without question the simple explanation that more resources leads to better subsequent adaptation does not match reality!

Current Functioning

It is commonly assumed by both social scientists and the general public that the best predictor of future behavior under stress is how well the person is currently functioning. Conventional wisdom has it that those who function more adequately will be able to meet and cope effectively with adversity. Although simple in the abstract, close examination of this proposition quickly becomes complex because there is little consensus on how to describe adequate functioning. Diverse theoretical perspectives and the implicit and explicit beliefs and value systems behind them come to the fore.

Moreover, beyond the conceptual problems posed by such diversity are the methodological dilemmas posed by the need to assess the current functioning of elderly people drawn from a variety of circumstances. Our respondents ranged across an age span of thirty years and included at one extreme those who were functioning reasonably well in the community and, at the other, state mental hospital patients who had in previous periods of their life exhibited debilitating mental illness. A broad range of approaches was required to assess adequacy of current functioning if assessments were to be at all equivalent across studies. The framework we adopted to measure current functioning includes three general areas that collectively represent the general consensus of the theoretical and empirical literature in this area: first, measures of both overall psychological or mental health and specific reflections of mental impairments such as levels of anxiety and depression; second, morale, measured in terms of life satisfaction and self-esteem; and third, indices of social functioning.

MEASURES OF CURRENT FUNCTIONING

Measures of Mental Health.   Previous work in this area offers a number of alternative procedures for assessment. Various psychological tests (for example, the Minnesota Multiphasic Personality Inventory) or, clinical interviews, and previous history of adjustment have all been used to differentiate individuals with regard to level of "mental health." Although our assessment methods varied from study to study, our major approach to testing the hypothesis that mental health was associated with stress adaptation was to use Block's (1961) Q-Sort. (See technical note 5.)

The Q-Sort technique, which provides a subtle and complex approach to assessing psychological health, was appropriate for the Home for Life and the Deinstitutionalized Elites studies because of the complex and diverse interview data that were obtained. In the Unwilling Old Ladies study we used ratings of ego pathology as the measure of mental impairment as reflected in stories told in response to the TAT (Dana 1955); and in the Death of an Institution study, we used observers' ratings of psychiatric symptoms. In addition to these measures, in the Home for Life and Deinstitutionalized Elites studies we used comparable measures of depression and anxiety. Thus, in all four studies, assessments were made of psychiatric symptoms, but in only two of the studies did we have a direct measure of mental health, the Q-Sort. In the Death of an Institution study, mental illness was assessed by the extent to which such manifest psychiatric symptomatology as visual and auditory hallucinations, delusional material, and repetitive motor activity, hyperactivity impaired the patients' ability to function effectively in their environment. For the most part, ratings of psychiatric symptomatology were made by hospital staff and adjusted by the observations of the research staff. Symptoms judged to be present by the hospital staff were not counted, however, unless verified by the observer.

Measures of Well-Being. Perhaps the simplest and most direct assessment of current social-psychological status can be found in measures of well-being or morale. Such measures represent the sum total of the individual's sense of self—his or her personal summary of beliefs about the self and his or her position in the world. They index, from a phenomenological point of view, current equilibrium. Because measures of well-being were not available in the Unwilling Old Ladies study, the first investigation in which such assessments were made was in the Home for Life study. Well-being was measured by ratings of life satisfaction (Neugarten, Havighurst and Tobin 1961) and by judgments based upon the sum of positive self-descriptive statements using the Leary (1954) Self-Sort Task (described in chapter 10). Only life satisfaction ratings were available in the Deinstitutionalized Elites study, and the use of observations rather than subjective reports in the Death of an Institution study precluded measures of well-being and self-esteem.

Measures of Social Functioning. In each of the four studies, role interaction and the quantity and quality of interaction were assessed. The extensiveness of a person's social network represents a resource, much like the individual's health status. The quality of interaction with those individuals in the person's social network represents, on the one hand, a resource that can be called upon in times of crisis, and on the other hand, an important component of current functioning. Although it is an ambiguous distinction, for the purposes of exposition, it seems reasonable to consider social interaction as comprising two distinct conceptual areas: resources that can be called upon (which was discussed in the first section of this chapter) and current social functioning (which is discussed here).

Although conceptually an attempt was made to develop similar measures of these areas for all of the studies, the differences among the samples necessitated modifications for each. Role interaction was indexed by the amount of contact with others made in the context of various social roles within the past month. Among respondents dwelling in the community, eight roles (children, siblings, other relatives, friends, roommate/neighbor, work, organization, and spouse) were assessed on four-point scales, ranging from 0, which implied no contact, through 3, which reflected a high degree of contact or involvement. For mental hospital patients, eight roles were assessed, representing the possible different interactions in a mental institution.

The quantity of interaction reflected the number of people (other than relatives) with whom the respondent interacted, as well as the social activities in which the respondent knew other participants and was known to them. The rating is a combined score for interaction with individuals or in groups and was made on the basis of current interaction. Four weighted scale points were included: 0—relatively isolated; 2—one or two friends; 4—an important focus of activity; and 6—a constant round of activity. In the mental hospital studies, staff and observer judgments were used rather than respondents' testimony regarding their activity.

The last social functioning index was of the quality of interaction, based on ratings of frequency and types of interaction that respondents had with others. We attempted in this scale to assess the meaning others had for the individual; that is, the degree of intimacy or isolation psychologically experienced by the respondent. (See technical note 6.)

PREDICTION OF FUTURE ADAPTATION BASED ON CURRENT FUNCTIONING

Mental Health. In each of the four studies, we examined the relationship between mental health (or its converse, psychological impairment) and adaptation to relocation. As noted, measures differed in complexity from study to study. In the initial investigation, the Unwilling Old Ladies study, no significant difference was found in ego pathology ratings of stories told in response to the Murray TAT between those who adapted and those who failed to adapt after relocation.

In the Home for Life study, the primary measure, as noted earlier, was the Block Q-Sort. Here, too, we found no differences between those who adapted successfully and those who failed in adaptation (as shown in table 7–1). Similar negative results were found for indicators of psychopathology—specifically, measures of depression and anxiety—using as data responses to a sentence completion test reflecting both state and trait characteristics and traits reflected in a standard personality inventory, Cattell's 16 Personality Factor Test (Cattell 1962). That is, neither the projective assessment of these affective aspects of psychopathology nor their assessment as traits by the inventory predicted subsequent adaptation. Measures of both anxiety and depression were available for the control group, but the Block Q-Sort was not; results were similar, except that there was a trend (p < .10) for control subjects who were more anxious on the sentence completion test to show subsequent maladaptation a year later.

Among Deinstitutionalized Elites respondents we found, as shown in table 7-2, some evidence that high scores on the Block Q-Sort, reflecting better mental health, were related to subsequent decline, which obviously is a reversal of expectations. Other measures of psychopathology, however, based on assessments of deviant behavior, did not yield significant differences between those who successfully adapted subsequent to their move and those who did not.

In the Death of an Institution investigation we relied on staff and observers' ratings of psychiatric symptoms: visual and auditory hallucinations, delusional material, repetitive motor activity, hyperactivity, and so forth. We found that the group who died manifested the least number of psychiatric symptoms; the difference between the dead and the alive was statistically significant at the .05 level (as shown in table 7-3). Those who improved, deteriorated, and remained unchanged, however, did not differ in psychiatric symptomatology. An examination of the same measure in the control sample yielded similar negative results. Perhaps the low incidence of such symptoms among those who subsequently died reflected their impoverished physical and cognitive status; the indicators we chose (such as hallucinations) may require more capacities than many of these respondents possessed.

None of the studies, therefore, offered evidence linking psychological impairment to subsequent maladaptation under stress—or, for that matter, predicting the course of adjustment among controls when a major crisis or challenge was absent. Despite the long theoretical history suggesting that the psychologically impaired are less able to cope adequately with stress, our analyses consistently revealed no evidence supporting such a view. The implications of these consistent negative findings will be considered after we examine the other indices of current functioning.

Well-Being. Neither life satisfaction ratings nor self-esteem, as shown in table 7-1, were significantly associated with subsequent adaptation to stress in the Home for Life study, nor did these measures predict adaptation among control respondents. Life satisfaction ratings, the single measure of well-being used in the Deinstitutionalized Elites study (table 7-2), again did not distinguish between those who maintained homeostasis subsequent to relocation and those who declined. Measures of well-being were not available in the Death of an Institution or Unwilling Old Ladies studies.

Although our data set is incomplete because we do not have findings from two of the four studies, measures of well-being and self-esteem, when available, are unrelated to subsequent adaptation. These findings, then, are similar to those reported for measures of psychological impairment and mental health. The similarity is, in part, linked to the conceptual relationship between morale and mental health. High levels of psychological deficit are associated with low levels of reported well-being, as well as diminished self-esteem. The reverse, however, is less true; good ego functioning was not found to be linked to high levels of well-being or self-esteem.

Social Functioning. Whereas measures of life satisfaction and self-esteem represent a phenomonological perspective on current functioning, social functioning connotes an external perspective. Although examining how well a person performs in his or her social roles is a traditional method of evaluating adequacy of functioning, we believed it to be all the more important among the elderly. The decrements associated with aging frequently manifest themselves in social roles and social behavior; thus we chose to focus on this area as one useful perspective for understanding how well the elderly were doing. The first investigation that provided adequate measures was the Home for Life study. Assessed were the level of normative role functioning still available and both quantity and quality of social interactions. These three areas of measurements (see table 7–1) did not predict subsequent adaptation to relocation, nor did we find that social functioning was associated with future adaptation among the control respondents.

In the Deinstitutionalized Elites study a variety of scales based on interviews with both staff and patients were developed to assess social functioning. Included were a measure of interpersonal behavior using staff observations, ratings of role activity during the past month in eight social roles, and ratings of the amount and quality of interpersonal contact. Only one of these measures, amount of interpersonal contact, was significantly associated with adaptation subsequent to relocation (see table 7–2). The association, however, was in an unexpected direction: The respondents who had more interpersonal contacts were those who subsequently declined. One explanation for this finding is that those who had developed the most attachments in the therapeutic discharge unit had the most to lose in the move.

This unexpected finding led to a similar but more detailed approach for measuring social functioning in the last study, the Death of an Institution. Five scales were developed: sociability index, total interaction with staff, total interaction with patients, attachments to others in the environment, and role functioning. Separate comparisons between those who died and those who did not and among those who deteriorated, improved, and did not change revealed statistically significant differences on four of the measures, as is shown in table 7–3. Specifically, we found that those who died were rated significantly lower than survivors in role functioning and in attachments to others in their environment. In contrast, the deteriorated, prior to relocation, had the highest levels on all four measures; they had significantly greater social functioning than the no-change group. Although the elderly who improved had higher means on the four measures, none of the results were significantly different from those of respondents who did not change.

Thus, our findings in the final study parallel, to some extent, those from the Deinstitutionalized Elite study. Both, of course, were based on elderly residents of mental hospitals. Adequacy of social functioning was highest among those who subsequently showed decline. The more detailed outcome classifications used in the Death of an Institution study helped clarify these observations. Those who died—the most precarious respondents—were functioning poorly in all life areas, and social functioning was no exception. Among the respondents who survived relocation, those who deteriorated and, to a lesser and not statistically significant extent, those who improved showed the best social functioning when contrasted to those who did not change—a pattern similar to the one reported earlier in this chapter for cognitive functioning.

In most respects, however, the findings on social functioning matches the other findings on current functioning in mental health and morale: Good social functioning does not constitute a powerful predictor of subsequent adaptation. Although it reflects current mastery in adaptation it is not in and of itself a characteristic of elderly people that is linked to future adaptation. In general, then, whether we look at indices of high degrees of mental health, life satisfaction, self-esteem, or social functioning, although we are identifying elderly people who show mastery of their current lives, from such a portrayal we cannot identify their future course without other information. Paradoxically, as revealed in more than one of our four studies, those who function best are frequently those who have most seriously deteriorated after the crisis, a finding explained by contextual characteristics rather than by characteristics of the individual.

Effective Resources: The Case of Mrs. A.

Mrs. A., first introduced in chapter 3, has already been described as having made a successful adaptation following relocation, despite serious losses that initiated her decision to live in a home for the aged and the consequent increased sense of loss and abandonment (chapter 4). We saw in chapter 6 that her strategies for coping with the threat and loss symbolized by the move successfully contained the negative emotions that often are engendered by such symbols. Here we will briefly characterize Mrs. A.'s resources and current functioning prior to relocation.

RESOURCES

Mrs. A. was well oriented in time and place, and on the cognitive functioning tests she was well above the cut-off levels that demarcated pathognomonic signs of dysfunction. On the Mental Status Questionnaire, for example, she made only one mistake when she said it was August rather than early September.

Similarly, her energy level was quite adequate, as reflected in her TAT ego energy score; but, although her scores were above the mean for the waiting list sample of the Home for Life study, they appeared to reflect a recent contraction of ego energy (based on her Time 1 scores when a respondent in the community control sample). As noted earlier when discussing her TAT stories (chapter 4), she projected indecisiveness into her stories and then ended them rather abruptly, especially for a rather fluent and talkative woman. For example, to Card 2 (farm scene) she told the following story: "To my idea this party wants to take the girl for a ride and the mother is not consenting. She looks too stern. The girl is not happy about it." This brief, rather terse, but complete story reflects both her excellent cognitive capacity and her contraction in ego energy.

Regarding her physical health, Mrs. A. needed help to go outdoors and to walk up and down stairs, but she had little difficulty in moving around her apartment, dressing (including putting on her shoes), or washing and bathing. Thus her self-care capacity was rather good, particularly considering she was on the threshold of entering a long-term care facility. In addition, she rated her health as better than others her age. When asked, however, how her energy was "compared to last year," she glumly responded, "worse." Although, as noted earlier, Mrs. A. used her impairments to justify the need for institutional care, she retained a high degree of capacity for self-care.

Mrs. A.'s personal resources, in the form of available others, were readily apparent. For ten of the eleven items on the Personal Resource Questionnaire, which focused on the availability of specific others to turn to in times of need or times of joy, she was able to name at least two specific persons. To the remaining query, which was "If you were collecting money for a charity drive, what three people would you ask for contributions?" she answered "When I was younger I had a lot of people I could ask, but now I wouldn't press anybody. I'd rather just give the money myself." Named as resources in response to the other ten queries were personal friends, her children, a daughter-in-law, and even a grandson, who was named as second to her son as the person she would call on if she "felt like having the company of a man."

CURRENT FUNCTIONING

The correlation between the Q-Sort for Mrs. A. and the Q-Sort for a person with optimum mental health was .74, which was the highest correlation in the sample (the mean for the sample was r=.17). Sorted into the pile "most like" Mrs. A (corresponding to a rating of 9) were the descriptions such as "arouses liking in others," "satisfied with self," "physically attractive," "cheerful," and "verbally fluent." Sorted, on the other hand, into the pile "least like" her (corresponding to a rating of 1) were the descriptions "vulnerable to real or fancied threats," "brittle ego defenses," "self-defeating," "concerned with own adequacy," and "self-pitying." The portrait that emerges is indeed that of a psychologically integrated woman of eighty years of age.

On the sentence completion test, Mrs. A. revealed virtually no anxiety but a moderate amount of depression, which was at the average level for the sample. Responses to this test were divided into six categories of negative affects. Examples of Mrs. A's responses in each category follow:

1. *Despair:*
   Time is . . . "sometimes very long when you are alone."
2. *Abandonment—Loneliness, death of others, and separation:*
   Sometimes I . . . "feel very lonesome."
   Brothers and sisters . . . "I haven't got any. They are all gone."
   I would . . . "like to see my children—the ones in California and Arizona."
   I miss . . . "my sister and my husband very much."
3. *Mutilation—Death, physical pain, decline in health and vigor, and illness:*
   Death is . . . "a big relief to people who are suffering or have an incurable disease. It's a blessing to them."
   The weakest part of me . . . "is my eyes."
   The worst thing is . . . "my eyes at present."

I wish I . . . "was well enough to travel."
I feel . . . "weak sometimes."
I look forward to . . . "being well so I can see my children in California and Arizona this coming year."
When I look in the mirror . . . "I see an old lady."

4. *Anxiety—Fear of death of self, fear of death denied, signs of fear, diffuse fear, and push of painful memories from the past:*
None.

5. *Unhappy regarding self—Subjective unhappiness and shame or inadequacy:*
I feel . . . "very bad about [my] situation of today."
If only I were . . . "independent."

6. *Unhappy regarding others—Abused by others, others as negative, and implicit onerous moral expectations of others:*
None.

Collectively, the responses reveal Mrs. A's specific concerns with abandonment and illness, which were also noted in the chapter on threat and loss. Her underlying fear was of being abandoned, and she used illness to justify the need for her move into the institution.

Mrs. A. was one of the more socially active people in the sample while awaiting admission to the home. She was very involved not only with her children but also with grandchildren, other family members, friends, and neighbors. Concurrently, her feelings of well-being assessed by the life satisfaction rating were appreciably higher than others in the sample. She was rated 22, and the mean was 15.9. Self-esteem, however, computed from responses to the self-sort test, was at the average level.

Mrs. A.'s resources and current functioning form an intelligible and coherent portrait of a rather competent elderly woman who was coping admirably with the strain she was under while awaiting imminent relocation. Apparently, the extent of her resources and her level of functioning equipped her well for the relocation and suggest reasons for her successful adaptation following relocation. As reflected on these dimensions, Mrs. A. appeared to be at minimal risk before the move.

Yet the findings reported in this chapter suggest that only some of her excellent resources and none of her superior functioning would have predicted subsequent successful adaptation. In the Home for Life sample of which she was a part, only cognitive capacity, ego energy, and health resources predicted adaptation, but these resources generally were also predictors for those not under the stress of relocation (see table 7–1). Social resources, as well as all measures of current functioning (mental health, well-being, and interpersonal functioning), were not predictive of subsequent adaptation to stress.

Summing Up

It is certainly understandable why severe cognitive and physical impairment were associated with maladaptation. It is equally understandable why social resources and social functioning may not be associated with successful adaptation. Although social resources reflect the capacity to form interpersonal relationships, the presence of more meaningful relationships before relocation also entails the loss of these relationships when moving to a new environment. Thus, the greater potential loss may offset the better initial resources. Not as readily understandable, however, is why mental health and its converse, psychopathology, were not associated with adaptation.

The view that individuals who are "psychologically healthy," well-integrated, psychologically mature, and have high ego strength are better able to deal with crises or stress antedates scientific psychology. This common belief is reflected in most contemporary human stress studies. For some, it is synonymous with predicting adequate coping with stress because, the very definition of psychological health implies the ability to cope with both normative life crises and situational crises in ways that are destructive neither to the individual nor to others. Perspectives on the nature of positive mental health or good adjustment, however, are widely divergent. (For a still relevant discussion of various approaches to positive mental health see, for example, Jahoda 1958.) Despite such wide divergence, there appears to be a general consensus which is reflected in the following quote from Grinker and Spiegel's (1945) report on the now classic study of airplane pilots during World War II: "In the presence of a previous emotional disorder, small amounts of stress to which an individual is sensitized may lead to severe symptoms. Conversely, men who have considerable psychological stability can withstand large amounts of stress before giving way to crippling symptoms" (p. 55). Many studies on the relationship between psychological factors and illness echo a similar theme (Lothrop 1959; Pascal and Thoroughman 1964; Thoroughman et al. 1964; Weiner 1956; Pancheri et al. 1978; Greenfield, Roessler, and Crosley 1959).

Although much of this type of research suffers from serious methodological limitations, the general theoretical principle is clear. Those who have lower ego strength or higher psychological impairment are, all other things being equal, less likely to be able to adequately address highly stressful situations. The very concept of healthy or optimal psychological functioning contains at its center the view that individuals with better "mental health" are those who will show the best response—whether the response is in reaction to illness, to unusual stress situations, or to their life course. Vaillant's (1977) seminal contribution to adult development, for example, is based on a framework using mature or immature adaptive style as a basic division among adults.

The belief that "well-adjusted" individuals are more successful in coping with crises is contradicted neither by empirical data nor by some of the special considerations regarding the psychology of aging. Although specific coping or defense strategies that are usually considered maladaptive, such as denial, may be related to successful adaptation under specific conditions, the view that overall psychological health is related to successful adaptation is not generally counterindicated. Among others Frankl (1963) and Mechanic (1974) argue convincingly that there are times when engaging in reality-distorting defensive activity is one of the few adaptive things that the individual can do, particularly when the means to make constructive effort to alter the danger is lacking. This view, that generally nonadaptive strategies may be adaptive under special circumstances, does not contradict the consensus that in general psychologically healthy people will deal more adequately with crisis.

Based on our findings, we believe that in order to develop an adequate framework for predicting the effects of stress, several important conceptual revisions must be entertained in the simple hypotheses that greater resources predict greater adequacy in coping. We did find that physical and cognitive resources fit the overall view that people who are very low in such resources will have less success in addressing even minimal amounts of stress. Beyond some unfortunately imprecise level however, this relationship is not linear. Predictions of subsequent adaptation based on level of physical and cognitive resources beyond this minimal level must take context into account. Factors within the social surroundings can counteract the ordinary negative effects associated with inadequate personal resources. In short, beyond some irreducible level, resources cease to provide a framework for predicting subsequent adaptation to stress.

The required revision in our thinking about the predictive efficiency of a framework based on adequacy of functioning involves even more complex considerations. Recall that no matter what criterion were used for evaluating functional adequacy—mental health, morale, or social functioning—the findings were uniformly negative. Although such perspectives do reflect important information on the status of people at a particular point in time, they do not necessarily reflect the ability to successfully weather future stress. We believe they are bereft of this kind of information for two very important reasons—the first, having to do with the general conceptual models of stress and adaptation; and the second, with the special circumstances of studying individuals in the last decade or two of life. The general resources and functional abilities of individuals, we believe, are neither sufficiently precise nor sufficiently specific to the particular stressful conditions to which people must adapt. In contrast to the predictive success of management of threat by strategies specific to the situation, which was reported in the previous chapter, general capacities appear less predictive. As is true in the field of personality research, without a sensitivity to situational conditions, the general characteristics of individuals are poor indicators of subsequent behavior. All stresses are not alike; and our evidence certainly shows that even when it can be reasonably assumed that a stress is severe, all individuals affected cannot be assumed to be equally stressed. We believe, therefore, that the search for general, high-level abstractions about people must inherently fail in predicting adaptation. This view is certainly not a prevalent one in the current field of psychology, but a recent review by Stone, Cohen, and Adler (1979) contains ample evidence for contradictory findings regarding how generalized predictors are associated with differential reactions to stress and to illness behavior.

Perhaps most relevant to the issues considered in this book, we believe that the model we have applied in this chapter—particularly as it concerns the mental health and psychological impairment of the elderly—represent an incomplete and inaccurate portrayal of adequacy of functioning during the last decade or two of life. It is, of course, our desire and goal throughout to explore the relevance of psychological predictors for aging and stress. We will return to this thesis throughout the remaining chapters. Suffice it to say here that the models of psychopathology of ego strength or other concepts used by investigators in this area are out of tune with the realities of this particular life stage.

Technical Notes

1. Although cognitive functioning is not a unitary dimension, but rather is composed of a number of discrete abilities, there is probably a sufficient overlap among abilities to justify a general dimension. The strategy used in this study was to first identify specific cognitive functions that would most likely be associated with adaptation to stress before developing a general or composite score. We began with the measurement of such simple functions as orientation in time and place, using the Mental Status

Questionnaire (Kahn, Pollack, and Goldfarb 1961) and the Face-Hand Test a common neurological examination which requires the person to locate simultaneous bodily tactile stimulation. Both instruments are designed to indicate major functional decrements in orientation to reality. The ability to process, retain, and recall new information was assessed by the paired-word association tests (Inglis 1959), a task that requires learning pairs of unrelated words. Orientation to time was measured by asking for time estimates during the passage of one minute. At a more complex level of cognitive functioning, because we were interested in how well the individual can organize visual stimulus, we used the Bender-Gestalt designs as a copying instrument to determine the subject's organizational ability (Pascal and Suttell 1951). How well the elderly can process complex stimuli was assessed by the Dana (1955) scoring system to assess perceptual organization and perceptual range in responses to the Murray TAT cards (Nos. 1, 2, 6BM, 7BM, and 17BM). Flexibility—how well a person can change set—was assessed by the degree to which the respondent could make cognitive distinctions when asked to describe a series of stick figured drawings, each showing the human body in a different posture (Reitman and Robertson 1950).

The average intercorrelation among those cognitive tests was .40. Three aspects of reliability were examined for these tests: stability, split-half reliability when appropriate, and interjudge reliability when required. The results of these reliability tests (presented in the order indicated when more than one was used) were Mental Status Questionnaire, .91; Face-Hand, .40; Word Learning, .39; Clock Time, .68, .84; Bender Gestalt, .66, .43, and .94; TAT Perceptual Accuracy Measures, .60, .41, and .84; and Reitman Stick Figure Test, .45, .54, and .93. A factor analysis suggested that six of the seven tests—all but the estimate of one minute—form a coherent cognitive factor. The modest level of intercorrelations may reflect both different specific functions and such extraneous factors as particular physical handicaps (such as impairments in vision or hearing) or particular habit strengths (such as the degree of comfort in using a pencil to copy designs). When test scores are used separately, they reflect specific cognitive abilities; when test scores are summed, the global measure reflects overall cognitive functioning.

2. Thirteen hours of observation on each patient in the Death of an Institution study were made in the unit in which he or she resided. Observations were made by a minimum of three different observers during the two-week period that the research team spent on the unit and together encompassed each segment of the patient's day, from the time he or she

arose to bedtime. Using a narrative style, the observers recorded anything the patients did or said during the observation period, including where they went; what they did; with whom they interacted; how they behaved when around observers, other patients and staff and when alone; and how they responded to normal and unusual stimuli in their life space. In addition to this structured observation, informant interviews were conducted with the staff person most knowledgeable about each patient. Whenever possible, the patient himself or herself was interviewed. These were informal, brief contacts, planned over a period of time. Once a relationship had been established with a patient who was able to communicate verbally, these "conversations" frequently extended into areas of the patient's past life, future plans, feelings about the impending closure of the hospital, satisfaction with his or her current life, and so forth. Because of the spottiness of patient interviews, these data are treated as supplemental to the observation and staff interviews. Rating scales were developed to assess patients' verbal comprehension, verbal ability, awareness of environment, responsiveness to the environment, extent of remaining in contact (ability to engage in such normal adult activities as keeping personal possessions in order and managing money without supervision), functioning in the hospital routine without staff intervention, performance of complex tasks such as sewing and other hobbies, use of space off the unit, and so forth.

3. Since the emphasis in our study was on developing a framework based on psychological and social factors, in three of the studies—Death of an Institution, Home for Life, and Deinstitutionalized Elites—the samples were purposely biased to exclude the very ill. In these studies we did not examine the full range of physical problems associated with aging. In the Death of an Institution study, residents who at the time of move were residing in the infirmary were not included in the study, thus excluding the physically incapacitated. The emphasis in the Home for Life study on highly complex and subtle psychological measures required that we systematically exclude individuals who showed exceedingly poor physical and cognitive functioning. This does not mean, however, that all the subjects in this study were healthy or elite individuals. Indeed, most had diagnoses that included the most common diseases associated with the seventh and eighth decades of life, but at the point of admission, these diseases were sufficiently under control so that they did not interfere with the subjects' ability to function in the old-age homes. The Deinstitutionalized Elites sample, which was selected for discharge by the hospital staff from over two thousand older people, represented, both physically and

psychologically, the elite of that population. Although only in the Death of an Institution study was there full range of physical incapacity, in all four studies there was considerable variation in physical functioning.

4. Rosen and Neugarten (1964) rated four dimensions: (1) the ability to integrate a wide range of stimuli; (2) the readiness to perceive or to deal with complicated, challenging, or conflictual situations; (3) the tendency to perceive vigorous and assertive activity; and (4) the tendency to perceive or to be concerned with feelings and affects as these play a part in a life situation. Their data on a sample of 144 cases suggested that these indicators, based on TAT responses, showed a modest decline across age groups from forty to seventy-one.

5. The Block Q-Sort consists of one hundred items describing a broad spectrum of personality characteristics. (See appendix F.) In this procedure, a trained rater first reads a case history that includes material from both the current and past life of the subject. The rater then describes the person by sorting the Q-Sort cards into nine piles, from most to least like the person. Items are to be sorted according to a normal distribution, fewer items at the extremes and more in the mid-point of the nine-point continuum. After sorting, the items are scored 1 to 9, based on the pile sorted into. The items are then correlated with the scores as signed to the items when sorted for the "optimally adjusted person." This was determined by Block using the consensus of the ratings of trained, experienced clinicians.

Because Block's optimally adjusted person was not age specific, we asked a clinical psychologist experienced in working with the aged to sort the items for "an optimally adjusted elderly person." This Q-Sort was sufficiently correlated with Block's original Q-Sort of optimal adjustment ($r=.83$) to accept Block's weightings for each of the one hundred items as appropriate for our elderly population.

For interrater reliability, Q-Sorts were made by two raters on twelve selected cases; these sorts were then correlated with the criterion Q-sort of optimal adjustment to obtain a mental health score. Using Spearman's rank difference correlational method, the two raters achieved a rho of .88. When the actual descriptions of the twelve cases rated by two judges were intercorrelated with each other, reliability was .73.

The adequacy of the Block Q-Sort measure of mental health for our sample is suggested by its correlations with two standardized tests that we had available in the Home for Life sample. The Cattell 16 Personality Factor (PF) Test (Form C; 1962) has a measure of global anxiety that Cattell sees as representing degree of neuroticism. The correlation between mental health and anxiety was $-.29$, a small but significant correlation in the expected direction. The rating of life satisfaction (Neugarten, Havighurst, and Tobin 1961) is another measure that reflects adjustment; a high correlation (.75) was found between the Q-Sort and this measure.

6. As might be expected, correlations among social functioning measures were relatively high, from the low .40s to the high .70s. In all four studies, quality and quantity of social interaction appeared to be more closely related to each other than either of these measures was to role activity. For all measures, interjudge reliability was adequate, the highest being for role activity (.89) and the lowest for quality of interaction (.70). Similar high correlations were found for stability of the measures over time, the highest here being for role activity (.85) and the lowest for quality of interaction (.67).

8

Personality and Adaptation

THE RELATIONSHIP between personality dispositions and adaptation provides a conceptual bridge between the study of risk factors discussed in the preceding chapter, and the developmentally oriented chapters that follow on "Distance from Death," "The Self," "Reminiscence," and "Hope." Although personality dispositions have been considered in countless studies of adaptation to stress, issues relating to life span have invariably been ignored in these studies. In turn, although personality dispositions have been the focus of many studies that have addressed developmental issues, insufficient attention has been given to their role in adaptation to stress. Thus, coordination between these two areas of inquiry is woefully lacking. We hope that through the investigation of adaptation among the elderly, a beginning link between these two unrelated traditions can be achieved.

A range of specific aspects of people that are relevant to adaptation have already been considered. Examined in chapter 5 were characteristics congruent with environmental demands; in chapter 6, strategies employed to cope with threat and loss; and in chapter 7, resources and adequacy of current functioning. In the latter chapter some complex characteristics of people were investigated, in particular, level of mental health, anxiety and depression, self-esteem, and social interaction—all indicators of how alloplastic and autoplastic demands of current circumstances were being met. In turning to the study of personality dispositions, we recognize that not only is there a lack of consensus regarding the viability of personality as a coherent construct, but even among those who maintain that personality is a heuristic and meaningful theoretical construct, a consensus on definition is difficult to achieve. Staub (1980) provides a set of useful thumbnail sketches reflecting this diversity. According to the various authors he cites, personality is:

> ... the culmination of all relatively enduring dimensions of individual differences in which he (an individual) can be measured [Byrne 1974, p. 26].

> ... the distinctive patterns of behavior (including thoughts and emotions) that characterize each individual's adaptation to the situations of his or her life [Mischel 1976, p. 2].

> ... a relatively enduring pattern of interpersonal situations that characterize human life [Sullivan 1953, p. 111].

> ... the dynamic organization within the individual of those psychophysical systems that determine his characteristic behavior and thoughts [Allport 1961, p. 28].

> ... a person's unique pattern of traits [Guilford 1959, p. 5].

> ... the most adequate conceptualization of a person's behavior and all its detail [McClelland 1951, p. 69].

We examined personality dispositions in order to summarize characteristic adaptational styles that could distinguish among groups of people. The individual differences considered in relationship to threat and loss in chapter 6 were assumed to be situationally specific, whereas personality dispositions, in contrast, are assumed to characterize the general styles people use to adapt to everyday situations as well as to crisis situations. Given the diversity of definitions of personality, others may conceptualize the characteristics of individuals that we have previously examined as reflecting personality dispositions. The framework developed to study adaptation to stress includes a distinction, albeit somewhat artificial, between attributes of people that reflect general tendencies transcending the specific situation and coping styles that are specific to the stress situation. Because the distinction is somewhat artificial, when problem-solving strategies were discussed in chapter 6, we included concepts that can be considered personality dispositions. For example, a generalized belief system such as locus of control, which has received much attention of late, was assessed by items specific to the situation, which were interpreted to reflect a belief about the respondent's ability to exercise command over the kind of environmental change he or she was confronting and not as a general belief or personality disposition. A similar posture was assumed when conceptualizing and measuring a defensive strategy such as denial. We are, in short, attempting to distinguish those adaptational styles which we have labeled personality dispositions both from situational specific psychological dimensions, such as problem-solving strategies, and from individual differences that contribute to adaptive potential, such as cognitive abilities or levels of mental health. Life stage specific issues to be considered in chapters 10, 11, and 12 will also encompass attributes often conceptualized as belonging to the domain of personality.

The rationale for assessing personality dispositions was based upon the assumption that persistent past strategies are sensible indicators of how—and how well—people will deploy their resources in meeting future crises. The caveat described in the previous chapters, however, must be repeated. Although assessments were made before the relocation, the situation produced effects before the actual move. Respondents anticipated the situation and developed an array of coping strategies prior to the actual relocation; and, to be sure, psychological threat existed and affected their psychological performance. Thus, assessments of personality dispositions made prior to the actual physical move were not free of contextual effects. Because of this contamination, our primary measures are based on ratings of large segments of data rather than on standard personality tests, which are, we believe, more open to contextual influence. It was assumed that ratings based on extensive data can tap relatively stable personality characteristics.

What personality dispositions are most relevant to adaptation among the elderly? Because our goal was to distinguish among people on the basis of dispositions that were not intrinsically linked to the stress context, we went beyond the studies of human stress to the research on life span psychology to identify likely personality dispositions for measurement.

Collectively, personality studies of the adult life span, as well as those focused primarily on the aged, do not provide a rich supply of specific hypotheses for selecting personality dispositions linked to adaptation. (See technical note 1 for a review of relevant studies and issues.) A review of stress studies was undertaken with the same quest—to find specific personality traits that mitigate the negative consequences of stress. We examined a variety of studies, including investigations of the link between life stress and illness; research on the effects of specific stressors such as surgery on health; studies that link certain personality dispositions to recovery from illness; and studies that explored the role of personality in adapting to extreme circumstances, such as prison camps and migration. Among these studies, with their diversity of stress conditions, variety of criteria for adaptation, and multiplicity of methods of assessing personality, there have been some successes, some failures, and frequent contradictions in linking personality dispositions to stress adaptation. (See technical note 2 for a review of relevant studies and issues.)

The absence of an empirical consensus on relevant personality dimensions led us to approach the task with a variety of strategies. Personality tests and ratings based on observation and interviews that were previously found by other investigators to be successful predictors were used. Most of those measures chosen for our investigation were drawn from life span studies, particularly those that focus on the elderly, rather than studies of stress. We chose for special emphasis a method that did not require high specification and prior commitment to a limited number of personality styles. This strategy involved using the Q-Sort (Block 1961), described in the previous chapter as a means for assessing mental health, to generate personality dispositions through factor analysis of the intercorrelations among the one hundred items.

Methods

As described in the preceding chapter, Q-Sort ratings of mental health levels were based on the discrepancy between the rater's description of the individual and the ideal description generated by the collective judgments of clinicians. The one hundred Q-Sort items are useful not only for developing personality dimensions, but also for making comparable assessments when there are differences in the data base. Replication then becomes possible across studies that vary in richness and kind of data. The task in sorting the Q-Sort items is to describe the person using all available information—interviews, staff observations, and projective tests. The one hundred items, which are shown in appendix F, range from interpersonal behaviors, such as "is critical" or "seeks reassurance," to items reflecting motivations, such as "feels a lack of personal meaning in life" and "is vulnerable to real or fantasied threat." Some items are geared to a wide variety of ego defenses, such as "tends toward overcontrol of needs" and "is insightful"; while some items reflect values including "genuinely values intellectual and cognitive matters," "has high aspirations for self" and "is concerned with philosophical problems." In short, a wide range of characteristics are contained in the one hundred-item array, from observable behavior to aspects of the person that can only be inferred. At least two alternatives were possible for developing the personality dispositions based on factor analyses of these Q-Sort descriptions. One was to merge together the two samples for which we have Q-Sorts—the Home for Life study sample and the Deinstitutionalized Elites study sample—and submit the intercorrelation of Q-Sort items for the combined sample to a factor analysis; the other was to conduct factor analyses on each sample separately and then compare the extracted factors. (See technical note 3.) We chose the latter method, primarily because of the differences in the two samples that have been noted throughout this book and also because of the differences in the two kinds of data that were available for making Q-sort ratings. Our plan, then, was to generate factors for the two studies separately, using principal component analyses and orthogonal rotations, and then to compare the resulting dimensions.

Although the Q-Sort was used to develop a common methodology for two of the studies, the remaining strategies for assessing personality were quite specific to each study. The Q-Sort strategy was unreliable for assessing personality dimensions in the Unwilling Old Ladies study. The raters found the interviews too narrowly focused and insufficiently complex to make the subtle judgments required by the Q-Sort. When judgments were made, the raters reported low levels of confidence for many of the items, particularly those that referred to internal states. Thus a decision was made not to use the Q-Sort with this sample. However, data, regarding feelings about the impending change, current activity patterns, interpersonal relationships, and attitudes toward the past and future were useful for developing a five-fold typology for characterizing the dominant strategy employed by the Unwilling Old Ladies to deal with the interpersonal world, including coping with the news of impending relocation. The five types were the acceptors, the self-invested, the angry, the withdrawers, and the deniers.

The most salient characteristic of the acceptors was their awareness of the limitations of their capacities, which thus included an awareness of feelings about the impending move. Generally, they were people who were engaged in life and related actively to others and, moreover, maintained a balance between undue optimism and destructive pessimism. The second type, the self-invested, were characterized by a seeking of gratification for primitive dependent needs, as was reflected, for example, in constant efforts to gain medical attention. Their relationships to others was rather tenuous and shallow. They generally complained a great deal and were dissatisfied with life. The third type was composed of individuals best described as angry. Bitter and pessimistic, they were suspicious of people and tended to be distant from them. The fourth type, the withdrawers, generally showed flattened affect and withdrew from life. They tended to feel that they had little control over their lives and approached life with a minimal amount of investment. The fifth type, the deniers, shared some characteristics with the withdrawn, but generally were more effective. They were, however, rigid, compulsive individuals who seemed to have a strong need to exclude the negative aspects of their lives.

Our initial approach was thus descriptive; and although we believe that these stylistic categories capture something essential about people and particularly the elderly in the variety of attitudes toward life and adversity, we recognized quite soon that the typology did not represent a systematic approach to personality; nor were these categories of sufficient scope for developing an understanding of personality and adaptation. Hence, in the next study, the Home for Life study, we approached the assessment of personality more systematically, using not only the Q-Sort, but also standard personality inventories and the nine traits developed to assess congruence with adaptative demands of institutional environments that were discussed in chapter 5.

The Home for Life study permitted the most intensive test of the hypothesis that personality characteristics are associated with adaptation to stress. Beyond the Q-Sort, we developed several approaches for studying personality, including two standard personality inventories, Form C of the Cattell 16PF (1962) and the Leary Interpersonal Task (1957). Although several projective tests, including the Murray TAT and a sentence completion test, were used to measure specific "personality" dimensions described in previous chapters, we did not rely on these tests to assess general personality dispositions. We believe that such assessments are open to serious biases, particularly when used for elderly respondents.

Projective tests, such as the Thematic Apperception Test, are particularly sensitive to level of cognitive ability, as well as problems of test-taking set. A not infrequent response to the TAT by the elderly was to view them as tests of memory; or, alternatively, to perceive the test as having one "correct answer." For example, a respondent would stare at Card 1 and after a long time would finally say "That's a boy with a violin," with a feeling of relief and a belief that test requirements had been met. Or, after staring for some time at the card, would indicate that the person depicted was not of their ethnic group and therefore how could they know what was happening. A certain amount of playfulness and willingness to engage in fantasy are necessary if aspects of personality are to be projected into the stories told by respondents in response to the cards. This often did not occur among our elderly respondents, however, and thus the interpretive meaning found in the responses of many of the elderly are suspect.

In utilizing the Cattell 16PF, we found that the wording of the items was too often misinterpreted by our respondents. Even after simplifying the language, the items proved too complex for the elderly respondents, and we did not pursue this measure in the other studies. Instead we relied on the Leary Interpersonal Task, translating his checklist into forty-eight self-descriptive items made intelligible for our respondents. From the selection of items in the Leary Interpersonal Task, two scores can be computed that correspond to two basic dimensions of "personality": dominance-submission, and affiliative-hostile. Only through careful development of items and by asking respondents to either accept or reject the item as self-descriptive rather than to rate the item, we were able to use this instrument to yield reasonably stable dimensions of personality (as described in detail in chapter 10). The self-sort task, however, was still too complex for mental hospital patients, and hence was relied on in only the Home for Life study.

Ratings of nine personality traits (activity, aggression, narcissism, authoritarianism, status drive, trust, empathy, extrapunitiveness and nonintrapunitiveness) were developed as component traits of the congruence measure, which was described previously in chapter 5. Here, we employed these traits individually, as indices of personality dispositions.

In the Deinstitutionalized Elites study, the Q-Sort was the sole method used to measure personality dispositions. Assessments were not made of personality traits in the Death of an Institution study because systematic interview data were not collected.

Findings

First, we shall briefly examine findings bearing on the relationship between personality dispositions and adaptation that are unique to each study. Then we shall report more fully on the Q-Sort, since it provides an opportunity for replication across two studies.

As noted, in the initial study of the Unwilling Old Ladies, we relied on a five-category typology. The proportion of those who adapted successfully versus those who showed deterioration subsequent to relocation were similar among three of the types. Thus, of eighteen acceptors, ten had adapted successfully after relocation and eight had not; of the twelve self-invested respondents, seven had successfully adapted and five had not; and of the seven angry respondents, four had successfully adapted and three had not. However, among a total of eight withdrawers and deniers, only one subsequently had a positive adaptation, while seven had become maladapted. Although these findings suggest that the latter two personality types may be linked to subsequent deterioration, the results did not reach adequate statistical significance, and, as we shall see, more robust evidence exists for the predictive power of personality dimensions.

In the Home for Life study, as shown in table 8–1, there was a trend for

TABLE 8–1
Personality Dispositions and Adaptation

Measure	Outcome Group (means)		
	Stable or Improved	Deteriorated or Died	p^a
	Home for Life		
	(N=44)	(N=41)	
Self-Sort			
Dominance	.02	−.37	.08
Affiliation	.06	.41	.09
Cattell			
Introversion	21.10	21.10	N.S.
Traits			
Activity	3.4	2.4	.001
Narcissism	3.6	2.7	.002
Aggression	3.5	2.4	.001
Status Drive	3.4	3.0	N.S.
Trust	3.3	3.2	N.S.
Empathy	3.3	3.1	N.S.
Extrapunitiveness	3.2	2.9	N.S.
Nonintrapunitiveness	3.1	2.9	N.S.
Authoritarianism	3.3	2.9	N.S.
Q-Sort			
I Self-Confident	−.15	.15	N.S.
II Intellectual	−.02	.02	N.S.
III Aggressive-Passive	.31	−.34	.002
IV Introversion	.03	−.03	N.S.
V Socially Responsible	.02	−.01	N.S.
	Deinstitutionalized Elites		
	(N=42)	(N=40)	
Q-Sort			
I Indulgent-Ascetic	−.09	.21	N.S.
II Optimistic-Depressed	−.11	.06	N.S.
III Rational-Irrational	−.05	.00	N.S.
IV Aggressive-Compliant	.20	−.20	.05
V Complex-Simple	.14	−.14	N.S.

^{a}N.S. = not significant.

high dominance and low affiliation on the self-sort task to be associated with successful adaptation subsequent to relocation. The effects of these traits seem to be stress-specific, since such trends were not found among control respondents. The personality dimensions of the Cattell 16PF did not distinguish those who adapted from those who did not adapt to relocation. Of the nine traits measured by the ratings scale, three significantly distinguished between the maladaptive and adaptive. (See technical note 4 for details on the influence of gender.) Those high on aggression, on narcissism, and on activity were less likely to suffer maladaptive consequences subsequent to relocation. (See technical note 5 for description of factors generated from intercorrelations among the nine traits.)

In the next chapter we will explore characteristics associated with distance from death. Because there are identifiable psychological changes associated with nearness to death, an attempt was made to distinguish such changes from prediction of maladaptation. These findings, based on an analysis excluding respondents who died, indicated that the results linking personality traits to subsequent adaptation were not a result of distance from death. (See technical note 6 for details of this analysis.)

PERSONALITY DISPOSITIONS DERIVED FROM THE Q-SORT

The Q-Sort constituted our major strategy for assessing personality; it lends itself to maximizing the information available on each respondent, provides a method for replication across studies, and is less subject to errors resulting from test-taking set that are characteristic of standardized personality inventories when they are administered to the elderly.

In both the Home for Life and Deinstitutionalized Elites studies, five factors were extracted from the Q-Sort ratings. As shown in table 8–1, in each of the studies, one of the personality dimensions predicted subsequent adaptation at a significant level—Factor 3 in the Home for Life study and Factor 4 in the Deinstitutionalized Elites study. As shown in table 8–2, the item arrays of the two factors reveal considerable similarity. In the Home for Life study, the positive pole contains attributes of rebelliousness, assertiveness, and hostility, whereas the negative pole contains attributes of submissiveness and brittleness. In the Deinstitutinalized Elites study, the positive pole again contains characteristics of rebelliousness and hostility, as well as suspiciousness, unpredictability, and self-defensiveness, whereas the negative pole contains submissiveness, meekness, a connotation of unassuming warmth, closeness, and the calling forth of caring behavior from others. Thus, loadings for both factors suggest that the common attribute of the positive poles is aggressiveness and that the common

Q-Sort Items in the Aggressiveness–Assertiveness Factors

	Home for Life			Deinstitutionalized Elites	
Item No.	Item	Loading	Item No.	Item	Loading
	Positive Pole (Aggressiveness)			*Positive Pole (Aggressiveness)*	
62.	Tends to be rebellious and nonconforming	.72	1.	Is critical, skeptical, not easily impressed	.79
52.	Behaves in an assertive fashion	.70	38.	Has hostility toward others	.76
94.	Expresses hostile feelings directly	.65	36.	Is subtly negativistic	.68
65.	Characteristically pushes & tries to stretch limits	.60	62.	Tends to be rebellious & nonconforming	.68
37.	Is guileful & deceitful, manipulative, opportunistic	.50	34.	Over-reactive to minor frustrations	.66
95.	Tends to proffer advice	.44	49.	Is basically distrustful of people	.64
1.	Is critical, skeptical, not easily impressed	.42	27.	Shows condescending behavior	.59
74.	Is subjectively unaware of self-concern	.40	37.	Is guileful, deceitful, manipulative, opportunistic	.56
			50.	Is unpredictable & changeable	.54
			48.	Keeps people at a distance	.53
			65.	Characteristically pushes & tries to stretch limits	.52
			12.	Tends to be self-defensive	.43
			44.	Evaluates motivation of others in interpretive situations	.43
			23.	Extrapunitive	.41
	Negative Pole (Passiveness)			*Negative Pole (Compliant-Passive)*	
30.	Gives up & withdraws in face of frustration	−.73	17.	Behaves in a sympathetic or considerate manner	−.81
14.	Genuinely submissive	−.54	35.	Has warmth	−.79
17.	Behaves in a sympathetic or considerate manner	−.52	54.	Emphasizes being with others; gregarious	−.66
45.	Has brittle ego defense system	−.51	5.	Behaves in a giving way to others	−.65
25.	Tends toward over-control of needs and impulses	−.48	28.	Tends to arouse liking & acceptance in others	−.65
42.	Reluctant to commit self to any definite course of action	−.48	14.	Genuinely submissive	−.63
21.	Arouses nurturant feelings in others	−.46	19.	Seeks reassurance from others	−.60
72.	Tends to perceive contexts in sexual terms	−.43	11.	Is protective of those close	−.49
9.	Is uncomfortable with uncertainties and complexities	−.42	77.	Appears straightforward, forthright, candid	−.49
47.	Has a readiness to feel guilt	−.40	88.	Is personally charming	−.49
			75.	Has a clearcut, internally consistent personality	−.47
			58.	Enjoys sensuous experiences	−.45
			93.	Behaves in appropriate sexual manner	−.40

attribute of the negative poles is passivity. (We have not shown the item arrays for the other factors since they did not prove to be significant predictors of subsequent outcome. However, the interested reader can determine the arrays by first examining technical note 7 which contains the Q-Sort item number for items in each factor with loadings greater than .40 and then referring to appendix F for the content of each item.)

Elderly respondents who scored high on aggressiveness were able to maintain homeostasis and remained intact despite undergoing the stresses associated with relocation. The role of personality in predicting subsequent outcomes when encountering stress (but not, as the results from matched controls in the Home for Life study indicated, under ordinary life conditions) is strengthened by the finding that in the one study in which we had a variety of methods and measures to assess personality, a personality dimension that was similar across measures proved to be predictive. Both trait ratings, one of the standard personality tests (the Leary Interpersonal Task), and the Q-Sort factors, indicate that a dimension of aggressiveness predicted subsequent outcome. These personality dimensions were associated with one other. (For the set of nine rated traits, rather than use the three traits that were significant—activity, narcissism, and aggression—we used the single factor dimension of nonpassivity, which was based on those three ratings.) The correlation between nonpassivity, and dominance, measured by the Leary Interpersonal Task, was .36; between affiliation, measured by the Leary, and nonpassivity, −.29; and between nonpassivity and the Q-Sort factor of aggression, .41.

The finding that the same personality disposition, aggression, predicts successful adaptation in two contrasting samples—a group of mainly foreign-born, aged urban Jews and a group of elderly people who have spent a good deal of their adult lives in state mental hospitals—affirms the robustness of this particular personality disposition in predicting adaptation. Not only were the two samples of elderly decidedly different from one another, however, but also the stressful situations were dissimilar. In the Home for Life study, before relocation the elderly were living in, and reasonably adapted to, the community; they then moved into long-term care facilities that they associated with being abandoned.

In the Deinstitutionalized Elites study, on the other hand, the elderly state mental hospital patients moved into community institutions that were, by and large, superior to the one in which they had previously resided. The differences in samples and situations indeed suggests the importance of aggressiveness as a predictor of successful adaptation. Furthermore, in the Home for Life study, different methods of assessing personality dispositions revealed that a similar trait based on different measures was significantly and singularly predictive of adaptation.

The empirical fact of this association is clear, and the replication, of course, lends confidence to the finding. The discovered relationship between aggressiveness and adaptation does not in and of itself, however, provide a direct pathway for understanding the processes that may underlay the observed empirical association. Thus, next we will systematically examine a series of alternative explanations that may account for the observed relationship.

PROCESSES LINKING PERSONALITY TO ADAPTATION

Explanations for the association between aggressiveness and adaptation depend upon the extent to which personality disposition is a surrogate for other, perhaps even more basic processes that form part of the chain of causal factors between stress and adaptation. Thus, we examined the relationship between aggressiveness, measured by the Q-Sort, and six other factors to explore alternative explanations: (1) level of threat and loss, to explore whether aggressiveness is mediated through the degree of threat and loss experienced; (2) problem-solving strategies, to explore whether persons high on aggressiveness command better problem-solving strategies for minimizing the effects of threat and loss (which, as we have previously shown, are associated with subsequent adaptation); (3) intensity of stress, defined either by levels of environmental discrepancy or by the actual quality of the relocation environment, to determine if the association between aggressiveness and successful adaptation can be accounted for by the more parsimonious explanation that those who possess aggressive dispositions were exposed to less environmental stress; (4) health, cognitive, ego energy, and social interaction resources, to determine whether individuals high on aggressiveness are those who have more resources—individual characteristics that have been shown to be predictive of subsequent adaptation; (5) mental health, life satisfaction and self-esteem, which reflect more adequate current functioning, to see if these factors determine the capacity for aggressiveness; and (6) certain individual attributes specific to the last decade or two of life which were found to be associated with adaptation (and are to be described in chapters that follow) to see whether they are associated with aggression.

In brief, a series of personal and situational characteristics were examined as potential antecedent and intervening variables to determine possible causal relationships between aggressiveness and adaptation. For the initial examination we chose the rather straightforward method of correlating personality dispositions and the "intervening" variables. If results had warranted it, the next step would have been multivariate analyses, including path analysis, but as we shall see, the findings did not justify further exploration.

Aggressiveness and Threat and Loss Levels. In the Home for Life study, our major independent indicators of threat and loss were the scale developed to measure early memory loss and the measure based upon the discrepancy in performance when telling stories to the Institutionalization TAT and to the Murray TAT. As shown in table 8–3, in the Home for Life study, higher levels of aggressiveness were associated with more anticipated losses but less threat. As shown in table 8–4, in the Deinstitutionalized Elites study, aggressiveness was not associated with a greater likelihood of loss expressed in the earliest memory, but was associated with less anticipated satisfaction.

Collectively, therefore, these findings do not provide consistent evidence that the elderly who had high scores on aggressiveness felt less threatened or experienced less loss. Rather, the evidence is marginally suggestive that those in the Deinstitutionalized Elites study may in fact have experienced somewhat more apprehension. The evidence is inconclusive in the Home for Life study because the two indicators of threat and loss reflect opposite tendencies. The inconclusive relationship does not clarify the findings reported in chapter 4 that although there was no association between levels of threat or loss and long-term adaptation, threat and loss levels did predict short-term emotional reactions, particularly depression. Possibly, the paradoxical findings can be clarified by understanding the role of problem-solving strategies, as suggested in chapter 6, and specifically the relationship between these strategies and aggressiveness.

Aggressiveness and Strategies for Coping with Threat and Loss. A review of the data presented in tables 8–3 and 8–4 reveals that there were no significant correlations between aggressiveness and the problem-solving strategies shown in chapter 6 to be associated with subsequent adaptation. (The relationship between aggressiveness and congruence is a negative one; highly aggressive people were less congruent.) Although aggressiveness—the personality disposition that predicts adaptation—was not associated with these strategies, other personality dispositions were indeed positively correlated with these strategies at modest but significant levels, as is also shown on tables 8–3 and 8–4. Thus, on the basis of the examination of the problem-solving strategies addressing threat and loss,

TABLE 8–3
Correlates of Q-Sort Factors:
The Home for Life Study

Measure	I Self-Confident	II Intel-lectual	III Aggressive	IV Introverted	V Socially Responsible
			Factor		
Threat and Loss					
Earliest Memory Dramatic			.21	−.23	
TAT Discrepancy			−.30		
Expected Loss	−.25	.15	.20	−.24	−.22
Problem-Solving Strategies					
Working through					
Denial					
Congruence	−.28				
Resources					
Cognitive		.32			
Health					
Energy				−.26	
Social			.25	−.23	.36
Current Functioning					
Mental health	.28	.65			.69
Sentence completion test—anxiety	−.25	−.23			
Cattell anxiety	−.22			−.31	
Sentence completion test—depression	−.32				−.38
Life satisfaction	.45	.34			.49
Self-esteem		.25	.24		.30
Number of roles			.20		.52
Quality social interaction		.38		.34	.31
Developmental Indices					
Self-validation adequacy				−.25	
Past evaluation		.26			
Past affect		−.23		−.37	
Life review		.27		−.22	
Introspection				−.26	
Hope					.48
Personality Disposition					
Dominance	.28		.25		.41
Affiliation			−.24		.31
Introversion	.33				.41

Only correlations significant at the .05 level or beyond are reported.

TABLE 8–4
Correlates of Q-Sort Factors:
The Deinstitutionalized Elites Study

	Factor				
Measure	I Indulgent	II Optimistic	III Rational	IV Aggressive	V Complex
Threat and Loss					
Feeling, discharge	.24		.32		
Anticipated satisfaction				−.30	
Expected loss					
Earliest memory loss					
Problem-Solving Strategies					
Congruence			.23	−.41	
Realism					
Information		.25	.28		
Resources					
Cognitive			.35		−.26
Health	−.34	.01	.32		
Social		.25	.42	−.39	
Current Functioning					
Mental health		.50	.67	−.46	−.28
Anxiety	−.26		−.46	.33	
Life satisfaction		.57	.48	−.32	
Roles		.25	.42	−.39	
Quantity interaction		.25	.34	−.30	−.24
Quality interaction		.23	.43	−.34	
Stress—Environmental Quality					
Congruence					
Fostering	−.26	.28	.38		
Affiliation	−.25	.25	.31		
Autonomy		.36	.28		
Recognition					
Succorance		.38	−.24		
Stimulation			.31		
Personalization		.28			
Resource richness		.44			
Warmth	.26		.24		
Tolerance of deviancy					
Overall quality	.26	−.36	−.32		

[a]Only correlations significant at the .05 level or beyond are reported.

there is no evidence that individuals with more aggressiveness utilize more effective problem-solving strategies.

There was a reasonable expectation that the mobilization reflected in the disposition toward aggressiveness would be linked to more effective problem-solving strategies, particularly the strategy of working through threat and loss associated with relocation. To the extent that an individual is generally mobilized, it was assumed, he or she would cope actively with the event. Since such an association was not found, however, a general mobilization is apparently not transformed into a specific ability to confront and master the symbolic meaning of the threat and loss situation. Thus, coping strategies and aggressiveness are independent predictors, and we must look elsewhere for an explanation of why aggressiveness predicts adaptation.

Aggressiveness and Stress Intensity Defined by Environmental Press. To what extent is aggressiveness associated with the stress levels generated by environmental press? This question could only be pursued in the Deinstitutionalized Elites study because respondents in the Unwilling Old Ladies and Home for Life studies were relocated to common environments. Independent measures for assessing environmental press were also available in the Death of an Institution study, but data of the complexity required to assess personality dispositions were not available. As shown in table 8–4, neither congruence between needs and environmental opportunities nor social psychological characteristics of the new environment were associated with aggressiveness. Personality dispositions that were not predictive of subsequent adaptation were, however, associated with facilitative environments, highlighting the lack of association between aggressiveness and environmental quality. Thus, aggressiveness as a predictor of adaptation is apparently not based on lower levels of environmental stress.

Overall, therefore, we have been unable to develop evidence that threat and loss intensity or the strategies our respondents used to cope with threat and loss, or the levels of stress generated by the environment are associated with the aggressiveness, the personality disposition, that predicted outcome. The observations that other personality dispositions were, however, associated with measures in three areas strengthens the conclusion that the survival potential of aggressiveness is not explained by less threat and loss, by better problem-solving strategies for coping with threat and loss, or by less environmentally induced stress. Next to be examined is the relationship between aggressiveness and resources and levels of current functioning, some measures of which have been shown earlier to be predictive of subsequent adaptation.

Aggressiveness and Resources. In the Home for Life study, only one significant correlation was found between aggressiveness and resources: Respondents high on this disposition reported fewer people in their usable social networks. Most important, however, was the absence of associations between aggressiveness and both health and cognitive resources. The findings were similar among Deinstitutionalized Elite respondents: there were no significant correlations between aggressiveness and cognitive and health resources. Once again, other personality dimensions were associated with cognitive and health resources, but clearly the adaptive success of people high on aggressiveness is not a function of their command of high resources.

Aggressiveness and Current Functioning. Various definitions of current functioning were examined in chapter 6, including levels of mental health, indicators of psychopathology such as anxiety and depression, levels of life satisfaction, self-esteem, and social functioning. As shown in table 8–3, for the Home for Life study sample, there were only two appreciable associations between aggressiveness and current functioning. Those high on aggressiveness had better self-esteem and more social roles, but neither of these variables was found to be predictive of subsequent adaptation. As also shown in table 8–3, other personality dimensions, particularly the first, second, and fifth Q-Sort factors, were more closely associated with better levels of current functioning.

In the Deinstitutionalized Elites study, as shown in table 8–4, all correlations were above .30 and all correlations reflected a negative association between aggressiveness and good current functioning. Individuals high on aggressiveness had lower mental health scores, more anxiety, less life satisfaction, fewer social roles, less social interaction, and a poorer quality of interaction. In short, those who were high on aggressiveness were consistently those whose current functioning was, if anything, less adequate. This observation may again be profitably contrasted with other personality dispositions. Factor 3, the dimension of rationality, for example, revealed very strong associations with mental health; low anxiety; high life satisfaction; and high social functioning, as reflected in role activity, amount of social interaction, and quality of social interaction. The personality disposition labeled aggressiveness, although portending subsequent positive adaptation, runs counter to the traditional view of covariates of successful adaptation in being inversely related to positive mental health and to optimal functioning. Rather, this trait was found in people usually thought of as poorly adapted.

Aggressiveness and Developmental Issues. In chapters 10, 11, and 12, psychological issues will be examined that have particular relevance for the last decade or two of life—the self, reminiscence, and hope. For completeness, we should briefly indicate in this chapter, the association, if any, between aggressiveness and these life-stage issues, since as will be seen, they all have bearing on adaptation. Information about developmental issues was generated primarily in the Home for Life study. Turning once again to table 8–3, it is evident that the ability to maintain a coherent and consistent self-identity, addressing and integrating one's personal past, and the extension of self into the future (hope) are not associated with aggressiveness. Consistent with the findings for the other alternative processes, other personality dispositions were associated with some of these developmental dimensions.

Our examination of the correlates of aggressiveness, therefore, has not yielded associations that elucidate mechanisms accounting for the role of aggressiveness in adaptation. In the language of causal analysis, the path from the personality disposition of aggressiveness to adaptation appears to be a direct one, or at least one that is not mediated by any of the individual differences that we have assessed. The finding that other personality dispositions—dispositions not predictive of adaptation—were more often associated with relevant characteristics of the person or the stress situation strengthens the argument that a direct path exists between aggressiveness and adaptation. Our findings certainly do not reflect a lack of associations between personality dispositions and such fundamental characteristics of people as availability of social resources, coping, ego strength, well-being, and so forth; rather, it is the relative lack of association between these characteristics and the specific personality style predictive of subsequent adaptation—aggressiveness—that demands explanation.

Before examining the implications of these findings, we will look briefly again at Mrs. A. Based on the case material presented in previous chapters, the reader will probably recognize that Mrs. A did not possess the survival prone characteristics of aggressiveness. Her scores bear out this assumption. On the Q-Sort factor of aggressiveness she had a mean score of +.58 (the sample mean is, of course, 0). When we examined the specific items, her slight positive score stems from items reflecting nonpassivity, rather than the aggressive, hostile stance characteristic of very high scores on this factor. Her other Q-Sort scores mirror her self-confidence, intellectuality, extroversion, and sense of social responsibility. On the Leary interpersonal dimensions, her score again reflects a resolute but not domineering quality and an affiliative rather than hostile, distancing. Similarly, her ratings on the nine congruence traits portrays a person who is neither excessively extrapunitive nor intrapunitive, somewhat introspective, rather friendly, and, as is perhaps most important for her consequent adaptation, assertive. She does not represent an extreme example of the profile discovered in this chapter to be associated with successful adaptation. What is reflected in her scores is an absence of a personality characteristic, passivity, that is associated with maladaptive reactions to stress. It is probably this aspect of her general personality disposition that served her well, but certainly she is not marked by the extreme mobilization characteristic of the aggressive disposition.

Implications

A variety of antecedent and intervening variables were explored for the purpose of specifying processes linking particular personality dispositions to adaptation. We were unable to find evidence that respondents in the Home for Life and Deinstitutionalized Elites studies who were high on aggressiveness were more likely to experience less stress, to have more successful strategies for coping with threat, or to possess more resources for addressing stress. In short, within the limitations of our studies, we have been unable to identify, through the empirical examination of six alternatives, a mechanism to explain why individuals high on aggressiveness are able to weather stress successfully. In this section we continue this search by looking at some possible theoretical perspectives for understanding the role personality plays in stress adaptation.

To help identify such a mechanism we initially turned to other studies of stress and asked whether aggressiveness is a trait ordinarily found to predict successful adaptation. Obviously, the finding that this trait does predict successful adaptation, under different circumstances and with different populations, does not in itself lead to understanding underlying processes. Findings similar to the ones we have described would, however, aid in limiting the range of possible explanations and in this sense further understanding.

Few investigators, however, have focused on the trait we have identified. Most studies of personality dispositions as predictors of reactions to stress have focused on the conventional dimensions that reflect ego strength or mental health. Yet, rare as it may be, a few investigators have singled out a disposition similar to the one we have identified. Nardini (1952) observed that among World War II prisoners in a Japanese prison camp, lack of aggressivity was a frequent precursor of death. Similarly, Cannon (1942) in his classic work on "voodoo" death, suggested that even

Personality and Adaptation

the most healthy individual may succumb to death if his or her passivity is extreme. Apparently when an individual is under a great deal of external pressure, giving into it leads, at least in these two examples, to death.

A parallel to the observation of Nardini and Cannon, as well as to our finding of an association between a psychological precursor and subsequent deterioration, can be found in the work of Engel and Schmale (Engel 1968; Engel and Schmale 1967; Schmale 1972; Schmale and Engel 1967). They have suggested that an emotional state reflecting helplessness and hopelessness in patients who have experienced loss can exacerbate the development of disease when either a somatic predisposition exists or there are external pathogens. They characterize the emotional state as "a sense of psychological impotence, a feeling that for briefer or longer periods of time one is unable to cope with the changes in the environment, the psychological or social devices utilized in the past seem no longer effective or available" (Engel 1968, pp. 359–360). This state in many ways resembles the emotional counterpart of the nonaggressive or passive disposition that we have found to be associated with maladaptive outcomes to stress among the elderly. The emotional state these authors implicated in disease, however, is apparently a reaction to loss, whereas passivity is assumed to be a persistent personality disposition.

Engel and Schmale attempted to identify the underlying biological mechanisms for the association between the emotional state of helplessness and hopelessness and the development of disease. They see the emotional state as representing a conservation of energy and a withdrawal of activity. At the level of the central nervous system, they postulated

> a predominance of parasympathetic activation and a relative sympathetic inactivity plus an overall mixture of hormonal influences which favor anabolic activity over catabolic activity. Such a combination of influences promotes internal survival at a reduced rate of functioning as well as protection against an unfavorable external environment [Schmale 1972, p. 29].

Thus, the interaction with the environment, when a somatic disposition exists to acquire a disease or when an external pathogen is present that can cause disease, is not to mobilize physiological resources but rather to withdraw from activation. The counterpart in behavior is the absence of either flight or fight when confronted with environmental stress.

The apparent similarity of Engel and Schmale's findings to the finding described in this chapter illustrates the dilemmas of investigators who use personality constructs to account for individual differences in stress reactions. Although Engel and Schmale postulated an emotional or affective state in response to loss, while we in this chapter are suggesting a generalized personality disposition, the description of these two supposedly distinct concepts are not altogether dissimilar. Despite this similarity, we believe that the aggressiveness personality disposition—as well as its opposite, passivity, which resembles helplessness as described by Schmale and Engel—are conceptually distinct. In our work we have attempted to fractionate a number of concepts into more coherent and basic components rather than use more generalized constructs such as those developed by Schmale and Engel. In chapter 4 we examined loss and reactions to loss; while in chapter 12 we describe the concept of hope and its converse, despair, which also resembles, to some extent, the emotional state identified by Schmale and Engel. Of greater importance are the findings presented in tables 8–3 and 8–4, which indicate that aggressiveness-passivity is not linked to level of loss; nor is it linked to our measures of hope. Although it would be intriguing to see the findings of these investigators as corresponding to our own results, the underlying theoretical bases of their work and what we are presenting in this book are distinct. The labeling process used in the area of stress often merges what to us appears to be distinctive concepts: despair, depression, generalized personality disposition, and various coping strategies directed toward the symbolic levels of stress. Superficial resemblances, unfortunately, do not make for robust and precise theories.

A process postulated by Sacher (1965; 1977) merits attention in searching for a mechanism to explicate our empirical findings on aggressiveness. Sacher has suggested that the ability of humans to live as many years as we do—our life span—is a function of the capacity to maintain integration when subunits are disintegrating. Specifically, Sacher first determined that among mammals there is a "functional relation between length of life and brain weight" (when controlling for body weight) and then concluded that "species longevity depends on the cybernetic capability of the phenotype" (1965, p. 103). Thus, for the human phenotype, the ability to live longer is a function of the capacity of the central nervous system to maintain integration and organization. In turn, for any member of the species, processes that diminish cybernetic integrative functions hasten deterioration and death. Integrative functions are apparently enhanced by aggressiveness and diminished by passivity, particularly when the individual is confronted with extreme disorganizing environmental stress that necessitates integration to maintain and reestablish homeostasis.

Although Sacher's research suggests the role of aggressiveness in insulating the elderly against deterioration and death when confronting stress, it is not clear why a similar role for aggressiveness was not evident in adapting successfully to everyday life. Perhaps only when the organism is faced with extreme situations—as we believe respondents were in the situations of relocation described in this book—can we see the linkage between such disparate levels of analysis as personality and biological processes. The "error and noise" of measurement inherent when using life as a laboratory may mask much of what are actually meaningful linkages. Extreme situations do, we believe, permit a small window for observing these complex relationships.

A very different explanation of why aggressiveness leads to successful adaptation in a highly stressful situation may lie in the specific nature of the stress-inducing circumstance in question. Is there any reason to believe that the tasks confronting the elderly respondents in the relocation setting is helped by an aggressive stance? Aggressive people are not likely to be ignored in institutional settings, which ordinarily emphasize overt compliance. Perhaps such a style commands attention, and such individuals may garner more of the available resources. Other personality dispositions that were not predictive of successful adaptation could provide equally plausible explanations for meeting the unique demands of institutional life. The traits described in chapter 5 that comprised congruence are one illustration; another is the finding that people with certain personality dispositions are more likely to successfully establish meaningful relationships within the new environment because they possess interpersonal qualities attractive both to the staff and other residents. Elderly people rated high on such personality dispositions would, theoretically, have an equally high potential to successfully garner the resources of the new environment. If we had found that trait to be predictive of successful adaptation, a plausible argument could be made as to why such elderly were successful. We do not, therefore, give much credence to a position that the particular trait we have isolated, aggressiveness, is successful because of the specific tasks facing the individuals in the new institutional environment.

Most plausible, although still highly speculative, is the argument that aggressiveness facilitates adaptation to stress for the elderly because it reflects the mobilization necessary to retain the psychological and biological integration for counteracting the propensity toward disequilibrium and deterioration. Moreover, the combative or fight stance may make this trait successful in confrontations with stress because our respondents are elderly. Although a modicum of mobilization or aggression is needed for an elderly person to transcend underlying deterioration and maintain homeostasis, the degree and kind of aggressiveness we have identified as associated with adaptation under stress appears rather extreme. Because the trajectory in the latter half of life is apparently toward increasing passivity, however, the counternormative trajectory—the fight stance—is successful not because it is universally adaptive under all stress conditions or across all stages of life, but rather because it addresses this fundamental dilemma of the elderly. Marking these elderly as unusual is their refusal to give in to deterioration or to accept even appropriate dependency, their willingness to blame external forces for present plights, and their capacity to rage against these forces. Gutmann (1975; 1977) has made similar observations in his cross-cultural research, noting that whereas the normal trajectory is toward an oral passivity, those who deviate in adopting a combative stance reap its survival benefit.

Modest support for the nonnormative characteristic of this trait in old age and its special role in adaptation was found by Lieberman and Cohler (1975) in their "Ethnic Study," a community survey of Irish, Italian, and Polish ethnics ranging in age from forty to eighty, half of whom were born in the United States. The central thrust of that study was to examine the effects of the cultural environment (defined in terms of ethnic affiliation) on patterns of adaptation, measured in terms of morale and on indices of psychopathology. The finding from that study relevant to our current concern were the trajectories shown by men and women on measures of aggressiveness and affiliation. Cross-sectional comparisons indicated that for men, age was associated with a lessening of dominance and an increase in affiliation. Women, as previously suggested by the Gutmann age trajectory hypothesis, became more dominant and less affiliative. Dominance was associated for both middle-age and elderly men with positive adaptation; those who showed more dominance at either stage of life were more successful. Among women, however, the pattern was different; for the middle-aged there was no association between dominance and adaptation, but among the elderly, women who showed the most dominance were most successful in their adaptation. Thus, dominance was associated in the middle years with successful adaptation for men but not for women, whereas in the later years dominance was associated with successful adaptation for both men and women. Among the elderly, then, it was the "off-trajectory" dominant men as well as the dominant women—who may also have been "off trajectory"—who showed the best adaptation.

We are suggesting, therefore, that the fight stance, a psychological position that may not be normative for the last stage of life, may nevertheless be uniquely adaptive for the very old. Placing this personality disposition in a life-stage perspective does not, in and of itself, explain the process. We believe, however, that locating the relationship within a particular life stage offers a direction for identifying mechanisms. Possibly the ultimate answer to the question of mechanisms will be that the nonnormative fight stance counteracts the conditions associate with old age, such as physical decline, despair, dissolution of self, and loss of prestige and status. If so, we await the further specification of the physiological processes that underlie the association between the fight stance and surviving intact. Thus, although the survival function of the fight stance seems to be a plausible hypothesis, based on our empirical work as well as that of other investigators, the reasons for the association still remain relatively opaque. In the chapters that follow, we will explore several aspects of inner life that in our view reflect solutions to the major psychological dilemmas for those in the last decade or two of life. Although the findings to be presented do not directly reflect personality in the sense that we have been discussing it in this chapter, they lend credence to the notion that specific adaptive issues are peculiar to the elderly.

Technical Notes

1. Life span psychology encompasses several types of inquiry that are relevant to our interests. Central to the field are the classical issues of consistency and change, which have been studied through a variety of research designs. There are literally hundreds of cross-sectional studies comparing people at different ages on various personality dimensions; less frequent are longitudinal studies that examine people's lives or specific psychological attributes over time. Some investigators have focused on structural changes defined rather narrowly by the limits of factor analytic methods, while others have examined stability and change by applying models useful for isolating the effects of age from the effects of cohort. Contrasts among investigations in the field of life span personality can literally fill a book, but that is not our purpose here. Excellent reviews are available elsewhere (see, for example, Neugarten 1977; Siegler 1980). By and large, as is perhaps best demonstrated in Neugarten's (1977) review of age and personality, little that is consistent can be sifted from the myriad of studies. A few personality characteristics have been found to be associated with aging, however, such as increased introversion, more interiority, and increased passivity. Assessments reflecting these dispositions were covered in our studies.

Another relevant line of developmental inquiry is reflected in investigations that focus directly on personality and adaptation. Investigators such as Brim (1974), Levinson et al. (1974), Neugarten and Datan (1974), Soddy (1967) and Vaillant and MacArthur (1972) have examined adaptational patterns in middle age. There is general agreement that people with different personality dispositions adapt differently to the tasks of middle age, although the specific patterns are not consistent across studies. Other investigators have focused on the periods beyond the middle years. Reichard, Livson, and Petersen (1962); Neugarten, Havighurst, and Tobin (1968); Friedmann and Orbach (1974); Back and Morris (1974); and Lowenthal, Thurnher, and Chiriboga (1975) have all described the relationship of various personality styles or types to adaptation to aging. In some of these investigations, meaningful age differences were found; in others, such as that Lowenthal, Thurnher, and Chiriboga, differences between men and women were much larger than were age differences. These studies do not lend themselves to many generalizations; there have, however, been some limited successes in relating particular personality styles to successful adaptation and some of these styles may be unique to successful adaptation in the latter stages of life.

2. Maddi and Kobasa (1981) have linked the personality dimension of commitment, control, and challenge to the consequences of life stress for illness and health. Moss (1973) develops the thesis that alienation—the failure to feel involved in an environment which provides congruent, effective, and accurate information—renders one vulnerable to disease. Length of cancer survival has been associated with more frequent expressions of hostility and other negative affects (Stavraky 1968; Derogatis and Abeloff 1978) and less inhibition and defensiveness (Blumberg, West, and Ellis 1954; Klopfer 1957). From their studies of pulmonary syndrome patients, Dudley et al. (1969) suggest that successful use of denial, repression, and isolation are linked to better physiological and psychological adjustment. Taking an active, involved role has been linked with recovery from severe burns (Andreasen, Noyes, and Hartford 1972). Boyd, Yaeger, and McMillan (1973) suggest similar findings for patients recovering from vascular surgery. Feelings of optimism, trust, and confidence before retinal surgery were found to be positively related to speed of healing (Mason et al. 1969). Gilberstadt and Sako (1967) found that those who died following open heart surgery were less guarded, had more energy, and were more socially introverted than those who survived. A replication by Kilpatrick et al. (1975) failed to confirm these findings. Cohen (1975) found that those who were inhibited and cautious stayed longer in the hospital whereas capable, conscientious, conforming individuals had minor complications post-operatively. A recent review by Cohen and Lazarus (1979) provides eloquent testimony to the disarray that marks the various at-

tempts to develop linkages between personality and adaptation in response to stress.

Descriptive studies of individuals in extreme situations suggest, for example, that psychopathological behavior predisposes one to adaptation and survival in concentration camps (Wolf and Ripley 1947). Gunderson (1964) found gregarious, active men to show better adjustment to Antarctic isolation. Personality studies in extreme situations suggest that the conceptualizations relevant under such conditions are not to be found in the usual model of the mentally healthy or optimally functioning person, as was found to be the case here and was reported in the previous chapter.

3. Criteria for factor extraction in each of the studies were identical. We set the minimum latent route equal to 1, and the minimum percentage of commonality equal to 10. In each analysis, five factors were extracted. In the Home for Life study, the latent route of Factor 1 (Self-Confident) was 21.4; of Factor 2 (Intellectual), 8.9; of Factor 3 (Aggressive), 7.4; of Factor 4 (Introverted), 5.9; and of Factor 5 (Socially Responsible), 3.9. In the Deinstitutionalized Elites study the latent route of Factor 1 (Indulgent) was 22.9; of Factor 2 (Optimistic), 12.1; of Factor 3 (Rational), 7.4; of Factor 4 (Aggressive), 5.0; and of Factor 5 (Complex), 3.9.

4. Because personality traits are usually sex specific, separate analyses were conducted for men and women on the nine traits. The findings were generally similar. Of the traits that differentiated the two outcome groups at statistically significant levels, activity and narcissism showed the same order of results for both men and women, but aggression was not significant for men. On authoritarianism, which did not significantly differentiate outcome groups, a trend toward differentiation was found among the men, which was not the case for women.

5. A further analysis which developed broader personality traits based on a factor analysis of the nine traits yielded four factors: punitive authoritarianism, nonpassivity, nonreflectiveness, and unfriendliness. The following are the traits making up each factor in the order of their loading: Punitive Authoritarianism was composed of the traits authoritarianism, extrapunitiveness, and status drive; nonpassivity consisted of narcissism, activity, and aggression; nonreflectiveness included low intrapunitiveness and low empathy; and unfriendliness consisted of extrapunitiveness and high status drive. The factor analyses did not substantially alter our findings because the only factor that showed a significant difference between adaptive and maladaptive subjects was the factor of Nonpassivity. This factor, of course, reflects its three component scales which were all signifi-

cant predictors. The intercorrelation among the three traits was modest: for aggression and activity, .26; for activity and narcissism, .36; and for aggression and narcissisim, .35. In comparisons of differences between men and women, the Nonpassivity factor was equally effective in discriminating adaptive from maladaptive individuals.

6. Those who died (thirteen of the forty-four, or 30 percent of the maladapted in the Home for Life study) were separated out and three groups were constructed from the remaining subjects: those showing marked decline, those showing some decline, and those showing no change. (The latter two classifications had earlier been combined to form the adapted group.) The congruence factor of nonpassivity (which combines the traits of aggressions, narcissism, and activity) was significantly associated with outcome groups. A linear analysis of variance revealed that nonpassivity was greatest for the no-change group and least for the marked-decline group, with the mean of the some-decline group between those of the no-change and marked-decline groups. This linear association suggests, therefore, that as nonpassivity increases, the likelihood of decline lessens.

7. Item numbers of Q-Sort personality items with loadings greater than ±.40 on other than Aggressivity Factor:

HOME FOR LIFE STUDY

Factor I (Self-Confident):	15, 18, 31, −34, −38, −44, −49, 56, 63, 67, −68, 73, 74, 75, −78, 80, 81, 84, 88, 92, 93
Factor II (Intellectual):	2, 3, 8, −9, 16, −19, −23, 32, −37, −39, −45, −50, 51, −53, −55, 57, 60, 64, −67, −69, 70, 71, −76, 77, −79, 83, 88, 90, 92, 98, −99
Factor IV (Introverted):	4, 7, 33, −43, 48, −57, 75, −82, 85, 86, −89, 97, 100
Factor V (Socially Responsible):	1, −2, −5, −11, 12, −17, 22, −26, −28, −29, 34, −35, 36, 37, 38, 48, 49, −54, 55, −64, 72, 78, 79, −83, −84, −88, −95

Personality and Adaptation

DEINSTITUTIONALIZED ELITES STUDY

Factor I (Indulgent): 2, 3, 4, 5, 8, −9, −10, −13, 15, 16, 17, 18, −22,
−23, 26, 28, 29, −30, 32, 33, −34, 35, −36,
−37, −38, −39, −40, −42, −45, −48, −49,
−50, 51, −53, 54, −55, 56, 57, 60, −62, 64,
−68, −76, 77, −78, −79, 83, 84, 88, 92, −97,
98, −100

Factor II (Optimistic): 1, −5, 8, −11, −14, −17, −19, 20, −21, 27,
−30, −35, 38, −42, 44, 49, 51, 52, 57, −58, 62,
−63, 65, −70, −75, −85, 87, 91, 94, 96, 99,
−100

Factor III (Rational): 2, −4, 8, 16, −19, 25, −46, −53, −58, 60, −61,
−67, 72, −76, 83, −84, −99

Factor V (Complex): −72, 74, 86

Part 4

THE PSYCHOLOGY OF OLD AGE

9

Distance from Death: A Strategy for Studying Development in Late Life

THIS CHAPTER initiates the section of our book that is directly concerned with the unique psychological characteristics of individuals in the last two decades of life. Central to such a life-style perspective is the view that the psychological sequelae associated with the increasing certainty of impending death is focal to the psychology of the elderly. Awareness of finitude is seen as an organizing concern for the aged. This view, although theoretically important in the psychology of aging (Butler 1963; Cummings and Henry 1961; Erikson 1950), has not been explored or refined in empirical studies of death and dying. It is not sufficient, for example, to simply demonstrate that aged and younger people have differing attitudes in order to address this critical theoretical issue. Rather, new research strategies are required.

Our interest in the psychology of death occurs at a point when this topic has almost become a preoccupation among social scientists, mental health experts, physicians, theologians, and humanists. This preoccupation is evidenced at meetings of national professional and scientific organizations, which nowadays are incomplete without a symposium on death and dying. Witness also the development of a scientific and professional society devoted exclusively to the subject—the Society for the Study of Thanatology—complete with a journal exclusively given to the exploration of death. The burgeoning social science literature on the topic ranges from investigations of attitudes toward death to inquiries into the social context of dying to broader concerns with how the mortality of human beings constitutes an existential crisis.

Choron (1974), Becker (1973) and Aries (1981) offer some impressive insights into fluctuations of concern with issues of death in the history of Western civilization; such a broad sweep of history does not, however, contribute to understanding more recent concerns with the study of the psychology of death. Although the reasons for the recent interest remains unclear, the interest for many, at least at a manifest level, is because death is a "fact of life" that has been too long ignored.

We feel a special kinship with some of the recent explorers of the psychology of death, because we share their perception that the study of death becomes a way of understanding aging. Erikson (1950), for example, in extending his study of development throughout the life span, reflects this shared interest in the psychological role of death at the end of life. The speculations of Butler (1963) and the work of Cummings and Henry (1961) similarly reflect the theme that old age must be understood in terms of how individuals cope with their approaching death. In a pioneering study Munnichs (1966) succinctly sums up this point of view:

> When we ask ourselves what are the most characteristic features of old age, one difference, compared with other periods of life, stands out most prominently, namely the fact that there is no other period following on old age. . . . The experience of death, that is to say, to realize and to know that life comes to an end, and adjustment to this fact, might possibly be considered as the focal point of the mentality of the aged. [p. 4]

Our excursion into studying death began with Munnich's assumption. The elderly know their life is nearing an end and must confront the psychological reality of their own finitude. Although social scientists may have long ignored this reality, it is not a topic ignored by the elderly themselves, nor (as our interviewers who were typically in their forties feared might be the case) is it a topic that the elderly dread discussing. Rarely did respondents decline to discuss death in personal terms unfettered by cultural euphemisms or literary metaphors. The respondent who avoided the topic was rare, and equally scarce was the respondent who talked of an afterlife. All devoted effort to considering their own death, and, to varying degrees, all were attempting to cope with what they experienced as an existential dilemma.

The seeds of a new research strategy were developed from the senior author's experience as a consultant to a home for the aged. The chief nurse in the home appeared to have an uncanny ability to predict accurately which resident was next to die, even though the resident's medical status appeared stable. Although the mystical theories she suggested offered little guidance, the comments she made suggested that she was actually basing her judgment on detectable early psychological changes associated with death. Apparently, certain psychological changes could be detected even many months prior to the resident's death.

Thus, a strategy emerged for distinguishing among the elderly according to their "distance from death." The development of a time line based on distance from death obviates the use of chronological age, which is an "empty variable." Distance from death varies greatly; among a sample of elderly people above sixty-five years of age, some may be six months away, and others over twenty years. The extent to which distance from death may be considered causally related to psychological characteristics among the elderly is the topic of this chapter.

Investigators of psychological changes during the process of dying have invariably focused both on a briefer period than several months or a year before termination and on younger people. Furthermore, they have generally relied upon clinical observations rather than careful measurements. Kübler-Ross (1969), for example, developed her stage theory of the process of dying through clinical observations when doing therapeutic work with dying patients. The many reports from psychoanalysts are similarly based on clinical experience, often with a single case. As will become apparent, the design of our studies has permitted us to compare individuals who are at different distances from their own death. By following people over time, many to the actual time of their death, it has become possible to study psychological processes associated with nearness to death. Our task, however, has been not only to identify psychological correlates of impending death but also to determine how such psychological manifestations become modified by the adaptational demands generated by environmental changes.

When our initial study was conducted in 1962, few precedents in the literature were available. Beigler (1957), using clinical interviews with the physically ill, noted a marked increase in anxiety several months prior to death. Kleemeier (1961a) reported observations on intellectual changes in an aged population approximately two years prior to death. Obrist, Henry, and Justiss (1961) found characteristic EEG changes preceding death. Jarvik and Falek (1963) observed intellectual changes similar to those reported by Kleemeier. More recently, Jarvik and Blum (1971) and Riegel and Riegel (1972) have reported similar findings. These studies suggested two alternative approaches to the study of psychological changes which occur prior to death: (1) a phenomenological approach focused on the reporting of the subjective experience related to the sensing of, as well as reactions to, biological decline; or (2) a nonphenomenological approach focused on the measurement of psychological processes assumed to reflect a general decline, in which awareness of decline is of secondary concern. Both approaches have been used in the three studies examining the psychological changes associated with distance from death that are presented here.

The First Exploration:
Psychological Changes Prior to Death

The first exploration was designed to determine whether systematic changes in ego functioning and emotional states occur in the elderly prior to death and, if they do, to differentiate such changes from changes associated with nonterminal illness. For this exploration, a small group of institutionalized elderly were administered brief tests every three to four weeks. Those who died within one year of the last testing were compared to those who lived for at least one more year.

Brief performance tests were administered every three to four weeks over a two-and-one-half-year period to a group of institutionalized elderly. Four tests were selected for which it had previously been shown that performance is not radically affected by repeated administrations or practice: the Bender-Gestalt design-copying test, the Draw-A-Person (DAP) Test, the estimation of one minute, and the Reitman Stick Figure task (which requires respondents to describe the posture depicted in twelve line drawings). Six scores reflecting ego functioning and emotional states were derived from these four tasks. (See technical note 1.)

The tests were administered in the same order for all respondents over all trials. The sample consisted of volunteers who had been residents for at least one year but less than three years in one of the three homes for the aged used in the Home for Life study. This was a population of elderly not previously reported in this book, although they are similar to the Home for Life institutional control sample described earlier. Respondents were told that the investigator was interested in developing psychological tests useful for assessing the elderly. Fifty people volunteered, from whom thirty subjects (seventeen women and thirteen men) were selected after excluding those who had incapacitating physical illnesses, gross neurological disturbances, or marked psychiatric disorders. Each respondent was tested every three to four weeks and paid a small amount of money after each assessment. The results reported are based on twenty-five respondents—four dropped out or died before a sufficient number of assessments could be made, and one died five months after the two-and-a-half-year study period. All were born in Eastern Europe, and all but one migrated to the United States prior to World War I. Most had been (or had been married to) small storekeepers or draftsmen. Educational level was difficult to determine with any precision, but generally seemed equivalent to an eighth grade education.

COMPARISONS BETWEEN DEATH-NEAR AND DEATH-FAR GROUPS

Results are reported in terms of comparison between two groups: those close to death (death-near group) and those further from death (death-far group). The death-near group consisted of eight respondents who died less than three months after completing at least five trials on the measures used in this study. The seventeen death-far respondents were still living a year after they had completed at least ten trials. For the death-near group, the time from last trial to death ranged from 2 to 11 weeks, with a mean of 5.4 weeks, whereas all the death-far individuals lived at least 52 weeks after completing the last trial.

To determine whether the death-near and death-far groups differed at the onset of the experimental period, a series of t-tests on the scores of the first trial were computed. Only one significant difference was found at the .05 level between the death-near and death-far groups. The death-near group had an initially smaller Bender-Gestalt area score than did the death-far group.

Figures 9-1 through 9-6 summarize the differences among the death-near and death-far groups. On the Bender-Gestalt Pascal scores (figure 9-1), the size of the Bender-Gestalt reproductions (figure 9-2), and the complexity of the DAP drawings (figure 9-3), the death-near respondents showed a pattern of declining performance over time. In contrast, the death-far group indicated a pattern of improving performance over time. Both groups generally showed similar curves on the time-estimation task (figure 9–4) and number of affect responses to the stick figure test (figure 9–5). On the intensity of activity score (figure 9–6) both groups generally showed an increase, but the death-near group reversed the direction after the fortieth week. (See technical note 2.)

Another method used to compare the two groups' change over time was to determine how many in each group showed improved or declining performance. Comparisons of change over time were made by comparing the first half of each person's trials with his or her last half. Three of the six measures, as shown in table 9–1, significantly distinguished the death-near from the death-far group. These differences were all in the same direction: Over time, more respondents in the death-near group showed a pattern of declining scores while more of the death-far group showed improved or stable scores.

Such changes are illustrated in figures 9–7 through 9–9, which show individual respondents' decline in Draw-A-Person complexity score, increasingly poorer performance on the Bender-Gestalt, and decrease in the size of the Bender-Gestalt reproduction over time.

Results indicate that death-near and death-far groups could be distinguished by changes in the tasks reflecting the adequacy of ego functioning: Bender-Gestalt performance (degree of disorganization), Draw-A-Person complexity (integrative capacity), and Bender-Gestalt size (ego energy). They were similar, however, on measures of affect—specifically time estimation (optimism-pessimism) and the activity and affect scores derived from the stick figure test. In addition to these analyses, the examiner's notes on test behavior (for example, mood) and "critical events" that had occurred the last testing session, as well as a content analysis of responses to the stick figure test, were examined in an attempt to further differentiate the two groups. Overall, this qualitative analysis revealed few consistent differences. These data did indicate, however, that the death-near group made more spontaneous comments about something being wrong or something "going on" or, at times, referring explicitly to the realization that they were going to die. Furthermore, four out of the eight in the death-near group gave an increased number of depressive responses to the stick figure test on the trial preceding death compared to earlier trials. Generally, however, depressive content was not more characteristic of death-near than death-far respondents; nor did the content analysis of the stick figure test reveal responses indicating increased anxiety or fear.

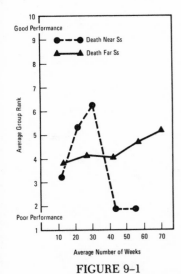

FIGURE 9-1

Trends in Bender-Gestalt Pascal Scores

Trends in Bender-Gestalt Pascal scores over time for the
N and DF groups. Each point ⊙ for the 8 DN Ss is an aver-
e group rank representing one-fifth of all trials for each DN
each point △ for the 17 DF Ss is an average group rank
presenting one-fifth of all trials for each DF S. High ranks
dicate good performance, low ranks, poor performance.

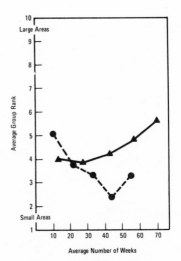

FIGURE 9-2

Trends in Bender-Gestalt Area Scores

Trends in Bender-Gestalt area scores over time for the DN
and DF groups. Each point ⊙ for the 8 DN Ss is an average
group rank representing one-fifth of all trials for each DN S;
each point △ for the 17 DF Ss is an average group rank representing one-fifth of all trials for each DF S. High ranks indicate large drawings, low ranks, small drawings.

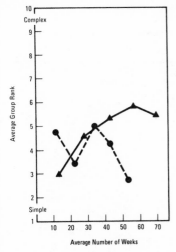

FIGURE 9-3

Trends in Draw-A-Person Complexity Scores

Trends in Draw-A-Person complexity scores over time for
e DN and DF groups. Each point ⊙ for the 8 DN Ss is an
erage group rank representing one-fifth of all trials for each
N S; each point △ for the 17 DF Ss is an average group rank
presenting one-fifth of all trials for each DF S. High ranks
dicate complex drawings, low ranks, simple drawings.

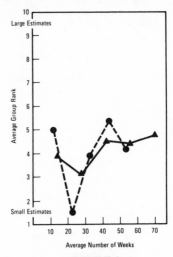

FIGURE 9-4

Trends in Time Estimates

Trends in Time estimates of a 60-sec. interval over time for
the DN and DF groups. Each point ⊙ for the 8 DN Ss is an
average group rank representing one-fifth of all trials for each
DN S; each point △ for the 17 DF Ss is an average group rank
representing one-fifth of all trials for each DF S. High ranks
indicate large estimates of the standard time interval, low
ranks, small estimates.

Reprinted by permission of *Journal of Gerontology*, Lieberman, M. A., "Psychological correlates of impending death."
Journal of Gerontology 20(2) (1965):181-190.

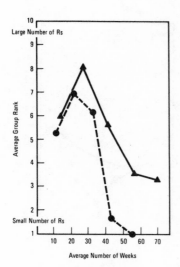

FIGURE 9-5

Trends in Number of Affect Responses
(Stick Figure Test)

Trends in number of affect responses over time for the DN and DF groups. Each point ⊙ for the 8 DN Ss is an average group rank representing one-fifth of all trials for each DN S; each point △ for the 17 DF Ss is an average group rank representing one-fifth of all trials for each DF S. High ranks indicate a high frequency of affect responses to the Stick Figure test, low ranks, small number of such responses.

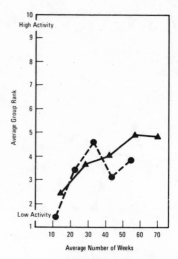

FIGURE 9-6

Trends in Intensity of Activity
(Stick Figure Test)

Trends in intensity of activity over time for the DN and DF groups. Each point ⊙ for the 8 DN Ss is an average group rank representing one-fifth of all trials for each DN S; each point △ for the 17 DF Ss is an average group rank representing one-fifth of all trials for each DF S. High ranks indicate high intensity of activity attributed to the stick figures, low ranks, low intensity.

Reprinted by permission of *Journal of Gerontology*, Lieberman, M. A., "Psychological correlates of impending death." *Journal of Gerontology* 20(2) (1965):181-190.

TABLE 9–1
Number of Subjects Showing Performance Changes

Test		Death-Near Group	Death-Far Group	p
Bender-Gestalt performance	Number declining	3	6	.01
	Number not declining	14	2	
Bender-Gestalt area	Number declining	3	5	.09
	Number not declining	14	3	
DAP complexity	Number declining	2	5	.02
	Number not declining	15	3	
Amount of activity Stick Figure Test	Number declining	2	3	.17
	Number not declining	15	5	
Number of affects Stick Figure Test	Number declining	12	5	.78
	Number not declining	5	3	
Time estimation	Number declining	6	2	.31
	Number not declining	11	6	

[a]Fisher exact probability test.

TIME OF DECLINING PERFORMANCE

The scores of each death-near person were examined to determine if changes in performance level occurred at particular points in time. The small N and the degree of response fluctuation from trial to trial prevented a meaningful quantitative analysis. However, inspection of each respondent's set of scores suggested that major shifts of performance on the test could be found as early as six to nine months before death. The earliest identifiable changes occurred in the Bender-Gestalt performance scores, followed by changes in the complexity of the drawn human figure, and finally by decreases in the size of the Bender-Gestalt figures.

The results already presented suggest that the two groups could be distinguished by the direction of changes in performance over time. Even though the death-near and death-far groups were similar at the onset of the study, were their performances different when the death-near group was closer to death? The groups were compared by choosing the last trial

COMPLEXITY SCORE—FIGURES
SUBJECT # 17 M

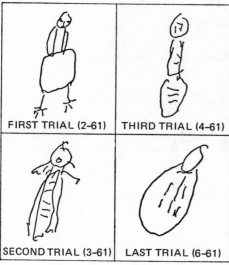

FIRST TRIAL (2-61)   THIRD TRIAL (4-61)

SECOND TRIAL (3-61)   LAST TRIAL (6-61)

FIGURE 9–7
Complexity Score—Figures
Subject 17M

BENDER GESTALT—PERFORMANCE
SUBJECT # 15 F

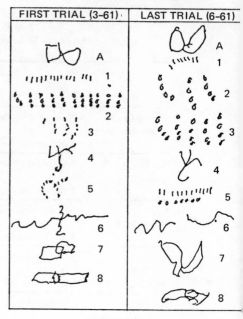

FIRST TRIAL (3-61)   LAST TRIAL (6-61)

FIGURE 9–8
Bender-Gestalt—Performance
Subject 15F

SIZE CHANGE—BENDER GESTALT
SUBJECT # 17 F

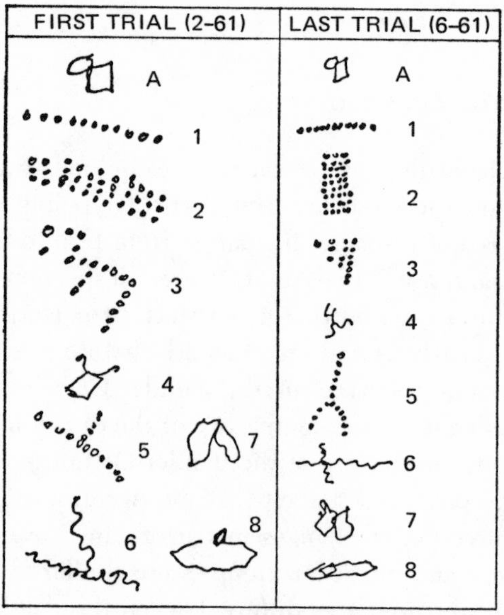

FIRST TRIAL (2-61)   LAST TRIAL (6-61)

FIGURE 9–9
Size Change—Bender-Gestalt
Subject 17M

Reprinted by permission of *Journal of Gerontology*, Lieberman, M. A., "Psychological correlates of impending death."
Journal of Gerontology 20(2) (1965):181–190.

of each death-near respondent and matching the death-far respondents for number of trials (to control for effects of practice). No significant differences were found in the comparison of absolute levels of performance on the six variables. Thus the two groups were distinguished by the changing level of performance over time and not by an absolute level of test performance at any single point in time.

EFFECTS OF ILLNESS

The test score changes found have been attributed to time of death. Could they have occurred in relationship to illness? A tentative answer to this question is available from analysis of twelve respondents in the death-far group who suffered major illnesses requiring hospitalization during the course of the study. If declines in test performance reflected nonlethal illness rather than imminence of death, the trial preceding hospitalization would show a lower level of performance than other trials for the same person. The mean score of each person in this group for all trials was used to identify good and poor performances for each of the six measures. We found that the trial preceding illness was as likely to be above each person's mean as below it. A second method of analysis utilized the total set of trials in evaluating the effects of illness on performance. The sum of scores of all the trials prior to illness was compared with the sum for an equal number of trials after the acute phase of the illness had subsided. Only seven of the twelve elderly could be used for this analysis; the other five had episodes of illness too early or too late in the series of trials for a before-and-after comparison. Performance levels were found to be similar before and after illness. These two analyses of the performance of death-far individuals who became ill and recovered suggest that illness per se was not the sole factor which affected the decline of performance found in the death-near group.

IMPLICATIONS

The findings of this study suggest that the terminal phase of life is characterized by specific psychological changes. Despite the small sample and high intra-individual variability on the psychological tests, the results indicate that systematic psychological changes that occur many months prior to death are measurable. The observed psychological changes are not the simple result of physical illness, since those who became seriously ill and recovered did not exhibit psychological changes similar to those found in elderly people whose death was imminent. The absolute level of ego functioning was also unrelated to impending death, which suggests that the absolute level at which aged individuals are able to cope is not associated with the distance from death. Rather, it is the change in the individual's level of coping relative to his or her own initial performance that is related to death.

Before death, respondents showed decreases (relative to their initial levels) in level of organization, as measured by the adequacy of the Bender-Gestalt reproductions; energy, as indicated by measurement of the Bender-Gestalt figures; and ability to integrate stimuli, as shown by a decrease in the complexity of the figure drawings. Changes in affect were not systematically related to approaching death.

Our reading of the results is that the observed psychological changes preceding death, particularly the lowered ability to organize and integrate stimuli, are best viewed in terms of the individual's decreased ability to cope adequately with alloplastic demands. Perhaps the aged person approaching death experiences upheaval because of currently active disorganizing mental processes, rather than because he or she fears approaching death. The observed psychological disintegration may not be a reaction to the unknowable, but may rather represent a general decline of the system preceding death, as reflected in the variety of physiological and psychological measures. If this interpretation is correct, some frequently reported phenomena in the terminal phase of life become more understandable.

Many observers commented on the psychological withdrawal of the dying patient and have suggested that the withdrawal is functional because it protects the individual from intense separation anxiety. We would suggest that withdrawal represents an attempt to cope with the experience of inner disintegration. Individuals approaching death pull away from those around them, not because of a narcissistic preoccupation with themselves, but because they are engaged in an attempt to hold themselves together— to reduce the experience of chaos and retain a sense of self.

Investigators of psychological functioning in the very old have been impressed by the greater range of interindividual differences among the old than the young in a wide range of psychological abilities. Explanations for these individual differences have run the gamut from the genetic to the effects of early life experiences to personality differences. The present study may point to another area of explanation worthy of investigation. Variations in psychological abilities among a given age group may be explained, in part, as an effect of distance from death. A group of seventy-year-old men, for example, may vary in distance from death from one to fifteen years. If, as we suggest, imminent death implies an experience of psychological chaos and lessened psychological effectiveness, the man of seventy who is closest to death could be expected to perform differently from an age mate who will survive him by an appreciable length of time. From this perspective, then, low correlations between age and psychological functioning may be a function of differences in distance from death.

Since the changes we examined in this explanation were primarily alterations in functioning, we set as a task in the next exploration the examination of symbolic processes, comparing those nearer and those further from death to determine if awareness of death played a role in the observed psychological changes. Some marginal evidence from the respondents studied suggested this as a plausible direction. Many of the elderly we studied sensed some type of change and felt it to be different from that of illness. The labeling of the subjective experience, however, varied with some respondents reporting only a vague sense of feeling "different," while others said that they were going to die soon. Comments such as these suggest that more thorough and sensitive phenomenological reports would be a useful avenue for research in the terminal phase of life.

The Second Exploration:
Emotional Life When Death Is Approaching

Among the 172 elderly respondents in the Home for Life study were 40 who had died within twelve months (mean=8.6 months) of their last interview. These 40 were paired with 40 who survived an average of three years beyond the last interview session. Matching was based on a hierarchical sequence of comparison criteria: living arrangement, sex, age, birthplace, marital status, and educational level. (See technical note 3.)

EMOTIONAL LIFE AND COGNITIVE FUNCTION

Although measures of cognitive functioning (I) were included to provide a basis for comparison with findings from the earlier study on psychological factors associated with impending death, the emphasis was on indices of emotional life. The measures tapped five affective realms: (II) emotional states (anxiety, mood tone, and so forth); (III) orientation to emotional life; (IV) health and body orientation; (V) self-image; and (VI) time perception. Table 9–2 contains a list of the dimensions, tests, and a brief description of each measure, as well as the interrater reliability

TABLE 9-2

Measures for Comparing Death-Near and Death-Far Respondents

Variable	Description
I: Cognitive functioning	
Impairment	
1. Mental status	10 questions, orientation in time and space score (Khan, Pollack, and Goldfarb 1961), $St = .91$.
2. Learning-retention	Paired-word association learning test (Inglis 1959); 3 pairs of unrelated words; scored number of trials to criteria, $St = .39$.
Complexity	
3. Visual organization	Designs 1, 3 and 8; from the Bender-Gestalt Test (Bender 1938); Pascal and Suttell Scoring System (Pascal and Suttell 1951). $R = (rho)$ 97; 2 raters, $St = .66$.
4. Perceptual adequacy	Murray TAT Cards 1, 2, 6BM, 7BM, 10 and 17BM; instructional set—demonstration procedure; scoring, Dana System (Dana 1955); $R = (po)$ (rho) = 85, (pr) (rho) = .72 St, total score $(po + pr) = .60$.
5. Time judgment	Method of time reproduction of 30- and 60-sec. intervals; $St = .68$.
II: Emotional states	
6. Expansive-restriction	Bender-Gestalt designs; enclosed area summed, increasing size associated with expansiveness, $St = .73$.
7. Anxiety	Cattell 16 PF (Form C) anxiety factor, $St = .46$.
Mood	
8. Life satisfaction	Ratings of interviews (Neugarten, Havighurst, and Tobin 1961) on five 5-point scales—zest vs. apathy, resolution-fortitude, congruence between desire and achieve goals, positive self-concept, and mood tone, $R = .84$, $St = .69$.
9. Anomie	Srole Anomies scales (Srole 1956). Degree of agreement or disagreement to 5 items about general world views. $St = .61$.
10. Acceptance of life	Factor analysis (principal component, Varimax solution) of 21 affect measures revealed 4 factors. The 21 measures included projective tasks (SCT, TAT, and Reitman); structural tasks, size of Bender-Gestalt Test and time estimate; self-report tasks; Cattell 16PF; Srole Anomie scale; and the Osgood Semantic Differentia; and interview items for judgments of mood in the earliest memory, life satisfaction, mood tone, and depression. Acceptance of Life (fourth factor) included (a) quantity of positive affect to Park Bench TAT Card, (b) acceptance of death in completion of SCT stem "To me, death is . . . ," and (c) positive attitude toward past life in completion of SCT stem "My past life . . . ."
11. Loss	5-point ordinal scale of subject's earliest memory (Tobin and Lieberman 1976). Scale from nonloss themes (1), loss defended themes (2), interpersonal loss themes (3), mutilization themes (4), death themes (5). $R = 3$ judges, 57% exact agreement, agreement of 2 or 3 judges on remaining 43%, $St = .46$.
III: Orientation to emotional life	
12. Emotional reactivity	See factor analysis, Variable 9 (third factor), Cattell Factor I and number of positive emotions seen in Reitman Stick Figure Test (Reitman and Robertson 1950).
13. Affective complexity	Interview, schedule on 8 affects: depression, happiness, guilt, pride, etc. 8 emotions; Guttman scaled for difficulty of talking and describing, $R = 100\%$ interjudge agreement. $St = .39$

| 14. Introspective stance | Adaptation of Gendlin (Gendlin 1964) rating system, 1–7, for degree of introspection, R = 76% one step below, St = .57. |
| 15. Introversion-extroversion | Cattell, 16PF, Form C, St = .50. |

IV: Health and body orientation

Functional health status	
16. Health evaluation	Self-report on the ability to get about, walk stairs, etc. (Shanas 1961), St = .59.
Body orientation	
17. Body preoccupation scale	20 sentence-completion items, degree of preoccupation based upon number of body references to items not calling for such response. R = 97% extract agreement, St = .46.
18. Body image scale	Negative or positive qualities associated with 3 sentence-completion items referring to body. R = 92% exact agreement, St = .56.
19. Negative body image	12 line drawings portraying the human form (Reitman and Robertson 1950), scored for absence or presence of negative body images. R = 99% exact agreement, St = .24.

V: Self-image

20. Self-esteem	Semantic differential (Osgood and Tannenbaum 1958). 5 self-evaluative dimensions, St = .25.
21. Contents of self-image	48 self-descriptive statements based upon 8 octant category system of Leary (Leary 1957). Instructional set, pick as few or as
Octant AP power-success	many of the 48 cards that describe his present self-image, St = .83.
Octant BC narcissistic-exploitative	
Octant DE hostile-aggressive	
Octant FG rebellious-distrustful	
Octant HI weakness-masochistic	
Octant JK conformity-trust	
Octant LM collaboration-pure love	
Octant NO tenderness-generous	
22. Mechanisms of self-maintenance	Self-image interview. Subject provides specific, concrete, recent example of each of the statements he or she chose from the self-sort. Scored (Rosner 1968) in terms of adequacy of examples (a) current, (b) past, (c) conviction, (d) wished for, (e) distortion categories. R = 79% exact agreement; St = .10, .69, .32, .10, respectively.

VI: Time Perception

23. Futility	Interview questions, meaning of time, planning ahead, meaning of future. 4-point rating system; R = 88% exact agreement, 2 raters, St = .62.
24. Extensionality	Sentence-completion test—3 items: "I look forward . . ." "An hour is . . ." and "Time is . . ." 3-point rating scale. R = 93% exact agreement, St = .44.
25. Past	
26. Present	Past, present, future things, events or situations on the 5 Murray TAT cards. R = (rho) 65, St = .60.
27. Future	

NOTE: St = stability; T1-T2 correlations for population from which dead and control samples drawn; R = interrater or interjudge reliability.

Reprinted from Lieberman, M. A., and Caplan, A. S. "Distance from death as a variable in the study of aging." *Developmental Psychology* 2 (1969): 71–84. Copyright 1969 by the American Psychological Association. Reprinted by permission of the publisher and authors.

when appropriate, and stability coefficient. All the statistical analyses in this study are reported between members of matched pairs. A nonparametric test was used, the Wilcoxon matched-pair signed-ranks test, which is equivalent to matched-pairs t-tests. (See technical note 4.)

Twelve of the 37 analyses (variable 27 encompassed eight subscores and variable 22 had five subscores) were significant beyond the .10 level, as shown in table 9–3. These differences occurred in three of the six realms: cognitive functioning, orientation to emotional life, and self-image. Generally, those nearer to death manifested poorer cognitive functioning; were less affectively complex and less introspective than those further from death; portrayed themselves as less aggressive and more docile, dependent, and intimacy-oriented than their paired counterparts; and used less evidence from their current life to validate their self-image but relied less on distortion for validation. In some areas, however, anticipated associations with impending death were not found: for example, in anxiety and mood tone, whether measured by self-report or projective data, and in self-reports or projective indices of health and body image.

Significant differences in three psychological realms—cognitive functioning, orientation to emotional life, and self-image—were found between matched pairs. These findings substantiate the results of the previous exploration, in which impending death was found to be associated with cognitive decline. Most important was the finding regarding affects—not affect states per se, but rather, orientation to emotional life. Those closer to death are apparently not more depressed, as is frequently reported in clinical papers, but they do avoid introspection. The magnitude and consistency of differences on measures of orientation to emotional life suggests that this finding is not an artifact and that those approaching death are unwilling—or possibly unable—to look inward because at some level of consciousness they recognize their impending death. It is as if they avoid introspection because of the fear of what they might discover. Although the nature of this monitoring process is unclear, the pattern of findings does indeed suggest a reduction in introspection without necessarily a modification in type or intensity of affect per se. Despite the almost universal focus of the psychological literature on the association of proximity to death with anxiety and withdrawal from others, our data, including impressions of the interviewer, does not reveal this association.

The last set of findings from the matched-pair design suggests a slight but measurable shift in the content of self-concept, away from assertiveness in interpersonal interactions and toward dependency and affiliation—or, in the language of Bakan (1966), away from agentic aspects and toward communion. Although Bakan's concepts of agency and com-

Comparison of the Six Realms Between the Matched Pairs

Variable	Sample means		z	Variable	Sample means		z
	DN	DF			DN	DF	
Realm I				**Realm V**			
1. Mental status (E)[a]	2.1	1.4	1.41[b]	20. Self-esteem	23.1	24.1	.78
2. Learning-retention (E)[a]	14.9	13.8	1.75[c]	21. Self-image characteristics			
3. Visual organization (E)[a]	32.8	30.3	1.08	a. Power success (Octant AP)	8.9	9.6	.08
4. Perceptual adequacy	24.0	23.6	.12	b. Narcissistic-exploitative (Octant BC)	13.4	13.5	.12
5. Time judgment	23.7	22.0	1.23[b]	c. Hostile-aggressive (Octant DE)	9.8	12.5	2.30[c]
Realm II				d. Rebellious-mistrustful (Octant FG)	11.1	13.7	2.03[c]
6. Expansiveness-restriction	5.4	5.6	.89	e. Weakness-masochist (Octant HI)	14.1	13.8	.22
7. Anxiety	25.7	27.3	.58	f. Conformity-trust (Octant JK)	11.8	9.9	2.03[c]
8. Life satisfaction	16.9	18.0	.60	g. Collaborative-pure love (Octant LM)	16.1	14.3	1.85[b]
9. Anomie	12.4	12.6	.17	h. Tenderness-generous (Octant NO)	15.3	13.2	2.16[c]
10. Acceptance of life	9.7	9.5	.19	22. Self-image maintenance mechanisms			
11. Loss	3.2	2.8	.51	a. Current	39.0	44.4	1.33[b]
Realm III				b. Past	5.7	4.9	.28
12. Emotional reactivity	4.9	5.3	.57	c. Conviction	49.2	42.9	1.01
13. Affective complexity	2.0	3.5	2.95[d]	d. Wished	1.2	1.0	.44
14. Introspective stance	2.0	2.7	3.00[d]	e. Distorted	4.6	6.9	1.65[c]
15. Introversion-extroversion	21.2	21.3	.66	**Realm VI**			
Realm IV				23. Futurity	5.7	5.9	.01
16. Health evaluation	3.5	3.3	.37	24. Extensionality	6.6	6.9	.59
17. Body preoccupation	4.0	3.9	.09	25. Past	4.1	4.0	.57
18. Body image	1.6	1.4	.48	26. Present	0.8	0.8	.22
19. Negative body image	1.3	1.0	1.11	27. Future	0.8	0.7	.06

NOTE: All tests of significance were one-tailed on variables having clear positive-negative directions and for which the death group was hypothesized to be on the lower or less adequate direction; two-tailed tests were used for variable 21, for which such an assumption could not be made; DN = death-near; DF = death-far.

[a]Higher scores indicate more errors; in all other cases, higher scores indicate score of variable named.

[b]$p > .10$.

[c]$p > .05$.

[d]$p > .0001$.

munion represent a higher level of abstraction than is revealed in our assessment of self-concept, his application of these constructs in relationship to Freud's concept of death instinct offers a framework for explaining the apparent modification in self-concept and is consistent with the findings from the analysis of death symbols discussed later in this chapter.

A DIRECT INQUIRY INTO THOUGHTS AND FEELINGS ABOUT DEATH

All direct statements related to death that respondents made in the interviews were collated for both groups, and the responses for each person were typed on a card without identifying information. The raw data, then, consisted of eighty paragraphs compiling all statements each respondent had made about death. Two scales that could be reliably rated were developed to discriminate individual differences: a three-point scale rating degree of preoccupation with one's own death and a four-point scale of fear of death (interrater reliabilities were 67 percent exact agreement and 100 percent exact agreement, respectively).

The preoccupation scale consists of a three-point scale: Scores of 1 reflect intense preoccupation with the imminence of death; scores of 2 and 3 reflect lesser degrees of preoccupation. Respondents who are scored 1 see death as just around the corner and use concrete imagery of rapid progressive decay. For example, one such respondent's card read:

> I'll go to sleep [bitter], I ain't so strong; weakest part is not being well. Death is nothing, just going to sleep. One hour is just another hour gone. Time means nothing. Everyone tries to plan, but it is impossible. No future. I don't think about things.

Scores of 2 were given when there was an acute awareness of one's age and the lack of an extended future, and death was seen as occurring in the intermediate future. Scores of 3 reflect relative lack of such preoccupation; despite commenting on their own death, respondents experience subjective time is as containing activities and hope as is evident. An example is the following:

> I would like to be strong and healthy—death is unavoidable. One hour is a blessed thing. I look forward to living a long life with my wife. The thing I like about myself is that I am all together in one piece. Time is to forsee things ahead. Don't plan. Next year I would like to live and tell of good events of the past year. The future is to look ahead for better things to come. I think more about the future. The past is gone.

On the fear of death scale, the lower scores indicate a limited capacity to cope with fears, and higher scores were given when there was evidence the integrative mechanisms were used to reduce fear. Evidence for the mechanisms was frequently found in the respondents' "personal philosophy." Scores of 1 were given when there was an unambivalent wish to be dead with no evidence of fear. An example:

> I'll be sick and die. I don't think they'll throw me out of here. There's nothing to hope for, I'm a nothing. I'll get worse and that's all. I can't fool myself. Hope means to die and not to suffer. My body isn't perfect. The weakest part of me, probably I have many weak spots. I'm dissatisfied with myself. There are times when I just don't like to live. Death would be a relief, my dear. I can't walk, I can't see, I can't hear. Right now I like to think about summer. I look forward to it without pain and suffering. Time does not mean much. People die every day like flies here. Next year I would like to die. Future means death and pleasure from the family.

Scores of 2 were given when there was unmitigated fear associated with not existing. Scores of 3 were assigned for a feeling of personal hopefulness in the face of death's inevitability, which is often accompanied by reliance on something outside self for coping. An example of a rating of 3:

> Nothing more to worry about. Only thing is that they'll bury me. I fear I will die. Sometimes I feel disappointed because I feel young and I am not. Each day goes away and another comes. Dead is something I never was yet, I won't think about it until I die. No point otherwise. My mind is floating, nothing sure to me. Time here is worthless. Time is gone. I'd like to be a free man if I live. The future is for children.

This respondent has not developed a consistent attitude toward personal death, whereas those scored 4 have done so.

Respondents rated 4 evidenced relative adequacy to cope with fear of dying and death, using such processes as placing their own death in an interpersonal context, with emphasis on separation rather than death; viewing death as the interruption of ongoing life processes, with some emphasis on loss, but the losing of life rather than death itself being paramount; and focusing on the processes, the means, or the mechanism of death, so that the way of going rather than death itself is feared. An example of a rating of 4:

> I'm better than many people. I prepare myself always, I even have the stone next to my wife. I told the children that if I possibly . . . the best thing is just to go. Each day goes by. Death is like a shot; when she died it was just like a shot. Time is gone. I plan ahead. Next year I'd like to go to Europe, but I don't know if I can go. The future is the best thing if I have a companion. The future is to get a companion, go out together and not to lose one's mind.

The Wilcoxon matched-pairs signed-ranks test (one-tailed) was used to compare those near death with their matched pairs. As shown in table 9–4, those near death were appreciably more preoccupied with death than their matched pairs (Z=2.05, p=.02) and had a somewhat greater fear of death (Z=1.49, p=.07). (See technical note 5.)

Inspection of the distribution for scales measuring the attitude toward death showed low preoccupation and low fear for approximately 40 percent of the death-near group, suggesting either that the sensitivity of these scales was poor or that the phenomenon tapped by these measures applied only to a subsample of those near death. Further analysis was required to determine the significance of the large number of death-near individuals who did not respond as anticipated on these two scales. Perhaps the low degree of introspection previously noted as characteristic of those close to death was an important influence. Many of these individuals may have been unable to discuss their thoughts about death and dying directly. This possibility led us to develop measures less amenable to the respondent's conscious control.

DEATH SYMBOLS

Responses were analyzed to the set of institutional TAT cards (Lieberman and Lakin 1963) discussed in the earlier chapter on "Threat and Loss." Four types of symbols were analyzed: (1) direct references to death and dying, such as struggling to save one's life in drowning; (2) issues of rebirth; (3) inscrutable events or mysterious trips; and (4) death figures or the specter of death, such as a figure with hands folded or face covered. (The interrater reliability for absence or presence of death symbols by the subject was 85 percent agreement.)

TABLE 9–4
Scales Measuring Attitude Toward Death

	Number of Pairs	
Matched Pairs	Preoccupation with death	Fear of death
DN group scored higher than DF group	16	18
DF group scored lower than DN group	7	7
DN group scored same as DF group	17	15
Sample means		
DN	2.22	1.73
DF	2.60	2.18

NOTE: DN = death-near; DF = death-far.

Mr. R., a respondent in the death-near group, expressed several of these symbols in his responses to the Institutional TAT:

[Card 1: Packing scene] [Long pause] Well, he's opening up this box. Now let me adjust my spectacles so I can see better. He opened up that box and this lady . . . Well, all I can see is that he opened up the box and he was looking for something. What it was I don't know. This lady is also taking a glance into the box. They lifted up some objects but I don't see the type of objects they lifted up. I just can't tell what it is so that I can decipher it for you. It's a very invisible thing. Very undecipherable to me. I see some other people—about three of them—in the back there. I don't know who they are. They have no significance to me. And now I've told you my opinion of this picture.

[Card 2: Entering scene] This one is walking up the stairway of a threshold. There are one to five steps he's going to climb. All I can see is that he's carrying a satchel. Seems to me that he has a baby or something in front of him [pointed to white in front of man's face]. Or maybe it's a dolly instead of a baby. Anyway he's interested in looking at this strange thing. To me it's undecipherable. It's very faded and obscure. But I can see that this man seems to be old. Yes, he's really an old man. That's all I can tell you about this picture.

[Card 5: Roommate scene] Those two men are having a conversation. This fellow [left] is trying to convert him [right]. The old man on the right says, "I'm trying to change your opinion." Then he goes on to say, "You say you're going to live longer than Winston Churchill, but you're not." By the way, did you know I'm still waiting for the Messiah. Christian Messiah that is, has come, but we Jews have been waiting for the real Messiah for 5,000 years. I prophecy his coming.

The eighty respondents were rated for the presence or absence of one or more of the death symbols for each TAT response. The results of this blind analysis indicated that death symbols were rated as present for thirty-four of the forty death-near respondents and for only nine of the forty death-far controls (χ^2 = 32.2, df = 1, p = .001). Thus, although spontaneous comments did not reveal extensive preoccupations and fears, projective data did reveal that symbolization of death occurs among those closer to death. To what extent these symbols intrude into consciousness cannot be determined with any specificity. We can, however, pursue the questions of emotional reactivity toward death among those nearer to death.

EFFECTS OF ENVIRONMENTAL INSTABILITY ON REACTIONS TO DEATH

Although the findings presented so far show clear differences among individuals further from and nearer to death, they do not suggest that impending death is experienced as a major crisis. In the first analysis of

223

emotional life and cognitive functioning, indices of anxiety, depression, and body preoccupation failed to yield differences between the death-near and the death-far groups. Our direct analysis of fear of death, although showing some statistically significant differences between the two groups, also suggested that for a large number of those a year or less away from death, no evidence of heightened fear or preoccupation could be found. However, the third analysis, relying on death symbols, clearly did suggest that those close to death were registering it at some level of consciousness. We wondered whether a clearer appreciation of impending death's affect on the psychology of the elderly might be garnered if we were to examine individuals experiencing externally induced stress. Therefore we divided our sample into two groups on the basis of whether or not they were in a stress-inducing setting related to environmental change.

Twenty-two pairs were waiting to enter homes for the aged or had recently entered such homes (unstable environmental circumstance). Eighteen pairs had lived in the homes for the aged from three to five years or were living in the community (stable environmental circumstance). We thus compared the matched pairs, now divided into two groups, to determine whether psychological processes associated with nearness to death differed depending on whether the respondent was in a stress situation. The data presented in the first three analyses was reanalyzed on the basis of group differences, using matched pairs as the unit of analysis.

The psychological dimensions previously described in table 9–2 were reanalyzed. Differences between matched pairs were used as scores for a t-test analysis comparing those in the stable and unstable environments. Only four of the twenty-two measures were significant at $p < .10$, not beyond the level of chance for this number of analyses. When the two groups were compared on the death attitude scales by means of the Wilcoxon matched-pairs signed-ranks tests, however, the death-near respondents in unstable environmental circumstances showed more preoccupation and fear than the death-far respondents. No differences were found, however, in preoccupation and fear between death-near and death-far respondents in stable environmental circumstances. Approximately 40 percent of all death-near respondents had shown preoccupation and fear, and when the sample of pairs was divided between those in stable and unstable environmental circumstances, preoccupation and fear were characteristic mainly of those in unstable circumstances.

The presence of death symbols on the TAT was not useful for discriminating between the stressed and nonstressed groups, because all but six of the forty death-near respondents had introduced such symbols. We then sought a measure that would assess affective responses to these death symbols. For this purpose we selected the TAT discrepancy measure described in the chapter on "Threat and Loss." High discrepancy scores reflect affective incursions on perceptual accuracy associated with the Institutional TAT. For those in the unstable condition, the death-near members of the matched pairs were more likely to manifest impaired accuracy than death-far members. In 67 percent of the pairs, the death-near respondents had poorer performance, whereas the corresponding percentage for the stable sample was 23 percent ($\chi^2 = 9.33$, $p = .01$). Thus, the discrepancies scores for the death-near group in unstable environmental circumstances indicated that these individuals reacted with apprehension or anxiety when faced with the Institutional TAT, which they apparently interpreted as symbolic of death and dying. In contrast, individuals near death in the stable environmental circumstances produced an equal number of death symbols but did not react with apprehension. Thus, while those close to death and under crisis reacted with anxiety to stimuli associated with death, those close to death but not in crisis reacted to the same death stimuli with integrated responses.

The Third Exploration:
A Replication of the Second Exploration in a Probability Sample of Middle-Aged and Old Respondents

A longitudinal study of 386 community residents created an opportunity to further explore the distance from death hypothesis. This stratified probability sample of elderly and middle-aged individuals was used to validate the findings reported in the prior two explorations. Participants, all first- or second-generation Irish-, Italian-, or Polish-Americans ranging in age from forty to eighty, included 189 men and 197 women. Forty-one of the original group died (25 men and 16 women) prior to the follow-up conducted five years later. A matched-pair death-far group of 41 survivors was drawn from the pool of 319 original respondents who had been successfully located for the five-year follow-up. The 41 death-far respondents were matched hierarchically for sex, socioeconomic status, age, generation in the United States, and marital status.

The death-near and death-far groups were compared on awareness of impending death, using loss in earliest memory as well as death symbolism in the Murray TAT; perceptions or views of death; and several measures of mental health. (See technical note 6.)

Matched-pair t-tests were performed on all continuous variables. Death-near members of the pairs introduced significantly more loss themes in their earliest memories (mean = 2.4) than the death-far members (mean = 1.7, p < .05). When this measure was treated as a categorical rather than a continuous variable, the same finding emerged; over one-half of the death-near respondents (twenty-one out of forty-one) introduced loss themes in their earliest memories, whereas about only one-quarter of the death-far respondents (eleven out of thirty-nine scorable responses) introduced such loss themes. Death-near individuals were also found to have significantly more death symbolism in their TAT stories (p < .05). In an analysis in which only presence or absence of any death symbolism was considered, eighteen of the death-near respondents were found to have introduced at least one death symbol in their TAT stories, compared to only seven of the death-far group (χ^2 = 7.41, df=1, p < .01).

The death-near and death-far groups differed significantly in how they envisioned their deaths (χ^2 = 14.45, df=6, p < .05). The death-near showed a much higher proportion of "happy-magical" responses (ten compared to three) and "concern about suffering" responses (five compared to two) than the death-far group. Death-near and death-far groups were about equally divided in the response categories of "natural process" (seven compared to five), "denial" (seven compared to eight), and "finalism" (six compared to nine). The death-far group held an almost exclusive claim on the categories of "traditional religiosity" (eight compared to one) and "mystery" (three compared to zero).

Thus far, we have seen that death-near individuals exhibit a concern with death in their projective material (earliest memory reports and TAT stories) and that they envision death differently than their death-far counterparts. To address the question of whether psychological disruption accompanies the approach to death, measures of four characteristics were used: anxiety, depression, psychiatric symptoms, and self-perceived health. Three of these measures distinguished the groups. The death-near showed more depression (p = .05), more psychiatric symptoms (p = .05), and more self-perceived ill health (p < .01). The anxiety measure, however, did not differentiate between the groups.

The study provided confirmation for the general hypothesis developed in this chapter: individuals closer to death show distinctive patterns both in their ego functioning as measured in this exploration by mental health indices, and in their experience of approaching death. When asked to carry out two simple tasks (to report an earliest memory and to tell stories about three Murray TAT pictures), participants who were approaching death introduced significantly more loss and death themes into their responses than did a matched group of survivors.

The study also added some insights into how the elderly conceptualize their own personal finitude depending on their distance from death. Those near death were responsible for 77 percent of the happy-magical responses, which reflect a sense of personal urgency and almost desperate conviction that something happy, pleasurable, and good is waiting for them after death.

Conclusions and Implications:
The Role of Death in the Psychology of Aging

SUMMARY OF FINDINGS

Changes in Ego Functions. Ego functioning was found in all three explorations to diminish when the individual was nearer to death. The first exploration revealed that cognitive decrements were idiosyncratic; that is, absolute levels were not predictive, rather decrements were found only when a respondent's later trials were compared to earlier ones. We found in the second exploration that those nearer death manifested more cognitive impairment than their matched pairs who were further from death; and in the last exploration, that respondents near death showed more psychiatric symptoms. This cumulative evidence supports an association between decline in ego-functioning and impending death.

Deterioration in ego functioning with impending death can be explained as either the behavioral manifestations of central nervous system disorganization or as a reaction to disturbing affects caused by inner awareness of changes prodomal to death. Probably both explanations are accurate. Evidence for a reactive process is found in the lessened propensity to introspection and the greater passivity when portraying the self in interaction with others among those closer to death. Both kinds of evidence suggests some active process in which painful underlying or latent meanings and affects are screened from consciousness. The success of this process is suggested by the inconsistent evidence for differences in emotional states between those nearer and those further from death. In the first two explorations, differences were not found in emotional states, whereas in the third exploration there was a modest association between

227

depression and impending death but not between anxiety and impending death. There was also an increased prevalence of preoccupations with death and fears of death among death-near respondents in the second exploration. Because these preoccupations were neither intense nor ubiquitous, it appears that many if not most elderly people approaching death are able to contain the experience and thereby limit conscious pain.

Phenomenology of Death. What is the nature of the underlying experience of approaching death? Our most consistent findings were that death-near respondents introduced symbols reflecting death when telling stories to TAT cards and loss themes in the earliest memories of death-near respondents. What are the likely mechanisms of such symbols? As shown in the first study, acute illness crises, in which respondents recovered, did not produce such symbols. Neither did those who recovered from acute illnesses show the same pattern of decline as those who died soon thereafter. It seems equally unlikely that the signaling process was set off by self-detected changes related to decrements of aging—social and personal losses, physical incapacities, and the many onslaughts undermining self-image. Most if not all respondents had suffered multiple losses and physical decrements associated with advanced age. Nor did environmental setting generate such death symbols in those close to death. If environment influenced production of symbols, more institutionalized respondents should have shown death symbols, inasmuch as the old-age home itself is sometimes perceived as symbolic of death—as a "death house."

The kinds of symbols and losses introduced into projective responses suggest that a variety of meanings are attributed to an inner, possibly diffuse and ambiguous experience. For some, the meanings of the internal changes prodomal to death are narrowly focused on separation or bodily decay, while for others the meanings are not as specific, encompassing a sense of nonexistence itself. Despite the diversity of symbols employed to superimpose meaning on inner changes, the nature of the underlying psychological experience is probably the potential dissolution of the self. This issue of dissolution of the self, and how the elderly strive to maintain stability and consistency of the self, will be the specific focus of the next chapter.

The presence of these covert meanings suggests the usefulness of an explanatory model that includes signal anxiety. An out-of-awareness experience of prodromal disorganization or disintegrative somatic changes is detected and experienced as a threat to the self, with subsequent signal anxiety. In response to the signal, the detected changes are symbolized and attempts are made to defend against the anxiety. Although depressive affect may be associated with such symbolization, manifest anxiety is not. Only through further study will we be able to determine whether this absence of manifest anxiety is specific to the very old, who apparently are more accepting of their own finitude than are younger people. On the other hand, the elderly may be more likely than younger people to become cognitively disorganized in the absence of manifest anxiety because of a less efficient central nervous system. The burden of defending against internal threat may overwhelm an already weakened ego, a process that we found in studying perceptual adequacy.

IMPLICATIONS—TOWARD A THEORY OF AGING

Death as an Organizing Focus. What do these findings tell us about death as a core psychological issue in the last decade or two of life? In investigating death and dying as a psychological issue in the aged, it is important to distinguish among people with respect to socioenvironmental conditions as well as distance from death. Those near to death but living in stable environmental circumstances, although clearly registering the "event," as evidenced in the death symbols produced, showed no signs that they perceived it as a threatening event. They exhibited no storminess, no reactivity, no disruptiveness. Munnichs (1966) expressed similar observations:

> It was extremely surprising to us at the time that there was a great preponderance of confidence and lack of apprehension, though more than half of the number of persons interrogated admitted that they did think about the matter. ... We realized this unexpected result was that if death was awesome in character for only few exceptions, the field of experience during old age must be of a different nature from what is generally supposed. [p. 12]

Whether the experience signaled by approaching death is contained, however, depends on externally induced stress. Environmental change constitutes a severe crisis for the elderly; previous patterns of relationships, meanings of significant others, and the self-image are challenged and tested by disruption of the environment. Individuals in this crisis state may have been more distressed and reactive over impending death—not because their approaching death was of core concern, but because life had again impinged on them, forcing them to make new adaptations and to face anew previously solved problems including, perhaps, a previous resolution of the meaning of their personal death. If death were the essential threat, rather than the life yet to be reorganized, more signs of avoidance, denial, or other similar psychological mechanisms would be expected in response to impending death.

The variety of methods and populations used across age groups makes it difficult to say whether the aged give more attention to the issue of death than nonaged populations. The direction of the findings would support the view that death is perhaps a more overt issue for the aged. Clearly, death plays a part in their psychology. The respondents' willingness to talk openly about death suggests that they viewed it as a legitimate topic of discussion. Furthermore, many had worked out the meaning of death for themselves, and most had developed a personal viewpoint toward their own death. That death is a topic of conversational interchange among the aged does not indicate, however, that it is a critical psychological focal point toward which the last decade of life is oriented.

It seems appropriate, in the light of these findings, to question the salience of death as a ubiquitous issue during the final two decades of life. The view of death as an overriding issue to be grappled with or as an organizing specter during these years, although not contradicted, is not supported by our findings. It is not that death has no meaning for the aged, but rather that its meaning as a primary issue is limited to specific, restricted conditions. Death becomes a meaningful issue for the very old when distance from death is relatively brief, that is, a year or two prior to death. Perhaps the discrepancies between theories and empirical studies on the meaning of death are partly explained by this observation. If in the homogeneous samples used in our explorations, death had a different psychological weight depending on its imminence, clearly it would be difficult to substantiate a general theory about the importance or centrality of death and dying for a more diverse population spanning a twenty-five year range. It is likely that the issue of death is crucial much earlier in life, perhaps in late middle age. Munnichs (1966) develops a similar conclusion: "The elderly person between 50 and 65 is more conscious of the problems regarding finitude than the old person—70 and older." We now believe that the psychological teleology advanced in theories of aging does not fit the empirical findings because it is primarily an invention of the young.

How, then, may we best understand the elderly person's experience of and reactions to impending death? In particular, in our examination of the psychology of aging in regard to environmental crises, where do we place impending death? Compared to this crisis, impending death appears, relatively speaking, less disruptive. Still, impending death is not an issue that the aged can blithely ignore. Rather, what appears most important is that the elderly we have studied generally had dealt with their own personal demise before they reach their seventies and eighties. It is against such a background that the psychology of the aged must be understood as death becomes a proximate reality for them. There seems to be no question that the aged have, at some level, a recognition that death is approaching.

On the basis of the explorations reported in this chapter, the experience of impending death is reflected primarily in elderly people's sense of decreased adequacy, a sense of ego disintegration that manifests itself in lessened cognitive abilities as well as a lessened potential for maintaining a stable and consistent self, which is the core of the experience of approaching death. Coping involves withdrawal from the environment around them, an emotional constriction, simplification, and a turning away from their inner life. There is an increased passive stance to a world that no longer is experienced as controllable as death approaches. In general, these strategies are successful, so that manifestations of psychic pain, eruptions of anxiety, and unmanageable fears are not usual. Intense anxiety exists when circumstances not related to death impinge upon the elderly, so that they must renegotiate life once more. Only under these circumstances do a majority of the elderly approaching death experience the psychic pain and disruption so characteristic of literary accounts of approaching death.

Most impressive in our data is the ability of the elderly to face their own death—their relative equanimity and the adequacy of their coping strategies. We feel safe in concluding, therefore, that impending death is a crisis only under limited circumstances among the aged, and that the issue of death must be examined at earlier points in time to understand its contribution to a psychology of life.

Distance from Death: Implications for Theories of Adult Development. Although addressing personal death may not be a focal point for organizing the psychology of the last several decades of life, such studies may have important consequences for viewing adult development. Our explorations reveal the importance of distance from death as a useful matrix for explaining differences among the elderly. In explaining age-related phenomena, distance from death must be considered as causally related to changes in individuals, just as biological deterioration and social events such as situational crises are the "real" explanatory variables rather than chronological age. Differences among adults of various ages that have been explained by the "empty" variable of age, for example, may indeed be explained by distance from death. More specifically for the elderly, measuring time by distance from death becomes a more useful metric than chronological age for organizing psychological phenomena, particularly for understanding changes in psychological experiences and functioning.

The findings from the studies of distance from death have a central importance to those of us who are interested in the social and psychological aspects of adult development. These findings clearly document the problems faced in mapping out developmental change. In the three explorations reported in this chapter we found that as people approach death, in addition to the well-documented cognitive decline reflected in level of performance and decreased cognitive integration, there are significant changes in the affective realm. These changes include a decreased level of introspection—an unwillingness to look inside oneself—and a movement toward a communion orientation and away from an agentic one. Both psychological parameters have been shown by other investigators to be among the few that are likely to be characteristic of developmental trajectories over the life span.

The greater likelihood of the death of less adequate persons in the population from which consecutive age samples are usually drawn suggests that such samples are not homogeneous, but increasingly, as the age of the sample increases, become positively biased. Consequently, age trends reported in the literature underestimate the decline or change that would result if all persons had the same chance of survival; that is, if the population remained homogeneous. Persons who perform below average on cognitive functions at any time during late adult life are closer to death than their more able agemates. Differences in scores within adult age groups might, therefore, be a function of survival probability; those scoring low are closer to death and/or have already experienced their "terminal drop"; those scoring high retain their abilities and have a good chance for survival. Differences in levels of functioning among adult age groups (hidden by selective survival) reflect the increasing number of persons with terminal drop.

For example, Gutmann (1975), using cross-cultural data, has suggested that as people age they shift from active mastery to passive mastery and then to magical mastery, which has characteristics of a communion orientation. The possibility that psychological trajectories in the latter half of life can be replicated when data is organized by distance from death augments the importance the field must place on the mapping of changes using this metric. It is not sufficient, however, to discover systematic changes in later life. Changes such as those attributed to terminal drop can only become intelligible through conceptualizations that clarify the factors that cause the developmental changes.

A biological explanation is most commonly used to account for terminal drop, which assumes that manifest changes reflect a general physiological deterioration. A narrow focus on cognitive deterioration supports a parsi-

monious reduction of the explanation to the level of the underlying biological substrata. Yet the finding that a variety of psychological changes
are associated with terminal drop should caution us against reducing the
phenomenon to a simplistic biological model. Riegel and Riegel (1972),
arguing in the same vein, have postulated one alternative model for explaining terminal drop, the "sociological terminal drop mortality model."
In their model, some people are unable to cope with their environments
as well as others because they received less education, have had lower
income, worse nutrition, less medical assistance, and so forth. Consequently, their chances for survival are lowered and their performance drops
earlier in life than that of their more favored agemates. As a discipline we
simply do not now have the requisite data to determine either the correct-
ness of alternate explanatory models or—possibly of even greater importance—their compatibilities or incompatibilities.

APPLYING THE CONCEPT OF DISTANCE FROM DEATH

A recently completed study that examined the effects of cultural surroundings and personality on adaptation can serve as an illustration of the
application of the concept of distance from death. A random sample of
three cultural groups was gathered and interviewed (Lieberman and
Cohler 1975), including approximately four hundred first- and second-
generation Polish, Irish, and Italian men and women aged forty to eighty.
Although this was a cross-sectional investigation, the use of a random
probability sample provided a modicum of correction for the obvious errors of selection bias. The analysis of cultural effects was accomplished
through dividing the sample into two groups—those who successfully
adapted (high life satisfaction and low depression) and those who did
not—and then examining the groups on a series of psychological and social parameters associated with adaptation. Analysis of age differences in
the sample replicated Gutmann's trajectory; by interpreting cross-sectional differences as longitudinal changes, we found that men, as they age,
move from high dominance to greater submissiveness, whereas women
from relatively low dominance to high dominance. In the context of terminal drop, it is important to note that developmental trajectories were
only characteristic of those who adapted successfully. This paradox was
clearest among the women who were low in adaptation in their forties
and subsequently moved downward toward decreased dominance, a pattern that was totally different from that of their well-adapted counterparts. In other words, the poorly adapted (whom we presume were closer
to death) showed different psychological trajectories than their agemates

who were high on the measures of adaptation used in the study. We also found in the study of middle and elderly ethnics that personality characteristics interact with life stage and cultural affiliation and play a dominant role in accounting for individual differences in adaptation level (Lieberman 1981). This hypothesis was tested by contrasting the effects on adaptation of social characteristics and social resources on the one hand to the effects of personality characteristics on the other. For all life stages and for all cultural groups, personality characteristics were more robustly associated with successful adaptation than were social characteristics (expressed in percentage of variance explained). Moreover, the specific psychological characteristics that were found to be associated with successful adaptation levels were unique for each ethnic group and age cohort. (See technical note 7.)

But, although personality constellations unique to specific cultural affiliation were associated with successful adaptation in the middle years, this was not the case for later years, particularly beyond the seventies. Some personality characteristics were associated with successful adaptation in later life, to be sure, but they were not specific to ethnic groups nor, for that matter, were they specific to one sex or the other. Thus, there appears to be a common final pathway of adaptation processes in late life that transcends cultural variations.

How are we to reconcile these rather strong findings regarding the effects of culture on adaptation in middle life with the lack of substantive effects in later life? One explanation that fits the findings is selective survival—that is, individuals with particular psychological characteristics are more likely to survive through advanced old age. An explanatory framework to account for these data based on terminal decline and selective survival is clearly speculative. However, the increasing similarity among people in characteristics that reflect adaptation, albeit with marked cultural variation and sex differences, lends credence to such a model.

In summary, we are suggesting that constructing psychological theories of late life without sensitivity to the particular characteristics of a population—and specifically to those characteristics that have been associated with survival—may lead to gross overgeneralizations. Certainly, in many studies the selectivity of the sample is likely to be a major problem. It is well known that even in probability samples we underrepresent those who are least adequate, particularly as the sample's age increases. Yet these may be the very individuals who, if available for study (both as subjects selected into a sample and as survivors), would force us to alter our conclusions about the nature of adult development.

Technical Notes

1. The six scores derived from the four tasks were the following:

1. Bender-Gestalt figures (a series of simple geometric designs) were used as a copying task with no time limit. The adequacy of the reproduction was assumed to assess degree of cognitive organization. A large number of errors has been associated with psychiatric disability, organic brain damage, less adequate reactions to physical stress, and inability to cope with cognitive complexities of the physical environment. The test was scored according to the system suggested by Pascal and Suttell (1951). Scores obtained from the present population ranged from 3 (an almost perfect reproduction, reflecting high organization) to 200 (a grossly unrecognizable reproduction of the test figures, indicating considerable disorganization).

2. The size of the Bender-Gestalt reproduction was used as an indicator of ego energy, that is, energy available for dealing with stimuli from the outer world (Hartmann 1950). Evidence that the size of Bender-Gestalt drawings reflect available ego energy stems from comparisons of different psychopathological groups. A score for each performance was derived by measuring the area enclosed by each of the nine figures, and then summing the nine measurements for a total score. Scores ranged from nine square inches to sixty-four square inches. (The actual area of the nine figures in the standard designs is 29.4 square inches.) All area scores were converted by means of the square-root transformation prior to statistical analysis.

3. The free-hand drawing of a human figure—the Draw-A-Person (DAP) Test—was used to assess capacity to integrate stimuli. Inadequate drawings are assumed to reflect ego insufficiency (Modell 1951; Swenson 1957). Although the figure drawings are open to a wide range of interpretations, Swenson's review suggests that an interpretation such as the one made here best fits the empirical evidence. Scores were based on a frequency count of body parts shown and on the size relationships of body parts. One point was given for each body part and one point for each correct size relationship. The scores obtained from the present population ranged from 1 (a simple oval with no differentiated body parts) to 22 (a well-articulated drawing of the human figure). High scores indicate complex figures and were interpreted to reflect high ego sufficiency.

4. Respondents were asked to estimate the passage of a sixty-second interval. The time interval was signaled by a red light which they were instructed to turn off at the end of sixty seconds. Two contiguous trials were used. The task was suggested by the work of Feifel (1957), who found that, for a similar population of institutionalized aged, the length of the estimated passage of time correlated with measures of optimism and pessimism. The longer the time estimate, the most optimistic was the person's mood. Estimates for our population ranged from two seconds to eighty-seven seconds.

5. Twelve simple line drawings of the human figure (portraying a range of postures) were shown to the respondents one at a time (Reitman and Robertson 1950). They were asked to tell what they saw and to describe the feeling

235

and action states represented in the drawings. The first measure derived from this test was the degree of affectivity. Affect scores were based on the number of affective responses attributed to the twelve stick figures and ranged from 0 to 12.

6. Intensity of activity ascribed to the stick figures was measured on a five-point scale ranging from 0 to 4 for each figure, with higher scores indicating greater attributed activity. Total scores ranged from 0 to 30 on activity.

The degree of judgment involved in scoring these tasks is relatively minimal. Interscorer reliability was computed for all tasks in which there was some aspect of judgment (the Bender-Gestalt performance, Draw-A-Person complexity score, and the activity and affect ratings). Correlations ranged from a low of .84 for the judgment of activity level of the stick figures to .96 for adequacy of reproduction of the Bender-Gestalt drawings. Intercorrelations among the six scores were relatively low, ranging from −.01 to +.56, with an average of +.19.

2. The graphs are based on average ranks; thus they cannot be used to compare differences between the two groups at any one point in time. Differences between the groups, however, are represented by the the direction of the lines. In interpreting the graphs it should be noted also that each point on the graph for the death-near and death-far groups does not represent an equal time interval. For the death-near group each time point represents a range of 5 to 15 weeks, with a mean of 11; for the death-far group, they represent a range of 10 to 20 weeks, with a mean of 14. Thus, despite the longer period of observation for the death-far group and the increased age of the respondents, figures 9–1, 9–2, and 9–3 suggest that the effects of practice were greater than the effects of aging measured over a two-and-a-half year span. Decline in scores was associated with imminence of death and not with increase in age.

3. Of the forty who died within twelve months, twenty-two were in the original waiting list sample; eight of these had last been interviewed while on the waiting list and fourteen had last been interviewed two months after admission. Five others were members of the community control sample and had not applied for admission. The remaining thirteen were members of the institutional control sample who had resided in the homes for one to three years. These forty respondents from sixty-five to ninety-one years of age (the mean age was seventy-nine), and three-fourths were women.

4. The relatively low intercorrelations among the measures within each affective realm suggested that the degree of independence between variables was sufficient for examining each measure separately.

Realm I: (cognitive) average r = .34 (range .18 to .51)
Realm II: (emotional states) average r = .15 (range −.06 to .40)
Realm III: (orientation to emotional life) average r = .09 (range −.01 to .48)
Realm IV: (health and body orientation) average r = −.06 (range −.18 to .09)
Realm V: (self-image) the interdependency of data, that is, i.e., single source makes r's impractical to compute
Realm VI: (time perspective): average r = .04 (range −.22 to .28).

5. Although based on the same set of data, the two scales were sufficiently independent (death-near group: r = .43; death far group: r = .40) for separate analyses.

6. In addition, a variety of personality indices were examined: trust (Robinson, Rusk, and Head 1968); dominance/submission (Leary 1957); locus of control (Rotter 1966); sex-role rigidity (Lieberman and Cohler 1975); and authoritarianism (Adorno et al. 1950). Since none of these personality tests proved to distinguish between the death-near and death-far groups, they will not be reported on further.

7. For example, the particular mode used by Irish males in their forties to achieve a successful adaptation was not only different from that used by successfully adapted forty-year-old Irish females but also was distinct from those utilized by Italians or Poles in their forties who achieved successful adaptation. Apparently, each cultural group has a unique personality constellation associated with successful adaptation in mid-life.

To illustrate, the mean scores for the three ethnic groups differed significantly on authoritarianism, with the Polish sample the highest. More important, however, those people who live in a culture that stresses authoritarianism and who have high amounts of this trait in middle age (both men and women) are successfully adapted, whereas those in the Polish culture who show low levels of this trait are poorly adapted. Neither the Irish nor the Italian culture stresses authoritarianism, and we found fewer examples of high scores on this trait among those two cultures. Moreover, those among the Irish and Italians who are high in authoritarianism in middle age are poorly adapted, a sharp contrast to the adaptive characteristics of this trait for the Polish sample.

Findings are similar for other personality traits and aspects of inner life.

10

The Maintenance of Self-Identity

I F the task in early development is to acquire a sense of self; and in early adulthood, it is to maximize the use of the self for adaptation; then the task in later adulthood is to maintain a sense of self despite adversities that can erode identity. The essential problem in old age is to use whatever resources are available to maintain self-identity. How well the elderly accomplish this, particularly in the face of crises, and what processes they use to maintain the self is the focus of this chapter.

The Self in Psychology: A Brief Overview

The idea that conscious appraisal of oneself is a critical psychological mechanism extends back, in modern times, to William James (1890, 1892), who is considered by many to be the earliest "self" psychologist. Cooley (1902), a sociologist, also focused on the self as an organizing principle; but it was George Herbert Mead (1934) who developed the construct to its fullest. Like James, Mead believed the essence of the self was

The Maintenance of Self-Identity

the "I-me" distinction—the process by which people become objects to themselves; like Cooley, Mead saw the self as a social phenomenon, the product of interaction with others which reflected the experience of the self.

The "self" was popularized by Carl Rogers (1951; Rogers and Dymond 1954) in reaction to the dominant Freudian psychology, which at that time did not focus explicitly on the self. Rogers developed a "client-centered" psychotherapy, based on phenomenology: "The central construct of our theory would be the concept of self, or the self as perceived in the phenomenal field" (1950, p. 379). The major theorists of the self of this era, Lecky (1951) and Snygg and Combs (1949), made preservation of the self the primary principle. Self-preservation includes both stability of the self over time and consistency, unity, and organization of the self. As stated by Lecky (1951):

> All of an individual's values are organized into a single system, the preservation of whose integrity is essential. The nucleus of the system, around which the rest of the system revolves, is the individual's valuation of himself. The individual sees the world from his own viewpoint, with himself at the center. Any value entering the system which is inconsistent with the individual's valuation of himself cannot be assimilated; it meets with resistance and is likely, unless a reorganization is made, to be rejected. This resistance is a natural phenomenon, it is essential for the maintenance of individuality. The changing situations present continuous problems of adjustment, but the organization can make a unified movement in only one direction at a time, which explains why a single tendency can be dominant at one time. The striving for unity and organization or integrity is constant. The individual's organization of values makes itself evident in the regularity of his behavior. This organization not only defines his role in life but furnishes him with standards which he feels obliged to maintain. [pp. 88–89]

Most recently, Rosenberg (1979), in a creative and admirably ambitious effort to synthesize the current state of knowledge on self-concept, discussed both self-esteem and self-preservation as motives. The individual has "a wish to think well of oneself" (p. 53) and "the wish to protect the self-concept against change or to maintain one's self-picture" (p. 53). In his use of such phrases as "self-picture," it is obvious that to Rosenberg the self is more than self-esteem. He suggested that the self-concept comprises four areas: (1) content, consisting of social identity elements, dispositions, and physical characteristics; (2) structure, which refers to the values or criteria used to assess different self-attributions; (3) dimensions of the self, which include self-attitudes of stability or continuity, consistency, clarity, and accuracy; and (4) ego extensions, the incorporations of external elements into the self.

Psychology and sociology are not the only disciplines that have been interested in the self. Although Freud did not focus explicitly on the self (and accused Adler and Jung of being too preoccupied with this kind of noninstinctual, peripheral concern), he did recognize that the functions of the ego include self-reflective behaviors. He explicated processes involved in the development of the self, for example, in his discussions of the content of the superego and, specifically, of the ego ideal. It was not until the introduction of the concept of identity by Erikson in the 1950s (Erikson 1959), however, that the self came to the forefront in psychoanalytic theory. According to Erikson, the task in adolescence is to achieve a sense of identity, that is, crystallized feelings of a sense of selfness and continuity that persists throughout life. Other psychoanalytic theorists of the time who focused on the self as an important construct included Hartmann (1950), Sullivan (1953); later there were Jacobson (1964) and Guntrip (1971). Most recently, Kohut's (1977, 1978) theory represents a major reorganization of psychoanalytic thought on the self. A central aspect of his theory is that each stage in the development toward a mature internalized self is associated with a specific pattern of internalization of significant people in the person's life as well as self-evaluations.

Despite the diversity of approaches to theories of the self, the construct has persisted as a meaningful one in personality theory from the time of William James. Given this diversity, it is surprising that there is any consensus among theorists. Brittle as the consensus may be, however, three elements seem to be shared: first, the self includes evaluations and descriptions about "me" as an object; second, the self is a product of interactions that are, in turn, reflected in current interpersonal interactions; and, third, the self is the persona that each individual strives to enhance and to maintain.

The long and respected, albeit uneven tradition among the social sciences of interest in the study of the self has not led to an equally productive accumulation of empirical work. This is nowhere more apparent than in the study of the psychology of the adult. Intrinsic to many theories of adult development—and certainly implied in most of the work cited in this brief overview of theories of the self—is a bias from development in the earlier years. Neither the requisite detailed theory nor empirical support exists, however, for a life stage perspective on the self in adulthood. Speculation about and study of the self in adult development usually entails specification of systematic psychological changes over the adult life cycle. Despite three decades of research, however, such change remains elusive (Neugarten 1979). Neither systematic change nor stability is reflected in our current state of knowledge. Yet the conventional wisdom is that in spite of a plethora of changes in later life, each of us remains the same to ourselves. As Mischel (1969) has written: "The experience of subjective continuity in ourselves—of basic oneness and durability in the self—is perhaps the most compelling and fundamental feature of personality" (p. 1012). However, the literature Mischel reviewed regarding continuity and change in personality suggests otherwise: "Indeed we do need to recognize that discontinuities—real ones and not merely superficial or trivial veneer changes—are part of the genuine phenomenon of personality" (p. 1017).

At least one study, however, supports the notion that the self-concept remains stable throughout adulthood. Haan and Day (1974) and Haan (1976) used the Block Q-Sort on cases drawn from the Berkeley Guidance and Oakland Growth Study to organize traits into four groups: information processing skills, interpersonal reactions, responses to socialization, and presentation of self. They found that traits classified as reflecting the self-concept were the most stable from adolescence through the middle years.

Issues for Study

In this chapter we are concerned with some classical issues: the stability of and changes in the self as well as the processes individuals employ in their quest to maintain self-identity. We are studying the elderly under special circumstances of environmental change, circumstances that we believe mirror in a concentrated span of time the fundamental psychological tasks confronting the elderly in general: dealing with losses of various kinds, lessened control over their life, and the absence of clearly defined roles.

Situations that tax a person's ability to cope with adaptive demands may cause a diminution in self-esteem. Some situations may cause further damage to the self by reducing the capacity to maintain a consistent self-image. Goffman (1961), for example, characterizes the change in the self that results from becoming institutionalized in a mental hospital as "deselfing" or, to use his more dramatic phrase, "a mortification of the self":

> Whatever the forms or source of these various indignities, the individual has to engage in activities whose symbolic implications are incompatible with his conception of self. A more diffuse example of this kind of mortification occurs when the individual is required to undertake a daily round of life that he considers alien to him—to take on a disidentifying role. [p. 23]

We have assumed that the onslaughts associated with aging—losses of people and roles, denigration by society, confrontation with bodily disintegration and personal death—would similarly cause a "deselfing." We believe that the critical task of aging is to maintain a persistent perception of oneself by transcending internal and external losses. We studied the capacity for such transcendence among the elderly by examining them as they experience environmental upheavals and as they approached death.

We were interested not only in the fact of stability or change in the self-image, but also in the processes used by the elderly in maintaining self-identity despite upheavals in their lives. The maintenance of self-continuity is not a passive process. In interaction with others there is a constant search to reinforce and maintain the senses of selfness. Feedback, or validating experiences, are essential for maintenance of self-concept. In advanced age, however, opportunities for such validating experiences may lessen. Certainly, the major disruptions in life space that are the focus of this book not only disrupt ongoing sustaining patterns of interaction but may also diminish opportunities for reestablishing interactions that can validate the self.

Nevertheless, it may still be possible to perceive oneself as the same person when such opportunities are diminished, or even nonexistent. This may be accomplished through the use of such psychological processes as denying or distorting the meanings of interaction rather than accepting the direct reflection of oneself offered by others. The man in his mideighties, for example, who has always perceived himself as a powerful person whom others fear, may attribute the indifference of other men in the new setting to their fear of him when in reality they are simply preoccupied with their own problems. Another mechanism to assure continuity may be to ignore the present, in which validating experiences are not available, and focus on the past, where there is evidence that one has been, for example, a housewife to whom everyone turned for succorance and praise. Particularly for the elderly, the past may be the repository of memories that assure the maintenance of their self-identity in a deselfing environment.

Measuring Self-Concept: The Self-Sort Task

We needed a measure of self-concept that would meet several goals: provide a portrait of the self; assess stability and change in self-concept; provide information on processes used to maintain self-identity; and be easy to administer to very old people. A review of existing methods for assessing psychological constructs about the self proved disappointing; most measures that focus on self-concept are restricted to self-esteem. Indeed Wylie's (1974) extensive, if not exhaustive, review of self-concept instruments is primarily a review of measures of self-esteem or self-regard, indexed by self-administered attitude scales and assessments of congruence between "the ideal" and "the actual" self.

Although we did not begin with the intention of developing a new instrument, our review of existing measures led us to do so. It also led to criteria for an instrument appropriate for use with the elderly. With the age of our respondents uppermost in our minds, we set out to develop a measure containing unambiguous statements of self-reference that the respondents could either accept or reject as self-descriptive. We avoided the usual requirement that respondents grade themselves on self-descriptive items (on scales that range, for example, from "a little like me" to "a lot like me") as well as formats asking respondents to select most self-descriptive item from a set of two or more. We strove to develop a series of readily intelligible statements that would be self-descriptive for the elderly respondents and would provide information on the processes used to maintain self-consistency.

Leary's (1957) interpersonal personality theory provided useful categories for developing self-assessments based on consciously perceived attributes. He divided personality attributes into sixteen categories of interpersonal behavior that can be applied to any unit of observed, self-reported, or self-descriptive behavior. Categories are arranged to form a circle in which adjacent categories are more similar than nonadjacent categories, and categories on opposite sides of the circle are assumed to represent psychological opposites. The sixteen categories were then grouped into octants by pairing categories as follows: success–power, exploitative–narcissim, hostility–punitive, rebellious–distrustful, weakness–masochistic, conformity–trust, collaboration–pure love, and tenderness–generosity. In this scheme success–power is assumed to be the psychological opposite of weakness–masochistic, with the former reflecting a general trait of dominance and the latter of submissiveness. Likewise, collaboration–pure love is assumed to be the psychological opposite of hostility–punitive, with the former reflecting a general trait of affiliation and the latter of hostility.

THE SELF-SORT TASK

Based on Leary's scheme, a set of forty-eight statements were developed, with each of the octants represented by six items. (See table 10–1.)

These were used in a self-sort task, in which each respondent selects those statements that describe his or her current self. Respondents are first asked to sort a shuffled deck of cards containing the forty-eight statements into two piles: "like me now" and "not like me now." Then the respondent is asked to provide an illustration of current interpersonal behavior for those statements in the "like me now" pile. It was expected that most examples would reflect specific current interpersonal characteristics of the self-concept based on feedback or validating experiences derived from these exchanges. Adequacy in using the interpersonal environment to reaffirm self-concept could therefore be assessed by the percentage of items for which the respondent was able to give current validating examples. Statements were constructed separately for the two categories composing each octant and the three statements in each category, as shown in table 10-1, scaled from 1 to 3 according to their intensity using Guttman scaling procedures (Rosner 1968).

VALIDITY OF THE MEASURE

Wylie (1974), in her extensive review of the assessment of the self-concept, sees method variances as the single most serious problem for self-concept instruments. We asked, did the self-sort reflect pervasive qualities of the self that were not specific to the measure? To assess method variance, Edelhart (1965) scored self-concept measures in the Home for Life study sample using the Leary categories on six different tests: the self-sort task; an interview; the Murray TAT; the Reitman Stick Figure Test; the interpersonal role-playing task (respondents are asked to describe their "solutions" to a series of nine simple stories describing conflictual interpersonal situations familiar to an institutional population); and a specially revised Cattell 16 Personality Factor Questionnaire. The self-descriptions derived from these six tests were compared by computing a single summary score based on a weighting system developed by Leary. Edelhart found that "the self-concept scores on each of the six measures showed a closer correspondence than would be expected by chance (p=.001). Since similar self-concepts can be obtained from dissimilar measures, it is reasonable to conclude that the self-sort task yields a meaningful self-concept measure that is not an artifact of a particular type of test data.

We do not know, of course, whether a similar absence of method variance would have been found among respondents in younger age groups—the typical populations reported on by Wylie in her review. It is possible that the consistency in self-concept found across instruments may be a

Self-Sort Items with Self-Esteem Weights[a]

Octant Categories

Power
a. (+1) I enjoy being in charge of things.
b. (+2) I am a good leader.
c. (−2) I am somewhat of a dominating or bossy person.

Narcissism
a. (+2) I am a self-respecting person.
b. (+1) I am an independent and self-confident person.
c. (0) I am proud and self-satisfied.

Punitive
a. (+2) I am firm but fair in my relations with other people.
b. (+1) I can reproach people when necessary.
c. (−1) I am short-tempered and impatient with mistakes other people make.

Distrustful
a. (0) I am frequently disappointed by other people.
b. (−2) I am touchy and easily hurt by others.
c. (−2) It is hard for me to trust anyone.

Masochistic
a. (+1) I am able to criticize and find fault with myself.
b. (−1) I am easily embarrassed.
c. (−1) I am rather timid and shy.

Trust
a. (+2) I am a trusting person.
b. (−1) I prefer to let other people make decisions for me.
c. (−1) I will believe anyone.

Pure Love
a. (+2) I am a friendly person.
b. (+2) I am an affectionate and understanding person.
c. (+1) I love everyone.

Generosity
a. (+1) Generally I can be counted on to help others.
b. (+1) I often take care of other people.
c. (+2) I spoil people with kindness.

---

1. **Success**
a. (+2) People think well of me.
b. (+1) I believe that I am an important person.
c. (0) I frequently give advice to others.

2. **Exploitative**
a. (+2) I am able to take care of myself.
b. (−1) I am a competitive person.
c. (−2) I can be a cold and unfeeling person.

3. **Hostility**
a. (+2) I am frank and honest with people.
b. (0) I am critical of other people.
c. (−1) I frequently get angry with other people

4. **Rebellious**
a. (+1) When necessary, I can complain about things that bother me.
b. (+1) I will argue back when I feel I am right about something.
c. (−1) At times I act rebellious or feel bitter about something.

5. **Weakness**
a. (+1) I can be obedient when necessary.
b. (−1) Usually I give in without too much of a fuss.
c. (−2) Frequently I feel weak or helpless.

6. **Conformity**
a. (+1) I am grateful for what other people do for me.
b. (0) I am often helped by other people.
c. (0) I hardly ever talk back.

7. **Collaboration**
a. (+2) I am a cooperative person.
b. (0) I want everyone to love me.
c. (0) I agree with what everyone says.

8. **Tenderness**
a. (+2) I am considerate of others.
b. (+1) I am somewhat tender and soft-hearted.
c. (−1) I am too lenient with other people.

[a]Figures in parentheses represent self-esteem score weights assigned to each item.

special characteristic of the very old. As Zinberg and Kaufman (1963) note:

> The older patient is far less likely to "kid himself." His awareness of being stirred up by disagreements may be accompanied by a cynical disregard for his own feelings, because he understands himself in a sense too well, but he is more likely to know where the feelings come from and why he is upset. [p. 29]

Supporting this view are clinical impressions that previously ego dystonic feelings and impulses become recognized as acceptable. Zinberg and Kaufman state:

> Many feelings which are strongly resisted by younger people are accepted in the aged. The fact that people have destructive and envious urges are often admitted to consciousness without the anxiety and accompanying disorganization that may have occurred if the same feelings had reached awareness earlier in life. . . . They fear the judgment of others less because they see the future as unimportant." [p. 30]

Only through further empirical studies will we be able to confirm such clinical impressions. Our findings cannot distinguish between the effects of the method and a possible age-associated consistency in self-concept.

SELF-ESTEEM

Three judges rated the degree of self-esteem represented by each of the forty-eight items in the self-sort task on a five-point scale, ranging from positive to negative self-esteem. There was agreement among all three judges on twenty-six items and agreement between two of the judges on eighteen items. Thus, on forty-four of forty-eight items (or 92 percent) there was exact agreement by at least two of the three judges. The four items on which all judges disagreed were scored as neutral. The scoring of each of the forty-eight items is shown in table 10–1.

CATEGORIES OF SELF-VALIDATING EVIDENCE

The examples respondents provided for each self-descriptive item were categorized into one of five types. A rating of "specific present" was assigned when an example was given from current interaction. For example, to the statement "I enjoy being in charge of things," one respondent said, "I enjoy being in charge of the gift shop [in the home] and I also work in the library."

Given the nature of the task, as well as the importance of reinforcement in ongoing interaction with others for each attribute assessed, it was assumed that if an example from the present was not available, a specific example from the near past—although reflecting a lowered availability of day-to-day reinforcement of self—would be a meaningful way to provide validation for the attribute selected as "like me now." For example, for the statement "I enjoy being in charge of things," one respondent gave the example: "Where I worked years ago, they put me in charge of a department. I worked. I did a good job and people thought well of me."

Statements about self that did not contain specific examples would indicate less adequate self-validation. Thus, "general past" was the rating assigned when a specific example was not given, and the comment made by the respondent referred instead to the attribute as being a persistent characteristic. For instance, to validate the statement "I enjoy being in charge of things" a respondent said, "That's how I am, how I've always been." This kind of statement suggests that validation is solely from an internal feeling of conviction.

Next in the hierarchy would be responses indicating that the attribute in question was not necessarily possessed but was wished for or strived toward. "Wish to be" was, therefore, the rating assigned when a comment given to illustrate the item was a wish or hope, reflecting the sense that the respondent may not be certain that the attribute is characteristic of self but wishes that it were. For example, to the statement "I am a good leader" one respondent said, "I'm trying to be," while another said, "I wish I could be that way." In examples such as these, specific self-validating evidence may not exist now, may have existed in the past, or may never have existed at all. Although the respondents might claim certain self-characteristics as their own by their choice of statements on the sorting task, in fact, evidence might not be available to support the claim.

Last in rank of categories of adequacy, a rating of "distortion" was given for examples in which self-validation was based on fantasy, or in which there was confusion, contradiction, or actual distortion between the statement chosen and the example given. For example, to the statement "I enjoy being in charge of things" one person said, "My hair annoys me so; the dandruff. I'm in charge today, they all went out. I'm in charge of everything today." In the absence of more appropriate self-validating data, an individual may become confused, may stretch his imagination to provide a response, or may deny the choice of a particular statement as "like me now."

The ordering of the five categories was based on theoretical assumptions that we have made regarding the adequacy of evidence required to maintain a coherent and consistent sense of self-identity. (See technical

247

note 1 for computation of adequacy score.) Rater reliability was 79 percent exact agreement (Rosner 1968).

Findings

SELF-IMAGE STABILITY

Our initial question addressed the degree to which the elderly are able to maintain a stable and coherent self-image. This proposition was tested by contrasting respondents in the Home for Life study who were facing radical changes in their life space with those who did not undergo such environmental changes—the already institutionalized and the community control samples in that study.

Several different ratios were computed to assess stability of self-image. The first was a simple percentage of items sorted identically at three different measurement times by a sample of twenty study respondents, carefully matched to the respondents in the two control samples. As shown in table 10–2, the mean number of responses from pre-admission (while on the waiting list) repeated by the study sample two months after admission was 81 percent; one year after admission, 77 percent of the items selected were the same. These percentages are very similar to those for the institutional control sample (81 percent) and for the community control sample (83 percent), who were assessed at one-year intervals.

We found, however, that among the items that continued to be chosen were statements that almost all respondents selected. These "social desirable" items may have spuriously inflated stability scores. To control for social desirability, the seventeen items chosen on succeeding interviews over 75 percent of the time were eliminated. As shown in the second column of table 10–2, the stability of selection remained high, even with these "idiosyncratic" items, and all groups were again comparable.

A third stability score examined shifts in the proportion of items chosen within each octant. As shown in the last column of table 10–2, respondents shifted very little in the proportion of items selected within octants; the actual shifts were about one item per octant. Again, all groups were comparable, and stability remained very high. The average shift was only 3 to 4 percent.

Further support for the stability of self-concept among the respondents was found from an analysis of a group of sixteen elderly respondents who were administered the self-sort instrument weekly for six weeks beginning after their entrance into the institution. Stability of item selection from

TABLE 10–2
Stability of Self-Concept:
The Home for Life Study

Sample	N	Consistency of All Statements		Consistency of Idiosyncratic Statements		Shift in Percentage Selected within Octants	
		Mean	Range	Mean	Range	Mean	Range
		(in percentages)		(in percentages)		(in percentages)	
udy Sample							
ompared to pre-admission)							
2 months post-admission	20	81	61–99	72	40–99	3.7	0.83–5.9
1 year post-admission	20	77	56–95	66	33–92	4.1	1.21–6.9
ontrol Sample							
ompared to 1 year earlier)							
Institutional	22	81	47–96	71	30–99	2.9	0.92–6.5
Community	16	83	62–93	66	27–86	2.9	1.47–7.2

week to week remained as high for these sixteen as for any other group studied—despite the immediacy of the disruptive life change!

It is apparent that the elderly are remarkably capable of retaining a persistent self-concept. The radical shift in their life space and the confrontation to self-image implied by placement in a total institution has little impact on self-identity.

Consistency-of-self scores over time were computed for those near to death and contrasted with their matched control group (see chapter 9). A matched-pair t-test on twenty-one pairs (those near to death who had performed the self-sort task at least at Time 1 and Time 2) yielded a t of 1.53 (df=20), which was not statistically significant. This finding is similar to the observation on those being relocated. We expected that self-consistency would be diminished among both respondents under the stress of a life change and those approaching death, but this proved not to be the case. Again, we were impressed with the remarkable capacity of the elderly to maintain a coherent self under conditions that one would expect to lead to alteration.

THE PROCESS OF SELF-CONCEPT VALIDATION

The ability of the elderly to maintain a coherent and stable self-image, even in the face of highly adverse life changes affecting a wide variety of social, psychological, and physical functions, makes the exploration of mechanisms used to maintain such self-stability of singular relevance for understanding both the psychology of aging and stress adaptation. To explore these processes, we will examine the effects of age, environment, and distance from death on changes or differences in the maintenance of self-stability.

Effects of Age and Environment. For a comparison of mechanisms used to validate the self-image in different age groups, we chose a group that was also in transition, but was highly interactive in the period of potential self-change. For the comparison group we assessed twenty-four high school juniors and seniors on the self-sort task. The distribution of the responses in each category of self-validating evidence at the elderly's baseline (the first interview) was compared to the distribution for the high school juniors and seniors, as shown in table 10-3. As expected, the high school students relied almost completely on validating the self-concept through examples from the present, whereas less than one-half of the respondents in all three elderly samples provide validating evidence from the present. In turn, the general past, rarely used for validation by the adolescents, was prominent among the elderly.

In studying the effects of environment on maintenance of self-stability, contrasts in type of self-validating evidence used among the three samples of elderly respondents revealed differences only in the use of distortion. Paired comparisons revealed that those awaiting entrance into institutions and those already institutionalized utilized significantly more distortion than did respondents in the community control sample.

The analyses thus indicated that (1) the elderly used the present for validation appreciably less than adolescents, who rarely used any other mechanism; (2) use of the generalized past for validation was ubiquitous among the elderly; (3) the specific past was used sparingly by all respondents; (4) wish was rarely used for validation; and (5) distortion was used

TABLE 10-3
Sample Comparisons of Self-Validating Evidence

| Samples | N | Type of Self-Validating Evidence (percentage)[a] | | | | |
		Present	Specific Past	General Past	Wish to Be	Distortion
Home for Life Study						
Study Sample						
Pre-Admission	20	45.9	5.4	36.9	1.4	9.3
Institutional Control						
Sample—Time 1	22	47.4	7.5	36.3	0.6	8.3
Community Control						
Sample—Time 1	16	46.1	5.0	46.8	0.3	1.9
Adolescent Sample	24	94.1	1.5	2.4	0.0	2.1

[a]Percentages may not total 100 due to rounding of numbers.

rarely by adolescents and elderly in the community sample, but was used for nearly one out of ten self-descriptive items by elderly in the waiting list and institutional samples.

The Effects of Distance from Death. The forty-four pairs of death-near and death-far respondents were compared on the five mechanisms of validating self-concept. Thirty-nine percent of the death-near group used examples from the present, compared with 45 percent of the death-far group (DN 39% versus DF 45%); 6 percent of the death-near group and 5 percent of the death-far group used the specific past (DN 6% versus DF 5%); the generalized past was used by 49 percent of the death-near group and 43 percent of the death-far (DN 49% versus DF 43%); wish was used by 1 percent of each group; and distortion by 5 percent of the death-near group and 7 percent of the death-far (DN 5% versus DF 7%). A matched-pair t-test of Time 1 scores using a z transformation indicated that the death-near group used less present evidence than the death-far group ($p < .10$) and more distortion ($p = .05$) to maintain a stable self-image. The effects of nearness to death thus appear similar to the effects of both age and situation: Those near to death, although managing to maintain a stable self-image, do so by relying on less adequate processes.

To summarize our findings to this point, although the content of the self-concept is remarkably stable, the validating mechanisms to support self-attributes are contingent on context and stress. The elderly utilize concrete examples based on present interaction as well as comments about the general past that reflect the enduring sense of self-continuity. Adolescents, in contrast, are able to provide examples from the present for all self-selected attributes. Although crises do not affect stability of self-image, among the elderly who are under stress processes of self-maintenance are affected.

It should be underscored, however, that *all* the processes people use to maintain a sense of self-identity are successful—self-consistency was maintained even among those who used distortion. In a later section of this chapter, we will turn our attention to the cost of utilizing less adequate self-maintenance mechanisms to the person's ability to adapt under stress. This issue is separate from the fact that more primitive mechanisms do serve their ultimate goal—the maintenance of self-identity. Before examining the consequences for adaptation, we will first explore the source of these mechanisms.

Sources of Validating Mechanisms. So far, our findings on validating processes suggests that these processes are situationally determined rather than representative of enduring characteristics of people. To pursue this further, we examined the variability in validating processes by making

251

use of the longitudinal data available on the elderly respondents. We compared elderly undergoing the life change of relocation to elderly in more stable environments—the community controls and the long-term institutionalized. We found that the Time 1 and Time 2 distributions of the type of validating evidence used were not different for the groups in stable and unstable environments. The comparisons of two distributions at two different times, however, masks the variability of individuals. To circumvent this, percentage changes from Time 1 to Time 2 for each category of self-validating evidence were computed for each respondent, and then the average change for each category computed. This method of determining variability revealed substantial fluctuations.

As shown in table 10–4, respondents in the stressed sample exhibited an average shift of almost 22 percent in the use of present examples from pre-admission to two months after admission. Comparable instability was found for the other mechanisms. One-way analysis of variance and paired comparisons among the three samples revealed one significant difference: that between the community respondents and the other two samples combined. To further explore validating mechanisms, a similar analysis was computed using changes in mechanisms in each of the eight octants comprising the self-sort task. All three samples again manifested high degrees of instability. Among those waiting to enter institutions, the average shift in mechanisms per octant was 6.75 percent; those living in the institutions, 6.04 percent; and for the community elderly, 3.56 percent. The community sample again showed significantly less variability ($p. < .05$) compared to the other two samples.

The findings of instability are easily understood for those undergoing institutionalization who have lost previous social resources necessary for

TABLE 10–4

Average Change Per Respondent in Self-Validating Evidence

		Type of Self-Validating Evidence (percentage)[a]			
Sample	N	Present	Specific Past	General Past	Distortion
Study Sample (compared to pre-admission)					
2 months post-admission	20	21.6	5.5	12.6	5.9
1 year post-admission	20	17.0	5.2	13.6	5.8
Control Sample (compared to 1 year earlier)					
Institutional	22	14.4	6.4	14.3	7.2
Community	16	12.3	3.1	12.5	2.6

[a]There was less than a 1 percent change in all samples in the wish-to-be category.

ongoing feedback. The instability of self-validation mechanisms among the long-term institutionalized elderly is not so readily apparent; perhaps such environments may lead to distancing in interpersonal attachment, which limits the availability of stable others to provide self-validating feedback.

To assess the plausability of this explanation, we turned to information provided by the Personal Resources Questionnaire. Respondents were asked to name the people they would turn to in ten hypothetical situations (see chapter 7 for details). Stability of person named across time was found only for the community sample. Neither those becoming institutionalized nor those already institutionalized had stable interpersonal resources.

Findings examined up to this point indicate that the elderly rely on a variety of mechanisms to validate and maintain a stable self-concept, in contrast to the almost exclusive use by younger people of current feedback. When current evidence from others appears not readily available, the elderly turn primarily toward the generalized past, which appears to serve equally well for maintenance of self-image. We found a high degree of variation in mechanisms used among all the samples of elderly studied; those becoming institutionalized and those already institutionalized differed from the community-dwelling elderly only by degree. These findings support the view that the mechanisms the elderly used to maintain self-identity are more contingent on the characteristics of their social world than they are on specific personal characteristics.

We are not suggesting that the aged—or for that matter younger people—systematically demand of themselves, moment to moment, specific evidence to affirm a sense of self. More likely, in times of reflection, an individual may contemplate various experiences of the day or of the immediate past and evaluate his or her behavior as conforming to or falling short of previously established expectations of self. It is likely that such "internal conversations" are generated by activities in a variety of ongoing roles. It is the paucity of such roles among the elderly and the consequent lack of opportunities for input that result in a lack of current evidence to maintain their self-image.

THE SELF AND ADAPTATION

What are the consequences for adaptation of the inability of many elderly people to find current sources for self-validation in their environment? As we have indicated, despite major upheavals in the elderly's lives, consistency of self-image is the rule. What differs among our respondents is how such self-consistency was maintained. One approach to assessing consistency was to generate a measure of the adequacy of the processes used by the elderly in maintaining the self-image and then to determine how adequacy, as well as fluctuations of these processes over time, are associated with adaptation. Adequacy was based upon a weighted score, which ranged from the most adequate response, specific examples in the present and past ($+1$), to the least adequate, distortion (-4). Sums were computed for each respondent and, because of the shape of the distribution, transformed into z scores. When those who remained intact after relocation were compared by one-way analysis of variance to those who showed marked decline or had died, the intact group was found to have a mean score of 0.42 and the nonintact group, -1.84 ($F=5.0$, $p < .05$). In contrast, when we examined the scores among the elderly in the nonstress group—those who remained in stable living conditions, either in the community or in an institution—the mean score was 3.70 for the intact group and -0.23 for the nonintact ($p=.10$). Although this difference did not reach a high level of significance, it does suggest that adequacy of validating evidence may play a role in long-term adaptation regardless of the stress condition. (See technical note 2.)

The variability in mechanisms was examined next to determine whether individuals who fluctuated more are more likely to suffer poorer adaptation than these whose variability was lower. Such variability was high for most, and, as was previously noted, although there was some systematic difference among the samples of the elderly in the degree of variability in mechanisms used, no evidence was found to suggest that such variability was associated, in any way, with subsequent outcome. Findings do suggest, however, that how individuals maintain a consistent self-image—the adequacy of the mechanism used—has consequences for adaptation to the stress of relocation. Although the predictive power of adequacy of maintaining the self-image is to some extent mitigated by more robust predictors (as more fully explained in technical note 2), it is clear that those who employ inadequate evidence to maintain a self-image are more likely to suffer maladaptive consequences of environmentally induced stress.

Case Illustration

MRS. A.: POST-INSTITUTIONALIZATION STABILITY AND CHANGE

Mrs. A. was first interviewed for the community sample before she began to think about entering a home for the aged. We continued to follow her after she made her application while she was on the waiting list, through admission and her first year of life in the institution. Although she was seriously affected by losses prior to admission and under a great deal of stress throughout the three years of study, she maintained a remarkable degree of self-consistency and self-integrity.

After Mrs. A.'s admission, no major behavioral, physical, or cognitive decrements were noted. Stable functioning, of course, did not preclude subtle psychological changes. We did detect, for example, in her response to the question what are the worst features of your life now? a more receptive attitude toward death: "Why don't He take me? I've lived long enough." There was a change in Mrs. A.'s emotional states. Although she maintained a high level of feelings of well-being (as is apparent from her scores on the ratings of life satisfaction), she also showed increases in anxiety and depression. Mrs. A. became less hopeful and shifted toward a more negative appraisal of the world. Apparently, her attitude toward the world after admission reflected a disparagement of institutional life. The clearest example of the general change appeared in the shift from strong disagreement to strong agreement with the statement "These days a person doesn't really know who he can count on."

Mrs. A.'s response to the time dimension question also revealed this shift toward hopelessness. To the inquiry "In general, do you find yourself thinking about the past or the future?" she responded before admission: "I think about the past. If I think of the past I know what I am thinking about. But who can tell about the future? No one can!" After admission, she said, "If people knew what the future might bring, many people might commit suicide." Mrs. A.'s message might be interpreted as, "If I had only known what it really would be like to live in a home for the aged, I would have considered suicide"; or possibly, "If I were to change, to deteriorate as other old people do before my eyes, it would be better for me to die."

A change in preoccupation with the body was reflected in the introduction of themes related to bodily function in Mrs. A.'s responses to the sentence completion test. Before admission, among her responses to the thirty-two stems, Mrs. A. made three unsolicited allusions to bodily functions, whereas after admission she made six unsolicited allusions to bodily functions. Before admission these were

> I can't understand what makes me ... "weak."
> To me death is ... "a big relief to people who are suffering or have incurable sickness. It's a blessing to them."
> My only trouble is ... "my eyes at the present."

255

After admission

> I can't understand what makes . . . "me be so weak."
>
> My only trouble is . . . "that I'm not strong enough to do the things as I would like to."
>
> I wish I . . . "would be a little stronger than I am, so I could do something."
>
> I would like to be . . . "well, of course—which I never will, but I would like to."
>
> If only . . . "I would be well. I would like to do all I could to help others."
>
> The thing I like about myself . . . [she shook her head] "What can I say about myself? I don't know. Only thing I like about myself is I thank God he didn't paralyze my brain."

Before relocation, Mrs. A. indicated that she would welcome death if it would avert physical pain and suffering. In the second interview, however, after she was in the home but with no evidence of deterioration in physical status, she indicated that she had no qualifications regarding the benefits of death. In response to the sentence stem, "To me death is . . ." Mrs. A.'s addition at first was "a big relief"; after admission, it was "the best thing that can happen to anybody."

It may be that her experience among the home's sick inmates led Mrs. A. to believe that her only possible future was to become progressively more deteriorated. If so, she had indeed become incurable at that point. To paraphrase Ben Franklin, before admission she was long-lived, but afterward she was irreversibly and incurably old. Mrs. A.'s concerns with death and personal vulnerability were associated with actually entering and living in the institution. The same theme was echoed in her report of her earliest memory—for the first time, after relocation the same response was elaborated to include visions of epidemics and death. The series of Mrs. A.'s early memories were presented in chapter 4.

To what extent was Mrs. A. able to maintain a stable self-image when confronted with such feelings after institutionalization? We compared the statements she selected on the self-sort task as being like her when she was living in the community and part of our community sample to those she selected three years later after entering and living in the institution. When living in the community Mrs. A. selected twenty-six statements as self-descriptive (two above average); two months after admission to the home, she selected thirty-two statements. Of the twenty-six initially chosen statements, twenty-three (or 88 percent) were again selected three years later. Because fifteen of the statements she initially selected were among those selected by 75 percent or more of the respondents, eleven of the twenty-six statements selected were considered idiosyncratic statements. Of these, eight (or 73 percent) were selected again three years later. Mrs. A.'s maintenance of her self-concept is not only indicated by the percentage of all items and idiosyncratic statements chosen again three years later, but by the average shift in octants, which was 2.9 percent.

The items she selected, as well as those not selected, permit Mrs. A. to tell us who she is. The fifteen social desirability items chosen both times included the following:

People think well of me.
I am a self-respecting person.
I am frank and honest with people.
When necessary I can complain about things that bother me.
I am grateful for what other people do for me.
I am a friendly person.
I am an affectionate and understanding person.

Idiosyncratic items chosen both times reflect the intensity of Mrs. A.'s wish to be engaged and close to others, but not at the expense of her own personal worth. Items such as "I want everyone to like me" and "I love everyone" were selected along with "I can reproach people when necessary" and "I can argue back when I am right about something." Items rejected at both times also reveal the nature of Mrs. A.'s stable affiliative self-image. Not selected at either time were items such as: "It is hard for me to trust anyone," "I can be a cold and unfeeling person," "I am critical of other people," and "I frequently get angry with people." The combination of items selected and rejected at both times reveals a stable, complex, and fine-grained self-image that persisted over three years of adversity, including entering and living in an institution.

Contrasting with the stability in her selection of self-descriptive statements is the variability in the processes Mrs. A. used to maintain the self-image. Mrs. A. decreased the percentage of her examples in the present from 62 to 41 percent and correspondingly increased the percentage of validating comments classified as being from the general past from 31 to 50 percent. Also, whereas initially 7 percent of her examples were from the specific past, later none were; and although she had used no distortion initially, 9 percent of her responses were so classified subsequent to relocation.

Four self-concept items chosen by Mrs. A. at both points in time illustrate variability in the mechanism used for validation.

1. "I believe I am an important person." Initially the evidence was based on interaction: "I'm important to my family and friends. You should have seen how many New Years Cards I got." Three years later the evidence for the same stem was based on the general past: "I think I'm important to my family. I've always done the best I could for my family and they appreciate it."

2. "I can reproach other people when necessary." Initially the evidence was from the general past: "I always explain to them what I think is the best to be done. I don't really scold. I just give my opinion when they want it." Later the evidence was in the present: "If they don't do the right thing, surely, I tell them. Like when somebody said I'm not dressed right, I told them, It's my own business."

3. "I am touchy and easily hurt by others." Initially the evidence was from the specific past: "If people step on my toes they hurt my feelings. My brother-in-law opened a store and didn't consult me first. I felt hurt for a long time." Later the evidence was based on a distortion: "Sure I will. I wouldn't let anybody step on me! I have some kind of feelings! If somebody would say I said something and I didn't, I surely would defend myself."

4. "I can be obedient when necessary." Initially the evidence was from the present: "My son told me I wasn't well enough to come to his home for dinner tonight. I feel bad but I'm not going." Later the evidence was from the general past: "I do. Well, if someone would tell me what is the proper thing to do, I obey."

Mrs. A. showed the high stability in self-esteem from pre- to post-institutionalization. Initially her self-esteem score was 24. Later after entering and living in the home, it was 22. (The mean score for the entire Home for Life sample was 19.)

Despite marked changes in her inner life, the content of Mrs. A.'s self-image remained remarkably stable. Evidence used to support the self-image suggests the strain inherent in her effort for self-stability. Examples in the present dropped from 62 to 41 percent, whereas statements from the general past increased from 31 to 50 percent. Without reinforcement from the current interpersonal environment, Mrs. A. relied upon her sense of an enduring self-concept. For the first time, distortions appeared. Paralleling the stability of self indicated by the self-sort measures, the interviewer observed that Mrs. A. remained the same and adapted successfully. She displayed no manifest indications of an adverse reaction to becoming institutionalized. Indeed, her cognitive functioning and sensitivity to her environment improved from pre-admission while on the waiting list and her sense of well-being remained remarkably high. At the manifest behavioral level, all indications showed functioning similar to pre-stress levels or even improved.

258

Summary and Implications

This chapter set out to examine a core dilemma confronting the elderly—how to maintain a coherent, consistent sense of self-identity. Our investigation considered respondents undergoing events that threatened such consistency: radical life space changes involving loss of people and places and new demands for adaptation as well as approaching death and, possibly, awareness of it. We expected that such conditions would limit the ability of the aged to maintain a coherent and consistent self-image. We found, on the contrary, that they showed a remarkable stability of self-image when confronting radical life changes or closeness to death—a stability comparable to that maintained by elderly people who are not undergoing such upheavals. The consistency of the self-image despite such crises takes on all the more significance when it is contrasted to fluctuations and directional changes in behavioral, social, and cognitive measures of "inner psychological life" that result from relocation and nearness to death.

Only when we examined the processes used to maintain the consistency of the self-image did we begin to see the impact of these crises on self-concept. Unlike younger people who maintained a sense of self-identity by relying on current interaction, the elderly respondents require a variety of additional mechanisms for maintaining self-continuity. Primary among these were reference to specific past interactions and, even more often, to the generalized past—the sense of conviction that "I am who I always have been." When both the present and the past fail as sources of self-identity, the elderly are willing to forgo the reality principle, and use evidence based on wish and distortion in order to maintain self-consistency. The lack of an appreciable linkage between the processes used to maintain self-consistency and the high level of self-consistency suggests that the driving force is the maintenance of the sense of self-sameness through time, no matter what the cost.

The cost, however, may be too high. Those who turn to less adequate evidence in order to maintain the sense of identity are the very people whose ability to weather severe stress appears limited. Less adequate mechanisms for maintaining the self-image—defined as departing from the use of evidence from the present or the specific past to rely on the generalized past (conviction), wish, and distortion—predicts maladaptive reactions to radical changes in life space. Furthermore, those who are struggling with the approach of their own death also appear to be less able to adequately handle the maintenance of self-consistency—not by lessening their self-consistency, but by shifting to the use of processes for such maintenance that are less adequate.

Further understanding of the issue of how the elderly maintain a coherent and consistent self-image can be found in the apparent search for evidence to maintain a consistent self, which at times seems marked by desperation. We noted a marked increase among the elderly who were under stress in fluctuations over time in the type of processes used to maintain the self-image. Thus, despite the fact that self-image remains remarkably stable under conditions of stress, the processes used to maintain such consistency are highly variable, suggesting perhaps just how precarious the balance of maintaining self-identity is for some elderly people.

If, as we believe, a central (if not the crucial) issue for the very old is the threat posed to the sense of self-identity by both inner processes and external circumstances, what do the findings in this chapter imply about the psychology of the elderly? We believe our findings represent, above all, an eloquent testimony to the coping ability of the elderly, echoing similar observations made in the chapter describing management of threat and loss. We reported that despite the considerable loss involved in relocation, which often produced pain, maladaptive outcomes were circumvented by those who had developed coping strategies to address the losses. Indeed, many of the elderly people we studied were able to develop such strategies. Only the minority of elderly respondents who did not develop adequate coping strategies were likely to suffer serious long-term failures in adaptation.

A parallel observation can be made about the self. When faced with circumstances that threaten the death and dissolution of the self, most of the elderly people we studied developed ways of maintaining self-identity using processes that were not costly to their personal survival. Among those for whom such processes apparently do not function well and who turn to other, less adequate self-maintenance processes, subsequent adaptation is less certain. Approaching death and severe stress both pose real threats to the dissolution of self, a threat that is addressed by all—most with adequate, some with inadequate, processes. Paralleling the observations made on threat and loss, we found that the use of more primitive mechanisms to maintain consistency entail increased risk with regard to survival.

Technical Notes

1. An overall adequacy score was computed by weighting the five categories. Specific examples, whether in the present or past, were rated +1; statements of a general past, 0; statements of a "wish to be," −2; and examples of distortion, −4. Z-scores were calculated for the percentages of responses in each of the five categories. To develop a score for each individual, z-scores for each category were multiplied by the appropriate weight and the five weighted z-scores summed.

2. Similar analyses were computed using age, sex, and living arrangements as covariates. For the stress group, significance remained at the p=.05 level; for the nonstress condition, significance was p=.11. To determine the relative robustness of our measure of self-concept maintenance, we contrasted, in a series of step-wise regression equations, the best predictors of outcome from the various psychological realms we studied— cognition, health, hope, personality, and coping with loss and threat, as well as mechanisms for maintenance of self-consistency. Each of our predictors, excluding only cognition and health, were reduced when the other predictors were taken into account. In the regression equation, when self-consistency maintenance was entered as the first variable, it was significant at p=.04. However, the probability level was reduced by hope, to .13 when self-consistency was entered at step two; to .18 when it was entered as the third step after health and hope; to .37 when it was entered as the fourth step after cognition, health, and hope; to .40 when it was entered as the fifth step after personality was also placed in the equation; and to .47 after all parameters were entered in, with self-consistency maintenance as the last step. Clearly this analysis suggests that although self-consistency maintenance is a powerful predictor, in a comparative predictive framework both cognitive functioning and health are much more robust predictors. Furthermore, self-consistency maintenance is partially dependent on adequate cognitive functioning.

11

The Function of Reminiscence

NOVELISTS and purveyors of folk wisdom, as well as social scientists, have emphasized the special role of the personal past in the psychology of the aged. Throughout the popular and scientific literature, the elderly have inevitably been described as more interested in or even living in their past to resolve enduring psychological dilemmas. If we are to understand the unique psychology of the elderly and the link of their unique characteristics to adaptation, we can scarcely ignore this essential psychological realm. We saw in the previous chapter that the past served as a frequent and successful mechanism for maintaining a consistent self-image in the face of major referent group changes as well as when confronting debilitating stress. Now we shall explore the interrelated issues of how the elderly address their personal past and how these "internal conversations" contribute to successful coping both with losses and adaptive demands imposed by environmental change, and with nearness to death.

The role of the personal past in the psychology of the elderly can be conceptualized in a variety of ways. The observation that as people age they invest more of their current attention and interest in reminiscence could, at the simplest level, be a product of their barren present and limited future. The past may become the preferred modality, not because of any special psychological dynamic, but because both the present and the future offer little that is positive and attractive. The all too common losses of significant others, the marked changes in relevant reference groups critical to maintaining and enhancing the self, the failures of the body, and the obliteration of important social roles are all circumstances that may lead people to emphasize the past for comfort and gratification or to use the past to gain a sense of control when the current world ceases to afford opportunities for mastery. In reaction to the decreasing control they can exercise over their lives, when confronted with environmental instability, the elderly may develop a heightened interest and involvement in their past as a way of reestablishing control. If they cannot experience and demonstrate mastery by focusing on the future—which is highly indeterminate and fraught with anxiety—or on the present—which may only provide a reality that is bleak and barren—their past may still offer solace: It is still all theirs.

Emphasis on the past may, in addition, serve as a much needed source of social exchange. The major modality of social discourse for many elderly people is the recounting of their past. Tales about the self and past experience become the medium for social exchange. When they relate to younger people, recollections of bygone times can provide a special kind of interchange, because the elderly possess experiences in historical time that are not directly available to their juniors. Thus, the heightened involvement in the personal past may reflect the elderly's reaction to realistic appraisals of their life, in which the remembered past becomes a powerful and meaningful source of gratification, control, and social exchange.

This view of the past as an available resource to the elderly contrasts with the perspective held by some social scientists and novelists who posit reminiscing as a "required" developmental task of the last decade or two of life. One's life story, its pains and pleasures, its residual conflicts, its sense of continuity and discontinuity are seen as representing tasks to be addressed, reworked, realigned, and redirected. Some portions of the past must be let go, other aspects demand to be recherished. Remembrance is the last mountain to be climbed, the last issue requiring psychological effort. For Erikson (1959), the task is to validate existence by seeing the past as meaningful. He has suggested that

> the central dilemma for the aged is achieving integrity, a task that involves reconciliation to the personal past. Through the acceptance of one's one and only life cycle and the people who have become significant to it as something that had to be and that, by necessity, permitted of no substitutions. It thus

means a new and different love for one's parents, free of the wish that they should have been different, and an acceptance of the fact that one's life is one's own responsibility.... [p. 98]

Tolstoy (1863) in *Death of Ivan Ilych* described Ivan Ilych as having a life of comfort and superficiality until a protracted illness forced him to meditate. He then reviewed his life, accepted it as having been globally superficial, and thereby accepted death, freeing himself from the tortures he had been experiencing.

Butler (1963) has postulated an inevitable process of life review among the elderly in response to the nearness of death. This naturally occurring and universal mental process is characterized by the progressive return to consciousness of past experiences and particularly the resurgence of unresolved conflict. Simultaneously with the return to consciousness, these reviewed experiences and conflicts can be surveyed and reintegrated.

To Erikson, Tolstoy, and Butler, then, reminiscence is not simply a resource. There is, rather, an inevitability to reminiscing when confronting the termination of life as well as the possibility of gaining a unique human experience if conflicts can be resolved and one's life reviewed successfully.

Both of these views of past memories as resources or as a distinct kind of human experience differ from yet another perspective, which focuses more on the use of the past to be the same person one has always been. This third perspective was introduced in the previous chapter. Despite radical alterations in their lives, the elderly are able to maintain stable, persistent, and unique self-images by use of the past. The past becomes a way to define oneself in the present and not a way of resolving conflicts. The purpose of the selective reorganization and reconstruction of the past is not so much to accept one's life but rather to use the content of memories to support and reinforce the current "me." Thus, in reporting the past, the person tells both self and others a myth—a story intended to be believed in order to justify a life. Stated another way, the elderly person portrays him- or herself as the central figure or hero in a drama that is worth telling or worth having lived for. This "mythic hypothesis" postulates that the elderly's relationship to the past is one of reorganization to reaffirm the current self and not acceptance of one's life as inevitable to achieve resolution of conflicts and inconsistencies.

This chapter examines the elderly's use of the past from each of these three perspectives. We will explore the consequences of reminscence for a developmental model of personality and its implications for adaptation.

Methods

Our explorations of reminiscence use data gathered in face-to-face interviews of approximately three hours' duration with respondents in the Home for Life study. Three questionnaires were used:

1. The life history interview provided the respondents an opportunity to talk about such issues as what life was like for them as a child, what their parents were like, and what hardships they underwent. Open-ended queries were used to gather data about childhood, adolescence, and adulthood. Responses were rich in detail and vividly portrayed the lives of respondents.
2. The Evaluation of Life Questionnaire required the respondents to assume an evaluative perspective in examining their lives—whether they would want to live it over or change it, their major disappointments, the happiest events in their lives, and so forth. In contrast to the life history interview, which was administered first and generated detailed information, the Evaluation of Life Questionnaire gave respondents an opportunity to summarize and place their lives in perspective.
3. The third kind of data on reminiscence were responses to the On Memory Questionnaire, which required respondents to provide direct answers to such questions as, for example: "How important are your memories to you?"; to complete the stem "Thinking about the past makes me feel . . ."; and to indicate agreement or disagreement with the statements: "My memories are like spilled milk. One should forget and go on" and "My memories are like money in a bank for a rainy day."

Measures based on these data were developed in three areas related to the content and function of reminiscence: importance of the past, life review, and the past as myth or drama.

IMPORTANCE OF THE PAST

The first area focused on evidence that indicated the importance attached to the past. Two measures were developed: (1) a count of the number of words used to reconstruct the past in response to the open-ended queries in the life history interview, as a reflection of time devoted to reminiscent activity; and (2) a rating of the degree of affective involvement in such activity.

LIFE REVIEW

The second area was the life review, for which two kinds of measures were developed: reconciliation and life review style.

Reconciliation. The first set of measures indexed degree of reconciliation. Assessments were made of signs of reworking and reorganizing memories which indicated that life review work was accomplished. Data for these assessments were responses to the life history interview. Seven scales were developed to assess reconciliation, based on a rating of the entire life history. Each of the seven scales were rated on five points, ranging from low to high. (See technical note 1.) Following is a list of the scales with some highly simplified illustrations and excerpts to provide a sense of the scale points.

Reconciliation

1. *Significant figures seen positively.*

    Low: "Constant strain to please my mother, which was impossible. She didn't want us. She wanted a place to live . . . then off she went with another admirer."

    Moderate: "My father (I was told) was very kind and gentle. And I think my mother must have been the same until he died. . . . But I don't remember any warmth or closeness. We all admired her tremendously, but . . . no spontaneous warmth or closeness."

    High: "My father was a quiet, shy, wise man, large and tall and strong. I never disobeyed or deceived him. My mother was a lovely person in every way."

2. *Avoidance of negative (degree to which the respondent dwells upon positive aspects of the past).*

    Low (in answer to a question about how her parents got along): "Got along? What's that? My mother took such guff from that no-good bum that she never had time to care for us. He never even called us by name—it was 'come here, you' or worse."

    Moderate: "I resented deeply the fact that I did not have a mother and father as my schoolmates did, and suffered from the stigma of a broken marriage and a wayward mother. There were many hurts from unthinking children. . . . I had my pleasures, too, however, and loved and respected my grandparents sincerely, realizing even then how much I owed them for their care. To sum it up, I would say my childhood was pleasant with the necessities of life in abundance but few luxuries. Many happy times, but many lonely, resentful times also."

    High (respondent's earliest memory had to do with her impressions of Switzerland, how beautiful it was, how nice and how honest the people were): "The people in Switzerland were so wonderful. I loved it so."

3. *Absence of conflict.*

    A low score reflects major conflicts in which the respondent indicates predominantly unresolved problems: "With my parents there was arguing and a constant strain to please my mother, which was impossible. I was so happy to have her back and to be like other kids, that I had begged my father to try again. He didn't want to but took her back and established another house for her. I should not have begged him. She didn't want us. . . ."

Absence of conflict (if there is some indication of minor conflict but no directly stated conflict; or if there is a minor degree of conflict, rate fairly high on absence of conflict): "I remember a bad thunderstorm (I was about 3½) and climbing into bed with my parents. Then everything was all right. I haven't been afraid of thunder since. I remember learning to ride a two-wheel bicycle at about 4½ and was pleased I could do what my older sisters could do. I guess I've always been game to try things sooner than most."

4. *Lack of resentment.*

A low score represents high resentment: "Nobody will come to my funeral—everyone's too busy and wishes I would hurry up and die."

Moderate: "My father was very kind and gentle. And I think my mother must have been the same way until he died and she had to go to work. All my life everyone marveled at how well she managed and how cheerful she always was. But I don't remember any warmth or closeness. Perhaps she couldn't afford the expenditures of that energy."

Low resentment: "I am sure I was punished. My parents were the kind who would have believed in punishment, but only when deserved. I can't really remember any specific instances."

5. *Major values fulfilled in life.*

Low (respondent feels that he or she did not accomplish what he or she wished for in life): "Nothing ever turned out for me. I never had nothing."

Moderate (feels moderate degree of satisfaction with what he or she achieved in life; or, one kind of value was fulfilled, another not): "I wish I could have gotten married, but I did have lots of fun, traveling, seeing lots of things." "I had a small business, it wasn't big, but I did fairly well with that, we never suffered."

High (completely satisfied with life, in relation to values): "I have had a most blessed life. My children and my family all were wonderful. I have been most blessed."

6. *Ownership of life (the extent to which the respondent feels responsibility for what happened to him or her).*

Low: "There's nothing much worth remembering. I was married twice—neither of them was worth much. I divorced my first husband when I was forty—already an old woman from working so much and having so little. I'll tell you I never had no beauty parlors and pretty dresses when I was young like the women nowadays—had to chop wood to cook on and carry the water."

High (describes step-daughter's refusal to get married): "This other boy kept calling. She was never home, so I told him how much she wanted to see him and how much she cared for him. I even wrote him letters on her behalf. . . . So I married her to this boy who was Jewish [she is triumphant]. Well, what do you expect me to do? I couldn't have her living with us, could I? So I married her off."

7. *Acceptance of negative life events.*

Low (negative life events are mentioned but are not accepted; this may be evidenced by negative evaluation): "My whole life was rotten, never had anything decent to wear" (or by overwhelming or inappropriate affect): "Every time I think of my mother's death I cry and cry." "It makes me so angry that my folks never gave me enough love" (or by other evidence of resentment or bitterness in the way events are described).

High (if negative life events are mentioned with evidence of appropriate reaction, but no current strong feelings): "When my mother died, we all had a difficult time for many months." (This score implies that the negative affect has been neutralized or changed in some way.)

Evidence that an individual has accomplished a successful life review would be reflected in high scores on these seven indices: that significant figures in the past are, by and large, seen in positive, realistic terms; that conflicts do not manifestly intrude upon current life to the point of disruption; that the person has some sense of having fulfilled values and of owning his or her own life; and has reached at least a modest level of acceptance of the negative aspects of his or her life. In other words, our measure reflects not the presence of a process but rather the degree to which the individual shows that he or she has addressed specified tasks, which collectively are the end product of a life review. These seven measures cannot distinguish between those who are currently involved in the life review process and those who have never begun it.

Assessment of Styles. The second measure of life review consisted of an assessment of the style used in relating to the personal past: whether the respondent is primarily in flight from or avoiding his or her personal past; whether the respondent is currently involved in the life review process as reflected in evidence that suggests a reworking of past conflicts; or whether the individual has reached a life review resolution. To make the judgment of which of these three styles most captures a respondent's perspective on the past, and his or her stage in the process of life review, only data from the Life Evaluation Questionnaire was used. Our case ratings indicated that 51 percent of the elderly we studied were categorized as avoiding the past, 15 percent were involved in a life review process, and 34 percent showed evidence of resolution. Reliability based on the three categories was 100 percent. The following three case vignettes provide a detailed description of these three styles.

FLIGHT FROM THE PAST: "I LIVED FROM DAY TO DAY." As noted, more than half of the respondents displayed this pattern of reminiscence. A majority of those engaged in a flight from the past were in their sixties and seventies, were low in introspection, experienced difficulty in extending themselves into the future, and often used denial to fend off future

268

threatening events. They also evaluated their lives neutrally, with flattened affect.

Mr. S. was a sixty-nine-year-old bachelor who was born in Russia and emigrated to the United States when he was fourteen. He had lived with his unmarried brother and widowed sister in a small apartment for about thirty years. Working in a modest capacity as a shoe salesman for most of his adult life, he suffered a stroke of mild to moderate severity three months before being interviewed. A partial paralysis of his right side forced him to give up his job and apply for admission to a home for the aged.

Mr. S. was a portly man, with a rather slow, shuffling gait, who laughed a good deal, had twinkling eyes and a general "zest for life." Throughout his life, Mr. S. invested most of his time and energy in making a living not only for himself, but also for his brother and sister, whom he has partially subsidized for many years. Since his stroke the overriding concern of his daily existence has been the preservation of his health. When asked to describe himself he replied: "I'm just a broken down man—broken in health." Asked what he looked like, he continued: "Look at my face. I look healthy. A lot of things that don't show on my face." And when questioned about his personality, he said, "It's pretty hard. Just making the best of it."

Despite this somewhat depressed self-description, test data indicated that Mr. S. was somewhat less anxious and exhibited higher life satisfaction than the typical respondent waiting admission to the home. He was rated as possessing good mental health and displayed no signs of cognitive impairment. Clinical assessments of personality attributes characterized Mr. S. as a rather passive man with few activities and involvements, who tended to blame others for his own shortcomings, and employed aggressive techniques to gratify his desires. He was also seen as having a high status drive but experiencing difficulty in understanding or empathizing with the feelings of others.

Mr. S. can be viewed as a rather well-defended, nonpathological older person who tended to live his life pragmatically from day to day, focusing primarily on external realities. Conversely, his inner life appeared to be fairly constricted.

This relative impoverishment of inner life is particularly well-illustrated in the nonintrospective responses of Mr. S. to the affect questionnaire. He was assigned an introspection score of 12 for his description of all eight affects, placing him in the bottom quartile. While Mr. S. therefore displayed a general unwillingness to reflect upon his feelings, this tendency is most pronounced in regard to negative affects. When asked if he ever feels lonely, Mr. S. responded: "Nope—thank God that's something I've never felt." When the interviewer questioned this—"You never felt lonely?"—Mr. S. maintained, "That's right ma'am." The interviewer pursued: "When you were younger you were never lonely?" Mr. S. stated: "No ma'am I've always occupied myself by doing something."

Flight from the past is manifested clearly in the responses of Mr. S. to the Evaluation of Life Questionnaire. Mr. S. evaluated his life fairly positively, but with bland affect, merely listing events or offering generalities: "I had a nice life—I enjoyed it." He did admit that he "might have gotten married" were he to live his life over again. He consistently avoided reflecting on any negative experiences or unresolved conflicts from the past:

Interviewer:
> What have been the main disappointments in your life?

Mr. S.:
> Well, my sister got sick and she lost her son. All that was a disappointment.

Interviewer:
> Any other?

Mr. S.:
> No.

Interviewer:
> Any other bad things happen during your life?

Mr. S.:
> Sure, some, but it was a good life.

Interviewer:
> What were other bad things that happened?

Mr. S.:
> No use talking about them. They're over with. As long as we had food we were happy.

Interviewer:
> What was the hardest thing you had to face in your life?

Mr. S.:
> (shaking head) Life was okay.

This poor articulation of the past was also evident when Mr. S. was asked to compare himself in the present to the way he was at age forty. The only difference he could think of was a decline in health.

The extensive life history that Mr. S. provided further illustrated his constricted inner life. Despite the fact that he spent his early years in great poverty, struggled to earn a living during his first years in this country, and sustained the sudden deaths of his mother and brother-in-law, Mr. S. recited the narrative of his life with minimal affective involvement. Negative events were frequently denied or glossed over. For example, Mr. S. could think of no flaw exhibited by his father or mother. Perhaps the key admission made by Mr. S. was that even though he seriously dated a few girls, he never got married because "the family ran into hard luck—they always needed my help." Mr. S. characteristically ignored his inner feelings, defining himself primarily in terms of his instrumental role as a worker and his external responsibility as a family member.

Consequently, although Mr. S. was clearly an older person who was engaged in avoiding the past, this appeared to be the end result of a longstanding characterological tendency to not engage in introspection. This pattern of reminiscence provides little evidence that an active life review process will eventually occur. Rather, older people such as Mr. S. seem unpracticed in dealing with or conceptualizing their own emotional responses. They continue to avoid looking inward despite the shrinkage of social and work roles that accompanies old age. Mr. S. and other respondents like him do not generally exhibit extreme despair, disgust, or massive denial of death, however. Although they do not display any complex articulation of the future and do manifest some denial, they still often allude to death spontaneously as a genuine, albeit impersonal, contingency.

Mr. S. cannot be viewed as very poorly adapted. At the present time he lives as he always has, without looking inward. It is quite possible that if he survives for twenty more years he will still evaluate his life in the following manner:

Interviewer:
 How do you think you've made out in life?
Mr. S.:
 I done all right.
Interviewer:
 Compared to what you hoped when you started?
Mr. S.:
 I never thought none about it.
Interviewer:
 What do you think now about how you made out in life?
Mr. S.:
 No, I lived from day to day.

REWORKING OF CONFLICT: "YOU HAVE THE EXPERIENCES, YOU FIX THE MISTAKES." Only 15 percent of our respondents displayed this active pattern of reminiscence. They exhibited high levels of emotional reactivity and anxiety, tended to be rated low on life satisfaction, and often evaluated their lives quite negatively, but with a great deal of affect. Theoretically, the turmoil described can be seen as adaptive, designed to maintain identity and integrity in the face of impending death. During such a period, much previously unconscious material may suddenly be thrust into awareness. According to Butler (1963) it is through the life review process that long-standing unresolved conflicts are focused on, dealt with, and ultimately resolved.

Mrs. K. was a seventy-year-old widow with no children who lived alone in a small efficiency flat. She was born in Russia, married at age twenty-one, and emigrated to America three years later. For most of their lives together, Mrs. K. and her husband ran a small grocery store and lived in cramped quarters in the back room. Four years prior to being interviewed, Mrs. K.'s husband died after a long illness. The increasing loneliness of living alone and gradually failing eyesight ultimately led her to apply for admission to a home for the aged.

Mrs. K. was a short, stocky, gray-haired lady who was neatly groomed and moved with a slow, shuffling gait. She had a few minor heart attacks about ten years before, and "taking it easy" is a constant source of concern for her now. She is an extremely agitated person, with hands always in constant motion, and frequently becomes tearful with little provocation. She overwhelms others by pouring forth past experiences and events in a stream-of-consciousness fashion.

When asked to describe herself in the present Mrs. K. offers the following characterization:

Mrs. K.:
I am an average woman. I wasn't bad looking. I wouldn't win a beauty contest. I'm not pushing to people—that's why I'm lonesome.
Interviewer:
Is there anything else you'd like to say about yourself?
Mrs. K.:
I'm not a bad person—was in business my whole life. The wholesalers was taking my opinion. I'm an average person. I wasn't very bright and I wasn't very dumb. Is that right?
Interviewer:
Describe yourself now?
Mrs. K.:
I'm too old.
Interviewer:
How do you look?
Mrs. K.:
I'm not so tall—five feet two inches, you think that's right?
Interviewer:

Is there any more you would like to tell me?

Mrs. K.:

I'm average—not so good looking, not so ugly. My hair is now gray. It was brown. My hair was brown. I had long hair. I wore it in braids around.

Interviewer:

Anything else?

Mrs. K.:

I don't know. (*Gets very nervous.*)

Interviewer:

You wear glasses, don't you?

Mrs. K.:

Now I wear glasses.

Interviewer:

What things are important to you now?

Mrs. K.:

Now is not important. (*Cries.*) I am depressed. I am lonesome. I am pushing time to die is all.

This description, despite its rambling, associative quality, is striking in terms of the number of spontaneously introduced comparisons of the present with the past. It seems clear that Mrs. K. had thought about the past frequently and was well-practiced at making this sort of comparison between herself now and earlier. Her description of herself in the present as "depressed" and "lonesome" seems to be a conclusion arrived at after an emotionally charged immersion in the past.

Test data indicated that Mrs. K. possessed a fairly high level of anxiety, was rated below average on mental health, and had extremely low life satisfaction. Clinical judgments of personality attributes suggested that Mrs. K. was an assertive woman who was intensely involved with both external events and internal experience. She was also seen as a rather dominant person who was somewhat distrustful of others. However, she possessed a fairly well-developed capacity to understand and empathize with complex emotions in other people; perhaps her most characteristic personality trait was her frequent refusal to blame others for her own mistakes and misfortunes, turning aggression against herself instead with resultant self-castigation and guilt.

The test data also indicated that Mrs. K. displayed extensive articulation of both the past through memory and the future through expectation. This was true despite the fact that she exhibited slightly more signs of cognitive impairment than average.

This intrapsychic fluidity was perhaps most clearly evidenced in Mrs. K.'s responses to the affect questionnaire. She was assigned a total introspection score of 29 for the eight affects, placing her in the top quartile.

She supplied a particularly introspective and self-revealing response to the question, "Have you ever felt lonely?"

Mrs. K.:
I am all the time.
Interviewer:
Can you describe what it is like to feel lonely?
Mrs. K.:
How can I describe it. You are miserable, sitting by yourself. You can't do nothing. You start to think about your past, your future.
Interviewer:
Does this happen very often?
Mrs. K.:
Plenty often—to be alone is miserable. That's why I decided to go to the home. I'll be with people.
Interviewer:
How do you get over this feeling?
Mrs. K.:
When you are going out, you are talking, you are talking out of your misery.
Interviewer:
Is that what you do?
Mrs. K.:
How can I go out? Where can I go? Who can I talk to? If people are coming in, it's all right, too.
Interviewer:
Do they?
Mrs. K.:
Sometimes.
Interviewer:
Does your daughter come and keep you from being lonely?
Mrs. K.:
She comes sometimes.
Interviewer:
Do you always try and find someone to talk to?
Mrs. K.:
Sometimes I'm just sitting and thinking—mixing things up. Sometimes you want to go back through your life, figure the mistakes you have made.
Interviewer:
How long does this feeling last?
Mrs. K.:
If I'm not going somewhere, if I'm not doing something, it lasts a long time.
Interviewer:
All day?
Mrs. K.:
Sometimes, I try to go away sometime. Sometimes I want to think it over.
Interviewer:

What usually brings it on?
Mrs. K.:
    (*shrug*) It comes.

This moving and painful fragment provides a powerful description of the extreme inner turmoil evoked by Mrs. K.'s reminiscence. She also displays a marked willingness and strong ability to reflect effectively upon positive feelings.

The most dramatic illustration of Mrs. K.'s actual life review activity is to be found in her responses to the Evaluation of Life Questionnaire. Throughout the entire interview, Mrs. K. alluded to two major unresolved conflicts that plagued her. First, because of a gynecological operation when she was fifteen, she was unable to bear children, but did not tell her husband of this until two years after they were married. Second, she stopped sending money to her relatives in Europe, and shortly afterward many of them were killed in the Nazi holocaust. These unresolved conflicts burst into words with great intensity when the interviewer asked Mrs. K., "If everything were the same would you like to live your life over again?"

> I would make a little changes. I went into the business, I was not bright. I should look more. We did not have the choice. Right away we should support someone. I would be more supported if I had my family here. I would try and persuade them more. Then was different. They did not know. Only workers came to the U.S. Now they should know they need professional people. I start to beg my sister-in-law to let one of her twin boys come here with me. She has two. I have none. I support him heavily, but she will not let him come. If I didn't have that life, I could adopt children. I used to live on the west side in back of the store. I went places. They said I could not adopt children because it was not so good neighborhood. They say I do not have a proper home in the back of the store. I told them there was a grocery store across the street. They raised three children in back of the store. But by us was only rules and regulations. For children I am crazy. You think I don't want children? [Very agitated.] I was a good wife to my husband. I did my duty to him. I had an operation when I was fifteen and they say I cannot have children. And then when we got the business we lived in the store. We were afraid to get an apartment because already we had to send money home. We were afraid if we got an apartment we should not be able to pay the rent.

This outburst, coming as it did during the Evaluation of Life Questionnaire, which was preceded in the interview schedule by the extensive life history, is probably a summation of key themes that Mrs. K. had been focusing in her reminiscence. The high emotional pitch, the guilt, and the rapidity of association are all indicators of a pressing need to "set the house in order" as soon as possible.

Consequently, for Mrs. K. and for many other elderly people engaged in a life review, old conflicts are resurrected in the hope that through their resolution, the future can be faced with equanimity and death can be approached with confidence and grace. This may not be an explicit or conscious goal for older people such as Mrs. K., but their energies are harnessed into a problem-solving task, and the rewards that flow from a resolution of the problem are clear.

The past was the overriding focus of attention during the interview. While it is true that when asked, Mrs. K. was highly capable of articulating complex and realistic expectations of the probable effects of her imminent institutionalization; this capacity was exercised far less often than was her ability to reflect upon the past. In a sense, for her the past became the figure; the present, the ground. Or, as Mrs. K. stated in response to the question, "How do you think you've made out in life?":

> I could have made out better. You asked me once if I would change my life. I think everybody would. You are making mistakes. You have the experiences, you fix the mistakes.

RESOLUTION: "I REALLY DON'T HAVE ANY FEAR. I HAVE TO TAKE WHAT I CAN GET." Approximately one-third of the respondents were found to have previously engaged in and subsequently resolved an active life review. The older people we studied who had achieved resolution were generally in their eighties and nineties, were low in introspection, were rated high in mental health, and had a high degree of life satisfaction. They evaluated their lives positively, but with only moderate affective intensity.

The individual who has truly resolved his or her life may be regarded as a person who has restructured the self in such a way that the failures and never-to-be-recaptured joys of the past, as well as the personal dissolution of the future, can no longer inflict severe narcissistic wounds.

Mrs. T. was an eighty-seven-year-old widow born in New York who was living with her unmarried daughter in a comfortable house owned by one of her grandchildren. Her husband died about fifty years before; she supported herself and two small children by giving piano lessons.

Mrs. T.'s application for admission to an old-age home was necessitated by the fact that there was no one presently in the home to tend to her needs; her daughter worked all day, and her granddaughter was taking care of a number of young children. This in effect made Mrs. T. a prison-

276

er in her own room during the day, since the arthritis which had disfig-
ured her back and hands made it extremely difficult for her to negotiate
stairs without assistance.

Mrs. T. was a pleasant, smiling, well-groomed white-haired lady, who
appeared much younger than her age. She gave the impression of being
an emotionally modulated individual, well in control of her emotional
responses, yet still capable of sudden spontaneity or unexpected flashes of
wit.

When asked to describe herself she stated: "I can't say intelligent. I
can't say stupid. Generous when I can be. Admired by my old friends.
Loving my grandchildren and great grandchildren. I have a wonderful
family." Mrs. T., in her own acerbic style, conveyed the clear impression
that she knew who she was and was quite comfortable with it.

The test data indicated that she possessed a low level of anxiety and a
very high degree of life satisfaction. Clinical evaluations of personality
attributes characterized Mrs. T. as a woman who clearly asserted herself
through external activities and concerns, yet did not utilize hostile aggression to achieve her ends. Moreover, she did not often blame others for her
shortcomings, nor did she often evoke guilt feelings in herself through
self-castigation. She manifested high trust of other people and exhibited a
fair capacity to empathize with the feelings and problems of others.

Mrs. T.'s willingness to provide complex articulation of the past was
somewhat limited. Although on occasion she was quite able to provide
well-articulated expectations for the future, she did not display the high
proficiency clearly exhibited by most other respondents who were categorized as having achieved resolution.

This lack of involvement in intense intrapsychic activity is well-illustrated by Mrs. T.'s responses to the affect questonnaire. She was rated as
having an introspection score of 12, placing her in the lowest quartile.
Her verbalizations tended to be terse, well thought out and to the point,
but not intensely introspective. For example, she supplied the following
responses to the question, "Could you tell me about the time when you
feel depressed?":

Mrs. T.:
    When something is said to hurt me.
Interviewer:
    Describe it?
Mrs. T.:
    I just feel heavy. Sometimes tears come to my eyes.
Interviewer:

Do you have these feelings often?

Mrs. T.:

No.

Interviewer:

What do you do to get over them?

Mrs. T.:

Just take a book and read, or the paper. Listen to the television if it's a good story.

Interviewer:

What kinds of things make you feel depressed?

Mrs. T.:

Well, if you say something to hurt my feelings.

Here again, the distinctive quality emerges of a person who appears to be secure in her own self-knowledge and is not going to waste needless words or emotional energy to explore all the complexity of her feelings. This relative unwillingness to engage in introspection is qualitatively different from that observed among older people engaged in a flight from the past. For the latter group, a lack of introspection often seems associated with a denial of feelings and an avoidance of emotional realities. For those who have achieved resolution, however, low introspection may be the product of affective modulation and an attitude of serenity in regard to transitory emotional states.

The achievement of resolution is most clearly illustrated by Mrs. T. in her responses to the Evaluation of Life Questionnaire and in her lengthy life history. These data indicates that Mrs. T. regarded her life with a rather philosophic attitude; the good and the bad are both considered and weighed, with no undue remorse, with acceptance, and even with wit. For example, when the interviewer asked the question, "If you were going to live your life over again, what would you change?" Mrs. T.'s response was to point to the unmade bed in the room and proclaim, "Which I am." The interviewer then asked what she would leave unchanged, to which Mrs. T. replies, "Everything else." Through this gesture, involving as it did the fragile use of witty self-depreciation, Mrs. T. conveyed her belief that she herself had borne the major responsibility for her life experience, both the periods of satisfaction and the periods of disappointment.

Even when past conflicts were described, and Mrs. T. did not gloss over them, it is as if they were now being seen through the filter of understanding and tranquillity. A good example of this can be found in Mrs. T.'s life history where she described the personality and death of her husband:

Very nice. Very good-hearted. He was jealous of me. That was his trouble. If a man spoke to me or anything he would be upset. But otherwise we were very

278

close. I spoke to him about it and said don't you know me better than that. And then he felt ashamed. My marriage got better. Until he had his accident. We were only married a little over four years. He had an accident—he was getting out of a car, and a horse and wagon were passing. He was knocked down and hit his head. His brain was damaged and he was in the hospital four years. [Would you remarry?] No sir. I know what I had. But I didn't know what I would get.

In this excerpt Mrs. T. has not attempted to unrealistically idealize her dead husband, but instead presents what appears to be a relatively balanced picture of him, their relationship together, and the effects of his death. There was a strong sense from her account that this was once an issue for Mrs. T., with a multitude of strong emotions attached to it. Now, although still a salient conflict, it is neither distorted nor denied, and emotionally is only a shadow of its former self.

Mrs. T. appeared neither to flee from her past nor to focus intensely upon it. Rather, she seemed to have attained a certain perspective on her life and present situation. She was not apathetic, but tranquil; not pretending that all conflicts had been solved, but serene; not fearing death, but accepting its personal inevitability.

For many individuals who have achieved such resolution, the future is more interesting than the past—not because they deny the quickening approach of death, but because they seem to have made a certain peace with their past and have made most of the necessary psychological preparations for an unexpected stranger at the door. This is what Mrs. T. meant in her answer to the question, "What do you fear will happen to you as you grow older?" She responded: "That's a hard thing to say. I really don't have any fear. I just take what I can get."

PAST AS MYTH OR DRAMA

The third area of reminiscence measured was the degree to which the past was mythic or dramatic. Using the life history interview, six scales were developed to assess how the person restructured his or her past life. These scales were based on how significant people in the past were remembered as well as on the dramatic quality of the portrayal of interpersonal situations. The six scales were (1) parents as heroic, (2) spouse as heroic, (3) parents perceived primarily in terms of social relevance, (4) spouse perceived primarily in terms of social relevance, (5) early memory as dramatic, and (6) total life as dramatic. (See technical note 2) Descriptions of the scales and examples of statements representing points on the scales follow.

- *Parents Heroic and Spouse Heroic.* Ratings were based on extent to which significant figures were discussed as "bigger than life."

    Low: Parents are described in nonheroic terms. "Mother was a picky person, hard to live with."

    Moderate: Parents are described in particular superlative terms. "Mother was a good housekeeper, very meticulous, devoted to her children."

    High: Superlative, general terms are used to describe parents. "Mother was a lovely person in every way"; or, "Mother was one of the most wonderful women in the world. Everyone loved her."

- *Parents and Spouse Socially Relevant.* These ratings were determined by the degree to which significant figures are described in positive socially relevant terms rather than in relation to the self. We assumed that seeing significant others primarily in positive social roles unrelated to the self represents one mechanism for creating a mythology.

    Low: Parents and spouse are described primarily, but not exclusively, in terms of effect on respondent. "My parents were not too helpful to me. My mother was an intelligent person, but she spent most of her time nagging."

    High: Parents and spouse are described in primarily socially relevant terms—other characteristics may be briefly mentioned. "My mother was a wonderful cook, a good hostess, a talented singer. She took good care of us when we were sick."

- *Early Memories Dramatized.* These ratings indicated the extent to which the respondent's three earliest memories were dramatic. Dramatic events serve to focus interest on the respondent by eliciting pity or fear or making him or her seem important. This rating is given when the style of recounting the incident is designed to elicit a reaction (for example, one respondent described a situation in which her mother thought she was covered with blood, which was actually chocolate) or when the incident itself would elicit a reaction (for example, death).

    Low: "Life was pleasant in a country area. We lived in large white house in the country, and had several servants."

    High: "I had a mother, the most selfish creature on earth. . . . I gave the love to my sisters which my mother did not."

- *Total Life Dramatized.* This scale measured the degree to which the entire life history was described dramatically. The scale points are similar to those for early memories as dramatic.

As indicated, dramatization or the myth-making aspects of recounting one's personal past represent a reworking of the past. Unlike the life review process, however, in which the end point of the reworking is acceptance, integration, and the resolving of unresolved conflicts, dramatization or myth making functions to create a unique self for the individual and implies relaxation if not a renunciation of the reality principle. It has both intrapsychic as well as interpersonal or interactional aspects; thus, as seen in our rating scales, both aspects were used in the ratings.

Findings and Observations on the Remembered Past

The examination of information provided by respondents on the life history interview, the Evaluation of Life Questionnaire and the On Memories Questionnaire will be guided by the three general perspectives introduced earlier: the remembered past as a source of gratification and substitution; the remembered past as a developmental task; and the remembered past as a source of self-definition. Some of the questions we have raised require the inspection of age differences to determine whether there are relevant distinctions between those in the last decade or two of life and their younger counterparts.

A middle-aged sample of twenty-five respondents, not previously reported in this book, was drawn for our study of reminiscence. In order to provide a modicum of similarity to the aged respondents, we chose children who had parents in Jewish homes for the aged. The average age of these middle-aged individuals was forty-nine (the range was forty-four to fifty-five years), and they approximated the same sex distribution as our elderly respondents. Of course, their marital status was different: The elderly were primarily widowed, whereas the middle-aged were primarily married. They were, as expected, also different in educational level: the mean number of years of formal education was nine years for the elderly, and thirteen years for middle-aged sample.

Other questions about the elderly's use of their personal past require an examination of the effects of context; therefore, we will compare elderly respondents in conditions of stress (those on the waiting list to enter a home) to those in stable circumstances (the institutionalized and community control samples). Finally, we will examine the effects of nearness to death on reminiscence, because theories about life review assume that this process begins when individuals address their own finitude. Thus, three distinct comparisons of reminiscence measures will be made to determine differences by chronological age, by context, and by closeness to death. Then, as a final summary, we will consider the relevance of studying the elderly's relationship to their past to the issue of stress adaptation. Our question there is whether people who have successfully addressed the hypothetical developmental task of late life—the life review—have a greater ability to weather stress.

INVESTMENT IN THE PAST

We will begin our exploration by asking if our findings support the view that the aged are more invested and interested in their pasts than they are in their present and future. We examined the amount of involvement in the past, assessed by the total amount of time respondents discussed the past in our interviews. As anticipated, they spent significantly more time discussing the past than their middle-aged counterparts. On our second measure of involvement, which assessed the affective intensity of the past, we again found significant differences: The elderly showed more evidence that the past was "vivid" or "hot" compared to the middle-aged respondents.

These observations support the general view that the elderly invest more of themselves in their past than younger people. Recently, however, Cameron et al. (1977–78), used findings from a series of investigations of temporality across the life span to challenge the assumption that as people age they think and talk more about the past. They studied "consciousness sampling" among a very large and heterogeneous sample of respondents (overall N=7,300) by interrupting people engaged in a wide variety of activities and asking them to report on what they had just been thinking about. For all age groups (the range in age was from four to ninety-nine years old), at any given moment in time, participants were most likely to be thinking about the present and least likely to be thinking about the past.

Giambra (1977a and b), using a self-report technique (the Imaginal Process Inventory) to examine age differences in the temporal focus of daydreams, found no direct, linear relationship between age and reports of daydreaming about the past. A small but significant age association (r=−.11), however, was observed for future-oriented daydreams; older people tended to report fewer daydreams set in the future. When the relative importance of each time orientation was examined, those over sixty-five years of age were more likely to report daydreaming about the past then daydreaming about either the present or the future. In addition, the tendency to daydream about the distant past was reported most frequently by those in the oldest age group (seventy-five to ninety-one years of age). Kastenbaum (1966) studied uses of the past that are less accessible to conscious awareness. He asked groups of young and old people to complete twelve stories constructed to reflect neutral, pleasant, and unpleasant affective tones. He found that younger persons focused their stories primarily on the future, whereas older individuals tended to focus to a greater extent on the past and to integrate the past more successfully into thematic productions. Thus, while there may or may not be age differences in the frequency of reminiscence activity, it appears that there are qualitative differences in the use of the past across the life course. The relative ease with which the past is integrated into present experience, the cognitive restructuring of memories, and the emotional investment in reminiscence found among older persons all indicate that it is the nature of the reminiscence activity and the salience of the remembered past that are important toward the end of life.

These investigations obviously used different methods than ours, and thus their findings do not necessarily contradict our observation that the elderly are more invested in the past. In the introduction to this chapter we discussed a variety of reasons for increased investment in the past. We begin by examining the simplest hypothesis: The past serves the elderly because it is an effective substitute for a barren present and future. We approached this issue by examining how the elderly used their personal past when compared to middle-aged respondents. Three scales were constructed based on the eleven questions in the On Memory Questionnaire: (1) the past as a source of comfort; (2) the past as a source of instrumental or cognitive problem solving for current problems; and (3) the past as personally meaningful. Our findings were consistent and highly significant for all three scales: The elderly saw the past as more meaningful to them personally when compared to the middle-aged (p<.01); they were likely to use the past as a source of comfort (p<.01); and they used the past as a source of data for current problem solving less often than the middle aged (p<.01). These findings indicate that the elderly's greater involvement in the past is, at least in part, a function of its service as a source of substitute gratification.

THE LIFE REVIEW

Next we examined whether reminiscence served as a developmental function for the aged. For this we used our two approaches to measuring the life review.

Reconciliation. The seven scales used to measure reconciliation proved, all in all, disappointing. The anticipated results could not be demonstrated. We had expected that the elderly would show more evidence of engaging in a life review process than middle-aged respondents; and that those closer to death, particularly those who were approaching death with a low level of anxiety, would reveal evidence of having reviewed their past lives. (Recall that in chapter 9 we reported that those close to death in stable life circumstances showed little anxiety associated with approaching death.)

We found, however, that the elderly were significantly different from their middle-aged counterparts on only one of the seven scales: They were more likely to see significant figures in their past lives in more positive terms than did the middle-aged respondents. Only one scale showed evidence that those closer to death were different from those further from death: Elderly people near death dwelled more on the positive aspects of the past than did those who were further from death. Nor could we find substantial evidence that stress situations affected this process. Of twenty-one statistical tests (one on each of the seven reconciliation scales for each of the three contexts of age, living arrangement, and distance from death), only four were statistically significant, a number that could have occurred by chance alone.

Why did we obtain these negative results? Given an inquiry that has little historical precedence and only a handful of prior studies, it is hazardous to even speculate. Possible explanations include failure of conceptualization; inadequate operationalization of life review scales; low measurement reliability (this does not appear to be the case because reliability coefficients ranged from .59 to .85); insufficient sample of reminiscences from the source of data, the life history interview, to assess such a subtle process; and so on. Given the absence of empirical findings by others, it is difficult to draw any reasonable conclusions for our failure to empirically support the theoretical predictions.

Our best guess, however, is that we placed too much faith on developing evidence from a life history interview; that is, that we could detect information on reminiscence processes from the manner in which a person reported their life story. Thus, before dismissing such a critical construct as the life review, we will turn our attention to the typology of styles of relating to the past.

Life Review Styles. The typology of life review styles distinguished those who showed evidence of avoiding this process from those currently involved in a life review and those who showed evidence of achieving reconciliation. It was based on the respondent's perspective or judgment of his or her life in the Evaluation of Life Questionnaire rather than on the life history interview. Because we did not have these data for the middle-aged sample, we could not investigate the difference between the middle-aged and the elderly in life review type. Within the sample of the elderly, however, respondents ranged from their early sixties to their late nineties. Theoretically it might be expected that those in their sixties and seventies would be less likely to have achieved a resolution of their life review than those eighty and older. (The seven reconciliation scales were not correlated with chronological age.) For this analysis a distinction was made between "young-old" respondents in their sixties and seventies (N=79) and the "old-old" in their eighties and nineties (N=44). Based on the life review theory, it was hypothesized that the young-old would be more involved in the process of a life review, while the old-old would be more likely to show signs of resolution following a life review. Although less critical theoretically, we also hypothesized that the old-old would show less avoidance of the past. This was because it might be harder for the old-old to avoid dealing with the past when time is running out than it would be for the young-old, who might have a sense that time is still left. Before examining the relationship between life review style and age, psychological characteristics correlated with each of the three life review styles will be reviewed.

Respondents who were engaged in flight from the past generally possessed low emotional reactivity and poor articulation of the past as well as low regard toward the future. They also tended to utilize denial in regard to future expectations. Respondents engaged in the life review were found more likely to have high anxiety, strong emotional reactivity, and complex articulation of the past. Those exhibiting resolution tended to be characterized by a high degree of life satisfaction and well-articulated expectations for the future. Moreover, when we looked at other measures of reminiscence, we found those who were categorized as being involved in an active life review evaluated their lives negatively with a great deal of affect, whereas those manifesting resolution evaluated their lives positively with low levels of affects, and individuals engaged in a flight from the past tended to evaluate their lives in the neutral fashion, with flattened affect. These observations were seen as highly congruent with the formulation of the life review as a process involving psychic turmoil, confrontation of long-unresolved conflicts, and effective extension of the self through time. It was also congruent with a description of the resolution of the life review as producing the integration of past conflicts, a high degree of life satisfaction, and serenity.

Table 11–1 which shows the number of respondents falling into the various reminiscence types indicates some support for our expectations. Whereas 23 percent of the young-old were involved in an active life review, only 5 percent of the old-old were similarly classified. Stated another way, 90 percent of those showing an active life review were in their sixties and seventies. The respondents classified as resolved—those manifesting evidence that they had reorganized their lives and were currently experiencing a sense of equanimity—did not show as clear an age pattern, however: 32 percent of the young-old were rated as resolved, compared to 57 percent of those over 80. Overall age differences for the three types were significant at p<.01 (chi=square=10.07, df=2).

The finding that about one in three of the young-old evidenced resolution led to several further analyses. First we examined the effects of con-

TABLE 11-1
Life Review Type and Age

Life Review Type	Young-Old (younger than 80)		Old-Old (80 and above)	
	N	Percentage[a]	N	Percentage
Flight from the past	36	46	17	39
Active review	18	23	2	5
Resolution	25	32	25	57
Total	79	101	,44	100

[a]Percentages do not total 100 due to rounding.

text. In both groups—those under stress, as well as the stable controls—flight from the past was more characteristic for the young-old than the old-old (in a ratio of about two to one). Again, under both conditions, an active life review was more characteristic of the young-old. When we looked at resolution, however, the evidence was contrary to the expectation that resolved life reviews would be more characteristic of those in their eighties and nineties. Although this was true for respondents living in stable circumstances, the younger respondents under crisis showed significantly more resolution: Of the seventeen people in the stable samples who showed evidence of resolution eleven were over eighty; among the group on the waiting list (the unstable condition) of the thirty-three who showed evidence of resolution, only fourteen were over eighty. Thus, although the distribution of life review types is similar for the subsamples, only in the unstable condition is resolution more characteristic of the young-old than of the old-old. These findings led us to examine those groups whose life review style was unexpected, such as the young-old who showed signs of resolution and the old-old who showed signs of flight from the past.

If the young-old can be considered further from death than the old-old, the life review hypothesis would suggest that the elderly of the same reminiscence types but at different ages would have different psychological characteristics. We first compared those in the young-old and the old-old groups who flee from the past. The young-old who flee from the past may be avoiding reminiscing; the old-old who adopt this attitude may have earlier engaged in a life review but been unable to achieve a genuine resolution and thereafter adopted an attitude of resignation reflected in flight from the past. Differences between these two groups, however, were not found on the psychological variables described earlier in this chapter as associated with life review types, such as evaluation of the past, affective intensity of reminiscences, degree of life satisfaction, and expectations for the future.

We next compared the old-old and the young-old who had achieved resolution. The young-old may have resolved their life reviews during their sixties or seventies by achieving integration of long-standing conflicts but may not fully manifest the attitude of serenity observed at later ages. Again, however, comparisons between the two groups on psychological dimensions revealed no significant differences. Nor were differences found between young-old and old-old engaged in active life reviews. Thus age per se was found to have no bearing on the hypothesized life review process. Stated another way, we could neither differentiate between the young-old who had achieved a resolved life review (the unexpected pattern) and the old-old who had the same life review style nor between the young-old who manifested flight from the past and the old-old who similarly manifested flight (the unexpected pattern).

The only contrast in this series that led to a meaningful finding was among those who showed evidence of having resolved life reviews: Most of the young-old who had achieved resolution were under conditions of high stress. As has been discussed in previous chapters and has been detailed in elsewhere (Tobin and Lieberman 1976), those awaiting entrance into homes for the aged are marked by high levels of anxiety, emotional reactivity, depression, diminished self-esteem, and difficulty in maintaining a stable self-concept. Could such a set of psychological reactions, and the underlying feelings of abandonment and loss, set off an early life review? There is nothing in the theory of life review that would have led us to expect this. Yet, our findings show that although a resolved life review is primarily characteristic of people in late old age, younger elderly people awaiting entrance into homes for the aged (a stressful, disruptive situation) are more likely to have achieved a resolved life review. The finding is all the more puzzling, however, because we found no additional evidence that an active life review is more characteristic of the stressed groups.

Introspection and Life Review.   The link we found between age and the goal-directed reworking of the past is supported by some observations on introspection. In a study using the same population investigated in this chapter, Gorney (1968) found an appreciable negative association ($r = -.41$) between introspection on feelings and chronological age. He reported that 16 percent of the young-old were in the lowest quartile on introspection, compared with 35 percent of the old-old; conversely, 26 percent of the young-old were in the top quartile on introspection, compared with only 10 percent of the old-old.

Phenomenological psychologists have generally considered the willingness to reflect on feelings as an adaptive ability. In particular, reflective behavior has been understood as the primary means whereby an individual both experiences memory with fresh affect and newly symbolizes his or her present feelings (May 1958). While some theorists have suggested that introspection is somewhat related to cognitive and perceptual complexity (Merleau-Ponty 1962 [1945], 1963 [1942]; Sokolwski 1964), temporality has been consistently recognized as the primary dimension involved in introspective behavior (Ellenberger 1958). Minkowski (1933) has gone so far as to provide an elaborate scheme in which every self-referential act may be conceived of as relating to a particular temporal dimension. Such other phenomenological psychologists as Boss (1963) and Straus (1966) share with Minkowski the notion that successful adaptation in the present is largely determined by an individual's ability to easily introspect upon zones of the past (memory) as well as some of the future (expectation).

The ability to engage in introspection on feelings during aging may facilitate the formation of a strong self-concept in the present by providing a ready tool for integrating the remembered past and expected future. The aged individual's ability to effectively reflect upon feelings is thus conceived of as directly related to his or her ability to creatively utilize reminiscences of the past in order to adapt in the present to expectations for the future.

Before examining the linkage of introspection and life review, it might be helpful to describe how we assessed level of introspection. Introspection was empirically defined using the model and measurement approach developed by Gendlin (1962). Gendlin's framework uses a special technique, the focusing interview. We applied a similar measurement model to the affect questionnaire, an interview schedule which asked people to reflect on a variety of both positive and negative emotions. For example, we would ask the individual, "Could you tell me about the times when you feel very lonely?" or "happy," "sad," "proud," and so forth. The following responses to the question about loneliness illustrate several of the seven introspection scale points. (See technical note 3).

LEVEL 3: No I do not feel lonely. [Emphatic] You can quote me as saying that in spite of the fact that I live alone, I have no time to be lonely. I have so many things to occupy my time with that I just don't give the whole thing a thought. [Not ever?] Well, maybe once in a while. [When?] Sometimes on a Sunday when my daughter is busy. [What do you do?] I do nothing. I like to be alone sometimes so I can give my thought to things that are really important to me. Oh, there are many friends I could call to come over but I don't. I'm certainly not in want of friends. They would be only too happy to come over with me. But it is good for me to relax a lot. I sleep a good deal because the doctor told me that I must.

Although this highly verbal subject makes a halting start toward exploring her feelings, her description is largely limited to externals, and she does not consistently maintain an inward frame of reference.

> LEVEL 5: I have that feeling sometimes but I don't give in to it. I tell myself it's nonsense. You can find things to do to keep busy if you really want to. I may pick up my telephone and call somebody. Yesterday, for example, I felt quite lonely. Somehow it's always worse on Sunday—a family day. So I made arrangements to go to the bridge club downtown. I really had a wonderful time. . . . [Are you lonely at other times?] There come times every so often. It's just that now that I'm older everything becomes an effort for me. It takes initiative to get up and do something. [What do you do to overcome this feeling?] I look at a TV program or I read a book. But you can't do that all day long. Life is not so easy when you get older . . . [trailing off]. But I do try to keep my friendships in good repair. When one hasn't married and had a family, friends become very important to you.

This subject is both exploring and elaborating her feeling in a purposeful way. While there is a moderate intensity to her experiencing, and some explanation of inner awareness, there is little clarification of the full complexity of the feeling.

> LEVEL 7: I very rarely am lonely. I suppose once in a while one does get that way but with me it's not very often. I just don't let myself feel that way long. I don't think it's healthy. I think a woman like myself who has no immediate family may be expected to get a feeling of loneliness once in a while. When I was sick in the hospital and my roommate would have a great deal of family come and visit her I would feel quite lonely. Of course my nieces and nephews were very good to me, but it isn't the same as having a very immediate family be attentive. I also feel lonely when I am invited to a friend's home for a holiday meal and they have all the family there too. It reminds me of the fact that I am not now a member of a large family. But on the whole I don't give way to these thoughts of loneliness. It's definitely infrequent feeling with me. I keep myself as busy as possible. Now I would say loneliness is not frequent enough experience with me to diminish my enjoyment with people and things in life.

This respondent displays a sure and insightful understanding of her inner processes; she draws upon various introspective strands to formulate a new and more appropriate insight into the nature of her feeling.

What is the link between life review style and introspection? Theoretically, respondents currently in the midst of a review should show the highest level of introspection; those highly resistant to reworking their past should exhibit the least introspection; and those who we have categorized as having resolved life reviews should show relatively low levels of introspection. To test this, an analysis of variance (using z-transformed introspection scores) and life review type were computed and found to be highly significant (p $<$.001). The mean z-score for introspection for those categorized as being in the midst of a life review was z = .75; for those who were resolved, z = .01; and for those who avoided examining their past, z = $-$.25, showing the lowest level of introspection.

To summarize, there is a strong link between age and introspection as well as an association between level of introspection and life review status. Together, these findings suggest that a low level of introspection characterizes the old-old because the majority of them have already accomplished a life review and show signs of resolution. We would also speculate that the young-old show high levels of introspection because more of them are in the midst of a life review. The capacity to introspect probably reflects a fundamental characteristic, which waxes and wanes over an individual's life span depending on specific psychosocial issues associated with various life stages. Thus, we would expect that introspection would increase at transition points such as the movement from adolescent into adulthood and at other major normative transitions or eruptive crises that constitute challenges. We believe, however, that heightened introspection associated with the life review represents more than an ordinary response to a transition. Simply focusing on the past is not necessarily linked with an intensified turning inward. Indeed, we found no appreciable association between level of introspection and intensity of involvement in the past.

Life Review and Distance from Death. The link between life review and approaching death—the dynamic proposed by Erikson, Butler, and others—did not find support in our study. In contrast, we found that those closest to death showed significantly less reminiscence activity and significantly less introspection when compared with matched controls. Nor could we find in either of the strategies used to assess life review (the seven resolution scales and the life review types) any evidence to suggest that those approaching death were more likely to be engaged in a life review process or to show evidence of resolution. Only one of the seven scales was significant in the direction originally expected: Those closer to death used less denial of negative events in their past lives compared to those further from death (p=.10). For life review types, we could find no significant differences among the various types and distance from death. Thus, the association found between age and life review suggests that the process may be more complex than heretofore anticipated. The confrontation of personal finitude, as we were able to study it in terms of distance from death, did not appear to stimulate a life review.

Life Review and Adaptation. Implicit in the developmental perspective on reminiscence, which posits it to be a fundamental and universal psychological task of old age, is the view that a successful negotiation of the life review has significant psychological payoffs. Theoretical statements about such psychological payoffs are unfortunately vague. The life review has of course been analogized to other developmental tasks confronting people throughout the life span. Thus, by implication, success or failure in accomplishing this task is expected to have consequences. A direct and simple translation of Erikson's and Butler's views would lead us to expect that those who have accomplished this task would show more serenity and equanimity. As we have noted earlier, those rated as having resolved life reviews did in fact show a higher degree of life satisfaction and a more articulated sense of self and expectations for the future.

Furthermore, we would expect that those who accomplished this task of late life would manifest optimal levels of functioning, good mental health, and the ability to withstand and cope well with threat and stress. The variety of constructs used to assess optimal or successful functioning, however, has a long and problematic history in psychology. As we have found and reported throughout this book, certain preconceptions of success (such as the Q-Sort model of mental health developed by Block and discussed in chapter 8) are in fact not appropriate for the elderly in the particular set of circumstances of our investigation. The finding regarding the life review are similar to the findings reported in chapter 8 that levels of mental health were not associated with successful adaptation. The primary criteria used throughout this book for defining adequacy of functioning is the ability to weather stress.

We investigated the relationship between life review types and subsequent adaptation for the sample undergoing stress as well as samples who were in stable life circumstances. (As noted earlier, the distribution of life review types was similar among respondents irrespective of stress conditions—those waiting to enter institutions, those already in institutions, and those living in the community.) Our findings were clearly negative: No significant association was found between life review and subsequent adaptation in any of the subsamples. Overall, we found subsequent adaptive failure among 38 percent of those who avoided the past, 35 percent of those involved in the process of life review, and 30 percent of those who had resolved life reviews. Our findings were no different when we examined the seven scales used to address life review. Thus, aside from a high degree of life satisfaction as well as a clear and specified future, individuals who had resolved their life reviews successfully did not exhibit other signs that they were more mentally healthy or had higher ego strength than those who had not resolved their life reviews. Nor could we develop evidence that having engaged in and successfully resolved the issues of one's personal past has implications for the ability to address the future crises. We are left, therefore, with the evidence that those who have resolved their life review are more likely than others to have a modicum of equanimity or peacefulness (as measured by their stated levels of life satisfaction) and optimism about their future. Yet, more complex measures of optimal functioning (based on judges' ratings) did not show such relationships. We have also shown, however, that those involved in the process of life review do show more anxiety, which can be interpreted as consistent with theoretical postulates regarding the life review. Overall, however, we must conclude that the notion of the life review as a major dynamic of the last phase of life was not supported by our findings.

Role of the Past in Supporting the Self-Image. Our third perspective on how the elderly utilize the personal past is linked to maintenance of the self-image. Like the life review, this is an active process in which the past is restructured, not in the service of conflict resolution and reintegration this time, but rather in the service of defining and defending the present self. We investigated the way that the past serves the current self through the creation of a mythic and dramatic view of the self that provides a sense of uniqueness. As discussed earlier in this chapter, six rating scales, receiving scores from 1 to 5, were developed based on our analysis of the life history material that collectively assess the degree of myth creation and drama about the past. As shown in table 11–2 we found that the elderly more frequently created myths and dramatized their past than did the middle-aged respondents; that on four of the six scales, the stressed respondents more frequently emphasized myth and drama than did those in the stable circumstances (those living in the community or already living in institutions); and that, on two of the six scales, those closer to death were more likely to dramatize their past lives than those further from death.

These consistent statistically significant findings that age, closeness to death, and stress affect how respondents used the past have implications for how the self is viewed, particularly the self in relationship to the past. Our theoretical expectations are that as people age, particularly in the last decade or two of life, their ability to maintain a consistent, coherent, and positive self-image is challenged. As discussed in the preceding chapter, how people respond to this challenge has profound implications for their

TABLE 11-2
Past as Myth or Drama

Scale	Age			Stress			Distance from Death		
	Aged (N=35)	Middle-aged (N=25)	p	Stressed (Waiting list group) (N=81)	Non-stressed (controls) (N=26)	p	Death near (N=24)	Death far (N=24)	p
Parents heroic	3.0	2.3	.01	2.7	1.7	.01	3.6	3.2	.05
Spouse heroic	3.4	2.5	.01	3.4	2.9	.05	3.2	3.0	N.S.[a]
Parents socially relevant	3.5	3.0	.05	3.8	2.8	.01	3.3	3.5	N.S.
Spouse socially relevant	3.6	2.3	.01	3.8	3.1	.01	3.8	3.4	.05
Early memory dramatized	3.7	2.3	.01	3.6	3.4	N.S.	4.3	3.7	N.S.
Life story dramatized	3.0	2.7	.01	3.5	3.3	.10	3.3	3.5	N.S.

[a]N.S. = not significant.

capacity to adapt. The response of many elderly persons to the task of maintaining a consistent self-image was to draw on their past self as a source of confirmation. Now we find that a pattern of relating to the past by creating myth and portraying people and events dramatically is more characteristic of the elderly than the middle-aged; of those under stress than those not under stress; and of those closer to death than those further from death. These people literally create a unique sense of self in historical time.

We could not distinguish empirically between the intrapsychic and interpersonal aspects of this process—that is, to what extent this characteristic of creating a mythic, dramatic sense of one's personal past serves inner psychological functions and to what extent it is an interpersonal transaction used by the elderly to bolster a vulnerable self in a relationship. It is likely, however, given the degree of reorganization implicit in the creation of a mythic past, that it serves mainly an intrapsychic function. The fact that such myth making is associated not only with aging but also with nearness to death supports this view. As described in chapter 9, those near to death are involved in a number of intrapsychic tasks. Stress, nearness to death, and aging all present the individual with diminished self-esteem, and basic dissolution of one's personal sense of self. Given such an onslaught, it is not surprising that many individuals will forgo commitment to the reality principle in order to serve a higher purpose—the maintenance of selfhood.

Progress Toward an Acceptable and Accepted Past: The Case Of Mrs. A.

LIFE HISTORY INTERVIEW

Interviewer:
    What is the very first thing you can remember in your life?
Mrs. A.:
    When I was very little, two years old, I went out to the yard, and a little chicken had just been hatched and I didn't know anything. I picked him up and the mother hen flew on my head. My mother told me she was still nursing me because she didn't want to get pregnant again. After all, I was the eighteenth child.
Interviewer:
    Can you remember any other things?

Mrs. A.:
> Not very much. My childhood wasn't so hot. I went to school and I was a good pupil. I used to get second prize.

Interviewer:
> What was life like for you as a child?

Mrs. A.:
> I didn't have much of a child life. My parents were already too old when I was born. When I finished elementary school I went to work in a business, and there I slaved until I freed myself.

Interviewer:
> What were your parents like?

Mrs. A.:
> They were nice. My mother was a pretty little woman. She worked in the kitchen or made rugs. She was always busy.

Interviewer:
> What about your father?

Mrs. A.:
> My father was a very nice person. He modernized himself. He used to go all over. My mother stayed home because she was always busy, pregnant, or nursing.

Interviewer:
> Tell me about your brothers or sisters?

Mrs. A.:
> I don't remember very much about them. One sister went to Israel and died shortly after. . . . We were seven living—five girls and two boys. My oldest sister had two children. My brother had six children. Then came a sister. She had three children. Then another sister, then my older brother. Eleven died before I was born.

Interviewer:
> How did your parents get along?

Mrs. A.:
> They got along very nice. I never heard my mother and father quarrel or say a bad word. We were raised with love and respect.

Interviewer:
> Were you ever punished?

Mrs. A.:
> Not very much. My father used to say "Run, or I'll hit you." So if we ran we were lucky. I don't remember ever my mother or father hitting me.

Interviewer:
> Was your father the boss?

Mrs. A.:
> I don't think so. We knew that they each had their rights.

Interviewer:
> Did you get things from your parents?

Mrs. A.:
> If I needed something they gave it to me. They never refused me. I wasn't too demanding. We were a very contented family.

Interviewer:

What kind of people did your parents like?

Mrs. A.:

They liked to be with people who were honest. Because they were honest people. My father was a very respectable man.

Interviewer:

Were there any they disliked?

Mrs. A.:

I don't know. My father used to say, "If you have to quarrel, don't quarrel with somebody more stupid than you."

Interviewer:

Were there any other important people in your life?

Mrs. A.:

My grandfather was a wonderful man. He told me seventy years ago that we would have a lot of the scientific things we have today. He was right.

Interviewer:

Did you have any difficulties or hardships?

Mrs. A.:

I don't remember, because I had so little of a childhood.

Interviewer:

Did you have any sickness?

Mrs. A.:

I don't remember having any . . . Well, in some ways I was happy. I don't remember too much.

Interviewer:

What did you do as a teenager?

Mrs. A.:

From eleven to nineteen I worked in the business. I used to sing at parties. I had a good voice—a soprano. I didn't go dating because I didn't want to get married there. I wanted to get away. I wanted freedom. I left after my mother died.

Interviewer:

How old were you?

Mrs. A.:

About nineteen.

Interviewer:

How did you feel?

Mrs. A.:

We felt bad. Although she was bedridden for a couple of years.

Interviewer:

What was your life like?

Mrs. A.:

Very dull. . . . There were people who were important, but I don't remember any of them. My father was very important to me.

Interviewer:

Did you ever rebel?

Mrs. A.:

Not very much. I just took everything in stride. I still am like that.

Interviewer:
What were your feelings toward your brothers and sisters?
Mrs. A.:
My older sister. I was very close to her. She was like a mother, a sister, and an advisor rolled into one.
Interviewer:
Tell me about the boys in your life when you were a teenager.
Mrs. A.:
I didn't have time for love affairs. I had my cousins. We were a very large family and a very close one.
Interviewer:
Which person did you admire most?
Mrs. A.:
My father and brother.
Interviewer:
Why?
Mrs. A.:
Because they were smart.
Interviewer:
What person did you most want to be like?
Mrs. A.:
I don't think I had anybody I wanted to be like.
Interviewer:
What was school like?
Mrs. A.:
It was like every school. We had teachers. We had subjects. I was very good in arithmetic. . . . I liked to work. I had a very good memory. I was conscientious.
Interviewer:
Did you suffer any hardships?
Mrs. A.:
When my mother died it changed my life because I made up my mind to come to America.
Interviewer:
What happened?
Mrs. A.:
I decided and I talked it over with my father and he thought it was a good thing to make a life for myself. So I came alone. One sister came a few months later. So I married myself off and raised a family.

In response to a series of questions about specific hardships (separations, danger, and losses), Mrs. A. stoutly indicated that there were "no unusual problems."

Mrs. A.:
Life was so-so. Not very happy and not very sad.
Interviewer:

Why sad?
Mrs. A.:
Because lots of times I didn't like what was going on [referring to life in Russia].

QUESTIONS ABOUT ADULTHOOD

The next set of quotations summarize Mrs. A.'s responses to questions about adulthood.

Interviewer:
What were the important events in your life?
Mrs. A.:
I came here when I was twenty. My trip was pleasant. I came here with a friend. I didn't come like other immigrants. I didn't have to go to Ellis Island. I came to one of my aunties. Everything was wonderful to me. Because it was new and different. I shared a room with two of my cousins. Then I got a job in a store where they sold costume jewelry. I was very conscientious and they made me an assistant floorlady. After a couple of years I met my husband. He fell in love with my voice. He used to live nearby. Unfortunately, he got sick during an epidemic and he died after we were married seven-and-a-half years. My first baby was born nine months and four days after we were married. The next one came eleven-and-a-half months later.
Interviewer:
Go on.
Mrs. A.:
When my boy was two-and-a-half, I didn't feel well. There was a strike and my husband was supposed to strike but he got a card to say come back to work and he went back and the strikers got hold of him and beat him up. We moved seven times in one year, and it was after an operation. I had a hard time. We were afraid. My second husband I knew before I married my first. He was divorced. Normally, I wouldn't marry a divorced man, but I knew his wife and I knew what kind of person. He had two children, and his wife didn't want them so I took them and raised them up like my own.
Interviewer:
What was your life like?
Mrs. A.:
I always worked hard. I raised the children.
Interviewer:
How did you feel?
Mrs. A.:
I used to sing all the time. I was happy.
Interviewer:
Why?
Mrs. A.:
I used to enjoy housekeeping. I used to enjoy taking care of my children. I used to sew for them. I used to crochet in the evenings.

298

Interviewer:
What else?

Mrs. A.:
When we were in business we used to get a season ticket to the opera. I always like music.

Interviewer:
What were your children like?

Mrs. A.:
The only problem was with Eleanor. She was a bleeder and I had to watch out for her. I took a nursing course to understand how to help her. I always carried a first-aid kit with me. I used to take her to the clinic.

Interviewer:
Why?

Mrs. A.:
They all had the usual things that all children go through. They had the measles. They had their tonsils out.

Interviewer:
What were your husbands like?

Mrs. A.:
My first husband idolized me. We were in love. He was a self-educated man. He read a lot. He went to Europe several times. He was an Austrian. My second husband was very good to me. He never refused me anything. I think he was still in love with his first wife if I'm not mistaken. We married really for convenience.

Interviewer:
Did you get along?

Mrs. A.:
We never ever argued. My children never heard arguments. They didn't fight or argue either. I had a happy marriage—both times. If the first one wouldn't have been happy, I would never dare to married again. I think marriages get better over time.

Interviewer:
What were your main difficulties during these years?

Mrs. A.:
It was up and down but I always took it in my stride, and made the best of it. The worst things were the loss of my two husbands, but God forbid, I didn't lose a child.

Interviewer:
How did you feel?

Mrs. A.:
Well, I reacted very bad. It was very sudden and I had two small children. My husband's sister-in-law took us into her home and I worked and she took care of my children. Then a year later I married again. I didn't marry because I needed a man. I married because I wanted my children to have a father and not be orphans. He adopted them right away. My son went and said the prayer for the dead for both fathers.

Interviewer:
What happened next?

Mrs. A.:

My second husband died in 1963.

Interviewer:

How did you cope?

Mrs. A.:

I sold the house in California and came to Chicago because my children were here and my sister and all my family. I always made a profit on my property. I bought the house for $18,000 and sold it for $26,000.

In a review of crises that occurred during adulthood, Mrs. A. included sickness:

Mrs. A.:

I had four operations.

Interviewer:

When?

Mrs. A.:

Serious operations in 1915, 1945, 1963, and in 1953 I had a stroke but recovered in two weeks—I'm still a little lifeless in my lower hip.

Interviewer:

Did you ever have an accident?

Mrs. A.:

I had one accident with a streetcar in 1948. I was run over and broke my ankle and had my foot in a cast for the whole summer.

Interviewer:

Were you ever in a dangerous situation?

Mrs. A.:

The only time when there was a threat of a pogrom in Europe, I carried a pistol under my coat.

In response to a direct question, Mrs. A. indicated that she recalled no major incidents of deprivation or abandonment.

EVALUATION OF LIFE

Interviewer:

What kind of life have you had?

Mrs. A.:

Sometimes I pinch myself to see if I'm alive—because when I start to think about it I've had so many ups and downs I wonder how I'm still alive. Nobody goes before the alarm rings and it doesn't ask you first.

Interviewer:

If everything were to be the same, would you like to live your life over again?

Mrs. A.:

No. Never!

Interviewer:
What would you change?
Mrs. A.:
It's hard to explain. The only thing I wouldn't want to go back to is my childhood. I was glad when I married.
Interviewer:
Why?
Mrs. A.:
I was happy with my marriages and my children are wonderful.
Interviewer:
What were your main satisfactions?
Mrs. A.:
My children were good students; they were successful. So to that extent I achieved my goal. But I can't really say what were the main satisfactions.
Interviewer:
What were your main disappointments?
Mrs. A.:
I don't know. I don't remember. I suppose I must have had some in eighty years, but they couldn't have been very important because I don't remember them.
Interviewer:
What was the hardest thing you've had to face?
Mrs. A.:
When I decided to come to this country. My brother didn't want me to leave. I had a hard time getting him to let me go.
Interviewer:
What else?
Mrs. A.:
Well, when my husband died and I was left with two small children.
Interviewer:
When were you happiest?
Mrs. A.:
I never had outstanding happiness and I never had outstanding sorrows, I was just in the middle.
Interviewer:
When were you unhappiest?
Mrs. A.:
No real unhappiness. It was balanced.
Interviewer:
What was your proudest moment?
Mrs. A.:
That was when I came to my grandson's bar mitzvah. They put me on top of the world.
Interviewer:
If you could choose to be any age, what age would you choose?
Mrs. A.:
Between fifty and sixty.

Interviewer:
Why?

Mrs. A.:
Because it's not too young and it's not too old. You can do lots of things at that age. You can accomplish things.

Interviewer:
How do you think you've made out in life?

Mrs. A.:
I think I didn't make out so bad. I accomplished what I set out to achieve when I came to this country. I made my children independent and gave them the education which I didn't have, and I'm very proud.

Interviewer:
How do you feel you've made out compared to what you hoped for?

Mrs. A.:
I made out as I hoped.

Interviewer:
What are the best things about being the age you are now?

Mrs. A.:
The best thing would be if I could keep a little apartment, but as it is, I'm very satisfied. I have friends and I'm in congenial surroundings. I don't demand very much. I like to adapt myself to my surroundings.

Interviewer:
What are the worst things?

Mrs. A.:
I have too much leisure and nothing to do. At the home I'll be able to work with ceramics and there'll be more action.

Interviewer:
What things are important to you?

Mrs. A.:
My children are very important to me. I love to hear from them and see them and I would like to go to the coast to see my daughters.

Interviewer:
What do you expect to happen as you grow older?

Mrs. A.:
I hope it shouldn't happen I should be worse than I am. My biggest hope is that my mind should be clear and I should not be worse. To be better I cannot hope . . . I'm afraid that I shouldn't be in a position not to do what I'm doing now. . . . The first thing their arteries are getting bad. They get weaker all the time. But you have to expect it.

ON MEMORIES QUESTIONNAIRE

1. How important are your memories to you?

Important. Sometimes you like to think over what you have done. I went through very much in my life. Sometimes I pinch myself to see if I'm still living. [How important are they now compared to when you were fifty?] Memories are more important now—when I was fifty I was busy then. I was in the prime of work. I didn't have time to think. There was too much to do.

2. Do you agree or disagree—Right now my memories are the most important thing I own?

Disagree. Sometimes I try to count to forget them. [Why?] I want to go to sleep.

3. Do you agree or disagree—My memories are like spilled milk—one should forget and go on?

Disagree. You can't forget a conversation that brings them back as long as your mind is in order.

4. Complete the sentence: When I feel sad or lonely, thinking about the past . . .

Only makes me feel worse because I went through very much hardship. I didn't have such an easy life. And since my husband went away, I lost all my laughing power.

5. Is the following statement like you now—During the last several years I spent a lot of time trying to make sense out of what my life was?

Somewhat like me. I'm happy we gave the children the education they wanted and every one is on their feet. I know we did right there.

6. Some people say: "My memories are like money in the bank for a rainy day?" What do you think?

Yes. It's a good feeling to think you have something to back you up in your life. That what you did was right and good.

7. If some scientist were able to discover a pill that would make us forget our pasts, would you be interested in trying such a pill?

No.

8. Are there any things you'd like to forget?

The bad things I went through. Sickness, death, money troubles.

9. Are there any things you'd like to remember?

The brighter things. Companionship with my husband. How we were always together twenty-four hours a day.

The following summary analyzes Mrs. A.'s responses in each of the three areas of measurement discussed in this chapter.

The Importance of the Past.   Mrs. A. talked slightly less about her life than other respondents did, and she also tended to use less affective intensity than her peers. She described herself, for example, as having been happy by saying "I used to enjoy . . ." rather than with words reflecting a greater immediacy, for example, "I felt . . ." Thus, although she discussed her feelings, there was a tendency to distancing the affect.

REMINISCENCE SCALES.

Life Review. Mrs. A. was scored very high on the scale measuring positive views of significant figures—above the sample mean—because she consistently described her parents, for example, in a very positive manner: "My mother was a pretty little woman" and "Father was a very nice person." On past life viewed positively, Mrs. A. provided a balanced view of her past, noting both the good aspects and the painful experiences; thus, she was scored at the mid-point, the mean for the group. On absence of conflict, Mrs. A. scored higher than the mean. Although she made comments throughout her interview suggesting the absence of conflict ("We were raised with love and respect"; "When my mother died it changed my life because I made up my mind to come to America"), unresolved conflicts were suggested by other comments indicating she was unable to reconcile her past ("I had a hard time"; "We were afraid"). On lack of resentment, she was scored high because of such comments as, "It was up and down, but I always took it in stride and made the best of it." On major values fulfilled, she was again scored high, based on statements such as, "It's a good feeling to think you have something to back you up in your life. That what you did that was right and good."

Mrs. A.'s ownership of life, on which she also was scored high, is clear in statements such as, "When my mother died I made up my mind to come to America. I decided and talked it over with my father and he thought it was a good thing to make a life for myself. So I came alone. One sister came a few months later. . . . So I married myself off and raised a family." The statement of her own responsibility, along with the support from her father, reflects her view of life as having been hard but having taken place in a network of caring. On the last scale, acceptance of the negative, Mrs. A. was scored at a median level. Her husband's caring apparently left her with a residue of conflict and underlying depression. Her attitude of acceptance and pride in her accomplishments is not completely offset by her disappointment in having had some major and irreplaceable losses in her life.

Life Review Style. Mrs. A. manifested some minimal signs of flight from the past, when asked whether she disagreed with the statement, "Right now my memories are the most important thing I own," stating "Sometimes I try to count to forget them. . . . I want to sleep." She also manifested many aspects of resolution, however, as reflected in her high scores on three of the reconciliation scales—major values fulfilled, of ownership of life, and acceptance of the negative. Overall, the evidence suggests that she is actively involved in reviewing her life. For example, when asked whether she agreed or disagreed with the statement, "My memories are like spilled milk—one should forget and go on," she answered, "Disagree. You can't forget a conversation that brings them back as long as your mind is in order." She said the statement, "During the last several years I spent a lot of time trying to make sense out of what my life was" was "Somewhat like me." She then added, "I'm happy we gave the children the education they wanted and everyone is on their feet. I know we did right there." Apparently, she was in the midst of sorting out her past, of cataloging the good and the bad, what she did that was right and where she might have failed.

The Past as Myth or Drama. Mrs. A. was scored at the mid-point for parents and spouse as heroic. Her father, for example, was described as "a very respectable man" and, as noted earlier, "a very nice person." Scores for social relevancy of parents and spouse were not similar however. Mrs. A.'s parents were described in socially relevant terms, but her spouses were described in personally relevant terms. Her mother, for example, was a "pretty little woman . . . always busy, pregnant, or nursing"; this was scored high on social relevance. Her husbands, although described both ways, tended to be described more in nonmythic terms. Mrs. A.'s earliest memory, somewhat dramatic in content, though not in style, was of going into the yard, picking up a little chick, and having the mother hen fly at her head. Her second memory was similar in its underplayed style: "My mother told me she was still nursing me because she didn't want to get pregnant again. After all, I was the eighteenth child." Her third memory again presented a somewhat dramatic statement in matter-of-fact terms: "I went to school and I was a good pupil. I used to get the second prize." Her score for dramatization of earliest memories was lower than the mean. Again and again, Mrs. A. tells us that there were good things in her life, but more often than not, she received the second prize, reflecting the recurrent theme of hardship. Not overly dramatic, her recollections of her total life were scored lower than the norm for her aged peer group. Overall, Mrs. A. reported her past in a somewhat less mythic or dramatic way than most elderly respondents in the sample.

Mrs. A.'s relationship to her remembered past is complex. She sees her life as neither totally good nor totally bad and remembering as neither reassuring nor totally discouraging. She has accepted much of her past and it has become part of her sense of self. Overall, she is well on her way to resolution, but in comparison to some others, she does not manifest a complete integration. Use of mythic past for self-definition is not characteristic of Mrs. A.

Summing Up

There is a small but growing body of research on reminiscence in the latter half of life. In examining the implications of our findings it may be helpful to begin by reviewing the current state of knowledge.

Research findings specifically on the life review process are inconsistent. Ferrono (1981) studied reconstruction of the past among middle-aged and elderly adults. Earliest memories elicited during interviews conducted in 1974 and again in 1978 as part of a panel study of personality and adaptation (Lieberman and Cohler 1975), were examined for changes in manifest and latent content. On the basis of his findings that there were greater changes in early memories among the elderly, Ferrono postulated developmental differences in reconstruction of the past. For those in middle-age, it appears that the reminiscing process involves reworking negative aspects of the past, resulting in similar memories but higher levels of loss over time. Older adults, however, seem to maintain consistent levels of affect—possibly as a result of resolving previous conflicts—but appear to be involved in a final rewriting of the life biography. Fallot (1977), who focused his study of reminiscence on the life story, asked middle-aged and elderly women to complete a mood adjective checklist before and after a life history interview. However, he did not find age differences.

Studies of the universality of a life review process have also been inconsistent. Romaniuk (1978) found that approximately 80 percent of a group of elderly people in retirement homes responded positively when asked if they had experienced a life review in which "past events and experiences—successes, failures, accomplishments, mistakes, high and low points, milestones, etc.—are reviewed and evaluated in arriving at an overall picture of one's life" (p. 127). He concluded that this finding supports the contention that the life review process is a universal phenomenon experienced by all elderly persons. In contrast, studies examining reminiscence protocols obtained from open-ended interviews have reported that the life review process is by no means universal (Coleman 1974); and more often than not is found among only a few respondents (Fallot 1977; McMahon and Rhudick 1967; Postema 1970).

The empirical literature on the association between reminiscence and emotional states is also inconsistent, but it does support the link between affects or conflicts expressed in reminiscence and emotional states. McMahon and Rhudick (1967) found a positive association between frequency of reminiscences and the absence of depression. Havighurst and Glasser (1972) found significant positive correlations between self-reported frequency of reminiscence and pleasant affect, a high degree of life satisfaction, and positive self-concept. The frequency of reminiscence reported by elderly men residing permanently in a Veterans Administration hospital was found to be positively associated with adjustment, but was more likely to be associated with negative rather than pleasant affect (Boylin, Gordon, and Nehrke 1976).

In contrast to this group of findings, Oliveira (1977) reported that elderly men and women living in the community who were classified as either high or low reminiscers were equally likely to report an absence of depression, high degree of life satisfaction, a positive self-image, and plans for the future. The only significant differences found between high and low reminiscers were that high reminiscers enjoyed reminiscing, felt more relaxed when they reminisced, and felt better about their past lives. Coleman (1974) also found that frequency of reminiscence and emotional states were unrelated. But when he considered both style and content of reminiscence, a positive relationship emerged between reminiscence and emotional states. Individuals who reported dissatisfaction with their past lives and who attempted to integrate and reevaluate the past were found to be less depressed and have a higher degree of life satisfaction than those with unsatisfactory life histories who tended not to reminisce or life review. Among those who were satisfied with their pasts, individuals who did and did not reminisce were equally well adapted. Postema (1970) examined the relationship between frequency and style of reminiscence and evaluated self-concept among a group of elderly men. Like Oliveira and Coleman, he observed no relationship between quantity of reminiscence and self-concept. Style of reminiscence, however, predicted positive self-concept, with defensive and well-adjusted reminiscers more likely to report positive views of the self than conflictual or avoidant reminiscers.

Tobin and Etigson (1968) investigated the relationship between memory content and current stress. Earliest memories were elicited from adolescents, young and middle-aged adults, and elderly adults. The memories were then coded for the presence of loss themes. Tobin and Etigson concluded that current circumstances are indeed incorporated into the reminiscence process. Furthermore, the congruence in level of loss in the memories of adolescents and elderly adults suggested that these life stages involve a heightened experience of crisis or stress, which is then reflected in memory.

There are no studies relating reminiscence to either outcome of stress or long-term adaptation among those not undergoing stress. Thus, as is readily apparent, the empirical research on reminiscence in the latter half of life is still in its earliest stages. Reminiscence is, to say the least, an elusive construct to measure; findings are often ambiguous, and questions concerning the characteristics and adaptive value of reminiscence in the latter half of life essentially remain unanswered. However, a few consistent if tentative points deserving further empirical consideration have emerged from the trends and patterns of findings reported in the literature. Reminiscence appears to be a psychologically salient but by no means universal phenomenon that is not restricted to any period of life. Indeed, the use of reminiscence may wax and wane over the course of a lifetime in relation to the press of current needs. Clearly, there are individual differences in the form and content of reminiscence; common patterns involve either conflict-ridden evaluations of negative aspects of the past or glorified presentations of the life story. There also appears to be some association between reminiscence and emotional states, but the relationship is with style or the affective content of reminiscence rather than with the frequency of reminiscence.

Despite the spareness of systematic studies to guide us, we shall undertake a reexamination of the theoretical formulations postulated by developmentalists regarding the special meaning of the personal past in the last decade or two of life. The common view that the elderly are more interested and involved in the past than they are in their present and future can be supported by our findings. Perhaps more important is our observation that focusing on the personal past can be explained in large part by the current circumstances of the elderly, and that the past serves as a simple but powerful source of gratification and as a mechanism for increasing interpersonal attention. Beyond this rather straightforward observation lies the complex and developmentally more important idea of the restructuring of the past. The personal past is not only a source of gratification but also a source of challenge—an arena for investment and work.

We have pursued two hypotheses that address the reworking of the past. One, labeled the "life review," assumes the existence of a normative process characteristic of all elderly, a task involved in the closing of one's life whose resolution can lead, if successful, to serenity, and if unsuccessful, to turmoil. Such a task challenges the best in people; it implies maturity, a sensitive appreciation of reality and problem solving at the highest level. The other hypothesis views the reworking of the past as the creation of a myth or drama of the past self—a process whose characteristics resemble defensive strategies. Like the life review, it involves considerable effort and reorganization, but rather than reconciliation with one's personal past, such reorganization is the creation of an image. It serves, we believe, to resolve a critical dilemma posed by the issues of old age and leads not to serenity but rather to stability.

We have developed some evidence that the life review does take place among some elderly. It is subtle, and from the measurement point of view, it is difficult to specify the exact nature of work on past conflicts. Although we have little doubt that it occurs, our evidence does not lead directly to understanding the implications of such reworking. We did not find, as we had anticipated, that such reworking would lead to an acceptance of finitude, nor did we find unambiguous evidence that such work would lead to better adaptation in late life. We found clearer evidence that the elderly more often rework their personal past for the defense of a meaningful self-concept. We have not heretofore seen this distinction made theoretically, but we believe that our evidence underscores the need to be more specific and ask more precise questions, such as: What is the function of the restructuring of personal memories? and How is it done? The concept of life review suffers from an affliction similar to that of other psychological concepts introduced in investigations of adult development, in which heuristic descriptive constructs are intertwined with the implicit value that humans function only at the highest level. We believe that our field is not served in this manner. The generation of a truly developmental psychology of later life does not require such value judgments.

In summing up, we are reminded that the sensitive observations of Erikson, Butler and others were made in a psychotherapeutic context. Aside from the obvious caveat that such a population is highly selected, it should be noted that the life review process—involving as it does a sorting out and restructuring of the past—is a task that demands high levels of inner skills not necessarily characteristic of most people. Perhaps a meaningful life review requires a setting emphasizing problem solving and a supportive context to accomplish this difficult and demanding process.

There obviously are some who, without benefit of a special setting supporting introspection, have engaged in a meaningful life review—witness the work of Tolstoy, Proust and others. Perhaps we have been in error in assuming that the special skills needed to carry out a successful life review—a lifelong habit of introspection and heightened preoccupation with themes of mortality and immortality—are characteristic of most men and women.

The life review represents a powerful set of ideas, but we believe a set too narrowly focused. To understand the full implications of the personal past at the close of life, alternative hypotheses must be considered, including reorganization in the service of mythmaking and utilization of the past as a resource for comfort and gratification, for a sense of control and mastery, or for social exchange. The intricacy and subtlety of the diverse processes we have identified, and the difficulty of assessing them, leave us unable to determine whether, on the one hand, there are any universal processes involving reminiscence in old age; or, on the other hand, whether there are systematic and predictable differences in the use of the past among individuals, so that some elderly reorganize their past through mythmaking to support the stability of self, other elderly confront their past to achieve resolution, and still other elderly use their past primarily for comfort or as a vehicle for social exchange.

Technical Notes

1. Interrater reliability was calculated for each of the seven scales as follows: significant figures, r=.83; past positive, r=.69; conflict resolution, r=.59; lack of resentment, r=.71; values fulfilled, r=.71; ownership of life, r=.85; and acceptance of negative aspects of life, r=.63. Intercorrelations among these seven scales were moderate, averaging .35 and ranging from .15 to .66. A factor analysis, of twenty-two life history scales, confirmed that these seven scales do address a unified concept, which we have labeled *reconciliation* (Revere 1971).

2. Interrater reliabilities for these five-point scales, determined by Pearson product-moment correlations, were the following: parents heroic, .81; spouse heroic, .80; parents socially relevant, .77; spouse socially relevant, .73; early memory as dramatic, .72; and total life dramatic, .88. The average of the intercorrelations among these five scales was .26; the correlations ranged from 0 (parents heroic and social relevancy of parents) to .45

(dramatization of the earliest memories and dramatization of total life). In general, correlations were not as high as for the reconciliation scale.

3. Validity of the introspection ratings was ascertained by interviewing a subsample of ten respondents using Gendlin's focusing techniques and then correlating introspection scores for the focusing interview with scores for the affect questionnaire. Eight of ten respondents received identical ratings on both measures. The interrater reliability for the affect questionnaire was 89 percent agreement within one point, and the stability coefficient over a one-year interval was .67.

12

Hope and Despair

UNTIL quite recently, the word *hope* was not likely to be found in the working vocabulary of the behavioral scientist. The term has theological, philosophical, and literary connotations rather than scientific ones; and most of what has been written about the subject has come from such perspectives (see, for example, Bloch 1953; Camus 1955; Marcel 1962; Moltmann 1969; Riezler 1950; Smith 1965; Tillich 1965). In his 1959 presidential address to the American Psychiatric Association, Karl Menninger (1959) noted that

> Our shelves hold many books now on the place of faith in science and psychiatry, and on the vicissitudes of . . . love. . . . But when it comes to hope, our shelves are bare. . . . It seems almost to be a tabooed topic, a personal matter, scarcely appropriate for public discussion. [pp. 481–482]

We did not anticipate using hope as a core psychological dimension in our research strategy. Hope began to emerge slowly as a construct worthy of consideration as we studied in detail the elderly undergoing radical changes in life space. Some elderly, upon relocation, would literally turn their back to the world in total resignation. We initially viewed this as clinical depression, and, as discussed in chapter 8, invested great effort into developing sensitive indices of this condition; however, the resignation we witnessed was not what we had been accustomed to thinking of as depression. These elderly people often did not show the signs usually associated with such states: They did not portray the dynamics of guilt (although the existence of depressive guilt in the elderly is questionable), but above all psychomotor retardation and labile affects were usually not to be seen. Moreover, the elderly individuals who signaled such despair appeared to have a more eroding impact on us than the usual reaction to a typically depressed elderly person. We found as clinicians that our personal "strategies" for warding off the affective contagion of hopelessness and resignation were less useful. The elderly who manifested this state did not project themselves into the future. They, even more than those manifestly depressed, existed in the present, bereft of both a future and a past, and seemed unable to extend themselves in either direction.

Hopelessness is not a universal reaction to age-associated traumas and losses. Most elderly people who have suffered through painful life circumstances do not exhibit hopelessness. Indeed, many whose bodies are withered and who have lost numerous significant others through death are able to cope with their present reality and simultaneously relate to their personal past. More important, they can also project themselves into the future, anticipating with great pleasure events such as a weekly card game, an outing a month hence, and the graduation from college of a favorite grandson. Positive anticipations that are realistic and achievable may not, however, be readily available to those in the last decades of life, and anticipation of future gratification may be even more difficult for elderly people who are undergoing environmental change. Unlike the unlimited future of the young adult, the elderly—faced with the inevitable losses of significant others, of a failing body, and of impending personal demise—are confronted with the unique psychological task of extending the self beyond both their own past and present. This task is made all the more difficult by the realistic limitations of the last decade of life and the onslaughts that are sure to have occurred or will occur.

Thus, hopefulness and its unfortunate opposite, despair, became a psychological issue worthy of study. The concept of hope provided us not only with a way of decoding the stories the elderly were telling us but also with a way of thinking about reactions to stress in the latter half of life.

The Concept of "Hope"

A HISTORICAL OVERVIEW

Starting in the early 1960s, a number of psychiatrists (Erikson 1964; Frank 1961, 1968; Frankl 1963; Melges and Bowlby 1969; Schachtel 1959) and psychologists (Birren 1964; Cantril 1964; Farber 1968; Mowrer 1960; Stotland 1969) argued that hope refers to a distinctive psychosocial phenomenon that influences many aspects of human behavior and should be amenable to scientific investigation.

Although it has on occasion been regarded as a human weakness (Camus 1955), the weight of opinion seems to be that hope—at least in its "realistic" (Birren 1959) or "genuine" (Tillich 1965) forms—is a valuable affective-conative attribute that functions to sustain adaptive striving in the face of threat. It has been speculatively implicated as contributing to favorable outcomes in such diverse situations as survival under conditions of extreme environmental stress (Frankl 1963; Wolff 1957); the placebo effect (Frank 1961); and effective interaction in teaching and healing (Menninger 1959; Frank 1968). Several clinical studies have found that the lack or loss of hope, as assessed impressionistically or by self-report, is related to the onset of disease (Schmale 1958) and is correlated with fatal illness (Greene, Young, and Swisher 1956; Küber-Ross 1969; LeShan 1961). One social psychological investigation concluded that the loss of hope is the basic lethal element in suicide (Farber 1968). However, neither documentation that hope is in fact implicated in human beings' adaptive capacity nor adequate conceptualization consistent with research in nonclinical settings seems to have been achieved.

This increasing interest by social scientists in hope as a relevant psychological dimension, however, has not generated adequate constructs for operationalization that could lead to useful measures. Thus, belatedly, we set about to develop a theoretical foundation that could lead to development of a measure for empirical investigations (Haberland 1972). Because our studies were not directed at the onset to the development of measures of hope, procedures were developed for both conceptualizating and indexing the concept through a "bootstrap strategy." By no means, then, have we developed an optimum or, perhaps, even a useful measure for others, but we do believe we can offer some insights into this important psychological state.

The hope-despair continuum might be construed heuristically as a distinct social-psychological state that differs in several respects from such related concepts as optimism-pessimism and elation-depression. The most critical distinguishing factor is that the psychological act of hope, on the one hand, and the state of despair, on the other, are inextricably linked with life-situations involving extraordinary stress; under such conditions, the individual's adaptive capacity is respectively enhanced or diminished. This position is perhaps most clearly expressed by the existential philosopher Gabriel Marcel (1962), who regards hope as an active reaction against the sense of captivity or alienation resulting from threats such as disease, estrangement, separation, loss, and exile: "The truth is that there can strictly speaking be no hope except when the temptation to despair exists. Hope is the act by which this temptation is actively or victoriously overcome" (p. 36).

DISTINCTION BETWEEN HOPELESSNESS AND DEPRESSION

Although there is reason to believe that hopelessness (or despair) differs from the traditional psychiatric syndrome of depression, the basis of the distinction is not easy to specify; the two concepts seem to be best viewed as referring to analytically distinct phenomena that may empirically merge under certain conditions or at some levels of intensity. When they are discussed in the same context, hopelessness tends to be regarded as somewhat more basic or specific than depression. Gaylin (1968), for example, asserts that despair is the "essential ingredient" in the depressive process. According to LeShan (1961), despair is more severe, "much more barren and hopeless," than depression. Melges and Bowlby (1969) argue that hopelessness—defined as "a feeling that the future holds little promise" with regard to how plans relate to goals—is the central and most basic "underlying dynamic" in the psychopathology of depression. In a similar vein, Lichtenberg (1957) says that despair is necessary to, but not sufficient to comprise, depression, which he defines as "a manifestation of felt hopelessness regarding the attainment of goals when responsibility for the hopelessness is attributed to one's personal defects."

These formulations are consistent with our own position insofar as hopelessness is linked with a lack of personal control over the achievement of desired outcomes. They differ from our position in that (with the exception of LeShan) they deal with hopelessness primarily in terms of its significance for the psychopathology of depression; we are emphasizing the independent significance of hope-despair in terms of its implications for coping with situations involving threats against the person. (The distinction between hope-despair and depression is suggested by the only moderate association between the hope measure to be described subsequently in this chapter and a measure of depression based on the Gottschalk, Springer, and Glaser (1961) method, $r = -.29$, $N=83$.)

HOPE AND ADAPTATION

With the exception of the few studies referred to earlier, there seems to have been little empirical research either on hope per se or on the relationship between the measurement of hope and successful adaptation. Some experimental work with animals has been interpreted as showing that hope is a prerequisite for survival-striving (Richter 1957) and even for learning in general (Mowrer 1960). Descriptive studies support the conclusion that a subjective experience similar to what is commonly called *hope* functions to motivate persistent activity and thereby sustain life in situations of extreme stress. These include reports of human behavior under such extraordinary conditions as involuntary internment in concentration and prisoner-of-war camps (Frankl 1963; Wolff 1957; Bettelheim 1943; Bondy 1943; Cohen 1953; Nardini 1952; Strassman, Thaler, and Schein 1956; Tas 1951; Wolf and Ripley 1947). Observers have frequently noted that, in such extreme situations, mass fluctuations of the overall death rate and individual cases of death often could not be entirely accounted for by the nature of the external stressor or by the medical condition of those who died. Descriptions of extreme apathetic withdrawal reactions—the psychological core of which was a state of having "given up" in the conviction that all further effort was useless—suggest that the proximate cause of at least some of these deaths was a noxious emotional state that could properly be labeled "hopelessness"—a personal reaction to stress that was often heightened by the feeling of having been socially abandoned by one's own people (Frank 1961).

A Conceptualization of Hope

A DEFINITION OF HOPE

Although the conceptual model to be presented here focuses on intrapersonal properties, it should be noted that hope is construed not as a stable personality trait but as a consequence of a series of interactions between the person and a particular life situation; namely, a situation characterized by a severe threat to personally valued conditions of existence. And although hope involves affect (affect being one of the dimensions of the model), hope is not synonymous with a temporary affective state or mood. Rather, it is a set of personally significant affective-cognitive predictions that the individual makes about the future, which have a degree of conative "force." Phenomenologically, it involves the pleasurable anticipation that things will somehow change for the better and that, at least in part, the application of individual effort is likely to make some difference in the outcome. Within this framework, then, the following working definition was proposed: Hope is the confident expectation of personally significant gratifying change in that zone of experienced time which is the intermediate future.

THE NATURE OF HOPE

Although hope is defined in terms of expectations or desires, it is not synonymous with them. Hope is distinguished from expectation by its quality of "transcendence." One expects or wishes for concrete objects and events in the immediate future, but hope transcends expectation; it "goes beyond" what is presented in everyday experience, both by referring to temporally more distant events and in having a more abstract goal. Thus, for Menninger (1959), hope consists of the positive expectations in a particular situation "which go beyond the visible facts"; for Lewin (1951), it refers to a similarity "between reality and irreality somewhere in the psychological future." The human capacity for symbolic representation allows the individual to link the concrete with the transcendent and "to hope" in the full sense of the term. Whereas expectation refers to a specific object in the immediate future, hope surpasses the immediate, residing in that zone of experienced time which is the "intermediate" future (Minkowski 1933) and having as an object a goal that is "incalculable," often in the nature of "salvation" (Marcel 1962). Another way of saying all this is that genuine hope involves a broadly focused life outlook that has as its object the achievement of "meaning" (Smith 1965), which often becomes realized in situations involving tragedy, suffering, and the threat of death.

THE DIMENSIONS OF HOPE

The foregoing considerations suggested that the components of the hope-despair construct might be conceptualized as deriving from a psychological universe composed of a number of fundamental dimensions, seven in all, which are implicit in the working definition. Since hope is embedded in temporal experience—expecially, but not exclusively, involving representations of the future—it was assumed that an exploration of three major facets of "time perspective" (Lewin 1951) would provide data for one set of empirical indicators of an individual's level of hopefulness. These three dimensions are extension, direction, and density. The remaining four dimensions of our construct, which are of an extratemporal nature, are locus-of-control, affect, and two different aspects of the goal-seeking quality of hope—gratifying change and a sense of purpose in life. These seven theoretical dimensions, and the components of each, will now be described.

Temporal Dimensions. In order to hope, one must be able to symbolically extend the self beyond its present moment in time into the not-yet-lived future, and also, it would appear, into the already-lived past, since hope for the future may be based on memories of past satisfaction (French 1952; Melges and Bowlby 1969; Verwoerdt and Scherer 1965). This ability to extend the self in time was investigated through the examination of time perspective—the total length of time conceptualized by the person, the complete temporal span extending beyond the moment. The dimension has two components, past-length and future-length.

To have the ability to extend the self into the moderately distant future or past does not mean that the person habitually does either. Whereas *extension* refers to the linear quality of time perspective, *direction* refers to a "cognitive posture" indicating the particular temporal realm that the person prefers, or toward which he or she tends to be experientially "pointed" (Vischer 1946). This dimension, then, has three components: future direction, present direction, and past direction.

Density, which concerns the quantitative aspect of personal time, refers to the degree to which the individual's future is perceived as being populated with events. Included are undesirable and affectively neutral expectations as well as those highly desirable ones usually associated with hopefulness. Perhaps the critical aspect of hope is more in the number of acceptable alternatives available than it is in having a single, highly desirable future goal. This is implied, for example, in an analysis of the psychological problems of aging (Vischer 1946) in which "hope" is described as involving the perception of "the future as a field of manifold possibilities"; this "belief in future possibilities," in turn, fosters "that will to life which enables the individual to bear the burdens of the moment" (p. 282).

Extratemporal Dimensions. The *locus-of-control* dimension consists of two contrasting orientations: internal control, the belief that the outcomes of behavior are primarily contingent upon personal skill and effort; and external control, the belief that behavior is primarily determined by impersonal forces, such as powerful others, chance, or fate. Since hopelessness is often linked with feelings of "helplessness" (Schmale 1958), "apathy" (Strassman, Thaler, and Schein 1956), and "giving up" (Nardini 1952), the implication is that the realistic or genuine form of hope—the type that should sustain adaptive striving in the face of threat—will be associated with internal rather than with external control. Internal control is viewed as a personality factor that predisposes one toward hopeful behavior when the situation "tempts" one to act otherwise. The assumption is that this basic sense of mastery generates an attitude of confidence in affecting outcomes, which decreases the likelihood of both the purely fantasied response to trouble that is "magic hope" (Schachtel 1959) and the pervasive sense of doubt concerning one's ability to construct a meaningful future that is "despair" (LeShan 1961).

The next dimension of the model is *affect*. The kind of affect that should be related to hope is, in the terms of Schachtel (1959), the directed and sustaining tension of an "activity affect," which is experienced as pleasurable, rather than the diffuse discharge of an "embeddedness-affect," which is felt as distress. The suggestion is that when hope exists, as indicated by the other components operating in concert, pleasant affect will accompany and sustain the conative act.

The goal-seeking and sense of meaning implicit in hope is conceptualized in terms of two dimensions, one "self-actualizing" and the other "self-transcending." Hope implies the desire for *gratifying change* in terms of personally significant values and goals. This dimension, which involves the ability to imaginatively extend the self into the future in an improved condition, was examined in terms of the degree to which the person believes he or she is presently, has in the past, and will in the future achieve goals that contribute to his or her development. Viewed in this manner as the pursuit of valued goals that have been set with reference to the outer world, hope bears some similarity to the concept of self-realization and is, in a sense, a special avenue through which self-realization can be achieved: "'Realizing oneself' means being engaged in an endeavor which combines 'the real,' i.e., the objective world, and 'the self,' i.e., the subjective world" (Weisskopf-Joelson 1968). In the case of self-actualizing goals, hope gives meaning to life by integrating internal fantasies with external realities.

Meaning may also be seen as originating in the effort to actualize values that exist in a world beyond humankind—values that transcend the individual (Tillich 1965; Frankl 1963; Weisskopf-Joelson 1968). It has been argued that the striving for a sense of ultimate *purpose-in-life* is the primary motivational force of man; and that "the real aim of human existence cannot be found without transcendence" (Frankl 1963, p. 175), the former being a by-product of the latter. In this view, hope bestows meaning by integrating different spheres of reality in a new sense, relating the realm of transcendent values to the realm of human lives. This achievement of meaning, in turn, allows hope itself to serve as an organizing or "integrating principle" (French 1952) which, in situations of extreme stress, "is of fundamental importance in holding a person together and keeping him going" (Buhler 1968, p. 38). This self-transcending dimension was investigated in terms of the degree to which the person recognizes and is motivated by a sense of ultimate purpose-in-life.

Procedure

The complexity of the conceptual framework developed for hope and the fact that our interest in it emerged slowly subsequent to our major data-collection effort necessitated a rather cumbersome procedure in order to pursue the empirical study of this concept. The first stage was that of index construction with a pilot sample. It involved the development of a pool of indicators; the construction of a pilot index of hope embodying the elements set forth in the conceptual model; and the administration of a battery of instruments to a pilot subsample ($N=15$). The subsample was selected from the three situational subsamples from the Home for Life study (those awaiting entry into the institutions, those already living there, and the community control group). The second stage was the assessment of hope levels for all respondents for whom we had available data, using as a basis the hope scores developed for members of the pilot subsample. In this stage, measures that had previously been gathered were correlated with the pilot hope index as well as its several component variables. A multiple regression analysis was then used to select the best combination of measures as an approximation of the pilot hope index.

THE ASSESSMENT OF HOPE: PILOT SUBSAMPLE

The assessment procedure undertaken with the pilot subsample was based on the seven conceptual dimensions of hope outlined in the previous section, the variables that constitute these dimensions, and the scores or indicators generated from data collected by means of a specially constructed test battery. The battery consisted of ten instruments, seven of which were used to provide indicators of the variables entering directly into the conceptual model and three of which (attitude scales, an interview, and a measure of optimism-pessimism) provided criteria used to examine the construct validity of the basic measures.

The seven variables constituting the pilot hope index were: future density—the number of personally relevant events expected; future length—the span of future time conceptualized; past direction—the tendency to be oriented toward or to think more about the past then the present or future; internal future locus-of-control—the belief that desirable future outcomes are more often determined by personal endeavor than by impersonal or chance factors; pleasant future affect—the tendency to view the events that fill the personal future with positive affect; personal gratifying change—the self-actualizing tendency to project the self into the future (specifically, two years into the future) in an "improved" condition; and, finally, a self-transcending sense of ultimate purpose-in-life. (For test details, see Haberland 1972.)

Pilot hope scores were computed for the members of the pilot subsample. Each variable was weighted equally by ranking on a seven-point scale, giving a possible summed score for a respondent ranging from 7 to 49. The resulting index, which ranged from 11.5 to 46.0, was normally distributed, with a mean of 29.6 and a standard deviation of 10.7.

THE ASSESSMENT OF HOPE: STUDY POPULATION

Since the test battery was administered only to those respondents from the study population who were also members of the pilot subsample, the problem of assessing hope for the population of the Home for Life study had yet to be resolved. The two essential steps by which this was accomplished were first, to determine for the pilot subsample, by means of multiple regression analysis, that weighted combination of variables from the data base that were most closely predicted by the pilot hope index; and second, to use the regression equation to "predict" and compute a hope indicator score for each respondent in the Home for Life study.

The regression analysis yielded a multiple correlation coefficient of .89 with the pilot hope index, a relationship which resulted from the differential contribution of five measures. In the order of their relative contribution to the criterion, these variables were (1) anomie, assessed by a five-item scale (Srole 1956) which, at its extreme pole, measures the individual's perception of his or her social and cultural milieu as essentially disordered, valueless, and devoid of meaning; (2) willingness to introspect (Gendlin 1964; Gorney 1968), a self-reflexive process whereby the person introspectively examines his or her feelings; (3) self-esteem, as assessed by the self-sort task; (4) time perspective, derived from three sentence-completion items scored for the degree to which future time is perceived as pleasant, filled, and fleeting; and (5) overt time perspective, assessed by three questions dealing with the value of time, the tendency to make plans, and expectations of future gratification for self and significant others.

Before examining the relationship of hope to adaptation, we will briefly discuss some observations bearing on the validity of the measures used to index the concept. Hope, as discussed in the introduction to this chapter, is conceived of as a contextually influenced psychological state. Our study of individuals living in the community who were making application to enter old-age homes provides a useful context for demonstrating the validity of our measure. It will be recalled that the study involved three groups of elderly: those awaiting entry into homes for the aged, and two matched groups, one already living in such institutions and one of aged living in the community who had no plans in the immediate future for making such application. The psychological and social limitations of institutional life and the fact that such institutions are "homes for life" lead us to expect that the institutionalized aged would show the least hopeful stance; those living in the communities and successfully engaged in life would probably show the highest level of hope; and those waiting to enter institutions would be expected to show hope levels somewhere in between. We found, as we had anticipated, that the community group was the most hopeful; the institutional residents the least hopeful; and the waiting list group in the middle. (All the mean differences between each pair of groups were statistically significant beyond the .05 level.)

Our assumption that context influences level of hope was further borne out by the hope scores of the eighty-five respondents from the waiting list who actually became residents of old-age homes. During the typical interval of six months between the first assessment of hope prior to institutionalization and the second assessment subsequent to institutionalization, there was a statistically significant decline in the mean level of hope ($p < .01$ level). This finding supports the general theoretical perspective we have developed on hope and indicates that the summary measure used to index hope is potentially useful. As reported in a previous work (Tobin and Lieberman 1976), many psychological parameters show slight improvement, but more frequently show high stability from pre-institutionalization to a few months subsequent to the institutionalization. The finding that hope does not show this pattern, but instead declines significantly from pre- to post-institutionalization, may reflect its special relevance for understanding the circumstances and the attendant psychological issues confronting the elderly.

Case Illustration

Let us return to Mrs. A. one last time. The effect of environment on hope levels, as well as the way hope changes with changes in life circumstance, is illustrated by the reactions of Mrs. A., first interviewed as a community respondent, as she moved toward institutionalization. By now it is apparent that she was an admirable woman who weathered the storms of changes in her life circumstances. There was little in her case report to suggest anything other than great stability. Ego functions remained constant, the self was stable, and overall there were few changes in her pattern of reminiscence. We did, however, detect an increased concern, if not a preoccupation, with death. This shift was vividly portrayed in the changes in earliest memory from before to after institutionalization. Had hope similarly changed?

Before admission Mrs. A. was realistic about herself and her situation. At the time, the interviewer said that "she knew the score," emphasizing her willingness and capacity to address successfully the impending relocation. Her response to the Srole Anomic Scale reflects Mrs. A.'s hopeful *weltanschauung*. She was undecided about the first two of the five statements ("In spite of what some people say the lot of the average man is getting worse" and "It's hardly fair to bring children into the world with the way things look for the future"). But she disagreed with the third statement ("Nowadays a person has to live pretty much for today and let tomorrow take care of itself") and strongly disagreed with the fourth ("These days a person doesn't really know who he can count on"). She returned to being undecided on the last statement ("There's little use in writing to public officials because often they aren't really interested in the problems of the average man"). Thus, although neutral on three statements, she communicated that a person cannot live only for today but must attend to tomorrow and also that a person can count on others. Both messages appeared throughout her interview.

At this time, before admission, she was particularly looking forward to family activities, for example, she completed the stem "Each day . . ."

with, "I'm waiting for calls from my children which I do not get." She did not anticipate that entering into a home for the aged would disturb these relationships because between visits she would have people and activities and be in a secure environment. Her morale was high, as reflected in her scores on the life satisfaction ratings, shown here along with the interviewer's rationale for each rating:

1. Zest versus apathy, rated 5: Mrs. A. was given the highest score on this scale because she showed an active interest in people and events.
2. Resolution and fortitude, rated 4: Mrs. A. appeared to have maintained a philosophic attitude while coping with many different situations.
3. Goodness of fit between desired and achieved goals, rated 5: Having provided a good education for her children, who she felt loved her, Mrs. A. expressed feelings of pride that reflected the successful accomplishment of her goals.
4. Self-concept, rated 4: Mrs. A.'s good self-image was manifested in her sense of importance to her family who, according to her, "think I'm tops." Pride in her appearance and her ability to take care of herself and to get along with others indicate a good self-image.
5. Mood, rated 4: The interviewer noted a balance between Mrs. A.'s different moods. Thus, although she spoke of occasional depression, she also described her attempt to master it and to count her blessings.

After Mrs. A.'s admission to the home, the interviewer's rating of life satisfaction was identical. The first evidence of change in Mrs. A.'s emotional attitudes surfaced in her responses to the sentence completion test. The stem, "To me, death is . . ." was completed before admission by referring to others who suffer terribly from incurable illness for whom death is "a big relief." After admission, she completed the stem with ". . . the best thing that can happen to anybody." Before coming to the home, Mrs. A. indicated that death would be welcomed if it were to avert physical pain and suffering. Now that she was in the home, however, even though she showed no evidence of deterioration in physical status, she indicated that she had no qualifications regarding the benefits of death.

What had changed was the fullness of meaningful events in her distant future and her capacity to control the course of her future. Whereas before admission Mrs. A.'s thoughts were full of future family events, now she was focusing more narrowly on the activities in the home. In response to the stem, "Each day . . . " she earlier referred to her family; now she responded " . . . I look forward to what is going to happen. Listen to the announcements of what they are going to give." References to her family are still introduced, but her embeddedness in the institution is paramount; and with the institution's ascendence, the future becomes foreshortened.

In response to queries regarding future plans, before admission Mrs. A. talked not only of family but also of community activities in the intermediate future. After admission she said that she "made little plans for the future." She continued to look forward to activities, but increasingly in the more immediate future. Increasingly, too, planning for future happenings is out of her control. The shift toward lowered hope is most clearly reflected in her responses to the Srole Anomie Scale. Mrs. A. unequivocally communicated that she must live only for today and that she can count on no one. Whereas prior to admission she was either undecided about or disagreed with the last three statements, now she strongly agreed with them: "Nowadays a person has to live pretty much for today and let tomorrow take of itself"; "These days a person doesn't really know who he can count on"; and "There's little use in writing to public officials because they really aren't interested in the problems of the average man." Thus, although Mrs. A. could be described as retaining her feelings of well-being and although she showed only negligible signs of depression, she had made a meaningful and significant movement from relative hopefulness toward relative despair.

Findings

HOPE AND ADAPTATION

Hope scores were computed for the entire Home for Life study sample of 85 respondents waiting to enter homes for the aged, as well as for the two matched control groups—elderly people residing in the community and not planning to enter homes for the aged ($N=35$) and long-term residents of old age homes ($N=37$). Based on the previous discussion on the effects of context on hope, we analyzed the relationship of hope to subsequent adaptation separately for these three subsamples. Using z-transformed scores, we found that means for the waiting list sample were $-.04$ for those who were unchanged and $-.21$ for those who declined or died ($p<.02$); for the community respondents, .90 for the unchanged and .60 for those who declined or died (not significant); and for the institutional controls, $-.13$ and $-.89$ respectively ($p<.05$).

Those who maintained their level of adaptation had higher levels of hope compared to respondents who declined or died. Even in the nonstress circumstances—the institutional group and the community group—higher levels of hope are associated with greater likelihood of not showing subsequent marked decline or death. Our finding that subsequent levels of physical, mental, and social functioning are predicted by hope suggests that the level of hope, in and of itself, is not a unique predictor of adaptation under high stress situations alone. Rather, it seems associated with future levels of adaptation, and of course is sensitive to different environmental contexts. The predictive power of hope for subsequent adaptation is not simply a product of poorer functioning at Time 1 (before relocation), since our criteria of marked decline, as outlined in chapter 2, is based on relative functioning—that is, on significant idiographic changes based on the specific level of each person at baseline.

As indicated at the beginning of this chapter, the concept of hope emerged subsequent to the major data collection. The framework was applied to reexamining the Unwilling Old Ladies study to determine if it was possible to assess hope. This review of data and measures revealed that the measure of depression resembled our concept of hope more than it did clinical depression. The ratings of "depression" were based on respondents' evaluations of past life. High ratings were given when evaluations were negative—when, for example, there were frequent expressions of consistent deprivation, lack of accomplishments, and a diffuse, lifelong unhappiness. The "depression" ratings also reflected the respondent's view of a negative future, such as conscious expectations of illness and infirmity, increased isolation, lack of gratifying experiences, and death. In general, respondents rated high on "depression" indicated an almost complete surrender to their fate and a feeling of powerlessness to assume any meaningful direction for their lives. In all cases, a negative past and an empty future were found together. In contrast to the emotional state of those rated as depressed, while many of those rated as not depressed spoke of various losses and regrets, they did not dwell upon them in a morbid and preoccupied fashion. Thus, they did not view their past lives as having been empty, unfulfilled and generally dissatisfying. Also, the respondents rated as not depressed tended to feel that while death was an imminent possibility, they had no intention of "giving up" just because they were old and dependent on others for sustenance.

Reliability of the ratings of depression was checked by selecting ten interviews at random, five from those rated as "depressed" and five from those rated as not "depressed." The percent of agreement with one other independent scorer was computed, and 100 percent agreement was found between the two raters.

Support for the reinterpretation of the "depression" ratings as "hope-despair" can be found in the correlates of the ratings of depression. Those rated "depressed" did not show more cognitive disturbance, showed no differences on ego pathology (the Dana scoring of the TAT cards), and, perhaps most important, did not cluster in any particular personality type (the acceptors, the angry, the self-invested, the withdrawers, and the deniers described in chapter 8). In fact, the most well-integrated type, the acceptors, contained several individuals who showed evidence of despair. The only association found was between ratings of depression and ratings of ego energy, based on response to TAT cards in which the depressed showed significantly less ego energy than did the nondepressed ($p<.05$).

Of paramount importance was the finding that those rated as depressed showed significantly more maladaptive changes than did the nondepressed group ($p<.05$). Of the twenty-three in this study who showed negative change, fourteen were "depressed," whereas of the twenty-two whose level of adaptation remained unchanged subsequent to relocation, seventeen were rated nondepressed.

Although these observations are only suggestive of the more complex model we have developed of hope, this finding is similar to the one where the more complex model was used and showed the same association between hope before relocation and positive adaptation subsequent to relocation. Furthermore, as described in chapter 7 in the Home for Life study we found no linkage between depression (using either projective tests or standard psychological tests) and outcomes. This adds further support that the ratings of respondents in the Unwilling Old Ladies study may indeed reflect hope and its converse, despair, rather than depression.

To illustrate some of the differences between the respondents rated as "depressed" or not "depressed," as well as to illustrate why the measure assesses hope and not depression, some excerpts from the prerelocation interview are presented here. In these excerpts, "I" stands for the interviewer and "R" for the respondent.

Respondents Rated as "Depressed."

Case No. 1:

I:

How do you think the coming years are going to be for you?

R:

I hope I don't have anymore. I'm hoping it will be very short and quick. I'm tired, dreadfully tired. And I've gone through so much all my life. I was so unhappy all my life. Then to have my boys go. That just capped it. I was ready to give up, and I would like to go NOW—would like very much to go.

Case No. 38:

I:

How do you feel about the years to come?

R:

Well, I wouldn't care if there weren't many.

I:

Tell me about that.

R:

I can't see that I have anything to live for. Can you?

I:

You mean you feel there is no point in going on at all?

R:

No, I don't. I wouldn't want to take my life or anything, but it's just as well if it doesn't last too long. I really feel that way. I can't see any point in it. There are a lot in here that have a lot of children and they won't take them home, they are letting them go, but that wouldn't have happened to me. [R is bitter over her son's death in an auto accident.]

Case No. 36:

I:

How do you feel about the years to come?

R:

Well, I don't think there will be too many for me and I don't dread the suffering and I have no fear of death. I do feel that I didn't get nothing from life like most women get.

I:

What do you mean like most women get?

R:

Well, it's everybody's due I think to marry, have a home of their own, have their own children and be successful and know that their children, as they are growing up, are being educated and successful.

I:

The fact that you didn't marry has been a big disappointment to you?

R:

No, I can't say it was, but I feel like I didn't get anything out of life. I was born and lived and will die before long and I have had nothing, only what little pleasure I could snatch and that was always through great suffering. And I have tried so hard, but it always seemed like something crossed me up.

Subjects Rated as Not "Depressed."

Case No. 19:

I:

Do you ever feel there isn't any point in going in life?

R:

Oh no, I sure don't. I'm going to live it from day to day and get the most out of it. You should. I hope when I get down there [the relocation institution] that I will be happy and take in some of the activities.

I:

In other words, you are looking forward to getting as much enjoyment as possible out of whatever the future holds?

R:

That's right. It would be terrible if you sat and felt sorry for yourself and felt what is the use of going on. You make yourself miserable and you are the only one that's hurt when you do that. I'm not going to let that happen to me.

Case No. 11:

I:

What kind of a deal do you think you got out of life?

R:

Oh, I think the Lord has been very good and gracious to me all of my life, probably more than I have deserved, and toward the end of my life I have had such a good home here and I feel that I will have a good home there. I have been treated very, very fine.

I:

How do you feel about the years to come?

R:

Well, I don't suppose there will be too many. I am eighty-eight now you know. But I think they will be happy years because I feel like I will be contented there [the relocation institution].

I:

Do you ever feel that there is no point in going on in life?

R:

No, no. I don't feel that way, no. I feel there is a great deal in life yet.

Case No. 26:

I:

What kind of a deal do you think you got out of life?

R:

Oh, a good deal. I did a lot of work in my life; I enjoyed it. I enjoyed my married life. My husband was in the Navy for eight years and I had to give him up and I done pretty good.

I:

Do you worry much about the future?

R:

No, I don't have a worry like that. I don't have nothing to worry about; nothing to lose and everything to gain.

The difference on future outlook and evaluation of their past lives are strikingly apparent. While not all were as emphatic in their attitudes, the responses to these interview questions from the majority of respondents appeared to provide support for the presence or absence of hopefulness.

HOPE AND DISTANCE FROM DEATH

So far, we have shown that hope levels are strongly affected by environmental context and that a high degree of hope increases the likelihood that homeostatic equilibrium will be maintained after a year's time. Conversely, those with a low degree of hope will in a year's time be more likely to show marked decline in social, psychological, and physical functioning. Our results also indicate, however, that hope bears no unique relationship to adaptation under stress, since similar results were found for both the community residents and the long-term institutional aged.

Given this lack of a unique relationship between hope and stress adaptation, we decided to use the "distance from death" design as outlined in chapter 9 to further explore hope and despair. We had previously demonstrated that the elderly who were approaching death were aware on some level of the imminence of death up to a year prior to death. We asked whether those who are closer to death show lower levels of hope. We identified, as described in chapter 9, forty elderly respondents from the waiting list, community, and the institutional samples who died up to a year after the last measurement point. As controls, we selected forty matched individuals, matched for environmental context (community, waiting list, or institution) as well as for sex and age. When compared on the hope measure, those closer to death showed lower hope levels than those further from death in 68 percent of the pairs, a statistically significant distribution of differences (p=.02).

A Reexamination of Hope

Given the observations made on those close to death in chapter 9 and the likelihood that at some level of awareness individuals register their approaching death, it is not too surprising that distance from death should significantly and appreciably affect hope levels. Because of this finding, we returned once again to our analyses of the stressed group (those awaiting relocation) and reexamined the relationship of hope to adaptation. This time, however, rather than examining outcome based on a comparison between those who remained stable and those who subsequently showed marked decline or death, we separated the marked decline group from those who had died. Our findings were now rather striking. In the nonstress group, the level of hope for those who remained stable was higher than for both those who showed marked decline and for those who died. In the stress sample, however, there was a marked departure from this general rule: Those who died had significantly higher levels of hope when compared to those showing marked decline as well as to those who showed no change. In other words, under the stress condition, the highest level of hope expressed by respondents prior to undergoing the stress engendered by relocation was associated with increasing deaths. Excluding the outcome of death, however, the relationship between level of hope and adaptation was the same, namely, those who markedly declined initially showed more signs of hopelessness.

Our observation that, under certain conditions, high levels of hope may be predictive of mortality calls to mind Menninger's (1959) argument that the tendency to disparage the importance of hope in human affairs—to condemn it as a weakness, a narcotic, or an illusion—is in part a manifestation of the unrecognized truth that hope, in order to effectively influence adaptation and survival, must exist in precisely the "right amount." He also made the point (Menninger and Menninger 1942, p. 214) that the devaluation of hope may be "a common device for preventing disappointment," that is, the refusal to believe in favorable possibilities which in extreme form is neurotic pessimism or misanthropy. These two issues raised by Menninger—namely, that there is an appropriate "amount" of hope and that "disappointment" may be one of its consequences—seem to provide some speculative ordering of our results.

Menninger also said (1959) that while a "deficiency of hope is despair and leads to decay," an "excess of hope is presumption and leads to disaster" (pp. 482–483). This statement describes the curvilinear relationship between hope and subsequent outcome actually found for the elderly under stress: a low level of hope ("a deficiency") led to marked decline in overall functioning ("decay"), and the highest level of hope ("an excess") led to death ("disaster"). To extend the likeness, an intermediate level of hope—apparently, under such conditions of stress, "the right amount"— led to successful adaptation (Haberland 1972, p. 105).

There are, indeed, many suggestions in the literature that hope may have negative effects. Whether in terms of a critical level or "amount" of hope, as postulated by Menninger, or its possible manifestation in pathological form, variously depicted as "illusory" (Camus 1955), "magical" (Schachtel 1959), or "foolish" (Tillich 1965), the potentially self-destructive consequences of hope have frequently been noted. That hope clearly implies disappointment has been pointed out, for example, by Bettelheim (1960), and the punitive effects of the disappointment resulting from illusory or otherwise inauthentic hope have been described from perspectives as widely separated as behaviorism and phenomenology. Mowrer (1960) holds that disappointment is punishing through its arousal of emotions such as anger, sorrow, and fear; and Binswanger (1968) likens it to "shock" and to becoming "uprooted" through a loss of relatedness to the social surroundings, psychologically experienced as "stumbling, sinking, and falling."

Considerations such as the foregoing suggest that hope may not be altogether effective in influencing adaptation to those conditions of relatively high stress involving environmental change. When the elderly person becomes socially and psychologically "uprooted" by becoming a member of a waiting list to enter an institution, and later moves from the status of waiting to the fact of residence, too much hope may be worse than having too little. When thwarted hopes are added to the burdens of a fundamentally vulnerable person in a difficult situation involving experiences of separation and loss, the need to redefine the self, and new demands for the exercising of competence, death may be hastened. For hope to be effective in adaptation, these results suggest, it must exist in the "right amount," the amount becoming critical under conditions of stress. We may conclude that, in general, the attribute of hope does seem to make a difference in the adaptive capacities of the elderly. Hopelessness, it appears, leads to morbidity no matter what the setting. Hope, more often than not, leads to adaptation; but under some conditions, to paraphrase Menninger, an excess of hope may be a presumption and may lead to disaster.

Part 5

CONCLUSION

13

Stress, Adaptation, and Development: A Reassessment

WE have examined three crises common to the last decade or two of life: adaptational challenges stimulated by changes in life space; losses; and the increasing certainty that life is terminating. Although such crises are not unique to the very old, how they are addressed and mastered is, in large part, determined by a person's life stage.

We share with many of our colleagues the belief that the psychology of the aged can best be understood through a life-stage perspective. The philosophy underlying our studies was embedded in the Committee on Human Development at the University of Chicago, which for forty years has provided the orientation that life stage is a crucial if not a determinant consideration in understanding the psychology of individuals. Although we recognized when we initiated our studies that no powerful theory of life-span development currently exists, we nevertheless anticipated that the life course would offer a perspective—and perhaps more important, a promise in the future—for understanding people. Our perspective, thus, is not characteristic of the traditional emphasis on continuity that Kagan (Brim and Kagan 1980) has so provocatively and critically described. Kagan examines Western thought and documents the pervasive belief that the experiences of infancy and early childhood have a lasting effect on adult behavior and personality. Evidence for this belief comes from diverse disciplines: Behaviorists argue that it is difficult to extinguish behavior learned during early childhood because of the special quality of the conditions of reinforcement in early life; for psychoanalysts, the source of lifelong anxiety is generated during childhood and only defenses are altered; social psychologists contend that the self-image is developed in childhood, and life is played out as a self-fulfilling prophecy. In the enduring dialectic concerning stability and change, the social sciences have emphasized continuity rather than change.

The pervasive view of continuity is captured in a quote from William James (1890, p. 121, called to our attention by Moss and Susman 1980, p. 530):

> Already at the age of 25 you see the professional mannerism settling down on the young commercial traveller, on the young doctor, on the young minister, on the young counselor at law. You see the little lines of cleavage running through the character, the tricks of thought, the prejudices, the ways of the shop in a word, from which the man can by and by no more escape than his coat sleeve can suddenly fall into a new set of folds. On the whole it is best he should not escape. It is well for the world that in most of us, by the age of 30, the character is set like plaster, and will never soften again.

In contrast, our investigation began with the perspective that adulthood, and particularly the last decade or two of life, is marked by as much change as continuity. A commitment to a general orientation does not necessarily provide a clear pathway to follow. Throughout this book, we have counterposed two distinct positions: theories of human stress that are static, age-irrelevant models concerned with specifying modifiers (intervening variables that alter the relationship between stress stimuli and consequent responses) and a developmental perspective in which modifiers of stress are conceptualized as unique to life stages.

This chapter reexamines the conceptual underpinning of our studies and the interpretation we have given to our findings. To place our findings in perspective, we shall pursue three separate, yet interrelated issues. First, in the section on "The Nature of Crises and Predicting Adaptation," we reflect on the set of questions that arise directly from the large body of psychological and sociological research on human stress, reexamining the issues discussed in chapters 4 through 8. What have we learned about the nature and source of stress? How were our findings affected by the way we conceptualized and measured adaptation? What do the mediators examined in chapters 6, 7, and 8 tell us about general models of human stress? In the next section, "Selective Survival: A Dilemma in Studying

Psychological Development in Later Life," we reexamine the models, methods, and designs customarily used in adult development in light of our findings on psychological aspects of selective survival. Then, in the final section, "Toward a Psychology of Old Age," we provide a framework for understanding the unique psychological characteristics of old age.

The Nature of Stress and Predicting Adaptation

The search by social scientists for conditions that affect the course of human life represents a growing and diverse collection of concepts and studies. We have added to the collection through an intensive examination of the movement of elderly persons from one environment to another so that we can better understand and conceptualize the sources of stress. In doing so, we began with the recognition that in the literature events are considered stressful either because they change the circumstances of people's lives, leading to new adaptative challenges, or because of the symbolic meanings they have for individuals. These contrasting assumptions reflect differences in psychological perspectives: One is a more mechanistic view in which stress is conceptualized as a consequence of the impingement of external forces that require adaptation, and the other emphasizes the unique capacity of humans to symbolize—to give meaning to—potentially disruptive events and circumstances. Although investigators generally perceive the critical events in life as containing both aspects—that is, adaptive changes, which are not interpreted as losses and the symbolizing of these events as losses—most studies emphasize one or another of these assumptions.

Much of the research on adaptation to stress focuses on modifiers—characteristics of the person and the social surroundings that alter the consequences of stress, either by modifying the source of stress or by mitigating the effects of the stress. A set of modifiers about which there is consensus has emerged over time: cognitive appraisals of the threatening event (the source of stress); social resources, such as the utilization of others for help; and internal resources, such as ego strength and coping strategies. Starting with this consensus, we began our exploration of the linkage between stress and adaptation by examining the sources of stress. First in chapter 4 ("The Impact of Threat and Loss"), we focused on the symbolic meaning of the event, relocation, which we conceptualized as anticipatory threat and subsequent loss. Chapter 5 ("The Crisis of Environmental Change"), next dealt with adaptative challenge operationalized as environmental quality, the extent of the congruence between individual style and the new environment's demands, and the degree of environmental discontinuity. Then, in chapters 6 ("The Management of Threat and Loss"), 7 ("Risk Factors: Prediction of Adaptation"), and 8 ("Personality and Adaptation"), we examined a series of mediators: management strategies directed toward threat including degree of coping effort, level of integration, and degree of mastery; personal resources, including cognitive capacities, health resources, available energy, and social supports; adequacy of pre-stress functioning, defined as mental health or ego strength; and finally, more enduring characteristics or qualities of the individuals, reflected in personality traits, dimensions, and types. To examine the predictive power of these mediators we attempted to replicate findings across four relocation situations.

Relocation clearly constituted a stress for the elderly despite considerable variations in the conditions of the relocation and of the populations relocated. In all four studies, approximately half of those moved showed adaptive failures—psychological disability, serious illness, or death. The fact of stress was not at issue; rather, our concern was to develop a predictive model that would account for individual differences in reaction to the common event. In reexamining the framework, our emphasis will be on three issues: (1) on consideration of the nature of stress, (2) re-evaluation of the mediating linkages between stress and adaptation, and (3) examining how adaptation can be conceptualized for the understanding of the association between stress and adaptation.

The most powerful set of outcome predictors was neither cognitive appraisals of threat and loss nor the mediators between stressor and reaction, but rather environmental quality, person-environment congruence, and environmental discontinuity—all aspects of environments that create adaptive challenges. Despite the fact that the situation was common to all our elderly respondents, the findings presented in chapters 4 and 5 clearly indicate that not all were equally stressed. When we examined the hypothesis that adverse outcomes (psychological impairment, illness, or death) were a function of adaptational challenge measured by the environmental circumstances of the new setting, the findings clearly showed that the level of stress, indexed by environmental variables, had the most influence on adaptation. Comparative analyses of outcome predictors in the Deinstitutionalized Elites and the Death of an Institution studies, encompassing environmental variables (amount of stress), as well as characteristics of the individual representing the stress mediators, revealed that the major source of variance in outcomes was accounted for by environmental variables.

When we examined the source of stress as a symbolic event portending threat and subsequent loss, however, our findings were not as clear-cut. Although level of threat was associated with short-term depressive reactions subsequent to relocation, neither level of threat nor the experience of loss were directly associated with increases in illness, deaths, or psychological impairment, the long-term outcome criteria. Thus, in the enduring, and perhaps unresolvable, dialectic between the symbolic and external perspectives on stress, the weight of the findings developed in our studies clearly suggests a view that adaptive challenge as a source of stress is to be preferred over the symbolic meaning of the change. This does not, of course, imply that threat was neither real nor palpable. High degree of threat did lead to increased depression after relocation. Rather, the findings imply that the association between the meaning of stress and its long-term consequences involves a more complex chain of mediators.

The critical factor in the association between stressors as symbolic threat and outcomes was found to be the management strategies that elderly persons use to contain and ward off the threatening implications of relocation. Three types of strategies, investigated in chapter 6, were the degree of coping effort, the level of integration or cognitive restructuring, and the felt degree of mastery over relocation. Management strategies were associated not only with the amount of depression experienced after the move, but also, and more importantly, to subsequent long-term outcomes. The most potent management strategy was the creation by aged persons of a view that they had mastery and control over their lives and the impending crises. The greater the perceived mastery and control, the less likely were depressive reactions after relocation which, in turn, affected long-term outcomes. The management strategies, particularly degree of mastery, are conceptually akin to what Lazarus (1966) termed "secondary appraisal"; and it was the success of these strategies that enabled the elderly respondents to diminish the perceived threat. Such effective management strategies imply a substantial degree of myth-making, an issue that will be addressed in the last section of this chapter. Suffice it to say here that autoplastic strategies work to diminish the negative meanings of relocation.

The finding that a major portion of the explained variance for success or failure in adaptation is accounted for by environmentally induced challenge does not suggest that this is sufficient for understanding the relationship between stressful events and outcome. As described in chapter 5, the more able elderly persons—those who function more complexly prior to relocation and who by and large have greater resources—are most affected for better or worse by the stresses of relocation. A revision of the view of person-environment interaction, at least among the elderly, is required. Although we found in chapter 7 that the highly vulnerable elderly—those whose health and cognitive functioning were below a minimum level—were more likely to suffer untoward consequences as a result of relocation, once that portion of the population is removed from the analysis, an explanation of person-environment relationship requires a more complex model. The well-functioning older people are the most responsive to environmental quality and environmental change; they are the ones whose adaptation is most critically affected by environments.

The weight of the evidence from our findings about resources and level of current functioning described in chapter 6 and chapter 7 about personality characteristics suggests that the psychological characteristics that predicted subsequent positive adaptation in our studies ran counter to the characteristics of the optimally functioning person usually expected to produce better outcomes, namely, greater cognitive, health, and social resources; higher energy outputs; better mental health; higher ego strength. Paradoxically, individuals functioning at the most optimal levels were not the most likely to be successful in adaptation. Nor did social supports play their expected role in mediating the consequences of stress, although again, this has usually been considered an enabling characteristic that leads to successful adaptation at earlier periods of life. Moreover, the dramatic findings portrayed in chapter 8 that personality constellations reflecting aggressiveness were associated with successful adaptation posits as adaptive a set of characteristics that would not be associated with favorable outcome earlier in life. Certainly, this constellation would not reflect optimum functioning in younger people. Our results regarding the coping strategies that successfully mitigate threat once again points to the unexpected. Strategies based on the dictates of reality, which have been found by investigators studying younger populations to predict adaptation, did not prove to be adaptive for our elderly respondents. Conversely, characteristics of people that would usually be considered predictive of maladaptation at earlier periods of life were found to predict successful adaptation among the elderly undergoing relocation.

In our view, the most parsimonious explanation of observations such as these is that there are major discontinuities in the psychological processes leading to successful adaptation in late life and that the characteristics that make for successful adaptation may be age specific. Unfortunately, this "post-hoc" conclusion can only be speculative because we obviously do not know what our respondents were like before we studied them. We cannot exclude an explanation that it is not that individuals have changed but rather that our findings are contaminated by the problem of selective survival. Yet we are inclined to propose that the elderly people we studied would have looked different at earlier points in their life span on the psychological processes that we have identified as being associated with successful adaptation in late life. Our retrospective study of their lives, based on intensive interviews in which they recounted these earlier periods, as well as the lack of constancy in many of the psychological characteristics that we studied over a short period of two to three years, persuades us that change rather than constancy is the rule for many of these psychological attributes.

Before proceeding to a discussion of selective survival, a brief commentary on the conceptualization of adaptation is warranted. The slowly accumulated knowledge regarding the psychology of old age has evolved from research strategies that have invariably included definitions of successful adaptation. Concepts used for operationalizing successful aging present dilemmas far beyond measurement issues. These are theoretical and philosophical issues that may be irresolvable. Yet the understanding of the psychology of old age may necessitate clarity for such conceptualizations. The solution used throughout this book was to concentrate on an equilibrium or homeostatic model, defining successful aging as the ability to maintain previous levels of social, psychological, and physical functioning despite major crises. Success for us connotes stability in the face of external change as the ultimate good. The findings described in the previous twelve chapters on the nature of stress, mediators of stress adaptation, and mediators specific to different life periods are statements of findings that reflect our definition of successful aging—the maintenance of homeostasis.

In some analyses, however, other conceptions of successful aging were introduced. Like many others, we assessed our respondents' well-being or happiness. We also examined a more complex, multifaceted perspective derived from dynamic personality theory: the Block Q-Sort measure of mental health. In chapter 11 on reminiscence, we investigated the meeting of the task often assumed characteristic of this life stage—resolution of the life review—as a criteria of successful aging. We also considered another age-specific task: the maintenance of an integrated and coherent self.

Are there any reasonable criteria for choosing among these different definitions of successful aging? They are conceptually and empirically distinct. We found that well-being, optimal functioning defined by mental health variables, and homeostasis were not associated with one another.

These are empirically, as well as conceptually, independent ways of looking at success and failure. We believe that the problem of choosing among conceptual definitions of successful aging cannot be avoided by the false hope that such differences only represent labels, underneath which lies a unitary concept.

Nor do we believe that the various concepts of successful aging would produce similar findings about the mediators linking stress to adaptation. Differences in such "findings" depending on the criteria used to index success were noted throughout the first twelve chapters. To illustrate, we found and replicated our findings in chapter 8, that a particular personality constellation—aggressiveness—was associated with successful adaptation based on the homeostatic criteria. Other personality dispositions, that were unrelated to successful adaptation, however were intimately associated with optimal functioning. One of these personality dimensions also predicted the successful resolution of a life review. Another example of the dilemma posed by the criteria used to define successful aging also comes from our exploration of the life review. Although we have noted that the issue of life review is much more complex and demands a revision of our thinking of how elderly use their personal past, we subsequently found, as reported in chapter 12, that although individuals who had moved through a life review and resolved it were no more likely to be counted among the successful outcomes in response to stress, they did show higher life satisfaction and more serenity.

It is not our intent here to now recast the framework we have developed for examining successful outcomes in response to stress; we do not believe it would be a useful or productive task to reexamine our findings using different criteria. We do, however, wish to call attention to the irreducible reality that our model of the psychology of aging and of stress and adaptation is based on the specific criteria chosen to represent successful aging. Our choice of a homeostatic model was, as discussed in chapter 1, based on both specific measurement and conceptual considerations. We believe such a choice provides the most general criteria for studies that depend on highly diverse populations under high stress conditions. We offer these observations to alert our readers to a very real dilemma in studying the elderly (as well as people of other ages). There are many ways of reasonably defining successful old age, and the stance of an investigator regarding these constructs does not simply reflect empty philosophical dilemmas. The empirical reality is that the psychology the investigator constructs about the nature of the last decade or two of life— or, for that matter, about earlier life periods—is intrinsically connected with the particular position he or she takes when defining the criteria of successes or failures in adaptation.

Selective Survival: A Dilemma for Studying the Psychology of Late Life

Death is not psychologically random; survivors under crisis differed on important psychological characteristics from nonsurvivors, and those closer to death showed different psychological qualities from those more distant from death.

Psychological vulnerability does exist, and when the elderly are faced with overwhelming external demands, death will be hastened among those who have few internal resources to call upon, adopt a passive stance toward the world, perceive threatening conditions as not under their control, have either excessive hopelessness or hopefulness, and use less adequate mechanisms for maintaining a consistent self-image. Recall that we found that these psychological dimensions did not predict outcomes among control respondents, aged people who were not undergoing stress. Some members of our control group subsequently suffered serious illness as well as death, but of course not at the same rate. The psychological characteristics described as predictors for the stress group were not found to predict those who, simply with the passage of time, had deteriorated.

The most revealing evidence of excessive mortality under conditions of stress was found in the Death of an Institution study, in which death rates for those undergoing relocation were compared to matched controls who were not relocated. Even in the other three studies, where a clear statistical demonstration of excessive death rates was not possible, increased rates of morbidity and psychological deterioration were suggestive. The distinction between morbidity and death may be simply a reflection of time sampling.

Independent of the observations that relocation is associated with excess mortality and that psychological characteristics measured prior to the stress predict subsequent morbidity or mortality, are the findings described in chapter 10 on distance from death. When a group of elderly respondents were studied every three weeks until their deaths, systematic psychological changes were found. When those close to death were contrasted with elderly individuals who were matched on demographic and situation variables but were not near death, differences on psychological measures were found, including a less stable and coherent self, increased passivity, lessened introspection, and more manifestations of death symbols.

It would be tempting to speculate that death that is hastened by stress reflects specific biological processes that are not present when death occurs "more naturally," at least among the very old. In adapting to stress, for example, physiological mechanisms associated with mobilization as well as with subsequent depletion may be evoked, which are not in evidence when death occurs in the absence of identifiable stress. Unfortunately, the nature of our psychological findings cannot provide us with evidence about physiological mechanisms. It is important to underscore once again, however, that not only were the designs different in the predictive and the distance from death studies, but more often than not, the psychological qualities or characteristics isolated were also distinct. Our inability to describe underlying biological mechanisms does not, however, invalidate the implications selective survival raises for the knowledge base of the psychology of old age.

Our findings on psychologically selective survival poses some fundamental questions about the paradigms used to study the psychology of elderly persons. How have investigators defined the psychological qualities and characteristics distinctive to this period of life? Four dominant perspectives on the nature of aging are discernible.

Much of the psychology of old age centers on documenting changes in the outer world: personal losses, the absence of social roles, the changes in the body (even the latter are theoretically treated as "environmental" or external conditions that change with the life span). This perspective examines how these "changes" affect the psychology of the elderly. Frequently, the examination of external changes is pursued in order to determine the degree of constancy inherent in personality despite documentable external or contextual change.

A second perspective sees old age as depletion. The focus is on describing change in the internal milieu of the elderly, such as decrements in cognitive capacities and energy. The prime issue is whether deficit and depletion occur and, if so, how much. Attempts to distinguish illness from age and attention to differences in findings depending on cross-sectional, longitudinal, and cohort analyses research strategies are characteristic of deficit or depletion models.

A third perspective is offered by investigators who have attempted to characterize adult life periods by contrasts with earlier ones. Different disciplines dictate the kind of issues, with some focusing on career lines, others on family life stages, and still others on psychosocial transitions. Those with this perspective who focus on personality characteristics discuss personality dimensions as if changes were linear, leading to statements such as, "As people age they become more passive, more dependent, more internally oriented." It is assumed that there are a fixed number of salient psychological characteristics and that the central task of the investigator is to describe changes in the amount of the particular characteristic at each point in the life stage.

Yet a fourth perspective is expressed by investigators who have sought to examine characteristics or dimensions for describing people that are uniquely linked to a particular life period. Their view is of the emergence of new qualities not characteristic of earlier life stages. Reminiscence, the relationship to one's personal past, is perceived by some investigators as qualitatively different in old age than in earlier points in the life line. Another thrust within this emergent view of adult development is represented by those personality theorists who have used factor analyses of basic personality tests to discover new "underlying structures."

We have characterized the study of aging as representing four discernibly different perspectives: an emphasis on changes in external conditions, the deprevation-depletion view, characterization of life stages in terms of unique tasks confronting persons at different points in the life cycle, and the assumption that new psychological qualities emerge in adulthood and old age that are not characteristic of earlier points in the life line. Specific studies may, of course, represent a mixture of these perspectives. What research strategies typify studies of the psychology of aging? Most studies represent either age-difference designs, longitudinal strategies, or stress-adaptation paradigms.

Studies on the psychology of aging, whether they use age-difference design, longitudinal strategies, or stress-adaptation paradigms, face the problem of biased sample because of selective survival. Thus, statements about differences between the psychology of early and late life based on cross-sectional studies, developmental trajectories drawn from longitudinal findings, or processes linked to successful adaptation could produce spurious findings; the psychological differences, trajectories, or processes found to be linked to life stage may be, in large part, a function of selective survival. Investigation of generalizations about the psychology of late life such as the increasing passivity among men, movement toward psychological interiority, lowered ego capacities, or increased difficulty in maintaining a coherent and consistent self-image showed that all these characteristics were affected by survival proneness.

The mechanisms underlying selective survival are at present opaque.

These findings, however, do sensitize us to an inherent dilemma involving the study of the aged, in which descriptive findings have only been loosely linked to underlying processes. If selective survival explains a meaningful portion of the variance associated with changes linked to life stage and, as we have suggested in chapter 10, the underlying processes involve a systemwide decline, we may in fact be required to examine a fundamentally biological process. To label it thus does not necessarily lead to a reductionistic position; it does, however, point to one fundamental mechanism that requires exploration.

Another insight for the psychology of old age offered by the effects of selective survival can be gained by considering the "squaring" of the survival curve (Fries and Crapo 1981). Squaring of the curve refers to a constant high rate of survivorship until advanced age, when there is a sudden drop due to high death rates. Comfort (1964) developed a set of curves that showed, for example, that the United States in 1900 and Japan in 1930 had similar survival patterns approximating a straight line in which survivorship declined at the same rate each year from middle age onward. Changes in these patterns in the United States and even more so in Japan from 1930 until now suggest that increasingly people are living until age 85 or so. Instead, if in the future the survival curve was squared, all people would die at approximately the same age. Under this condition both cross-sectional and longitudinal designs would be uncontaminated with "survival effects." Until then, we must contend with these confounding effects.

To illustrate how survival effects may skew psychological findings in old age, let us return to the example of personality trajectories through adult life described in chapter 10. The increased passivity of men with advancing age and the increased aggressiveness of women has been highlighted by a number of investigators, most prominently Gutmann (1977). This theme, however, can be found in a number of postulates about late life, including, implicitly, in the disengagement hypothesis, which postulates a decrease in outer world investments with increasing age. The constructs of aggressiveness and passivity are in the most general sense select characteristics of individuals in relationship to the external world. As we have shown in our own work, passivity is linked to selective survival. The distinction Gutmann draws between men and women may be systematically underestimating the amount of passivity for males, since passive males are likely to die off more quickly, and overestimating the increment of aggressiveness in women, since there is a marked difference in survivability between the sexes. The point is, of course, that we may construct a psychology of aging employing very elaborate psychodynamic social theories that may ultimately be based only upon differences in survival.

Toward a Psychology of Old Age

Collectively, our investigations have studied over eight hundred elderly persons aged sixty-five to ninety-five, most of whom (80 percent) were facing situations of high stress. They were examined intensively over a two- to three-year period. The findings described in the previous twelve chapters provide a base for reexamining the psychology of the very old. An appreciation of the issues must begin with a sensitivity to the reality of the psychological context in this stage of life. It is defined by a special perspective on the life span on one hand, and by a common series of assaults on the other. When one is in one's seventies or eighties, an awareness that one has lived a lifetime is unavoidable; the elderly approach the present and the future from this special perspective. The sense of personal finitude is real and palpable; only occasionally among all those studied did we find individuals who had not addressed and in many ways resolved this issue by constructing a personal philosophy for dealing with death. As we indicated in chapter 10, only those in the midst of a life crisis reengage the issues of death and finitude, apparently to resolve once again the anxieties that clearly were "settled" earlier.

We believe that the psychology of old age cannot be understood unless one takes into account this particular perspective on life as well as the age-linked assaults that are intrinsic to what it means to become old. The experience of external losses, of significant others, and of social roles are common to the aged, as are the narcissistic losses that include signs of bodily deterioration and the increasing functional incapacities; above all, the aged share the impending dissolution of the self through death. The psychology of old age must be placed in this context.

We believe that discontinuity with earlier periods of life is the rule when aging is viewed from the perspective of processes and psychological characteristics influencing adaptation. The discontinuity observed with previous psychological attributes is based on an external frame of reference. That is, the view that such characteristics as ego strength, social resources, optimal personality, and coping strategies are not psychologically enabling in old age is based on assessments from the observer's perspective. In contrast, we have come to see that the central issue of late life from the perspective of elderly persons is an overriding motivation to maintain a sense of self-continuity, self-integrity, and self-identity. The driving force, the key to understanding the psychology of the aged, can be found in self-psychology. The core task, maintenance of the self, represents the psychological survival of the elderly and may be usefully seen as analogous to physical survival.

Our premise, then, is that psychological survival is equivalent to maintaining a sense of self-continuity, integrity, and identity, and it is toward this conservation of self that psychological work among the elderly is focused. Moreover, this work occurs within the unique psychological context of the aged—of a life lived and of personal finitude coupled with the fact of personal and structural losses. Roles do change, the body does fail, and important people die. The self is challenged to its very core because the opportunities for maintaining a coherent and consistent self, which are ultimately dependent on input from the external world, are radically altered. The sense of self does not change; rather, what we see is the utilization of strategies by the elderly to maintain this sense of selfhood. At its most general level, the strategies represent myths—the myth of control, the myth of self-constancy—and the blurring of the boundaries between the past and the present. These myths, the blurring of the past and present, and our findings of an age-linked reduction in introspective behaviors suggest a simplification of self-identity—a process in which previously ego-dystonic impulses and thoughts are now acceptable if they reaffirm the sense of self-identity.

What were the findings that led us to see the central and crucial task of old age in these terms? The evidence for the creation of mythology appears in a variety of sources in our studies. The first encounter with mythicizing was in our examination of coping strategies for dealing with loss and threat. We saw, in chapter 6, efforts to alter the threatening situation in order to create an image of the previously noxious situation that would be congruent with the person's own desires—an effort to transform a loss of control into a perception of control over one's destiny. We found that to the extent an individual was successful in creating these perceptions, the likelihood increased that the person would remain intact under stress. Then, in chapter 10 on self-identity, we noted the various mechanisms used by the elderly to maintain a consistent and coherent self-image. The frequency with which they turn to their past for the maintenance of self-coherence stands in marked contrast to the behavior of younger persons who have greater opportunities for current feedback. But the most compelling evidence for the function of mythology in maintaining the coherent, valued self was found in chapter 11 on reminiscence. There we found that for the majority of these elderly individuals, the reconstructive efforts directed toward the past more often than not were focused on creating a self-in-the-past that reflected positively and sustainingly on the present self. Personal history was redrawn, not in the service of resolving conflicts and reorganizing one's life prior to death, but rather for the creation of an enduring and affirming self.

Our evidence for the centrality of self-consistency is perhaps clearer than our understanding of how the creation of myths function in this process. It appears that the creation of certain kinds of myths that will maintain the self is, by and large, adaptive. The sense of control and mastery over relocation and the sense of an enduring and affirming self based on a recreation of one's personal story are all adaptive. There are, however, limits to the degree of distortion possible; the evidence on self-mechanisms developed in chapter 10 suggest that beyond some level, distortions of current interactions to support a persistent self-identity increase rather than minimize the risk associated with stress.

In reexamining findings relevant to the psychology of the aged and the functional utility of myth creation in this process, we are not stating that elderly persons depart from the requirements of reality in all segments of their lives. Witness, for example, the fact that most aged people are able to face the increasing certainty of their own death (see chapter 9). By and large, they do not use the myriad of linguistical and cognitive devices available to alter the facts of life and its termination. This appreciation of reality and the demonstration of their having addressed and anticipated their own demise certainly did not lead us to see aging as synonymous with myth making. Our findings are more specific; they point to the utilization of myth in the service of a particular task—the maintenance of the self.

Myths, however, are not without their price; as just noted, serious departures, in maintaining self-sameness by distortion, diminished the probability of successful adaptation. There seems to be a point at which the price of creating myths and forsaking the reality principle may be dangerous. However, it also appears that a great amount of "bending" of reality is acceptable, or even essential, necessitating modification of our definition of mental health. We believe that the bottom line is a reassessment of the essential task of old age, which is not to address finitude, not the high-minded, purposeful reconstruction and reexamination of one's life for integrative purposes, and not wisdom and serenity. The task is rather to maintain a coherent, consistent self, an inner task more critical than the interactional task of maintaining an accepted self.

The simplification of identity does not reflect wisdom, nor does it reflect a resolution of one's past life. The very old person does not achieve a new sense of wisdom regarding the regularities of human nature or resolution of past conflicts; rather, he or she achieves the maintenance of a persistent self when internal and external realities are undermining it.

Like many of our colleagues who study the psychology of aging, we share a perspective that the action at this stage of life is internal and not transactional or interactional. In this sense, our views are perhaps reductionist, for we see the interactional and transactional aspects of old age through the eyes of the central internal task.

The failures of the traditional age-irrelevant models that predict adaptation to stress—particularly the failures in the portrayal of what is mental health, or what represents ego strength, or what kinds of people with what kinds of personality characteristics are adaptive—are, to a large extent, the result of an underlying view of human beings that emphasizes rationality. If we are right in our speculations that the ultimate issue is self-coherence and consistency, then the inclusion of such psychological attributes may be a systematic error of these models, for they would not be linked to the ability of people to create mythologies. Thus, different dimensions for evaluating successful aging may be required. If the preservation of self is the ultimate and meaningful goal, then studies examining the quality of life or mental health or morale may not be sufficiently sensitive to the fundamental dilemma of old age—the preservation of self.

How adequate can the study of lives be across different life stages when the very criteria of success may require us to adopt different images of success depending on life stage? We believe that our field has given too little attention to the appropriateness of various frameworks used for assessing successful adaptation. Psychologists have recognized for many years now that value judgments were being made, but we have just begun to recognize that we may have erred by bringing "values" from early life stages into old age.

Appendix A

Control Samples

Control samples were developed for three of the four studies. The need to rapidly interview the respondents in the Unwilling Old Ladies study did not provide the time to identify and interview a matched sample of elderly widows of veterans. Thereafter, in the next three studies, contrast samples were developed so that changes in the relocated elderly could be compared with changes in samples of similar elderly not undergoing relocation. It was not, of course, possible in these settings to randomly assign individuals to either a relocation or nonrelocation group and then assess changes in each group one year later.

THE HOME FOR LIFE STUDY

Two control samples were developed by selecting respondents from institutionalized, as well as community, populations. For each institution, a list was compiled of all one- to three-year residents. A total of 141 had been residents for this period of time. The time period was chosen in order to minimize the effects of both the initial "transfer shock," on the one hand, and the possibility of major debilitating changes associated with very advanced age, on the other. Three criteria were used for selection from this resident pool:

1. Ability to walk and provide independent personal care.
2. Ability to communicate well.
3. Lack of major debilitating physical or mental changes since institutionalization.

The aim was to select only those institutional residents who could, in terms of self-care and mental functioning, live in the community. As shown in table A–1, this sample was similar to both those awaiting entrance and the community sample. Further data contrasting the three samples appear in chapter 3.

The community sample is of special importance because these elderly people were in an earlier phase than the primary sample relative to the problems that direct old people toward institutionalization. The contrasts between them and respondents in the primary (waiting list) sample elucidate the effects of the transition from this earlier period to the period of anticipating institutionalization. A "snowball" technique was used for sample location. At their first interview session, institutionalized respondents were asked to give the names of their friends. Fifty-seven individuals were contacted. Ten did not meet the selection criteria because they were either married, under the age of seventy, or, in one case, already institutionalized. Seven individuals met the criteria but refused to participate, and five others refused after the initial session. This procedure generated a community sample that was similar except in education to both the waiting list sample and the institutionalized sample. (See table A–1.)

TABLE A–1
The Samples in the Home for Life Study

	Study Sample[a] (N=85)	Control Samples	
		Institutionalized (N=37)	Community (N=35)
Sex			
Male	24 (28%)	10 (27%)	5 (18%)
Female	61 (72%)	28 (73%)	30 (82%)
Age (years)			
Mean	80.0	80.0	78
Range	63–93	67–90	63–91
Education (years)			
Mean	4.6	5.9	8.3
Range	0–14	0–14	0–16
Marital status			
Single	11 (13%)	3 (8%)	6 (17%)
Widowed	57 (67%)	31 (84%)	29 (83%)
Divorced/separated	2 (2%)	1 (3%)	0 (0%)
Married	15 (18%)	2 (5%)	0 (0%)
Foreign-born	65 (76%)	28 (76%)	26 (74%)
Has at least one living child	65 (76%)	26 (70%)	27 (63%)
Has at least one living sibling	75 (88%)	23 (62%)	21 (60%)

[a]In all, 100 respondents were interviewed while on the waiting list, but because 4 died before admission and another 11 withdrew or delayed their admission, only 85 entered the homes.

TABLE A–2
Comparison of Study and Control on Baseline Variables (Time 1): The Death of an Institution Study

Variable	Study Sample (N=427)	Control Sample (N=100)	p
Sex[b] (percent female)	64	63	N.S.[a]
Age[b] (mean years)	76.00	75.82	N.S.
Years hospitalization[b] (mean years)	28.92	26.05	N.S.
Place of birth (percent U.S. born)	68	69	N.S.
Race (percent Caucasian)	89	92	N.S.
Marital status (percent ever married)	69	62	N.S.
Education (percent eighth-grade or less)	60	61	N.S.
Family interest (percent yes)	37	47	.10
Close friends (percent yes)	15	10	N.S.
Diagnosis:			N.S.
Organic brain syndrome senility, cerebral arteriosclerosis	21	17	
Organic brain syndrome alcohol, other organic disorder	14	17	
Schizo—paranoid	20	23	
Schizo—chronic	23	19	
Other functional disorder	22	24	
Total physical condition (mean) (6=bad; 28=good)	22.29	21.73	N.S.
Self-care score (mean) (11=total care; 66=self-care)	39.04	39.78	N.S.
Percent bedridden	17	16	N.S.
Total illness score (mean) (0=no somatic; 35=many)	9.70	9.84	N.S.
Patient declining condition from medical records (percent decline indicated)	32	33	N.S.
Past deterioration trend (percent yes)	29	34	N.S.
Future deterioration expected (percent yes)	30	45	.01
Group 5 illnesses			N.S.
None	36	39	
One	43	37	
Two or more	21	23	
Medical unit moves (percent one or more)	25	17	N.S.
Degree of contact (mean) (2=low; 28=high)	11.16	12.02	N.S.
Verbal ability (percent short answers or better)	62	68	N.S.
Verbal comprehension (percent understand all you say)	42	60	.001
Relating to others (percent nonrelated)	73	70	N.S.
Friendly/joking relation to staff	17	21	N.S.
Primarily indifferent to staff	52	52	N.S.
Sociability index (mean) (21 = low; 99 = high)	39.04	42.74	.01
Responsiveness to environment (percent quite and actively responsive)	34	41	N.S.
Meaningful occupations index (mean) (11=low; 46=high)	16.32	18.45	.02
Primarily sitter (percent frequently or solely)	50	37	.05
Total psychiatric symptoms (mean) (2=low; 28=high no. symptoms)	7.55	7.86	N.S.
Degree withdrawal (mean) (4=low; 16=highly withdrawn)	10.89	10.08	.10
Hostility index (mean) (6=low; 27=high) (many hostile behaviors)	9.28	9.83	N.S.
Disorganized thinking (percent yes)	29	27	N.S.
Regressed (percent yes)	15	7	.10

[a]N.S. = not significant
[b]Selection criterion

THE DEINSTITUTIONALIZED ELITES STUDY

A "delayed discharge" sample of twenty-six, twenty of whom became members of the study sample, were interviewed twice prior to relocation. The twenty-six were interviewed approximately three months prior to discharge and again approximately two weeks before discharge. The relatively short interval between times of data collection makes the sample useful as a contrast with respect to short-term adaptive reactions but not for long-term outcomes. Because most respondents in the control sample became part of the study sample, as anticipated, the two samples were nearly identical at the time of the initial interview.

THE DEATH OF AN INSTITUTION STUDY

To construct a control sample, 100 patients who were sixty-five years of age or older and who had been hospitalized for more than 90 days were selected at another state mental hospital. These 100 patients were selected by a stratified random sampling technique to match them with the study sample on age, sex, length of hospitalization, and overall self-care ability. The success of this matching is suggested by the data presented in table A–2. Of thirty four dimensions, the study and control samples differed significantly only on five. Control patients were more sociable and more active (37 percent were primarily "sitters," as compared with 50 percent); larger percentages were able to comprehend what was said to them (60 percent vs. 42 percent), and they were higher on an index of meaningful occupations.

Appendix B

Assessing Short-Term Reactions and Long-Term Outcomes

SHORT-TERM REACTIONS

In three of the four studies (Unwilling Old Ladies, Home for Life, and Deinstitutionalized Elites), adverse changes from pre-relocation to shortly after relocation were assessed. Our task was to use comparable measures in all three studies that reflected stress in terms of adverse reactions in physical functioning, cognitive functioning, social interaction, and affects.

Physical Reactions. Ratings of four levels of change (death, much poorer physical condition, somewhat poorer physical condition, and improvement in functioning or no physical change) were based on the observations of the interviewer, reports of staff members, and data supplied by the residents themselves. In all cases in which residents reported serious physical difficulties, corroborating data were sought from interviewers or in staff reports.

In the Unwilling Old Ladies study, the clinical psychologist who had gathered most of the interview data made the ratings of change in physical functioning. When two raters were used, in the Home for Life study, the interrater reliability was r=.80 on twenty cases. For the Deinstitutionalized Elites study the corresponding reliability was r=.71 for the study and control samples combined (113 cases).

Cognitive Reactions. The Mental Status Questionnaire or MSQ (Kahn, Pollack, and Goldfarb 1961) was used to assess cognitive change. The test consists of ten simple questions that reflect the respondent's orientation in time and place, such as "What is the name of this place (street)?" and "Who is the President of the United States?" It is scored for the number of wrong answers. Other measures (described in chapter 9) were also available, such as the Dana scoring of the TAT, and the Pascal scoring of the Bender-Gestalt design-copying test, but whereas MSQ data were available for all respondents, there were missing data for other measures. Changes on the MSQ, moreover, were highly associated with changes on the others (r=.60 or higher). Using the MSQ, a three-step procedure for obtaining change scores was followed: First, raw change scores were computed; second, raw change scores were weighted according to a system based on the distribution of changes in the Home for Life study sample; and third, a boundary weighting system was devised in which crossing the boundary indicated that a major positive or negative change had occurred, whereas changes that did not cross a boundary were judged to be minor. (A boundary refers to the cutoff point beyond which scores at any one particular time may be considered to indicate a previous deficit in cognitive functioning.) The purpose of establishing boundaries was to provide a meaningful assessment of change.

The change and boundary weights were applied in exactly the same manner for all three samples. Those with two more errors or two more correct answers in either direction were judged to have changed. The boundary line which differentiated those with defect from those without was a score of 4: Those with a score of four or more errors on the MSQ at either point in time were considered to fall within the defect region. An error score of 4 or more has been proposed as an indication of organic brain damage (Kahn, Pollack, and Goldfarb 1961). The rating scale contained five scale points: +2 for positive change across the boundary; +1 for positive change, but not across the boundary; zero for no change; −1 for negative change, but not across the boundary; and −2 for negative change across the boundary.

Social Interaction Reactions. Role counts, a rating of the quality of interaction in seven roles—parent; sibling; relative, including grandparent; friend; roommate or neighbor; worker; and organization member—were used to assess interaction. Each role was scored on a four-point scale, from 0 to 3, where a score of 0 was given if the respondent was not currently active in the role, and a score of 3 indicated a high degree of involvement in the role. As with the MSQ, these measures were found to have high correlations with other social interaction measures (amount and quality of interaction). A five-point scale of change from −2 (extreme deterioration in interaction) to +2 (great improvement in interaction) was developed.

Affective Reactions. Ratings on satisfaction with the environment were used to assess affective change. This scale was highly associated with composite or global measures of depression, using several measures that

356

were available within each study but were not available for all studies. (In the Unwilling Old Ladies study, the correlation between satisfaction with the environment and the global score was r=.87; in the Home for Life study, r=.79; in the Institutionalized Elites, r=.78.) The satisfaction with the environment scale had five points, ranging from −2 to +2. An examination of the frequency distribution for the raw change scores indicated that the direction of change as well as the starting point would have to be considered if ratings of change in affect was to be equalized at all levels. The following conversion system was therefore developed:

1. From −1, 1, 2, and −2 positions, a two-point change was required if the change went in a direction opposite to the algebraic sign of the initial status; a one-point change was necessary if the change went in the direction of the sign. For example, a change from 1 to 0 was not considered a change, whereas a change from 1 to 2 was.
2. A change from 0 at baseline required at least two points before it was considered a change.

Based on the conversion rules, a three-point rating scale for affective change was developed, namely:

- +1—given for change in the positive direction.
- 0—given for no (converted score) change.
- −1—given for change in the negative direction.

REACTIONS: PROCEDURES FOR ANALYSIS

Although measures representative of four theoretically distinct dimensions of change were constructed, at least two alternatives existed for the utilization of these measures in the subsequent analysis: Change could be considered either within each dimension separately or, alternatively, across dimensions in a single, combined measure. The choice between these alternatives was based on the degree of intercorrelation among measures: Low intercorrelations would indicate the existence of relatively separate dimensions of change, worthy of individual attention, whereas high intercorrelations would indicate an essential interdependency, such that the presentation of individual measures creates redundancy rather than additional information. Because intercorrelations among the four short-term measures of change tended to be low (eighteen correlation coefficients were generated, six for each sample, and the range was .01 to .44, with only three of the eighteen correlations reaching statistical significance), the decision was to utilize each of the four measures separately.

THE MEASURES OF LONG-TERM MALADAPTATION

In the measurement of long-term maladaptation, it was necessary to rely on measures and scoring procedures developed separately by the research teams of each study. Another difference from the assessment of short-term reactions in all four samples was that extreme negative decline on any one dimension of maladaptation covaried with extreme decline on the other dimensions.

THE UNWILLING OLD LADIES STUDY

The two principal investigators who had interviewed respondents and had rated short-term reactions returned nine months after relocation and identified those respondents who had died, as well as those who had shown extreme deterioration or had improved in physical, cognitive, social, or affective functioning. For the assessment of extreme deterioration or improvements, brief interviews were conducted and personal observations and staff impressions gathered; based on these data sources, current status was compared with pre-relocation status as reflected in the complete interview and test data gathered before relocation. Those who showed extreme decline on one dimension tended to show it on the others as well. Because of this attenuated procedure, only two outcome groups were identified: an intact survivors group and an extreme decline group (including those who died).

THE HOME FOR LIFE STUDY

Five categories of change were identified, the first four referring to physical, mental, or behavioral functioning or, more typically, some combination of all three. The five levels were (1) enhanced functioning, (2) no essential change, (3) some negative change, (4) extreme deterioration, and (5) death.

With the exception of the respondents who died, placement in a particular outcome category was not made on the basis of absolute status after one year, because respondents varied widely in capacities before admission. Instead, *relative* change, from pre-admission to one year post-admission, was the basis of placement. Variations in initial level required a classification system that took into account very different levels of baseline functioning and also equated the magnitude of qualitatively different changes.

Of the eighty-five aged persons who constituted the study sample, complete follow-up data after one year were obtained for sixty-one (or 72 percent). Respondents who died in the interim (fifteen in all) are included in this number. Only partial data were obtained for the remaining 28 percent. For these twenty-four respondents, incomplete data usually reflected inability to obtain full interview material because of extreme deterioration. There were, however, fourteen respondents who remained intact and able to be interviewed but refused to respond during all or most of the twelve- to fifteen-hour interview. Partial information was gathered on very deteriorated and resistant respondents through the administration of a short-form interview and also from informants. Data used in assessing level of adaptation one year after institutionalization included all available information, which consisted of eighteen structured instruments and nine focused interview sections.

Three areas of change were identified: physical, mental, and behavioral functioning. Changes in physical functioning included shifts in the interviewer's perception of functional self-care capacity as well as verified changes in physical status. Changes in mental functioning were defined in terms of orientation in time and space, and perceptual adequacy. Changes in behavioral functioning included shifts in both mood and behavior, including psychiatric symptoms.

Information about physical changes included: (1) changes in self-reported ability to care for self; (2) changes in self-reported physical symptoms and diseases; (3) changes reflected in comments about physical capacity that were interspersed throughout the interview; and (4) changes in physical appearance, self-care capacity, and ambulation as reported by the interviewer and also by institution staff. Although some respondents obviously had considerable physical dysfunction and distress before admission, no respondent was terminally ill at baseline.

Data involving mental changes included: (1) changes on the Mental Status Questionnaire, which assesses orientation in time and place; (2) changes on several tasks—the Bender-Gestalt design-copying test, the TAT scored by the Dana system, and the Paired Word Learning Test— that measured ability to organize information and respond to complex interview and test material; and (3) interviewers' assessments of change in mental status and functioning one year after admission. Data involving behavioral changes included: (1) all the interview material, (2) interviewers' assessments and ratings on the respondent's behavior during the interview, and (3) staff assessments of behavior.

For each of the three functional areas, a rating of change was made on a seven-point scale. These scales were then used in forming a global judgment of improvement, no change, some decline, or marked decline.

Placement in the fifth group, death, did not of course require weighting evidence.

Because of the high interrelation of change among the three areas of functioning (correlations above .90), placement for most respondents was rather easy. For those few respondents who did not manifest negative change in all three areas, the highest level of negative change was used in making the global judgment. For example, three of the twenty-five in the waiting-list sample classified as "marked negative changers" had become confused but did not show a marked change in physical functioning. It is important to note that those classified as marked negative changers tended to function so poorly after one year of institutionalization that if they were then applying for admission to the homes they would be considered too incapacitated to be admitted. Thus, the group showing marked decline was composed of respondents who had all shown adverse changes after one year of institutionalization to a functional status that tended to be below admission standards at that time.

THE DEINSTITUTIONALIZED ELITES STUDY

The initial sample consisted of ninety-three patients, but because three had incomplete initial data and eight others insufficient data to make assessments of outcome, the final size of the study sample was eighty-two. Of these eighty-two, data were available on fifty-nine patients to generate scores in the same four areas used to assess short-term effects. The other twenty-three were either too ill to be interviewed or refused all or part of the test battery. Clinical judgments, however, could be made from varied data, such as incomplete interviews or "conversations" with the patients; staff interviews; observations; and hospital records. Because the judgments on these twenty-three could only be global (we could not subdivide these judgments into physical, cognitive, social interactive, and affective areas), the effort was made to combine the change data in the four realms based on test information into a global score of improved, unchanged, or deteriorated. This gave a total of eighty-two patients on whom one of these three judgments could be made.

To combine the outcome scores in the four areas for the fifty-nine patients on whom there were complete data, change scores were generated for each of the four areas on a nine-point scale, from marked negative change (-4) to marked positive change ($+4$), and then collapsed into the three categories of improved, unchanged, or declined. A sign approach was then used for placement, but generally negative change in one area was associated with similar changes in other areas. Of the fifty-nine, fifteen (or 25 percent) were placed in an "improved" classification, twenty-six (or 44 percent) into a "declined" classification, and the remaining eighteen (or 31 percent) into "unchanged." On the other 25 patients, the judgments classified two (or 9 percent) as "improved," seven (or 30 percent) as "unchanged," and fourteen (or 61 percent) as "declined." The total sample of eighty-two patients, then, includes forty (or 49 percent) who declined and only seventeen (or 21 percent) who improved. The following are three examples of patients classified by judgment:

Case No. 011: Readmitted to hospital seven months after discharge. Hospital records indicate that "patient had begun acting out—became hyperactive and combative . . . tried to strike several aides—continual talking loudly and singing—disturbing other residents." Classified as *declined.*

Case No. 032: Refused the one-year follow-up interview. The predischarge and follow-up interviews look almost identical. Staff commented that "she seems to have adjusted well." Classified as *unchanged.*

Case No. 089: Couldn't be located for one-year follow-up interview. Patient left sheltered care setting to get married and find an apartment. Predischarge and follow-up staff interviews very similar. Staff comments that "she's adjusted very well." Classified as *improved.*

THE DEATH OF AN INSTITUTION STUDY

Outcome was grouped into four categories: death, deterioration, no change, and improvement. Measurement of the various types of change, however, required a series of steps for determination. Four broad areas of patient condition or functioning were considered: physical status, mental or psychiatric condition, level of awareness, and social-behavioral status. Multiple indices and a variety of sources of data were used to measure change in each of these substantive areas. Finally, the change scores for each respondent for each substantive area were combined to produce a measure of overall change. The following steps were involved in this procedure:

Sources of Data. Three kinds of data were used to assess change in each substantive area of outcome: difference scores, direct change ratings, and staff ratings of change.

Difference Scores. Difference scores were computed using variables that had been measured both prior to and following relocation, encompassing physical condition, psychiatric symptoms, responsiveness, verbal ability, major occupations, and interaction with staff. Variables used for this purpose stemmed either from the staff interview or from ratings made by the observers at both points in time. Difference scores were computed by subtracting Time 2 scores from Time 1 scores, and then establishing cutting points from the determination of the outcomes of deterioration, no change, and improvement. The critical ratio technique was used to establish cutting points for these variables.

Direct Change Ratings. One of the advantages of using the observational method in the pre-relocation setting was that it elicited a complex and fairly complete picture of the patient. Before the patient entered the relocation environment, the researcher reviewed his or her entire record, noting data for a variety of areas such as physical frailty, relationships with others, interest in and awareness of the environment, and feelings of depression and anxiety. During follow-up observation of the patient and conversations with other patients, and especially during informal interviews with the aides or technicians in the new facility, the researcher attended particularly to the ways in which the patient had changed since before relocation. For example, behaviors that were evident then, but that were not now visible in the new environment, were inquired about in the interviews with the aides; similarly, behaviors newly manifested in the relocation environment were explored with the staff to determine the extent to which they were typical of the patient during his or her stay in the new environment.

Using all sources of data, the researcher then rated the patient on a series of dimensions with regard to whether he or she had improved markedly, improved somewhat, not changed, deteriorated somewhat, or deteriorated markedly. On this five-point scale the interrater reliability was 77 percent exact agreement, with 96 percent agreement within one point on the scale.

Staff Rating. As a final means of measuring change, the supervisory nurse, charge technician, or facility operator was requested to make a judgment of the extent to which the patient had changed while in the facility or on the unit. These ratings covered physical condition, psychiatric problems, and cognitive functioning. The reliability of the information from this source was enhanced by instructing the interviewer to adduce specific examples of the particular kinds of behaviors upon which he or she was basing ratings. If no example was produced, a rating of "no change" was assigned.

Variables Used to Assess the Four Substantive Areas of Change. The following is a list of the variables used to measure change in the four areas, with the source of information noted after each specific variable.

Appendix B

A. Physical status
    1. Frailty: direct change rating
    2. Physical change: staff rating
    3. Total physical condition: difference score
B. Psychiatric status
    1. Psychiatric idiosyncrasies: direct change rating
    2. Mental change: staff rating
    3. Psychiatric symptomatology: difference score
C. Awareness level
    1. Awareness of routine events: direct change rating
    2. Awareness of unusual events: direct change rating
    3. Responsiveness: difference score
    4. Verbal ability: difference score
D. Social-behavioral status
    1. Interest in environment: direct change rating
    2. Relatedness: direct change rating
    3. Occupations: direct change rating
    4. Major occupations: difference score
    5. Sociability: difference score
    6. Total interactions with staff: difference score

Determination of a Single Change Score for Each Area. The next step involved deciding what constituted a "change" in each of the above variables. For the direct change ratings and staff ratings, a score of either "slight" or "marked" change was considered a change, and the scores on these variables were easily transformed into a three-part distribution of improved, unchanged, and deteriorated.

For the difference scores, the critical ratio technique for the determination of cutting points was used to determine how much of a difference between the Time 1 and Time 2 scores would be considered a change. Data on both the study group and the control group were included in these difference scores.

Each of the variables in a given area were then scanned and the cases arranged in order of the number of scores the patients received in each category. For the physical status area, for example, ten combinations of change scores on the three variables were possible: three "deteriorated"; two "deteriorated" and one "no change"; one "deteriorated," one "no change," and one "improved"; and so forth to three improvements. When all three scores were not clearly in one direction, all of the case materials on that subject were reviewed and a decision was made to classify the case in one or another of the three outcome groups. Generally, a patient was considered to have changed only if the majority of scores on the various items in a given area were clearly in one direction, or if the case materials indicated a clearly visible change from Time 1 to Time 2.

Computation of Overall Change Score. After the preceding steps were used to assign four scores to each individual, the four were combined into one measure of overall outcome. Because the four scores received by the patient indicated "real" or substantial changes, the decision was made to designate any patient who had changed in at least one area as having changed overall. That is, if the patient had received at least one score of improved or deteriorated in any of the four change areas, and if the other three scores were all "no change," overall change rating of either improved or deteriorated was given. Patients who evidenced inconsistent change ratings (that is, both improved in one or more areas and deteriorated in one or more areas) were individually reviewed and a decision of outcome made on the basis of the review. There were no cases, however, for which the final classification was ambiguous. For example, one common inconsistency was found in patients who had deteriorated in the social-behavioral or awareness realms because they had become more withdrawn, refused to interact, and appeared to be less interested in their environment; but at the same time had improved in mental functioning because they no longer displayed former psychiatric symptoms. Examination of the case material invariably indicated, however, that the patient had improved psychiatrically *only* because of withdrawal from the world, and psychiatric problems were not being acted out because of the extreme withdrawal. This gestalt obviously pointed to an overall deterioration and indicated placement in the deteriorated outcome group.

An Example of Change, Including Scoring Procedures. To illustrate the classification procedure, we will use as an example a woman placed in the deteriorated group because of social-behavioral changes. First to be presented is a summary of pre-relocation data gathered from a number of sources, followed by post-relocation data and then by an analysis of the change that had taken place.

PRE-RELOCATION. The patient was a seventy-year-old Caucasian female with a diagnosis of "dementia praecox" of the paranoid type who was hospitalized for nineteen years. At the time of the initial interview, she was described by observers as healthy, overweight, neat, and in good physical condition, and it was noted that she mopped, helped serve trays, and was very active.

Behaviorally she was typically very active and spent much of her time working: "I've observed her humming while working, and there is no question that she is a very helpful worker on the ward. She makes beds in the morning, she occasionally works in the linen room, and she is a very important helper during meals." She performed all these tasks voluntarily, never had to be reminded, and was often found in one of the "work" side rooms:

> When I asked the staff where Mrs. P. was, they said she usually spends nearly all day Sunday in the shower room and hopper room, quite to herself. It is her hair shampoo and fixing day. She also often soaks her right foot in nearly boiling water in one of these rooms to keep bad spirits away, and the skin on the right foot and ankle has a continually red appearance from this treatment.

Since Mrs. P. was not always working while in these rooms, she gave the impression of "hiding out." She did not like to go off the unit and did so only rarely. When she was not working, she would sometimes come out into the day hall to sit among the other patients.

Mrs. P. never interacted with the other patients on a social, conversational level; she frequently, however, "talked at" or "lectured" them in a hostile tone. She seemed preoccupied with topics of violence, frequently talking about killings and threatening situations. When she was in the midst of one of her tirades, the other patients simply ignored her. In addition, she would order other patients around in a bossy, authoritative manner. Staff members stated she "gets carried away with her importance," and she was described as "noisy, bossy." Her attitude toward staff ranged from belligerent to pleasant, and they reported that she had a good sense of humor and would converse with them, but that she also could be "curt, verbally abusive." She would interact socially only with technicians and usually "gets along well" with them; significantly, she knew the "techs" by name. Because she was the primary worker on the unit, she received certain status benefits from the staff: they let her share in activities they are doing, allowed her free access to the unit's work rooms, let her eat in the supply room if she so desired, and tolerated her deviant behaviors. She hoarded soap, with the staff making no attempt to stop her, and they did not interfere when she "talked at" other patients.

In summary, then, Mrs. P. made her presence known and interacted considerably with her environment—working, socializing with staff, "talking at" other patients, approaching the observers, and so forth.

POST-RELOCATION. The patient had been put on an 800-calorie diet and lost 48 pounds. Although she still looked healthy and strong, she had developed Parkinsonian tremors in her hands and feet and had experienced three falling incidents over the past year. She was clean and neat, wore no makeup, and was still able to care for herself.

Behaviorally, a very clear picture emerged from the observations:

> She is basically a sitter, and seems very tense and uncomfortable in her chair.

During the morning she sits with her legs crossed, her elbows on the chair arms, and her hands in her lap. Occasionally she sits forward in her chair looking toward the nursing station, but this is not a very frequent occurrence. . . . She only appears to vaguely watch events in her environment. . . . In the morning there was a great deal of activity in the day hall. . . . She again seemed to watch this activity vaguely, but also spent a great deal of the time staring off at nothing in particular. There were several occasions of loud noises which she did not look at. . . . This patient is very withdrawn, unobtrusive, quiet—a "good" patient. She does not interact with other patients or initiate any interactions with technicians, although she will respond briefly to their questions. In the morning there was a patient sitting next to her, but she did not look at this other lady or attempt to say anything to her. Later in the morning, when she got a toothbrush and toothpaste from one of the technicians, she again did not have eye contact and did not have any verbal contact other than to ask for the toothbrush and toothpaste. Several times when our eyes met as I observed her, she would immediately avert her own eyes.

By now, the patient did virtually no work around the unit. After several months of prodding by staff, she did begin to feed one other patient, but she did this in a mechanical fashion, with no verbal interaction with the other patient. She refused to do any other work, stating that she was in the hospital for a rest, was paying for her hospital care, and therefore did not have to work. She did not know the names of the technicians, but still remembered the names of the ones at her former hospital. Nearly all of her comments about her present environment were phrased as disparaging comparisons with her previous environment. The interviewer wrote after talking to Mrs. P.: "When she takes a bath here they had some kind of bad shampoo, which made her hair difficult to comb and tangly. Of course, they had very good shampoo at the previous hospital." Generally, she spent her time sitting, doing nothing. Although the interview with Mrs. P. indicated that she was highly aware of her environment, she did not manifest this in any way. She did not interact with staff or patients; she did not talk to herself; she appeared emotionless and flat.

ANALYSIS OF CHANGE. The change that is clearly indicated when the two case records are compared is reflected in the difference scores and direct change ratings in the area of social-behavioral functioning. On the variable Meaningful occupations index, she received a pre-relocation score of 27 and a post-relocation score of 13. Her sociability score went from 59 to 33 in the new environment. Similarly, the direct change rating of Meaningful Occupations was "marked deterioration" because she had moved from being a worker, groomer, antagonist, and interacter to becoming a "sitter." The direct change rating of interest in environment was also "marked deterioration," because her former involvement in the activities of the unit had changed to a near total lack of interest. Mrs. P. had changed from showing a high sense of territoriality, a definite niche in the status hierarchy, and a viable, if self-imposed, role of ward critic at Time 1 to a withdrawn and nearly completely isolated person.

This case, then, is an example of deterioration in social-behavioral functioning. In the areas of physical functioning and awareness, changes were not evident, whereas on all of the variables in the area of social-behavioral functioning Mrs. P. received scores indicating decrements. However, Mrs. P. was one of the patients who had one "deteriorated" score and one "improved" score, which had to be adjudicated in scoring for overall change. Because she no longer talked to herself, yelled at other patients, or scalded her foot in boiling water (staff had "dissuaded" her from these behaviors), she received a rating of "improved" in psychiatric status. Closer analysis, however, revealed that this diminution in bizarre behavior was really a function of her rather complete withdrawal from her new environment, rather than of a change in her psychiatric condition. When she was interviewed by the observer, much of the same delusional material displayed earlier was still evident. Accordingly, she was classified overall as "deteriorated."

Appendix C

Rating Congruence Characteristics
to Assess Environmental Fit

The data for each respondent were reviewed and synthesized for transcription onto file cards, with each of the nine personality variables listed separately and always in the following order:

- Activity-Passivity
- Narcissism
- Aggression
- Status Drive
- Distrust of Others
- Empathy
- Extrapunitiveness
- Intrapunitiveness
- Authoritarianism-Equalitarianism

Categories of data were included in the order specified for each variable. If a particular category of data was not administered to a given respondent and these data were required by the outline of data analysis, the absence of the data was noted on the file card. For several variables, the outline of data analysis noted that relevant data for some but not all respondents appeared in certain subsidiary sources of data. These subsidiary sources of data were reviewed after the data specified as invariant for each respondent were analyzed.

In general, the order of data to be analyzed for each variable followed the order of data as it appeared in the interviews. For each variable different sections of the interview were used.

A description of each of the variables follows as well as a description of each point on the scale measuring the variable. Numbers in parentheses refer to the rating assigned to that point on a five-point scale. "R" refers to "respondent."

1. ACTIVITY-PASSIVITY

This scale is essentially an *activities* scale. These activities are usually not "active" ones (although, in general, television and radio are, even for this scale, "passive" pursuits). Visiting friends or going to the park in order to talk with people, in this sample, may be viewed as "active" pursuits. This relative inactivity is probably due to the stress of being on the waiting list for a home in addition to being a derivative of the events that led to application to the homes in the first place.

Data used in scoring were primarily responses to items about health status and the daily round of activities. Comments by the interviewer were also helpful. The focus is on what R is doing *now*, although one may note an activity such as "I worked selling ties door-to-door until a few weeks ago; I could still do it if I wanted to."

High Passivity (1): Open, excessive passivity. Lack of drive or energy. Renunciation of activity and effort at self-maintenance; regression. R may retain a reasonable appearance but otherwise does very little to occupy his or her time. R makes little use of opportunities for activity that are available. Seems to spend much time in reverie and has little interest in the activities he or she still partakes in.

Passivity (2): R usually lacks drive, energy, but retains self-maintenance. R may complain about inactivity, but makes little effort toward activity; has considerable unfilled time. R's major activity may turn out to be regular visits made to him or her by others several times a week. Often get impression that R's ego resources for meeting his or her activity needs are meager.

Midpoint (3): Retention of a few (rather passive) age-appropriate activities and interests. R takes naps and accepts this; usually no special activity on weekends.

Activity (4): Strong efforts at self-care, considering R's physical status. If *number* of activities is low, much energy is invested in them from the standpoint of R's physical status. Time is well-filled, although there may or may not be many visits and/or organizational activity. Usually, R attends a couple of organizations and goes out to visit regularly.

High Activity (5): Unusual efforts to maintain activities, including outside activities. R may work on a part-time basis, or did so after application. These activities may in great part be of a passive nature, such as meeting with friends and playing cards, but time is largely filled, and R makes efforts to overcome obstacles.

2. NARCISSISM

This variable is concerned with the extent to which R is invested in his or her physical appearance and with his or her health or physical status as compared to age peers. In other words, is it important to R to "keep up" physically with younger friends; does he or she strive to maintain a healthy, youthful "front," and so on. Primary data used for ratings were descriptions of health status, capacities, and infirmities; of the current self as compared to earlier in life; and of the importance of physical appearance.

Very Low Narcissism (1): R has given up self-maintenance, regressed, and looks messy; this is often noted as R's worst feature by the interviewer. R may avow greater interest, but makes little effort even for the interviewer. Statements usually express disinterest in appearance (rare in this sample).

Low Narcissism (2): R expresses interest in his or her appearance but does not seem to make an effort at this time to have more than an "acceptable" appearance, although he or she may be defensive about the inability to do so. Some Rs may emphasize the unimportance of appearance in old age, in their present surroundings, or in general. Or, R may comment that qualities of personality or mental ability are of greater significance than appearances.

Moderate Narcissism (3): R wants to look good, is concerned that he or she be dressed correctly and so forth, but is matter-of-fact about appearance. May state explicitly that appearance is less important than it used to be—appearance is something one maintains but does not stress—and, indeed, makes no special effort for the interviewer. R may have some concern with physical front.

High Narcissism (4): R has considerable narcissistic investment in appearance or in maintaining a physical "front." R may play down the importance of clothes, jewelry, and the like "at my age" but "dresses like a duchess" and is proud of his or her appearance; may play down the importance of clothes but make many invidious comments about the dress and appearance of others and be a "bug" on cleanliness.

Very High Narcissism (5): R is preoccupied with the impression he or she makes on others and is proud of it. He or she may go all out to impress the interviewer by means of dress or demonstrations of physical capacity. R. is vain; he or she may be covertly or overtly sexy and interested in attention from the opposite sex; wants very much to be admired. Youthfulness or strength is an integral part of R's self-image.

3. AGGRESSION (WOMEN)*

Aggression is defined as action that is carried out in a forceful way to achieve ends. High aggression refers to a high level of assertiveness and goal-directedness, to capacity to push toward a goal despite obstacles. A high level of hostility or overt anger does not necessarily indicate high assertiveness. At the low end of the scale, R is not assertive; hostility may be suppressed or covertly expressed, but R is withdrawn and nonassertive.

Ratings were mainly based on the interviewer's assessment, the life review, responses to queries on a variety of affects, and self-sort items selected and examples given.

Very Low Aggression (1): R denies assertiveness in almost every instance, seeming instead to withdraw. R seems unable to assert herself even in situations in which interpersonal conflict would not occur. R may appear "helpless" or apathetic. Among her personal characteristics are the following: (a) R is a very quiet, compliant, unobtrusive person who places or has always placed others' needs before her own; R represses her own needs in order to propitiate others, is subservient; (b) R is verbal and friendly to the interviewer but lets people "walk over" her; she is timid and fears her own decisions, so she defers to those of relatives, or "gives in" to avoid confrontations and denies anger or expresses helplessness; and (c) R despairs of influencing others and has withdrawn, feels helpless, and may seem actually afraid of the interviewer.

Low Aggression (2): R is generally a very mild person, but on occasion goes after things, although she may be most uncomfortable in situations involving interpersonal conflict. Or, R may seem never to go after things directly but instead manipulates others in a passive fashion to supply her needs. R may use martyrdom and whining as weapons but at the same time conveys importance in influencing others and an inability to follow through in an assertive manner. Rather than mildness, R may convey strong anxiety with consequent withdrawing tendencies and a strong wish to avoid trouble.

Moderate Aggression (3): R is not particularly assertive, but focuses considerable hostility outward so that she may angrily tell others off. R has much potential for interpersonal conflict, and she seems not to shrink

---

* Points on this scale were rated separately for men and women because manifestations of this behavior were somewhat different.

from it when given the opportunity. Or, R may be very domineering in one or two relationships within the family circle but be markedly fearful of nonfamily figures and thus avoid them or defer to them. Or, R's aggressivity may be highly controlled and contained, expressed only in "appropriate" circumstances.

High Aggression   (4): R is *very* goal-directed in certain areas of life; she may be tough and argumentative, but is occasionally unsure of herself and withdraws. R is somewhat domineering or tends to assume leadership roles and actively assumes responsibility in social situations, but is not as intrusive and dominant as a 5. Or, a mild, unobtrusive front covers R's ability to assume control of people and social situations, so that she is strongly directive and powerful without seeming to be so.

Very High Aggression   (5): R runs everything, takes over; R is a leader. R may "pop off" unrestrainedly at every opportunity; she has a never-say-die attitude and is a formidable opponent. R may manipulate people but does so in an active, commandeering, openly assertive way as well as being belligerent and pushy; R is an iron-willed dictator who compels deference. R is instantly prepared to fight for her rights in almost any situation, and is highly intrusive.

AGGRESSION (MEN)

The same as for women in dimensionality, but manifestations in men may differ somewhat from women. In general, men in this sample are less aggressive than the women.

Very Low Aggression   (1): R may be extroverted or very quiet, but in either case he expresses impotence and helplessness in interpersonal conflicts; for example, if his child says something mean to him, he cries or feels he must "take it." The interviewer may remark that R is especially mild-mannered, passive, and subservient. R is "broken." R has a strong self-image of noncompetitiveness and unobtrusiveness; he views himself as a man who "never argues."

Low Aggression   (2): R seems to do his best to avoid conflict, but irritation slips through. R may be quite apathetic and humble, but manipulates others. In his job, R usually appeared to have been somewhat assertive. R may have an "underdog" air.

Moderate Aggression   (3): R is easily irritated, agitated, and negativistic, but he deals with these feelings by isolating himself. R is a quiet man, but he has a stubborn streak. At the present time, R seems to be quiet, even passive, but in earlier life he displayed decided masculine-assertive characteristics; for example, he may have reveled in a superordinate position as foreman in which he directed the work of many other men; he may have once loved to participate in competitive sports. In general, it seems that R has a potential for conflict, although he generally prefers to avoid it.

High Aggression   (4): R was quite competitive in his business and took on many organizational activities and responsibilities. Often has been a "doer," and still tries to control others. He is occasionally quite irascible, or he may be an egotist who persistently seeks to be the center of attention. Although R may express some timidity about crossing others, he will stand up for his rights if need be.

Very High Aggression   (5): R is verbally aggressive or is quarrelsome and maintains a masculine-aggressive pose; he is forceful and may even be physically aggressive, or was when younger. R was and still tries to be dominant over others. Or, R is an egotist who takes on organizational responsibilities as well as relentlessly seeking a limelight.

4. STATUS DRIVE

This variable taps the extent of preoccupation with and attention to status needs and characteristics and the extent to which behaviors are carefully controlled to reflect understanding of the expectations of the reference group. In part, status preoccupation is reflected in the sheer number of references to status made by the respondent, especially the number of different people so described. However, the respondent may describe few others, but make status the focal point of key interpersonal relationships and reveal an intense orientation toward reference group expectations concerning status.

The most useful data for these ratings were responses to the queries on the transition or on the self compared to earlier in the evaluation of life and the life review.

Very Low Status Drive   (1): No status concerns are apparent; R virtually never or never uses a status referent. R may have no secondary goals, focusing instead on primary goals such as nurturence, and the like. If R is male, he scarcely alludes to his life's work and makes no other references to his status. Or, a single status referent may be made that is nonspecific and peripheral in nature, for example, the ideal man should "make a good living and be good to his wife."

Low Status Drive   (2): R uses few status referents, usually evaluating others in nonstatus terms. Status referents that are used are nonspecific, for example, "we were ambitious" and unelaborated as well as intermixed with achievement goals. Concern with status may be deprecated by R, who prefers, perhaps defensively, to emphasize the intrinsic nature of work, personal characteristics, and so on. Or, status referents (such as money, manual occupation, education) seem to reflect something other than status concerns, such as an oral character syndrome (reflected in an interest in acquiring and spending money) or identification problems (for example, R became a manual worker in part out of fear of competing with his scholar-father, but R has always been ashamed of this lack of education).

Moderate Status Drive (3): Here, R's status concerns and referents are unambiguous. R recognizes and appreciates status but does not seem driven by it; he does not describe most people in status terms or only in status terms. Status goals are usually intertwined with achievement or other goals.

High Status Drive (4): R is quite status-oriented and often speaks of his own status (makes status referents) or that of others. However, these status referents are mixed with other goals and reflect recognition of characteristics other than status. Status, while important to R, seems secondary to other goals.

Very High Status Drive (5): Stresses high status or socioeconomic position of family, friends, or self. People are evaluated in status terms, education is valued for status purposes, and so on. R makes an effort to impress the interviewer in these respects. Rejects low-status characteristics of others. R may be highly status oriented and use status terms constantly, even when he is not fully aware of his status drive or of the implications of his comments. Status is usually an important life theme, permeating many relationships, with many elaborations on the status characteristics of self or others. Or, status may be the focus of *key* relationships in R's life.

5. DISTRUST OF OTHERS

This variable taps R's trust that other people may be counted on, the extent to which he or she expects pleasure or positive outcome from interpersonal relations and truly likes other people. At the low end of the scale, R is overly trusting; that is, he or she unrealistically expects favorable response from all others. At the high end of the scale, R may be misanthropic and even paranoid concerning others.

Data primarily consisted of interviewer's assessments, expectations of others as expressed in the Interpersonal Role-Playing task, the Self-Sort Task, and responses to questions about feelings toward relocation.

Very Low Distrust (Overtrusting) (1): This rating encompasses two general categories of people: (a) R "likes" other people, and goes out toward others. R expresses an expectation of pleasure in dealings with others as well as the feeling that others *could not* dislike R. R minimizes interpersonal difficulties or may not seem to recognize them, and is over-trusting in the sense of expecting only positive response from others. R probably disagrees with the Srole item. (Note: "overtrust" may have a brittle quality; the high degree of trust in others expressed by R may have its roots in, for example, a vast need for narcissistic supplies that help determine R's views of others as wonderful to him or her; or a highly defensive view of his- or herself as deserving of rewards from others; or a very simple personality combined with fortunate and undemanding life experiences.) (b) R is warm, open, seems also to truly like other people. R has experienced and expects positive response from others as well as plea-sure in interpersonal relationships, but adds that one cannot, after all, trust everyone (is realistic). R usually does not cite specific instances in which others let him or her down.

Low Distrust (2): R seems to have been a trusting person in earlier years who had and may still have zest in interpersonal relationships. How-ever, very recently changes in a key relationship (usually with children) have resulted in a loss of trust in the people involved, about whom R may even make remarks tinged with paranoia, reflecting deep disillusionment or despair. This distrust of the children has not generalized to other rela-tionships, and seems at variance with less recent characteristics of R. Or, R seems to like other people and enjoys interpersonal relationships, but also cites specific instances in which others disappointed R; R may be somewhat sensitive to interpersonal slights although R recovers fast.

Moderate Distrust (3): R has some warmth and has had some positive relationships in the past in which he or she placed trust; R generally ex-presses trust in his or her close relationships, but has reservations about the trustworthiness of people in general, the generalized other. He or she does not shut others out, but is skeptical of them.

High Distrust (4): R is cautious of other people; R may seem warm and friendly but expresses strong distrust of a particular category of peo-ple, for example, men. Wary of strangers; for example, may be afraid to walk among "low-class" neighborhood residents; may feel it is hard to find worthwhile company. R's feelings may often be hurt by others' thoughtlessness. There may be a lifelong pattern of distance from others, but with at least one fairly trusting relationship.

Very High Distrust (5): Suspicious of others; R attributes a "jungle-like" character to the world ("dog eat dog"); R dislikes people; is suspi-cious of the interviewer and the interviews, resistant to being questioned. Expects bad results from interpersonal relations or no pleasure. Lifelong

distance from any close interpersonal relationships. May even seem paranoid in remarks about past relationships and in expectations of the generalized other.

6. EMPATHY

This variable measures the ability to put oneself in the other person's
place; to imagine how the other person feels. This sensitivity is related to
projection, defined as a defensive process in which an objectionable internal tendency is unrealistically attributed to another person in the new
environment instead of being recognized as part of the self. The empathic
person, however, imagines accurately how the other person feels, and does
not simply project his or her own emotions; he or she can differentiate his
or her own feelings from those of others.

Data most useful for these ratings were interviewers' assessments, the
life review, and descriptions of children and friends in the interpersonal
focused interview.

Very High Empathy (1): Ability to put oneself in the other person's
place, to imagine how the other person feels. R routinely tries to intuit the
feelings and thoughts of others. He or she tries to "understand" the feelings and thoughts of others and has a concern for the feelings of others.
Differentiated rather than judgmental assessments of others are the rule.

High Empathy (2): R is warm and sympathetic and is able to tune
into others' feelings at more than the very superficial level. If R seems less
warmly interested in others or is currently distant from people, R nevertheless evinces concern with understanding others even though gaps appear; or, R seems very highly invested in one or two relationships in
which empathy is apparent.

Moderate Empathy (3): R is a sweet person (or a good guy) but his or
her ability to tune into others' feelings is limited; that is, R is sympathetic
as a matter of course, but may often misread others' feelings, particularly
as they affect R, in order to maintain R's self-image or view of his or her
place in the world. Or, the affects may be too complex for R—that is, R is
sympathetic but not especially empathetic (except for "simple" emotions
that cannot be misread). Or, R may be distant but seems to focus on the
feelings (with reasonable accuracy) of at least one significant other.

Low Empathy (4): R tends to focus on the surface of events, and most
interactions with others are superficial; R has little interest in the feelings
and/or motives of others (and often seems out of touch with his or her
own feelings), or R may seem puzzled about why people behave the way

they do. Or, R may seem to have some capacity for empathy that is combined with marked callousness and disregard for others when it suits his or her purpose, so that real empathy is limited. Judgmental rather than differentiated assessments of people may be the rule for R; or R may express little interest in others. R is self-centered and tends to interpret the behavior or feelings of others from his or her own point of view.

Very Low Empathy (5): R says, directly or indirectly, "How do I know what others think/feel?" and demonstrates the truth of this in his actions. If R ever interprets the actions of others, he or she does so to suit him- or herself or to fit his or her own fantasies, thus expressing no ability to put self in the place of the other.

7. EXTRAPUNITIVE

This variable measures the degree to which aggressive, hostile feelings are focused on others, in which others are blamed for frustrations, failures, and shortcomings. Others are blamed for difficulties that arise in R's contact with other people or in R's work. Extrapunitive attitudes include strongly critical and/or condescending opinions of others which are flavored with pique that R's gifts are unrecognized by these inferior others.

Data were obtained mostly from the interviewer's assessment, responses to queries on the transition, evaluation of life, self-descriptions of interpersonal relations, and responses to selections on the sentence completion test, particularly "Other people usually . . . ,"; "My father . . ."; and "People over me . . ."

Very Low Extrapunitive (1): R seems impunitive; or is well defended against any extrapunitive tendencies through apathy, reaction formation, or some other strong defense.

Low Extrapunitive (2): Mild extrapunitive indications; one or two peripheral instances that do not relate to major frustrations in R's life. If the frustration or failure mentioned is a major one (such as loss of spouse or of job), R blames generalities or fate, not other people, and does not otherwise tend to place blame outward. R may tend either toward not blaming self or others or toward defensive handling of blame. R may make a few deprecatory comments about others.

Midpoint Extrapunitive (3): Extrapunitive trends more prominent than above. A mixed group. R may be critical of others or express blame of his or her parents or children but does not dwell on this theme; or expresses moderate blaming tendencies combined with actions designed to punish others—such as martyrdom and/or moral imperatives. Or R is extrapunitive, and has many complaints about others, but is somehow guarded about expressing blame, or tends to externalize but not about major incidents.

High Extrapunitive (4): R is markedly critical and disparaging of others, is on the watch for instances in which others wronged R. R may feel he or she is mistreated, or may be strongly but inconsistently extrapunitive toward key people such as children.

Very High Extrapunitive (5): R blames others with self-righteous justification at every turn, and may even sound slightly paranoid. Or, R is *strongly* extrapunitive toward key people, such as children.

8. INTRAPUNITIVE

This variable measures the extent to which aggression is turned onto the self; self-blame and exaggerated guilt are important behavioral indicators. Exaggerated self-blame may be interpreted as an expression of strict superego. Intrapunitive tendencies are indicated by self-blame for difficulties that arise in one's contacts with other people, in one's work, or for personality shortcomings, by self-deprecation, and by thinking and attitudes that seem pervaded by doubt, hesitation, and indecision. An intrapunitive individual may express feelings of inadequacy, inferiority, and guilt, tending not to think very highly of himself or herself. Highly intrapunitive individuals may tend toward obsessional rumination about their faults and the mistakes they have made. Exaggerated feelings of guilt and self-deprecation may, of course, accompany a depression. (Very mild self-deprecation, say, of test performance, may reflect a wish for reassurance; but more than one or two comments along these lines reflect intrapunitive trends.)

The primary data used for these ratings were interviewers' assessments, discussion of parents and punishment they meted out in the life review, the life evaluation, comments on shame and guilt and responses to sentence completion items, particularly "My past life . . ."; "Sometimes I feel . . ."; and "The thing I like about myself . . ."

Very High Intrapunitive (1): R is very openly engaged in self-blame; or R evinces less open guilt and self-recrimination but has a severe, punitive superego that leads to considerable self-deprecation. Most individuals who express suicide wishes belong here (some are extrapunitive).

High Intrapunitive (2): R deprecates his or her test performance and asks for much reassurance, but is not as deprecatory of self as those who are rated 1. R evinces feelings of inferiority/insecurity but tries harder to rationalize or defend against these than those rated 1; or, the intrapunitive tendencies are milder and/or are less central in R's personality structure. Respondents who have made suicide attempts earlier in life should usually be rated here.

Midpoint Intrapunitive (3): Mild self-deprecation. R may also *not* deprecate self because it would undermine efforts to shore up a covert image of the self as bad.

Low Intrapunitive (4): R is pretty nonpunitive, usually. R may make one or two mildly self-critical remarks but in a context of positive self-acceptance or successfully defended self-image; less often, from R's mild remarks it is difficult to determine whether blame is directed, inward or outward.

Very Low Intrapunitive (Non-Intrapunitive) (5): No instance is found of self-blame or even self-criticism, or only traces throughout the interview. R usually feels successful in life; such an R may be nonpunitive, or quite extrapunitive, but evinces little trace of the covert self-deprecation often manifested by extrapunitive Rs.

9. AUTHORITARIAN-EQUALITARIAN

In an equalitarian individual, social and personal relations are conceived in terms of mutuality and permissiveness; he or she is democratic and "expressive." The authoritarian individual, on the other hand, structures social relationships in terms of status, position, dominance, and submission. In the authoritarian syndrome, R achieves social adjustment by taking pleasure in obedience and subordination. R has a simultaneous blind belief in authority and readiness to attack those who are deemed weak and who are socially acceptable as "victims," and identifies with strength, rejecting all that is "down" to dichotomize between in-group and out-group.

The primary data for these ratings were the interviewers' assessments, the life review, the life evaluation, responses to queries on affects, and descriptions of past and current relationships with children and friends.

Equalitarian (1): R is democratic and permissive in interpersonal relationships, which have a quality of give and take. R may well have explicit "liberal" attitudes. May express some criticism of relatives or associates but overall has a "live-and-let-live" attitude. Even in relationships in which R is dominant, he or she does not strive to control. (The R who is equalitarian in *all* instances is rare.)

Low Authoritarian (2): R seems generally permissive and democratic, with an attitude of giving as well as getting, but control is occasionally an issue that induces R to manipulate, for example, by provoking guilt in others. R may regret that the children are no longer dependent. Or, R may have conscious conflict in this area—is guilty about authoritarian attitudes that he or she did or does possess.

Authoritarian   (3): R prizes a hierarchical structure in key relationships, such as with children. R may tend to manipulate, with considerable provoking of guilt. R may tentatively reject a category of people, such as "men" or "young people" on a moralistic basis.

Moderately High Authoritarian   (4): R often has a high moral code against which others—such as children, young people, or minority groups—are judged and found wanting. R seems to have formalized relationships rather than personal ones. R may stress moral precepts in describing her interactions with others and is often very manipulative. R often condemns others and seems interested in keeping others "in their place." If male, R stresses autonomy and/or dominance based on moral strictures.

Very High Authoritarian   (5): Similar to a rating of 4, only more so. R lists many moral precepts broken by children or others, is markedly intolerant of others. R also upholds societal codes in a rigid fashion. Often, in R's childhood obedience was a supreme value and R was often overadjusted, "broken." R stresses dominance-submission (overtly, or on a moral plane) in a number of relationships.

Appendix D

Assessing Environments

Interview and observational data were used for each of the ten environmental scales:

1. Achievement Fostering
2. Individuation
3. Dependency Fostering
4. Warmth
5. Affiliation Fostering
6. Recognition
7. Stimulation
8. Physical Attractiveness
9. Cue Richness
10. Tolerance for Deviancy

The eleventh scale in the Deinstitutionalized Elites study, health care adequacy, was a ranking of the twenty-six relocation environments. The ten scales were slightly modified for use in the Death of an Institution study. The staff interview and observational schedules and the point values to be scored for each response follow. Items are labeled "Q" if they are questions to be asked of the respondents and "O" if they are observations to be collected. "R" refers to the respondent.

A. ACHIEVEMENT FOSTERING

1. Do the residents help out by taking care of each other? (Q)
   a. Seldom; rarely; not very often.   0
   b. A little; some do; occasionally.   1
   c. Many do.   3

2. Can you give me a specific EXAMPLE (incident) of one patient helping another? (Q)
   a. No   −1
     (If incident given, ask:) How did you REACT to that? What did
     you think and do?
   b. R tried to stop it; got annoyed, etc. (any NEGATIVE reaction).   −2
   c. No particular reaction indicated.   0
   d. R "thought it was nice" or any other POSITIVE reaction that was
     NOT COMMUNICATED TO THE RESIDENT.   1
   e. R communicated some kind of PRAISE, REWARD, or ENCOURAGE-
     MENT to the resident.   1
3. Can you think of a time when one of the newer residents came and
said that he or she wanted to do some work or help with the chores
in some way? (Q)
   a. No   0
     (If YES, ask:) Can you tell me about the incident—describe it for
     me? (Then ask:) How did you REACT to that?
   b. R felt that the resident couldn't do the work; got annoyed; or any
     other NEGATIVE reaction.   −2
   c. No particular reaction indicated.   0
   d. R "thought it was nice" or some similar reaction that was NOT
     COMMUNICATED TO THE RESIDENT.   1
   e. R communicated some kind of PRAISE, REWARD, or ENCOURAGE-
     MENT to the resident.   1
4. Did the person GET some kind of work or something to do? (Q)
   a. No   0
   b. YES   3
5. You seem (very) proud of some of your residents. What makes you
feel that way? Can you tell me something that one of the residents
accomplished that made you feel proud? (Q)
   a. R cannot think of an incident.   0
   b. Incident involves withdrawal, quiescence, or compliance with in-
     stitutional rules.   0
   c. Incident reflects initiative or some "therapeutic" effort on the
     part of the resident.   1
6. Do any of your older residents have JOBS of any kind outside (in the
community)? (Q)
   a. No   0
   b. YES (if yes, ask what jobs the residents hold.)   4
7. Are any of the residents HIRED and PAID for jobs within the home?
(Q)
   a. No   0
   b. YES (If yes, list all such jobs.)   2
8. Do any of the residents have other kinds of jobs or duties which they
perform? (Q)
   a. No   0
   b. YES (If yes, list all such jobs.)   2

9. Do you TRY to have any or all of them do some little job or other? (Q)
    a. R suggests that attempts of this kind are made for NONE or VERY FEW residents. 0
    b. Attempts are made for SOME residents—a minority. 1
    c. Attempts are made for MANY—at least half or more of the residents, even though they may not be successful. 3
10. Do any of the residents have HOBBIES or work at some kind of crafts—such as sewing, knitting, woodworking, painting, etc.? (Q)
    a. No or VERY FEW. 0
    b. SOME do—apparently less than half of the residents. 1
    c. It appears that MOST (more than half) of the residents do. 3
11. Do any of the residents belong to clubs or do volunteer work or anything like that outside the home? For example, do any belong to the YMCA, a union brotherhood, a religious club, or do volunteer work or anything like that? (Q)
    a. No 0
    b. YES (If YES, list all appropriate activities.)
12. (The following items should be weighted 1 for a YES, 0 for a NO.) (O)
    a. Are there any CLUBS to which residents belong and which hold meetings or have activities? _____
    b. Do residents serve on any COMMITTEES? _____
    c. Is there a CRAFTS DEPARTMENT—a facility which is intended for use, that residents DO use and/or are encouraged to use? _____
    d. Is there any SPECIAL EQUIPMENT FOR CRAFTS, such as sewing machines, pottery wheel, easels, woodworking tools, soldering irons, pottery mold, kiln, leather-working tools, etc.? _____
    e. Can the residents use the KITCHEN for cooking or baking? _____
    f. Do any of the residents have a PRIVATE KITCHEN? _____
    g. Are there any group RECREATIONAL FACILITIES, such as bowling, shuffleboard, tennis, badminton, billiards tables, pinball machines, etc.? _____
    h. Are any CLASSES offered to residents? A series of meetings on some topic, intended for education of some sort? _____
       Do residents do any of the following:
    i. Drawing or painting? _____
    j. Work or chores of any kind (aside from simply straightening one's own bed or clothes, etc.)? _____
    k. Sewing, knitting, or crocheting? _____
    l. Engaged in any kind of craft or hobby (such as making paper flowers, etc.)? (Do not include painting or writing that was scored above) _____
    m. Working (for example cleaning floors or windows, cooking or doing dishes together)? _____
    n. Joint participation in some hobby or craft? _____
    o. Committee meetings? _____
    p. Club or organized social meeting? _____

q. Attending classes or lectures? _____

r. Is there a day center or organization for the elderly (for example, YMCA, YWCA, vocational rehabilitation center, Jewish Community Center, etc.)? _____

B. INDIVIDUATION

1. DIFFERENTIATION: I wonder if you could take just a few minutes to tell me what kinds of people live here. It's hard to tell just from looking around. What are they like? (Q)
   a. R suggests there are MANY TYPES of persons here, that you can't just lump them together or describe them in a few words.   3
   b. R distinguishes roughly TWO TYPES, for example: "Most of them are old ... but some of them are pretty healthy."   1
   c. R describes residents as if they're all rather similar; does not describe individual differences, types, or idiosyncracies; for example: "I guess they're all generally old."   0
2. Variations in residents' sleeping rooms: (O)
   a. All rooms NEARLY IDENTICAL, except for minor details, such as different color rug or curtains, furniture arranged slightly differently, or some rooms slightly larger than others.   0
   b. Rooms QUITE SIMILAR, though some variation in shape, size, furniture arrangements, or number of occupants. Observer can see variation when looking for it, but not very striking.   1
   c. MODERATE VARIATION—rooms are distinct, but a general theme or style of decor runs through all rooms. Rooms vary considerably, but obviously "belong in the same building."   2
   d. DISTINCT VARIATION—as if particular effort was made to ensure that the rooms vary considerably; for example, one room may be Danish modern, the next provincial, etc.   3
3. Personalization of residents' rooms: (O)
   a. LITTLE PERSONALIZATION—resident may have family pictures, medicine, and the like, evident, but otherwise observer finds it difficult to feel that the room "belongs" to an individual.   0
   b. SOME PERSONALIZATION—residents may have many objects or furnishings which help individualize rooms, but rooms still rather similar. Observer may have some feeling of identification of the rooms with their occupants.   2
   c. MUCH PERSONALIZATION—residents have obviously spent some time and energy personalizing their rooms, as evident from pictures, books, notebooks, clothes lying about, plants and flowers, etc., as well as apparent personalization of furniture, rugs, curtains, bedspread, etc.   4
4. Stimulus information available: How DISTINCT are the various AREAS of the building? How much VARIATION and CONTRAST is there from one area to another? Of particular importance are variations in furnishings and in colors and textures on floors and walls, as well as,

e.g., differences in windows, woodwork, and fixtures from one area to the next. (O)

   a. MUCH DISTINCTIVENESS—as in the different rooms of a HOUSE, where kitchen, dining room, living room, and bedroom typically contain very different furniture, are often of different colors, have different floor coverings, and are decorated differently.   3

   b. MODERATE DISTINCTIVENESS—some variation, as in a modern LOW-COST APARTMENT, where furnishings and decorations (and perhaps colors) may vary from room to room, but wall textures are usually the same and floor coverings show little variation.   2

   c. SOME DISTINCTIVENESS—somewhat "institutional," but SOME areas may be distinct, such as a lounge or lobby, and other areas show SOME VARIATION in furnishings, colors, floor coverings, and/or textures. Corridors, if any, contain some furniture, area rugs, pictures, signs, etc., to provide some distinctive information.   1

   d. LITTLE DISTINCTIVENESS—most areas are QUITE SIMILAR, as in a typical 1930s hospital. Only the lounge, lobby, director's office, or one or two other rooms show any distinctiveness. Corridors, if any, are relatively "blank," providing little information. This category would ordinarily apply to an institution or hotel only. Most residents' rooms are quite similar.   0

   (Note: Rate only those areas of building where majority of the residents spend the majority of their time. Do not include areas that residents rarely enter.)

5. Personalization of residents' attire: Observer should note how many residents wear clothes provided by institution. (O)

   a. Institutional clothing, gown, or uniform is worn by all or most residents.   0

   b. Most residents wear used clothing (noninstitutional) provided by the home, or many wear institutional gowns or uniforms. Few wear their "own" clothes (provided by selves or relatives).   1

   c. Most wear their own clothes, but some wear gowns, uniforms, or used clothing provided by the institution, including unmarked used clothing.   2

   d. All residents wear clothes provided by themselves or by relatives.   3

C. DEPENDENCY FOSTERING

1. Can you give me a specific EXAMPLE (incident) of one patient helping another? (Q)

   a. No   0

   (If incident given, ask:) How did you REACT to that? What did you think and do?

   b. R tried to stop it; got annoyed; etc. (any NEGATIVE reaction).   −1

   c. No particular reaction indicated.   0

   d. R "thought it was nice" or any other POSITIVE reaction that was NOT COMMUNICATED TO THE RESIDENT.   1

    e. R communicated some kind of PRAISE, REWARD, or ENCOURAGE-
MENT to the resident.   2

2. How would you describe YOUR (or your STAFF's) JOB here in relation
to the residents? What are their main functions, generally? (More
than one response may be checked.) (Q)
    a. To provide housing—a landlord.   0
    b. To be a companion or friend to them.   1
    c. To be available when needed—primarily to provide necessities
and services, such as food, beds, clothes, etc.   2
    d. To watch them and take care of them in their declining years.   3
    e. To work with them and help them become more independent.   −1
    f. To make sure they obey the rules and that everything goes well.   0
    g. To keep them from harming themselves.   2
    h. To keep them from getting into trouble.   2

3. Do you TRY to have any/all of them do some little job or other? (Q)
    a. R suggests that attempts of this kind are made for NONE or VERY
FEW residents.   2
    b. Attempts are made for SOME residents—a minority.   1
    c. Attempts are made for MANY—at least half or more of the resi-
dents.   0
    d. Attempts of this kind are made for ALL residents—even though
they may not be successful.   −1

4. Why/Why Not? (Q)
    a. They're not well enough; too weak; couldn't handle it; it would
be too hard for them; etc.   2
    b. R indicates that some or many of the residents DON'T WANT jobs
of any kind and that, therefore, they shouldn't be forced to have
some kind of job.   1
    c. R indicates that it's "good for them" in some UNSPECIFIED WAY.   −1
    d. R suggests that "It makes them feel good," "feel proud," "feel
worthwhile"—some legitimate therapeutic goal is mentioned.   −2

5. How do the residents go about getting the things that they need, like
stamps, toothpaste, shoelaces, etc.? (Q)
    a. They just go out to the store and buy them.   −1
    b. Most of them just go out and buy the things, but some of them
have to have someone else (a friend or relative) get the things for
them.   0
    c. Some of them go out and buy their own things, and they usually
pick up things for the rest of those who can't go out.   1
    d. Some of them go out and buy things on their own, but most of
them get the things from staff or from relatives.   2
    e. The home (staff) gets or provides most of the things. If there's
something special they need, they ask the staff and we get it for
them.   3

6. I'd like to show/read you two statements. I'd like you to tell me
which one is MORE TRUE of the older people living here. (Q)
    a. "They are pretty fragile, so we can't let them be too active or
they might hurt themselves."   2

b. "Even though they might hurt themselves, we think that they should keep active and do just about everything for themselves." −2

c. (Respondent OBJECTS to choice, saying that "It's somewhere between 'a' and 'b,'" or that "a" is true of some and "b" is true of others.) 0

7. What would you judge to be the STAFF'S APPARENT ROLE vis-à-vis the residents? (O)

    a. LANDLORD: No duties regarding maintenance, such as feeding, giving medicine, etc.; nor does there appear to be any assumption of a therapeutic role. 0

    b. WATCHDOG or GUARD: To ensure that no one does anything wrong, hurts him- or herself or someone else, or runs away. 1

    c. CARETAKER: To provide for basic maintenance needs of the residents—to keep him alive and reasonably well. 2

    d. CARETAKER PLUS: Same as caretaker, but in addition, tries to befriend individual residents, keep them happy, or make them somewhat happier or better adjusted. At least, tries to deal with resident on somewhat more personal or "therapeutic" level. 3

D. WARMTH

1. Do the residents help out by taking care of each other? (Q)
    a. Seldom; rarely; not very often. 0
    b. A little; some do; occasionally. 1
    c. Many do. 3

2. Can you give me a specific EXAMPLE (incident) of one patient helping another? (Q)
    a. No 0
    (If incident given, ask: How did you REACT to that? What did you think and do?)
    b. R tried to stop it; got annoyed, etc. (any NEGATIVE reaction). −1
    c. No particular reaction indicated.
    d. R "thought it was nice" or any other POSITIVE reaction that was NOT COMMUNICATED TO THE RESIDENT. 1
    e. R communicated some kind of PRAISE, REWARD, or ENCOURAGEMENT to the resident. 2

3. How would you describe YOUR (or your STAFF's) JOB here in relation to the residents? What are your main functions, generally? (Q) (More than one response may be checked.)
    a. To provide housing—a landlord. 0
    b. To be a companion or friend to them. 3
    c. To be available when needed—primarily to provide necessities and services, such as food, beds, clothes, etc. 1
    d. To watch them and take care of them in their declining years. 0
    e. To work with them and help them become more independent. 2
    f. To make sure they obey the rules and that everything goes well. 0
    g. To keep them from harming themselves. 0
    h. To keep them from getting into trouble. 0

4. Evaluation: (O)
   a. R speaks of some (or all) residents with genuine pride or fond-
      ness. May pick out one resident whom he or she is obviously
      proud or fond of.   3
   b. R seems to feel reasonably warmly toward some or most resi-
      dents. No real pride or attachment evident, but R generally
      seems to "like his residents." No negative feelings expressed
      toward any residents.   2
   c. R displays both POSITIVE and NEGATIVE feelings. R obviously
      likes some residents but dislikes others—feels that some are very
      nice, good, helpful, etc., BUT others may be "sick," nuisances, etc. 1
   d. NON-EVALUATIVE: R's description of residents is bland, lacks af-
      fect. No evaluations are made explicit or implicit. It's hard to
      decide just HOW R feels, but apparently he or she doesn't seem to
      care one way or the other.   0
   e. NEGATIVE EVALUATION.   −2
5. How did you REACT to this accomplishment? (Q)
   a. R cannot remember, cannot describe, or says "no particular reac-
      tion."   0
   b. R "felt proud," "felt good," or some other positive reaction NOT
      COMMUNICATED TO THE RESIDENT.   1
   c. R PRAISED or CONGRATULATED the resident.   2
   d. Some SPECIAL RECOGNITION was made before the resident—for
      example, respondent was mentioned in a newsletter, given an
      award of some kind, mention made in a meeting of the residents,
      etc.   2
6. (If b or c above, ask:) How (or why) was resident aware? How did he
   or she know how you felt? (Q) (This may have been answered
   above.)
   a. R says "Resident could tell how we felt." "Resident just sensed
      it," etc.   0
   b. R indicates that they TOLD the resident how they felt, congratu-
      lated or praised him or her, etc.   2
   c. R indicates that it was OBVIOUS to the resident, because they
      made such a big thing over it.   3
7. How did the OTHER RESIDENTS REACT to this accomplishment? (Q)
   a. Other residents did not learn of the accomplishment, or no reac-
      tion indicated.   0
   b. Other residents "felt good," "felt proud," etc.—any positive re-
      action NOT COMMUNICATED to the resident.   1
   c. Some of the residents congratulated him or her—some praise
      proffered by the residents.   2
   d. Much praise, excitement, encouragement, etc., was generated by
      the residents—for example, "They made a big thing of it."   3
8. How do the residents go about getting the things that they need, like
   stamps, toothpaste, shoelaces, etc.? (Q)
   a. They just go out to the store and buy them.   0
   b. Most of them just go out and buy the things, but some of them

have to have someone else (such as a friend or relative) get things
for them.   0

   c. Some of them go out and buy their own things, and they usually
pick up things for the rest of those who can't go out.   1

   d. Some of them go out and buy things on their own, but most of
them get the things from us (staff) or from relatives.   0

   e. The home (staff) gets or provides most of the things. If there's
something special they need, they ask us and we get it for them.   0

9. Do residents ask you if they can go shopping for things that they
need, like clothes or shoes? Can you give me an example? (Probe for
a specific incident.) (Q)

   a. No INCIDENT cited.   0
(If incident is cited, ask How did you REACT to that?)

   b. R pointed out to the resident that it COULDN'T BE DONE; or any
similar NEGATIVE REACTION.   1

   c. No particular reaction indicated.   0

   d. R "thought it was nice" or some similar reaction that was NOT
COMMUNICATED to the resident (some efforts may or may not
have been made to procure whatever the resident needed).   1

   e. Some kind of PRAISE, REWARD, or ENCOURAGEMENT was communicated to the resident—that is, resident was encouraged to go
out or do things on his or her own; some EFFORT was made in this
direction.   2

10. (Casually, as if commenting on previous question:) I imagine many
of the older people must be pretty difficult, aren't they? (Q)

   a. R. OBJECTION: R says "Oh no, they're very nice" or "They're no
trouble at all" or "That's what a lot of people think, but once you
get to know them you really get to like them."   3

   b. SOME OBJECTION: R suggests that SOME of them are, but "MOST of
them are pretty nice" or "MOST of aren't much trouble at all."   1

   c. MODIFIED AGREEMENT: R suggests that most of them ARE difficult but that SOME of them are pretty nice or SOME of them aren't
any trouble.   0

   d. AGREEMENT: R says "That's right" or "Yes, it takes a lot of pa-
tience," or "You just have to learn to live with it."   −2

11. Are any of their ideas (about making changes in the institution)
PRACTICAL? (Q)

   a. Not very often.   0

   b. Some of them are fairly/pretty good.   2

   c. MANY of them are (or) "You'd be surprised."   3

12. (Casually—a "personal comment":) One thing I've noticed about
older people is that they often want to DO THINGS FOR THEMSELVES,
but when they do, they just make a mess of it. Have you noticed
that? (Q)

   a. No—R suggests that elderly DON'T WANT to do things for themselves.   0

   b. YES—Relatively unqualified agreement.   −1

   c. YES—QUALIFIED AGREEMENT: R suggests that that happens often, but that some of them CAN or SHOULD do things for themselves.   0

    d. YES—but R thinks that they should do as much for themselves as
possible anyway.   1

    e. NO—OBJECTS STRONGLY: May say "When you really get to know
them, you'd be amazed at how much they can do if you let them
(or encourage them)," or "They're not that way at all."   3

13. Interaction of Residents: (O)

    a. VERY LITTLE interaction or contact apparent: Greatest majority
of residents are NOT interacting—most are seen walking or sitting
alone, or in bed. If residents are in multiple-bed rooms, most are
NOT interacting. Lounges, if any, contain only a SMALL proportion of residents in close proximity with other residents.   0

    b. SOME INTERACTION APPARENT: Some areas, such as a lounge or
lobby, may contain slight concentrations of residents (in close
proximity), some other residents may be seen interacting in pairs
or small groups, but at least 50 percent of residents appear to not
interact much.   1

    c. Roughly equal distribution of isolates and groups. 40–60 percent
of residents appear alone or in company of others but not interacting, while 40–60 percent of residents are interacting or in
close proximity with others.   2

    d. MUCH INTERACTION: Majority of residents are seen interacting—
sitting, standing, or walking in the company of others. Relatively
few isolates observed.   3

14. Observations of Brief Verbal Exchanges (greetings, pleasantries): (O)

    a. SEVERAL INSTANCES observed: Seems common that residents
greet each other or exchange a few words when they meet or sit
next to each other.   4

    b. OCCASIONAL INSTANCES observed: "Some do and some don't," as
if some are friends and exchange a few words while others are
relatively isolated and rarely speak upon meeting another.   2

    c. FEW INSTANCES observed: Residents withdraw, avoid speaking,
or seem to be strangers.   0

15. Observations of conversations among residents (lasting twenty seconds or longer): (O)

    a. MANY CONVERSATIONS observed: Many residents seem to be
friends (or friendly) and could be observed sitting and chatting
with each other (beyond brief greetings or pleasantries).   5

    b. SOME CONVERSATIONS observed: Residents have some conversa-
tions, but limited to a few of the more "interactive" residents.   2

    c. FEW CONVERSATIONS observed: MOST residents seem content to sit
or read alone and are not interested in speaking with others—or
act as though residents do not know each other very well.   0

16. Extent of staff's General Involvement with residents: (O)

    a. Most staff members seem PERSONALLY INVOLVED with residents.
Members go out of their way to interact with residents, or their
manner suggests a sincere concern for residents. MUCH attention
paid to activities, whims, and welfare of residents.   5

      b. SOME INVOLVEMENT apparent, but mostly through staff's duties with residents—most of staff's contact with residents occurs as part of staff's duties (for example, giving out medicine), but this contact may be highly personalized, and SOME efforts may be made toward additional, informal contact.   3

      c. Most staff are primarily concerned with "their own work." Residents are left alone and/or ignored during most of observation period. Contact, when it occurs, is rather formal—little personal involvement evident.   0

      d. HOSTILITY seems to exist toward residents at some level. Contact is highly formal, curt, or abrupt. Some staff appear to feel that residents are a nuisance or are "in the way."   −3

17. Does CONFLICT exist among members of the STAFF? (O)

      a. No evidence for conflict observed.   1

      b. SOME evidence for conflict, perhaps inferred from the manner in which members address each other or give directions.   −1

      c. Definite evidence for conflict. Staff observed complaining to or about each other. Open harshness or anger or bad temper.   −3

18. After considerable observation, what would you judge to be the STAFF'S APPARENT ROLE vis-à-vis the residents? (O)

      a. LANDLORD: No duties regarding maintenance, such as feeding, giving medicine, etc., nor does there appear to be any assumption of a therapeutic role.   0

      b. WATCHDOG or GUARD: To ensure that no one does anything wrong, hurts him- or herself or someone else, or runs away.   −2

      c. CARETAKER: To provide for basic maintenance needs of residents—to keep them alive and reasonably well.   1

      d. CARETAKER PLUS: Same as caretaker, but in addition, tries to befriend residents, keep them happy or make them somewhat happier or better adjusted. At least, tries to deal with resident on somewhat more personal or "therapeutic" level than a mere caretaker.   3

      e. THERAPEUTIC: Sees role PRIMARILY as trying to IMPROVE the resident, his or her adjustment, or circumstances.   4

19. Physical contact between staff and residents: (O)

      a. Little or no evidence of physical contact, except accidentally. Staff may seem to avoid physical contact.   0

      b. Some physical contact—for example, resident may take a staff person's arm when climbing stairs or walking and/or staff and resident may briefly shake hands when meeting, but little else. Little physical contact evident, but no apparent avoidance of contact.   1

      c. Some staff members seen putting hands or arms on resident's shoulder; staff members holds resident's hand or arm during conversation; staff member teaches resident or helps resident by holding or guiding hands, arms, or legs.   2

      d. CLOSE physical contact observed, including hugging, embracing; contact between trunks of bodies; or extended intimate contact, such as prolonged resting of arm on shoulder, etc.   3

E. AFFILIATION-FOSTERING

1. Do the residents help out by taking care of each other? (Q)
   a. Seldom; rarely; not very often.   0
   b. A little; some do; occasionally.   1
   c. Many do.   3

2. How would you describe YOUR (or your STAFF's) JOB here in relation to the residents? What are the main functions, generally? (More than one response may be checked.) (Q)
   a. To provide housing—a landlord.   0
   b. To be a companion or friend to them.   2
   c. To be available when needed—primarily to provide necessities and services, such as food, beds, clothes, etc.   0
   d. To watch them and take care of them in their declining years.   0
   e. To work with them and help them become more independent.   1
   f. To make sure they obey the rules and that everything goes well.   0
   g. To keep them from harming themselves.   0
   h. To keep them from getting into trouble.   0

3. Availability of "Social Spaces": Is an area set aside for the use of some, but not all, residents consisting of some part of the building (such as a floor or wing)? Do individuals have control over WHOM they can communicate with and vice versa? (O)
   a. Area is available to ALL OR MOST residents.   3
   b. Area is available to ONE-THIRD TO TWO-THIRDS of residents.   2
   c. Area is available to LESS THAN ONE-THIRD of residents.   0

4. Use of "social spaces": (O)
   a. Used by more than HALF of residents.   3
   b. Used by ONE-FOURTH TO ONE-HALF.   2
   c. Used by LESS THAN ONE-FOURTH.   1
   d. Used RARELY (or not available).   0

5. What GROUP or SHARED ACTIVITIES can be observed? (Observer should score only for those activities that are ACTUALLY OBSERVED. Shared activities should only be scored if the residents are ACTUALLY SHARING the activity or participating TOGETHER.) (O)
   (Each NO = 0; each YES weighted as shown.)
   a. Watching TV?   1
   b. Playing cards?   2
   c. Walking together?   1
   d. Singing?   1
   e. Arguing?   2
   f. Having conversations (with staff or residents)?   1
   g. Visiting with outsiders?   1
   h. Working (for example, cleaning floors or windows; cooking or doing dishes)?   1
   i. Participating jointly in some hobby or craft?   2
   j. Attending committee meeting?   2
   k. Attending club or organized social meeting?   3
   l. Attending classes or lectures?   2

m. Any OTHER joint activities? (If YES, list each, scoring 1 point for each activity):

1. _____   3. _____
2. _____   4. _____

6. Interaction of Residents: (O)

   a. VERY LITTLE interaction or contact apparent: Greatest majority (more than three-fourths) of residents are NOT interacting—most are seen walking or sitting alone, or in bed. If residents are in multiple-bed rooms, most are NOT interacting. Lounges, if any, contain only a SMALL proportion of residents in close proximity with other residents.　　0

   b. SOME INTERACTION APPARENT: Some areas, e.g. lounge or lobby, may contain slight concentrations of residents (in close proximity), some other residents may be seen interacting in pairs or small groups, but at least 50 percent of residents appear to not interact much.　　1

   c. ROUGHLY EQUAL distribution of isolates and groups: 40 to 60 percent of residents appear alone or in company of others but not interacting, while 40–60 percent of residents are interacting or in close proximity with others.　　2

   d. MUCH INTERACTION: Majority of residents are seen interacting—sitting, standing, or walking in the company of others. Relatively few isolates observed.　　3

7. Observations of brief verbal exchanges (greetings, pleasantries): (O)

   a. SEVERAL INSTANCES observed: Seems common that residents should greet each other or exchange a few words when they meet or sit next to each other.　　3

   b. OCCASIONAL INSTANCES observed: "Some do and some don't," as if some are friends and exchange a few words, while others are relatively isolated and rarely speak upon meeting another.　　2

   c. FEW INSTANCES observed: residents withdraw, avoid speaking, or seem to be strangers.　　0

8. Observations of conversations among residents (lasting twenty seconds or longer): (O)

   a. MANY CONVERSATIONS observed: Many residents seem to be friends (or friendly) and could be observed sitting and chatting with each other (beyond brief greetings or pleasantries).　　4

   b. SOME CONVERSATIONS observed: Residents have some conversations, but limited to a few of the more "interactive" residents.　　2

   c. FEW CONVERSATIONS observed: MOST residents seem content to sit or read alone and are not interested in speaking with others— or act as though residents do not know each other very well.　　0

9. Physical contact between staff and residents: (O)

   a. Little or no evidence of physical contact, except accidentally. Staff may seem to avoid physical contact.　　0

   b. Some physical contact—for example, resident may take a staff person's arm when climbing stairs or walking and/or staff and resident may briefly shake hands when meeting, but little else.

Little physical contact evident, but no apparent avoidance of contact. 1

c. Some staff members seen putting hands or arms on resident's shoulder; staff member holds resident's hand or arm during conversation; staff member teachers resident or helps resident by holding or guiding hands, arms or legs. 2

d. CLOSE physical contact observed, including hugging, embracing; contact between trunks of bodies; or extended intimate contact, such as prolonged resting of arm on shoulder, etc. 4

10. Extent of staff's GENERAL INVOLVEMENT with residents: (O)

a. Most staff members seem PERSONALLY INVOLVED with residents. Members go out of their way to interact with residents or their manner suggests a sincere concern for residents. MUCH attention paid to activities, whims, and welfare of residents. 4

b. SOME INVOLVEMENT apparent, but mostly through staff's duties with residents—most of the staff's contact with residents occurs as a part of staff's duties (for example, giving out medicine), but this contact may be highly personalized, and SOME efforts may be made toward additional, informal contact. 2

c. Most staff are primarily concerned with "their own work." Residents are left alone and/or ignored during most of observation period. Contact, when it occurs, is rather formal—little personal involvement evident. 0

d. HOSTILITY seems to exist toward residents at some level. Contact is highly formal, curt, or abrupt. Some staff appear to feel that residents are a nuisance or are "in the way." −2

F. RECOGNITION

1. Can you give me a specific EXAMPLE (incident) of one patient helping another? (Q)

a. No 0

(If incident given, ask:) How did you REACT to that? What did you think and do?

b. R tried to stop it; got annoyed; etc. (any NEGATIVE reaction). −1

c. No particular reaction indicated. 0

d. R "thought it was nice" or any other POSITIVE reaction that was NOT COMMUNICATED TO THE RESIDENT. 1

e. R communicated some kind of PRAISE, REWARD, or ENCOURAGEMENT to the resident. 2

2. Can you think of a time when one of the newer residents came and said that he or she wanted to do some work or help with the chores in some way? (Q)

a. No 0

(If YES, ask:) Can you tell me about the incident—describe it for me? (Then ask:) "How did you REACT to that? (Q)

     b. R felt that the resident couldn't do the work; got annoyed; or any other NEGATIVE reaction.   −1

     c. No particular reaction indicated.   0

     d. R "thought it was nice" or some similar reaction that was NOT COMMUNICATED TO THE RESIDENT.   1

     e. R communicated some kind of PRAISE, REWARD, or ENCOURAGEMENT to the resident.   2

3. How did you REACT to this accomplishment? (Q)

     a. R cannot remember, cannot describe, or says "no particular reaction."   0

     b. R "felt proud," "felt good," or some other positive reaction NOT COMMUNICATED TO THE RESIDENT.   1

     c. R PRAISED or CONGRATULATED the resident.   2

     d. Some SPECIAL RECOGNITION was made before the resident—for example, respondent was mentioned in a newsletter, given an award of some kind, mention made in a meeting of the residents, etc.   4

4. Do you think that the resident KNEW how you felt? (Q)

     a. R says "No" or doubts that the resident knew.   0

     b. R says "maybe," "probably," or "I think so."   1

     c. R is quite sure that the resident was aware.   2

5. (If b or c above, ask:) How (or why) was resident aware? How did he or she know how you felt? (Q) (This may have been answered above.)

     a. R says "Resident could tell how we felt," "Resident just sensed it," etc.   0

     b. R indicates that they TOLD the resident how they felt, congratulated or praised him, etc.   2

     c. R indicates that it was OBVIOUS to the resident, because they made such a big thing over it.   3

6. How did the OTHER RESIDENTS REACT to this accomplishment? (Q)

     a. Other residents did not learn of the accomplishment, or no reaction indicated.   0

     b. Other residents "felt good," "felt proud," etc.—any positive reaction NOT COMMUNICATED to the resident.   1

     c. Some of the residents congratulated him or her—some praise proffered by the residents.   2

     d. Much praise, excitement, encouragement, etc. was generated by the residents—for example, "They made a big thing of it."   4

7. It always seems that after a while some residents manage to acquire some STATUS in the home. That is, they manage to MOVE UP somehow—for example, by getting a better choice of certain things, a better room, or something a little extra (assure R there's nothing wrong with this). How does that work here? For example (assure R that you DON'T mean favoritism on staff's part):

Do some of the residents manage to get BETTER ROOMS after they've been here for a while? (Q)

    a. It appears that it DOES occur.   2

    b. Appears to occur only OCCASIONALLY, or it happens, but it's not important as a mark of status, or only happens accidentally, not as a result of residents' working the system.   1

    c. Does NOT happen.   0

8. Do some residents manage to get some AUTHORITY over the others? (Q)

    a. YES (even if they only THINK they do).   2

    b. OCCASIONALLY (as above).   1

    c. No   0

9. Do some manage to get a better choice of special things, like food, clothes, furniture, mattresses, an especially good place to sit—something a little extra (a special PRESCRIBED diet does not qualify)? (Q)

    a. YES   2

    b. OCCASIONALLY (as above)   1

    c. No   0

10. Do some manage to get some special PRIVILEGES? (Q)

    a. YES   2

    b. OCCASIONALLY (as above)   1

    c. No   0

11. Are there any other ways in which they manage to acquire status of any kind? (Q)

    a. No   0

    b. YES (If yes, list each LEGITIMATE example of status acquisition.)   1

12. Do residents ask you if they can go shopping for things that they need, like clothes or shoes? Can you give me an example? (Probe for a SPECIFIC INCIDENT.) (Q)

    a. No incident cited.   0

    (If incident is cited, ask:) How did you REACT to that?

    b. R pointed out to the resident that it COULDN'T BE DONE; or any similar NEGATIVE REACTION.   −1

    c. No particular reaction indicated.   0

    d. R "thought it was nice" or some similar reaction that was NOT COMMUNICATED to the resident (some efforts may or may not have been made to procure whatever the resident needed).   1

    e. Some kind of PRAISE, REWARD, or ENCOURAGEMENT was communicated to the resident—that is, resident was encouraged to go out or do things on his or her own; some EFFORT was made in this direction.   2

13. (If incident given, ask:) How did the staff members REACT to this action on the part of the resident(s)?

    a. "It just made things worse around here," or they objected, etc. (any NEGATIVE reaction).   −1

    b. They didn't mind "too much."   0

    c. Staff thought it was a fine idea or any POSITIVE reaction that was NOT COMMUNICATED to the resident in any way.   1

    d. Residents were CONGRATULATED, ENCOURAGED, PRAISED, etc., in some way.   2

G. STIMULATION

1. How many SOCIAL WORKERS during the day? _____ At night? _____ (Q)
2. How many ACTIVITY THERAPISTS during the day? _____ At night? _____ (Q)
3. Do any of the residents have HOBBIES or work at some kind of crafts, such as sewing, knitting, woodworking, painting, etc.? (Q)
   a. NONE or VERY FEW.   0
   b. SOME do—less than half of the residents, apparently.   1
   c. It appears that MOST (more than half) of the residents do.   3
4. On a typical summer day, how many of your residents would ordinarily GO OUTSIDE OF THE BUILDING, for example, to go shopping, go for a visit, go for a stroll, or go out to sit on a bench? Would you say— (Q)
   a. MOST (two-thirds or more of the residents go out).   2
   b. MANY—ABOUT HALF (one-third to two-thirds go out).   1
   c. SOME (one-fifth to one-third go out).   0
   d. VERY FEW (less than one-fifth).   0
5. Are the residents ENCOURAGED to go outside the building for visits, to go shopping, or to go for walks on their own—or aren't they well enough for that sort of thing? (Q)
   a. YES—staff tries to get as many to go out as possible.   2
   b. YES—staff tries to get "those that are able" to go outside.   1
   c. SOMETIMES—but MOST of them are "too sick," or don't want to.   0
   d. No—it's entirely up to them if they want to go out—we don't
      push them.   0
   e. No (unqualified)—they're not well enough to go out.   0

6. Do you take some of the elderly residents out of the building occasionally? For example, do you take them: On shopping trips? (Q) _____

(For each item no. 6–9, rate:
0—if very rarely or never
1—if only a few times per year
2—if once or twice per month
3—if about once per week
4—if several times weekly.)

7. To ball games or other recreational events? (Q) _____
8. For rides or tours? _____
9. For walks? _____

10. Do OUTSIDERS ever come in to ENTERTAIN the residents? For example: Do professional entertainers ever come in to entertain, such as singing groups, dancers, pianists, etc.? (Q) _____

(For each item no. 10–14, rate:
0—if happens rarely or never
1—if occurs few times yearly
2—if once or twice per month
3—if occurs weekly.)

11. Do AMATEUR groups come in, such as church choirs or groups from the public schools, etc.? (Q) _____
12. Do LECTURERS come in to give talks, show travel movies, etc. (Q) _____
13. Do volunteers come in to "work with" the residents—for example, by helping them write letters, teaching them crafts, or just visiting? (Q) _____

14. Do outside CLERGYMEN come in to hold group or private services with residents? (Q) _____

15. NOISE LEVEL: (O)

Bedrooms _____
Hallways _____
Lounge _____
Dining _____

   a. VERY QUIET: Noticeable ABSENCE of sounds, as in a library. "Could hear a pin drop."   −1

   b. COMFORTABLE: Some sounds present. Environment shows signs of life, such as quiet speech or radio or TV playing at low levels. One could read without much trouble.   1

   c. SOMEWHAT NOISY: Many sounds present. Environment seems quite alive or busy. Street noises, speech, and/or radio and TV sounds evident. One could easily have a conversation, but might have difficulty reading.   2

   d. VERY NOISY: Sounds are very distracting, making it difficult to maintain a conversation without some strain. Street noises, shouting, very loud TV, floor-cleaning equipment, etc., produce a generally high and unpleasant noise level.   1

16. LEVEL OF ILLUMINATION (from any source, natural or artificial): (O)

Bedrooms _____
Hallways _____
Lounge _____
Dining _____

   a. AMPLE LIGHTING: Rooms are brightly illuminated, making reading easy in any part of the room, even for those with impaired vision.   1

   b. BARELY ADEQUATE: Light may be uneven, making reading possible only in certain areas of the room—for example, reading is possible near window or reading lamp, but difficult elsewhere.   0

   c. INADEQUATE: Lighting is very poor, with illumination very low in many areas of room. Few lamps available or give off little light; illumination from windows very low. Reading would be difficult in any area of the room, even with normal vision.   −1

17. Window areas: (O)

Bedrooms _____
Hallways _____
Lounge _____
Dining _____

   a. MANY WINDOWS: Structure has many large window areas, affording an excellent view of the outside (regardless of how "pleasant" the view is). Number or size of windows draws one's attention.   2

   b. ADEQUATE WINDOWS: Window area seems reasonable, such that area is neither dark nor very bright on a sunny day. One does not feel "closed in" but on the other hand, one's attention is not drawn by large window areas.   1

   c. FEW WINDOWS: Room tends to be dark, even on sunny days, in the absence of artificial lighting, and/or one may feel "closed in" because of limited number of windows. Large rooms may contain only one or two windows, or windows are very small, covered, or placed such that they admit very little light.   0

18. VIEW FROM WINDOWS—APPEAL: (O)

Bedrooms _____   a. ATTRACTIVE: Some windows overlook quite pleasant   1
Hallways _____   scenes, such as a lake, park, boats, hills, interesting ar-
                       chitecture, attractive city skyline, etc.
Lounge _____   b. NO APPEAL, BUT NOT UNATTRACTIVE: Windows over-   0
Dining _____   look views such as a reasonably "nice" residential area.
                   c. UNATTRACTIVE: Windows may overlook a slum, blank   0
                       adjacent walls, dingy old homes, relatively deserted
                       streets, refuse, etc. Observer may feel tendency to
                       avoid looking outside.

19. View from windows—interest: (O)

Bedrooms _____   a. INTERESTING: View overlooks things of interest, espe-   2
Hallways _____   cially things happening, such as children playing, traf-
                       fic, etc. One's interest might be captured for several
Lounge _____   minutes by the view of the outside.
Dining _____   b. SOME INTEREST: One might be drawn to look outside   1
                       only occasionally or for brief periods, for example, to
                       watch people or traffic passing. Outside scenes or hap-
                       penings may have only mild, brief, or occasional inter-
                       est.
                   c. LACKS INTEREST: View is dull or only rarely captures   0
                       interest. Looking outside would quickly lead to bore-
                       dom.

20. Resources available in the environment: Observer should check off each
resource as it is seen during his or her tours of the environment. Near the
end of the observation period, observer should ASK about the possible existence of ANY RESOURCES ON THE LIST THAT HAVE NOT BEEN CHECKED OFF
(not already seen). Score as shown for each YES, 0 for each NO. (O)

a. Do any residents have PRIVATE TELEPHONES? _____   1
b. Are PUBLIC TELEPHONES available to residents within building?   1

_____

c. Do any residents have PRIVATE TELEVISION sets? _____   1
d. Are COMMUNAL TELEVISION sets available? _____   2
e. Are MAGAZINES and BOOKS available to take to rooms? _____   2
f. Is any GAME EQUIPMENT available, such as cards, cribbage boards,   3
   Bingo sets, Monopoly sets, chess sets, dominoes, etc.? _____
g. Do residents have DANCES? (Check bulletin board, and ask.) _____   3
h. Are there any CLUBS to which residents belong and which hold   2
   meetings or have activities? _____
i. Do residents serve on any COMMITTEES? _____   2
j. Is there a LOUNGE, living room, lobby, or commons room avail-   1
   able to residents for relaxation or conversation? _____
k. Is there a READING ROOM or an area set aside for this purpose, or   1
   an area which seems to be used primarily for this purpose?_____
l. Is there a COMMISSARY (or a counter with candy, cigarettes, pen-   2
   cils, stamps, etc.)? _____
m. Is there a CRAFTS DEPARTMENT—a facility which is intended for   4
   use, which residents DO use and/or are encouraged to use?_____

n. Is there any SPECIAL EQUIPMENT FOR CRAFTS, such as sewing machines, pottery wheel, easels, woodworking tools, soldering irons, pottery mold, kiln, leather-working tools, etc.? _____   4

o. Can the residents use the KITCHEN for cooking or baking? _____   2

p. Do any of the residents have a PRIVATE KITCHEN? _____   2

q. Are there any group RECREATIONAL FACILITIES, such as bowling, shuffleboard, tennis, badminton, billiards tables, pinball machines, etc.? _____   4

r. Are any CLASSES offered to residents? A series of meetings on some topic, intended for education of some sort? _____   3

s. Is OUTSIDE ENTERTAINMENT sometimes brought in? (Check bulletin board and ask residents.) _____   2

t. Is there a CHAPEL or TEMPLE on the premises? _____   2

u. Are RELIGIOUS SERVICES conducted on premises at least once per month? _____   2

v. Do ANY residents have BIRDS or FISH as pets? _____   1

w. Do ANY residents have DOGS or CATS as pets? _____   1

21. Activities of Residents—checklist: Observer should check off each activity as it is seen—and ONLY those activities seen. Activity should NOT be checked if not actually seen.

    In LARGE INSTITUTIONS of fifty or more residents, observer should select only ONE FLOOR or wing for these observations, plus the common lounge, activity area, and dining area. This is required to control for the fact that in institutions having large numbers of residents, nearly all activities will be seen if one observes carefully enough, but the score will not reflect as accurately how ACTIVE the residents are.

I. What SOLITARY activities can be observed? (Check off only those activities which residents are engaged in while relatively ALONE—although resident may be in some proximity with others, the activity is essentially his or hers alone—the resident is not interacting with others.) (O)

a. Watching TV? _____   2

b. Listening to radio? _____   2

c. Writing (letters, poems, etc.)? _____   1

d. Reading? _____   1

e. Solitary games (solitaire, pool, crossword puzzle, etc.)? _____   2

f. Wandering? _____   2

g. Drinking (coffee, soda, etc.) or snacking (candy, etc.)? (Do NOT include a regular meal.) _____   1

h. Drawing or painting? _____   2

i. Doing work or chores of any kind (aside from simply straightening one's own bed or clothes, etc.)? _____   2

j. Sewing, knitting, or crocheting? _____   2

k. Doing laundry or ironing? _____   2

l. Engaging in any kind of craft or hobby (such as making paper flowers, etc.—do NOT include painting or writing that was scored above)? _____   2

m. Any OTHER solitary activities? (If YES, list each, scoring 1 point for each additional activity.)

1. _____   3. _____
2. _____   4. _____

II What GROUP or SHARED ACTIVITIES can be observed? (Note instructions for Item I above. Again, observer should score only those activities that are ACTUALLY OBSERVED. Shared activities should only be
scored if the residents are ACTUALLY SHARING the activity or participating TOGETHER.) (O)

a.	Watching TV? _____	2
b.	Playing cards? _____	2
c.	Walking together? _____	1
d.	Singing? _____	3
e.	Arguing? _____	4
f.	Having conversations (with staff or residents)? _____	2
g.	Visiting with outsiders? _____	2
h.	Working (for example, cleaning floors or windows; cooking or doing dishes together)? _____	2
i.	Participating jointly in some hobby or craft? _____	2
j.	Attending committee meeting? _____	2
k.	Attending club or organized social meeting? _____	2
l.	Attending classes or lectures? _____	2

m. Any OTHER joint activities? If YES, list each, scoring 1 point for
each activity:

1. _____   3. _____
2. _____   4. _____

22. Interaction of Residents: (O)

a. VERY LITTLE INTERACTION or contact apparent: Greatest majority (more than three-fourths) of residents are NOT interacting—
most are seen walking or sitting alone, or in bed. If residents are
in multiple-bed rooms, most are NOT interacting. Lounges, if any,
contain only a SMALL proportion of residents in close proximity
with other residents.   0

b. SOME INTERACTION APPARENT: Some areas, such as a lounge or
lobby, may contain slight concentrations of residents (in close
proximity), some other residents may be seen interacting in pairs
or small groups, but at least 50 percent of residents appear to not
interact much.   1

c. ROUGHLY EQUAL distribution of isolates and groups: 40 to 60 percent of residents appear alone or in company of others but not
interacting, while 40–60 percent of residents are interacting or in
close proximity with others.   3

d. MUCH INTERACTION: Majority of residents are seen interacting—
sitting, standing, or walking in the company of others. Relatively
few isolates observed.   4

23. Observations of brief verbal exchanges (greetings, pleasantries): (O)

a. SEVERAL INSTANCES OBSERVED: Seems common that residents
should greet each other or exchange a few words when they meet
or sit next to each other.   4

b. OCCASIONAL INSTANCES observed: "Some do and some don't," as

if some are friends and exchange a few words, while others are
relatively isolated and rarely speak upon meeting another.   2
   c. FEW INSTANCES observed: residents withdraw, avoid speaking, or
seem to be strangers.   0
24. Observations of conversations among residents (lasting twenty seconds or longer): (O)
   a. MANY CONVERSATIONS observed: Many residents seem to be
friends (or friendly) and could be observed sitting and chatting
with each other (beyond brief greetings or pleasantries).   5
   b. SOME CONVERSATIONS observed: Residents have some conversations, but limited to a few of the more "interactive" residents.   2
   c. FEW CONVERSATIONS observed: MOST residents seem content to sit
or read alone and are not interested in speaking with others—or
act as though residents do not know each other very well.   0
25. General amount of activity of residents: (O)
   a. VERY HIGH: Many or most residents seem very busy much of the
time. Activity predominates. Observer is impressed with amount
of activity—more than one would ordinarily find even in an "active" old-age home.   6
   b. HIGH AVERAGE: Activity level seems somewhat above average for
this age group—somewhat higher than one would USUALLY find
in an old-age home, but not extreme nor particularly impressive.   4
   c. MODERATE: Amount of activity seems about average or low average for this age group. Only some residents seem moderately
busy, but a large proportion are rather inactive.   1
   d. LOW: Few residents seem at all active. Residents seem phlegmat-
ic, inactive; spend most of their time just sitting, lying, or slowly
wandering.   0
26. Does the facility have a yard? (O)
   a. No yard or a yard that is extremely small—too small for more
than two or three chairs.   0
   b. Small yard that might be large enough to contain a few chairs or
benches or a small garden (such as the front yard of a Hyde Park
walk-up apartment building).   1
   c. Moderate yard—UP TO one-half square block, but not very appealing. May be bare, with few trees, flowers or benches; or may
be quite unkempt.   2
   d. Moderate yard—UP TO one-half square block. Yard is quite attractive, with trees, paths, flowers, hedges, or benches.   3
   e. Large yard—one-half block or more, but not very appealing (as
in c above).   3
   f. Large yard—one-half block or more, but quite attractive (as in d
above).   4
27. Neighborhood resources: For EACH, rate the distance from the home
as follows: (O)
   0—if further than twelve blocks
   1—if within six to twelve blocks
   2—if within four to six blocks

  3—if within two to three blocks
  4—if within two blocks
a. Public telephone _____
b. Public transportation (bus, el, subway) _____
c. Park (more than one-half square block in area) _____
d. Drug store or grocery store _____
e. Movie theater _____
f. Day center or organization for elderly (such as YMCA, YWCA, vocational rehabilitation center, Jewish Community Center, etc.) _____
g. Benches or chairs to sit on _____
h. Shopping center or general community offering a variety of stores

_____

i. Church _____
j. Library _____

H. PHYSICAL ATTRACTIVENESS

1. Level of illumination (from any source, natural or artificial): (O)

Bedrooms _____   a. AMPLE LIGHTING: Rooms are brightly illuminated,   2
Hallways _____   making reading easy in any part of the room, even for
Lounge _____   those with impaired vision.
Dining _____   b. BARELY ADEQUATE: Lighting may be uneven, making   1
     reading possible only in certain areas of the room—for
     example, reading is possible near window or reading
     lamp, but difficult elsewhere.
    c. INADEQUATE: Lighting is very poor, with illumination   0
     very low in many areas of the room. Few lamps available or give off little light, illumination from windows
     very low. Reading would be difficult in any area of
     room, even with normal vision.

2. Window areas: (O)

Bedrooms _____   a. MANY WINDOWS: Structure has many large window   2
Hallways _____   areas, affording an excellent view of the outside (regardless of how "pleasant" the view is). Number or size
Lounge _____   of windows draws one's attention.
Dining _____   b. ADEQUATE WINDOWS: Window area seems reasonable,   1
     such that area is neither dark nor very bright on a sunny day. One does not feel "closed in," but on the other
     hand, one's attention is not drawn by large window
     areas.
    c. FEW WINDOWS: Room tends to be dark, even on sunny   0
     days, in the absence of artificial lighting and/or one
     may feel "closed in" because of limited number of windows. Large rooms may contain only one or two windows, or windows are very small, covered, or placed
     such that they admit very little light.

3. View from windows—appeal: (O)

Bedrooms _____   a. ATTRACTIVE: Some windows overlook quite pleasant   2

Hallways _____	scenes, such as a lake, park, boats, hills, interesting ar-
Lounge _____	chitecture, attractive city skyline, etc.

b. No APPEAL, BUT NOT UNATTRACTIVE: Windows over-   1
look views such as a reasonably "nice" residential area.

c. UNATTRACTIVE: Windows may overlook a slum, blank   0
adjacent walls, dingy old homes, relatively deserted
streets, refuse, etc. Observer may feel tendency to
avoid looking outside.

4. View from windows—interest: (O)

Bedrooms _____	a. INTERESTING: View overlooks things of interest, espe- 3
Hallways _____	cially things happening, such as children playing, traf-
Lounge _____	fic, etc. One's interest might be captured for several
Dining _____	minutes by the view of the outside.

b. SOME INTEREST: One might be drawn to look outside   2
only occasionally or for brief periods, for example, to
watch people or traffic passing. Outside scenes or happenings may have only mild, brief, or occasional interest.

c. LACKS INTEREST: View is dull or only rarely captures   0
interest. Looking outside would quickly lead to bore-
dom.

5. Cleanliness of floors: (O)

Bedrooms _____	a. Floors kept VERY CLEAN: Obviously cleaned several 2
Hallways _____	times weekly and polished often. Very little dirt, if any,
Lounge _____	evident—"hospital clean."
Dining _____	b. FAIRLY CLEAN: Obviously some concern for keeping 1

floors clean, but not ENTIRELY successful. SOME dirt in
corners evident, many scuff marks, some dust, or very
little polish evident. Floors appear to be cleaned more
than once per week, but less than daily.

c. SOMEWHAT DIRTY: Floors may get a weekly once-over,   0
but considerable dirt is evident. Floors are rarely polished. Floors "feel" dirty.

d. VERY DIRTY: Caked-in dirt in corners. Looks as if not   −1
cleaned for weeks. Much litter, stains, dust, etc. "Flop-
house" appearance.

6. Condition of floors (aside from cleanliness): (O)

Bedrooms _____	a. LIKE NEW: Floor apparently applied in recent years 2
Hallways _____	and is well kept.
Lounge _____	b. GOOD CONDITION: Floor not new, but in good condition. 1
Dining _____	Little evidence of wear or deterioration. Close exami-

nation may reveal worn spots or general scuffing, but
not very evident. May be slightly worn in areas of
heavy travel, but not much elsewhere.

c. MODERATELY DETERIORATED: Deterioration or wear is   0
evident without close examination. Many worn spots,
cracks, or much scuffing apparent. Tile or linoleum
may be warped, wood may be worn down in spots.

    d. BADLY DETERIORATED: Badly in need of repair. Torn −1
edges of linoleum, gouges in concrete, loose strings or
holes in carpets, or cracks in wood. Might be dangerous
for walking.

7. Cleanliness of walls and ceilings: (O)

Bedrooms _____ a. VERY CLEAN: Spotless—"hospital clean." Obviously 2

Hallways _____ considerable care is taken to keep walls and ceilings clean.

Lounge _____ b. FAIRLY CLEAN: Obviously cleaned regularly, but may 1

Dining _____ be some accumulated dust, fingerprints, or soot evident on close examination.

    c. SOMEWHAT DIRTY: Considerable dust, soot, scuff marks, 0
and/or some stains evident. May be cobwebs in corners.
Seems to be cleaned regularly, but only at long intervals. Needs cleaning at present.

    d. VERY DIRTY: Needs a major cleaning. Obviously hasn't −1
been in a considerable length of time. Dirty to the
touch, much dust, grime and staining evident. "Flop-
house" appearance.

8. Condition of furniture: (O)

Bedrooms _____ a. LIKE NEW: Seems less than three years old and in like- 2

Hallways _____ new condition, as if in a relatively new house or motel.

Lounge _____ b. GOOD CONDITION: Does not appear new by any means, 1

Dining _____ but in good condition, generally. No holes or tears,
scratches or gouges, but, for example, arms of chairs
may be slightly worn or tables slightly marred or with
hairline scratches.

    c. MODERATELY DETERIORATED: Some small tears or holes 0
in upholstery evident or tables scratched and marred;
cigarette burns, etc., evident. Furniture, in general, has
seen better days but is not delapidated.

    d. BADLY DETERIORATED: Furniture in very poor condi- −1
tion. Requires reupholstering or could be scrapped.
Many holes, burns, tears, or scratches.

9. Cleanliness of furniture: (O)

Bedrooms _____ a. VERY CLEAN: Spotless, highly polished. Upholstery ap- 2

Hallways _____ pears new or recently shampooed or refinished. Practically no dust evident, no water rings, cigarette burns, or

Lounge _____ stains.

Dining _____ b. FAIRLY CLEAN: Some dust evident, a few water rings, 1
stains or ashes evident as if not cleaned for a few days
or a week. May be some grime in creases of chairs.

    c. QUITE DIRTY: Obviously in need of cleaning, dusting, 0
polish, and/or shampooing. Most persons would consider the condition of the furnishings rather untidy for a
home. Furniture may be stained, somewhat greasy, or
very dusty.

10. Condition of walls and ceilings: (O)

| Bedrooms ____ | a. LIKE NEW: As if applied in last five years. | 2 |

Bedrooms ____   a. LIKE NEW: As if applied in last five years.   2

Hallways ____   b. GOOD CONDITION: Not new, but well kept-up. Some   1
Lounge ____   hairline cracks or warping may be evident on close ex-
Dining ____   amination. May be some marks where furniture hits
                    walls.

c. MODERATELY DETERIORATED: Some cracks, gouges, or   0
warping apparent without close examination. Some
peeling of paint or paint very faded.

d. BADLY DETERIORATED: Badly in need of repair. Large   −1
cracks or holes. Some plaster has fallen. Appears as if
no maintenance has been done in years.

11. Odors: (O)

a. FRESH: Environment has a pleasantly fresh odor, or anything is   3
noticeably pleasant about the atmosphere.

b. NO ODORS: Nothing noticeable about the atmosphere. Normal.   3

c. SLIGHTLY OBJECTIONABLE: Air is slightly tainted in some way.   −3
May seem slightly stale, close, musty, or may notice presence of
slight cooking odors or smell of floor-cleaning compounds. Slightly objectionable odors apparent, but not too unpleasant.

d. DISTINCTLY OBJECTIONABLE: Unpleasant odors immediately ap-   −6
parent. Observer may feel anxious to leave because of odors—for
example, observer might find the prospect of having to eat in this
atmosphere rather distasteful.

12. General attractiveness of physical plant: including furniture, draperies, carpets, paintings, plants, flowers, color scheme, woodwork, walls, etc. Rating
should be based on all aspects of the interior physical plant, but ONLY those
areas of the plant that the RESIDENTS occupy, rather than the reception
room or director's office. Do NOT include psychosocial characteristics in
this rating. (O)

a. HIGHLY APPEALING: Environment has PERSONAL APPEAL for the   8
rater. Attractive enough to be desirable for one's own home, or
has attractive features that one might wish one had in one's own
home.

b. APPEALING: Overall effect is favorable. Attention may be drawn   6
to some interesting features which may be novel or appealing.
May evoke some admiration for whoever "put the place together" or suggests that furnishing or decoration must have been
done at some expense.

c. ATTRACTIVE: Overall effect is fairly positive. May be old, spar-   4
tan, or somewhat unimaginative, but done in good taste. Seems
fairly pleasing or comfortable and may have some attractive features. Adequate, pleasant, but not impressive or particularly
noteworthy.

d. NEUTRAL: Rater may not be impressed by either positive or neg-   2
ative features. Reaction may be, for example, "not bad for an old
place." Observer does not find it at all attractive, but doesn't find
it unpleasant either.

    e. SOMEWHAT UNATTRACTIVE: Physical plant is unattractive, and   0
observer may find a mild negative reaction. Physical plant may
be cold, garish, sterile, "institutional," cheap, or somewhat dirty
or run-down.

    f. DISTINCTLY UNATTRACTIVE: Observer's reaction is strongly nega-   −4
tive. Physical plant is distasteful, very unappealing, as perhaps a
flop-house or slum dwelling.

13. Inconveniences or hazards: (O) (Score for YES answer only.)

    a. Are FLOORS SLIPPERY (and possibly dangerous) in ANY places   −1
where residents occasionally travel? (Include only when presence
of water, grease, or extremely high polish makes floors slippery.)

    b. Are LOOSE OBJECTS—cords, vacuum cleaners, loose rugs, boxes,   −1
paper, etc.—lying around the floors which might prove hazardous? (That is, might an elderly person feel insecure in walking
around the building?)

    c. Are some areas (where residents occasionally travel) DARK   −1
enough to make walking difficult for elderly persons?

    d. Are there any warped floor tiles, torn carpeting or linoleum, etc.   −1
evident that might make walking dangerous?

    e. Are there ANY OTHER HAZARDS evident (such as broken glass, a   −1
low, unexpected step in an entrance, etc.)? If YES, list each, scoring −1 for each.

    1. _____   3. _____

    2. _____   4. _____

14. Steps, stairways: (O) (Score for YES answer only.)

    a. Is it necessary for residents to climb ANY STEPS in the building?   −1
(Include any steps to outside, a few steps into a split-level area,
etc.)

    b. Is it necessary to climb an entire FLIGHT OF STAIRS (from one   −1
floor to another)? (If all stairs can be avoided by means of an
elevator, answer NO.)
(If there are no stairs, mark NO for items c through f and do not
score.)

    c. Are steps INADEQUATELY ILLUMINATED IN THE DARK in any   −1
areas?

    d. Are steps AWKWARD in any way (curved, varied height, too high,   −1
etc.)?

    e. Are there any OBSTRUCTIONS or HAZARDS on the steps, such as   −1
loose treads, slippery tiles or carpets, lumps or tears on stair coverings, loose objects lying on stairs, etc.?

    f. Is any hazard or difficulty presented by PEOPLE SITTING or stand-   −1
ing on stairs?

15. Personal grooming of residents: Rate only those residents moving around in
the general living area (such as corridors and lounges). Do not rate those
residents in sleeping rooms. (O)
If MOST residents are reasonably well-groomed but a substantial minority
are NOT, assign the lower of the two ratings.

a. Residents are WELL-GROOMED, well-washed. Makeup is appropri-   5
   ate on women, men are clean-shaven, hair is combed. Residents
   dressed as if awaiting visitors or about to go outside.
b. Residents neither distinctively clean nor dirty.   2
c. Residents NOT well-groomed or clean. Women may wear no   −2
   makeup and have hair uncared for or wear inappropriate makeup, or makeup may be crudely applied. Men may be unshaven
   and/or uncombed.

16. Condition of residents' clothing (in general): Again, rate only those residents moving around in the general living area. (O)
   a. Clothing is VERY NEAT AND CLEAN: Freshly laundered and   6
      pressed. In the condition (but not necessarily the quality) that
      might be demanded of, for example, a sales person.
   b. MODERATELY CLEAN AND PRESSED: Clothes such as what might   3
      be worn by the average person while lounging at home or in
      yard.
   c. MODERATELY OR BADLY SOILED and wrinkled, with holes, dirt   −2
      spots, stains, threadbare, etc. Disheveled appearance. Minimal at-
      tention given to clothing.

17. Personalization of residents' attire: Observer should ASK how many residents wear clothes provided by institution. (O)
   a. Institutional clothing, gown, or uniform is worn by all or most   −2
      residents.
   b. Most residents wear used clothing (noninstitutional) provided by   0
      the home, or many wear institutional gowns or uniforms. Few
      wear their own clothes (provided by themselves or relatives).
   c. Most wear their own clothes, but some wear gowns, uniforms, or   1
      used clothing provided by the institution, including unmarked
      clothing.
   d. All residents wear clothes provided by themselves or by relatives.   2

18. Condition of building exterior: (In Chicago, even recently constructed
buildings may look dirty or sooty. Do not let this influence the rating too
much—try to focus primarily on the CONDITION of the building.) (O)
   a. NEW OR LIKE NEW: Building recently constructed (within five   3
      years) and shows no signs of deterioration.
   b. GOOD CONDITION: Building is not new and may show SOME signs   2
      of deterioration or age upon close examination. Walls or trim
      may be in some need of paint. Generally favorable appearance
      and condition.
   c. SOME DECAY: Obvious need for some repair or maintenance.   0
      Paint may be blistered or peeling in spots. Some mortar or bricks
      chipped or cracked. Roofing torn or warped in spots; steps may
      be worn, cracked or warped; windows may need new putty,
      some may be cracked. Building somewhat run-down but quite
      salvageable with some repair.
   d. DILAPIDATED: Building is quite run-down; needing EXTENSIVE   −2
      REPAIRS.

19. Condition of neighborhood: (O)
    a. Surrounding property in neighborhood is quite modern—most structures erected within past ten years: in nearly new condition and of relatively modern design. — 5
    b. Surrounding structures are ten to thirty years old, but well maintained. Present moderately good appearance. — 2
    c. Surrounding property is ten to thirty years old, but showing deterioration. Property has been allowed to deteriorate somewhat in recent years. — 0
    d. Surrounding property looks more than thirty years old, but fairly well maintained for that age. — 0
    e. Surrounding property quite old and badly deteriorated. Slum or near-slum appearance. — −2
20. Does the facility have a yard? (O)
    a. No yard or a yard that is extremely small—too small for more than two or three chairs. — 0
    b. Small yard that might be large enough to contain a few chairs or benches or a small garden (for example, the front yard of a Hyde Park walk-up apartment building). — 1
    c. Moderate yard—UP TO one-half square block, but not very appealing. May be bare, with few trees, flowers, or benches, or may be quite unkempt. — 2
    d. Moderate yard—UP TO one-half square block. Yard is quite attractive, with trees, paths, flowers, hedges, or benches. — 4
    e. Large yard—one-half block or more, but not very appealing (as in c above). — 3
    f. Large yard—one-half block or more, but quite attractive (as in d above). — 6

I. CUE RICHNESS

1. Neatness-orderliness/clutter (O)

Bedrooms _____
Hallways _____
Lounge _____
Dining _____

   a. NEAT: Area is very neat, orderly, or linear, as in a Danish-modern home or hotel room; or like a hospital waiting room. — 0
   b. SOME DISARRAY: Area looks lived-in. Some clutter or disarray: some furniture is scattered or not aligned, some odds and ends lying about, but generally reasonably neat. — 1
   c. MUCH CLUTTER: As in a student's room, a child's room, or an attic. Area is somewhat disorganized, dense, disarrayed, nonlinear. — 2

2. Complexity of building: (Rate the entire area in which residents spend time.) (O)
   a. VERY COMPLEX: Would require considerable care, learning, assistance, or directions to find one's way about the building. A slightly impaired elderly person might find it extremely difficult — 2

to eventually learn his or her way about the building. May be very spread out or have several wings; may be unsymmetrical and/or have several unmarked or "unexpected" areas.

b. SOME COMPLEXITY: Building is moderately large or a bit com- 1
plex—requiring some assistance, learning, or instruction during the first day or two of residence, but even a slightly impaired resident would learn his or her way about without too much trouble.

c. LITTLE COMPLEXITY: Size and complexity poses NO PROBLEM. 0
Building is small and/or simple, such as a relatively small one or two-story home.

3. Are RULES, INSTRUCTIONS, and REGULATIONS or various "do's and don'ts" posted on walls or bulletin boards (beyond "No Smoking" and "Exit" signs)? (Score 1 for YES, 0 for NO.)

4. Variations in ODORS: Observer should identify and locate each odor as encountered, making a final rating after all observations. (O)

1. _____ 4. _____
2. _____ 5. _____
3. _____ 6. _____

a. NO NOTICEABLE VARIATION in odors. 0
b. SOME VARIATION: Two different odors evident in two different 1
areas, or an odor in one area and no odor in other areas.
c. MODERATE VARIATION: At least THREE different odors (one may 2
be a "no odor") are encountered in different rooms or areas.
d. MUCH VARIATION: More than three odors encountered—many 3
areas seem to have their own distinctive odor (one may be a "no odor").

5. Variations in BRIGHTNESS: (O)
a. MUCH VARIATION: At least three different rooms or areas are 3
distinguishable by their level or brightness—for example, some areas are typically very bright, others are typically rather dark, and others may be "in-between."
b. SOME VARIATION: One or two areas may be distinguishable by 1
differences in brightness, or very slight differences noticeable in many areas.
c. LITTLE VARIATION: Practically no differences in level of illumi- 0
nation in different areas (for example, all areas typically very bright, very dark, or "in-between").

6. Variations in NOISE: Observer should note different noise levels as encountered, then make final rating after all observations. (O)

1. _____ 3. _____
2. _____ 4. _____

a. MUCH VARIATION: At least three different rooms or areas are dis- 3
tinguishable by the level or types of noises found there.
b. SOME VARIATION: Two areas may be distinguishable by differ- 1
ences in level or types of noises, or very slight differences noticeable in many areas.

    c. LITTLE OR NO VARIATION: For example, all areas very quiet, or   0
all areas somewhat noisy.

7. Variations in RESIDENTS' SLEEPING ROOMS: (Attention should be paid to wall
colors, colors of contents—such as curtains, bedspreads, etc.—shape of
room, arrangement of furniture, size of room, decorations type of furniture, window areas, etc.)

    a. All rooms NEARLY IDENTICAL, except for MINOR details, such as   0
different color rug or curtains, or furniture arranged slightly differently, or some rooms slightly larger than others.

    b. Rooms QUITE SIMILAR, though some variation in shape, size, fur-   1
niture arrangements, or number of occupants. Observer can see
variation when looking for it, but not very striking.

    c. MODERATE VARIATION: Rooms are distinct, but a general theme   2
or style of decor runs through all rooms. Rooms vary considerably, but obviously "belong in the same building."

    d. DISTINCT VARIATION: As if particular efforts made to ensure that   3
the rooms vary considerably. Variation is on the order of, e.g.,
one room may be Danish modern, next room provincial, etc.

8. Personalization of residents' rooms: (O)

    a. LITTLE PERSONALIZATION: Resident may have family pictures,   0
medicine, etc. evident, but otherwise observer finds it difficult to
feel that the room "belongs" to an individual. (Rating may apply
as well to areas of multiple-bed rooms.)

    b. SOME PERSONALIZATION: Residents may have many objects or   1
furnishings which help individualize rooms, but rooms still rather
similar. Observer may have some feeling of identification of the
rooms with their occupants.

    c. MUCH PERSONALIZATION: Residents have obviously spent some   2
time or energy personalizing their rooms. Personalization may be
evident from pictures, books, notebooks, clothes lying about,
plants and flowers, fishbowls, etc., as well as apparent personalization of furniture, rugs, curtains, and/or bedspread.

9. Stimulus information available: How DISTINCT are the various AREAS of the
building? How much VARIATION and CONTRAST is there from one area to
the next? Of particular importance are variations in furnishings and in
colors and textures on floors and walls, as well as, for example, differences
in windows, woodwork, and fixtures from one area to the next. (O)

    a. MUCH DISTINCTIVENESS: As in the different rooms of a HOUSE,   6
where kitchen, dining room, living room, and bedroom typically
contain very different furniture, are often of different colors,
have different floor coverings, and are decorated differently.

    b. MODERATE DISTINCTIVENESS: Some variation, as in a modern   4
LOW-COST APARTMENT, where furnishings and decorations (and
perhaps colors) may vary from room to room, but wall textures
are usually the same and floor coverings show little variation.

    c.. SOME DISTINCTIVENESS: Somewhat "institutional," but SOME areas   2
may be distinct, for example, a lounge or lobby and other areas
show SOME VARIATION in furnishings, colors, floor coverings,

and/or textures. Corridors, if any, contain some furniture, area rugs, pictures, signs, etc. to provide some distinctive information.

d. LITTLE DISTINCTIVENESS: Most areas are QUITE SIMILAR, as in a   0
typical 1930s hospital. Only the lounge, lobby, director's office or one or two other rooms show any distinctiveness. Corridors, if any, are relatively "blank"—provide little information. This category would ordinarily apply to an institution or hotel only. Most residents' rooms are quite similar.

(Note: Rate only those areas of building where majority of the residents spend the majority of their time. Do not include areas that residents rarely enter.)

J. TOLERANCE FOR DEVIANCY

1. Tolerance for deviant behavior: By tolerance we mean ignoring the behavior, not making a big fuss over it, not trying to force, bully, shame, coerce the patient into changing. Deviant behavior includes both psychiatric symptomatology (hallucinations, talking to self, repetitive motor activity, hoarding, etc.) and socially irritating behavior (cursing, bugging, threatening, self-abuse, verbal abuse, night unrest, etc.) (O)

SCORING: 1 = never observed; 2 = rarely observed; 3 = sometimes observed; 4 = frequently observed. NOTE: In computation, scoring is reversed except for items circled.

a. Staff RIDICULES or pokes fun at patient because of some   1 2 3 4
form of deviant behavior or infraction of rule.

b. Staff YELLS AT patient for some deviant behavior or infrac-   1 2 3 4
tion of rule.

c. Staff finds it necessary to COMMENT ABOUT the patient's de-   1 2 3 4
viant behavior.

d. Staff indicates that the patient's odd behavior is CUTE, amus-   1 2 3 4
ing, etc.

e. Staff CATERS TO patient's odd behavior by giving the objects   1 2 3 4
or opportunity for doing his thing.

(f) Staff IGNORES patients who are engaging in deviant behav-   1 2 3 4
ior.

(g) Staff TELLS PATIENT TO STOP engaging in some deviant be-   1 2 3 4
havior.

h. Staff REMOVES THE OPPORTUNITY or the objects necessary for   1 2 3 4
the patient's "deviant" performances.

(i) Staff EXPLAINS the patient's deviant behavior as HAVING   1 2 3 4
SOME CAUSE rather than simply calling it "bad" behavior (for example, "The patient acts that way because he or she is frightened since he or she hears VOICES calling him or her bad names").

j. Staff seen to provide care, to do for the patient WITHOUT   1 2 3 4
SEEMING TO HAVE A NEED TO LECTURE OR REPRIMAND patient on his or her deviant behavior.

2. Expectations of normalcy: The extent to which the staff seems to expect the patients to behave like reasonably normal adults, and not like "nut cases" or dependent "addlepated" children.

   (a) Staff gives APPROVAL AWARDS for normal behavior (praises, makes positive comment when patient does what told, helps him- or herself, eat properly, etc.). 4 3 2 1

   (b) Staff gives MATERIAL REWARDS for normal behavior (for behaviors as above, patients receive cigarettes, extra food, candy, coffee, etc.). 4 3 2 1

   (c) Staff gives PRIVILEGE REWARDS for normal behavior (patients receive permission to stay up a bit later, go to a local store, help around the home, not take medicine, watch a special TV show, etc.). 4 3 2 1

3. Tolerance of deviance: Have the respondent rate each of the following "symptomatic" or "deviant" behaviors as either:

   INTOLERABLE: Resident would have to move out of the home if he or she displayed the behavior, 0

   UNDESIRABLE: Resident could stay if he or she displayed the behavior, but the home would try to put a stop to it, or 1

   TOLERABLE: "That's to be expected; we'd put up with it." 2

   a. SUICIDE ATTEMPTS
   b. DESTRUCTIVENESS: Damages or destroys property, such as chairs, tables, lamps, magazines, windows, etc.
   c. ASSAULTIVENESS: Physical attacks on other persons—injures others.
   d. THREATENS OTHERS
   e. SMOKING IN BED
   f. DRINKING, INEBRIATION
   g. BOISTEROUSNESS: Noisy, creates disturbances.
   h. DRUG OVERDOSE: Takes too much of any medicine; intentionally or otherwise.
   i. WANDERING
   j. NEGATIVISM: Repeatedly refuses or disagrees with orders or suggestions.
   k. CONFUSION, DISORIENTATION
   l. INABILITY TO FEED SELF
   m. POOR SLEEP HABITS: Cannot sleep at night or sleeps at inappropriate hours.
   n. EXCESSIVE BODILY COMPLAINTS
   o. DEPRESSION: Cries frequently or is chronically sad or "blue."
   p. WITHDRAWAL: Avoids or resists contact with persons or activities.
   q. INCONTINENCE (of urine or feces)
   r. INABILITY TO DRESS SELF

Appendix E

Correlations Among Threat Measures

Table E–1 displays the intercorrelations among threat and threat management measures for three studies: the Unwilling Old Ladies, the Home for Life and the Deinstitutionalized Elites studies. Measures not available in all three studies do not appear in the table (see chapter 6).

TABLE E-1
Intercorrelations Among Threat Intensity and Threat Management Measures

Type of Measure	Measure	Feelings about Leaving	Expected Loss	Anticipated Satisfaction	Information Absorbed	Working Through	Extent of Accurate Appraisal	Congruence	Perceived Control Relocation	Perceived Control Alternatives
Unwilling Old Ladies Study										
Conscious appraisals	Feelings about leaving									
	Expected losses	.76								
	Anticipated satisfactions	.73	.70							
Strategies										
Degree of coping	Information absorbed	.22	.12	.13						
	Working through	-.09	-.04	-.14	.06					
Level of integration	Extent of accurate appraisals	-.09	-.11	.07	.40	.18				
Degree of mastery	Congruence	.66	.61	.76	.37	-.02	.07			
	Perceived control									
	Relocation	.36	.28	.25	.02	-.18	-.17	.37		
	Alternatives	.18	-.01	.09	.06	.10	-.02	.17	.28	
Home for Life Study										
Conscious appraisals	Feelings about leaving									
	Expected losses	.52								
	Anticipated satisfactions	.71	.52							
Strategies										
Degree of coping	Information absorbed	.14	.13	.22						
	Working through	.11	.03	.22	.29					
Level of integration	Extent of accurate appraisals	.17	-.10	.05	.16	.17				
Degree of mastery	Congruence	.70	.53	.90	.35	.28	.05			
	Perceived control									
	Relocation	.32	.17	.37	.33	.26	.30	.39		
	Alternatives	.28	.13	.37	.36	.30	.32	.38	.95	
Deinstitutionalized Elites Study										
Conscious appraisals	Feelings about leaving									
	Expected losses	.51								
	Anticipated satisfactions	.41	.24							
Strategies										
Degree of coping	Information absorbed	.01	-.13	.28						
	Working through	-.11	-.14	.02	.12					
Level of integration	Extent of accurate appraisals	.08	.00	.29	.20	-.09				
Degree of mastery	Congruence	.20	.13	.83	.34	-.02	.29			
	Perceived control									
	Relocation	.27	.02	.25	.35	-.18	-.12	.14		
	Alternatives	.28	-.01	.29	.55	.10	.44	.30	.44	

Appendix F

Block Q-Sort Items (Block 1961)

1. Is critical, skeptical, not easily impressed.
2. Is a genuinely dependable and responsible person.
3. Has a wide range of interests. (Superficiality or depth of interest is irrelevant here.)
4. Is a talkative individual.
5. Behaves in a giving way toward others (regardless of the motivation involved).
6. Is fastidious.
7. Favors conservative values in a variety of ways.
8. Appears to have a high degree of intellectual capacity (whether actualized or not). (Originality is not necessarily assumed.)
9. Is uncomfortable with uncertainty and complexities.
10. Anxiety and tension find outlet in bodily symptoms. (If placed high, implies bodily dysfunction; if placed low, implies absence of autonomic arousal.)
11. Is protective of those close to him. (Placement of this term expresses behavior ranging from overprotection through appropriate nurturance to a laissez-faire, underprotective manner.)
12. Tends to be self-defensive.
13. Is thin-skinned; sensitive to anything that can be construed as criticism or an interpersonal slight.
14. Is genuinely submissive; accepts domination comfortably.
15. Is skilled in social techniques of imaginative play, pretending, and humor.
16. Is introspective and concerned with self as an object. (Introspectiveness per se does not imply insight.)
17. Behaves in a sympathetic or considerate manner.
18. Initiates humor.
19. Seeks reassurance from others.
20. Has a rapid personal tempo; behaves and acts quickly.
21. Arouses nurturant feelings in others.

22. Feels a lack of personal meaning in life.
23. Is extrapunitive; tends to transfer or project blame.
24. Prides self on being "objective," rational.
25. Tends toward overcontrol of needs and impulses; binds tensions excessively; delays gratification unnecessarily.
26. Is productive; gets things done.
27. Shows condescending behavior in relations with others. (Extreme placement toward uncharacteristic and implies simply an absence of condescension, not necessarily equalitarianism or inferiority.)
28. Tends to arouse liking and acceptance in people.
29. Is turned to for advice and reassurance.
30. Gives up and withdraws where possible in the face of frustration and adversity. (If placed high, implies generally defeatist; if placed low, implies counteractive.)
31. Regards self as physically attractive.
32. Seems to be aware of the impression he makes on others.
33. Is calm, relaxed in manner.
34. Over-reactive to minor frustrations; irritable.
35. Has warmth; has the capacity for close relationships; compassionate.
36. Is subtly negativistic; tends to undermine and obstruct or sabotage.
37. Is guileful and deceitful, manipulative, opportunistic.
38. Has hostility toward others. (Basic hostility is intended here; mode of expression is to be indicated by other items.)
39. Thinks and associates ideas in unusual ways; has unconventional thought processes.
40. Is vulnerable to real or fancied threat, generally fearful.
41. Is moralistic (regardless of the particular nature of the moral code).
42. Is reluctant to commit self to any definite course of action; tends to delay or avoid action.
43. Is facially and/or gesturally expressive.
44. Evaluates the motivation of others in interpreting situations (accuracy of evaluation is not assumed). (Extreme placement in one direction implies preoccupation with motivational interpretation; at the other extreme, the item implies a psychological obtuseness—subject does not consider motivational factors.)
45. Has brittle ego-defense system; has a small reserve of integration; would be disorganized and maladaptive when under stress or trauma.
46. Engages in personal fantasy and daydreams, fictional speculations.
47. Has a readiness to feel guilt (regardless of whether verbalized or not).
48. Keeps people at a distance; avoids close interpersonal relationships.
49. Is basically distrustful of people in general; questions their motivations.
50. Is unpredictable and changeable in behavior and attitudes.
51. Genuinely values intellectual and cognitive matters (ability or achievement are not implied here).
52. Behaves in an assertive fashion. (Item 14 reflects underlying submissiveness; this refers to overt behavior.)
53. Various needs tend toward relatively direct and uncontrolled expression; unable to delay gratification.

54. Emphasizes being with others; gregarious.
55. Is self-defeating.
56. Responds to humor.
57. Is an interesting, arresting person.
58. Enjoys sensuous experiences (including touch, taste, smell, physical contact).
59. Is concerned with own body and the adequacy of its physiological functioning.
60. Has insight into own motives and behavior.
61. Creates and exploits dependency in people (regardless of the techniques employed, e.g., punitiveness, over-indulgence). (At the other end of scale, item implies respecting and encouraging the independence and individuality of others.)
62. Tends to be rebellious and nonconforming.
63. Judges self and others in conventional terms like "popularity," "the correct thing to do," social pressures, etc.
64. Is socially perceptive of a wide range of interpersonal cues.
65. Characteristically pushes and tries to stretch limits; sees what he or she can get away with.
66. Enjoys esthetic impressions; is esthetically reactive.
67. Is self-indulgent.
68. Is basically anxious.
69. Is sensitive to anything that can be construed as a demand. (No implication of the kind of subsequent response is intended here.]
70. *Behaves* in an ethically consistent manner; is consistent with own personal standards.
71. Has high aspiration level for self.
72. Is concerned with own adequacy as a person, either at conscious or unconscious levels. (A clinical judgment is required here; item 74 reflects subjective satisfaction with self.)
73. Tends to perceive many different contexts in sexual terms; eroticizes situations.
74. Is subjectively unaware of self-concern; feels satisfied with self.
75. Has a clear-cut, internally consistent personality. (*Amount* of information available before sorting is not intended here.)
76. Tends to project own feelings and motivations onto others.
77. Appears straightforward, forthright, candid in dealing with others.
78. Feels cheated and victimized by life; self-pitying.
79. Tends to ruminate and have persistent, preoccupying thoughts.
80. Interested in members of the opposite sex. (At opposite end, item implies *absence* of such interest.)
81. Is physically attractive; good looking. (The cultural criterion is to be applied here.)
82. Has fluctuating moods.
83. Is able to see to the heart of important problems.
84. Is cheerful. (Extreme placement toward uncharacteristic end of continuum implies unhappiness or depression.)
85. Emphasizes communication through action and nonverbal behavior.

86. Handles anxiety and conflicts by, in effect, refusing to recognize their presence; repressive or dissociative tendencies.
87. Interprets basically simple and clearcut situations in complicated and particularizing ways.
88. Is personally charming.
89. Compares self to others. Is alert to real or fancied differences between self and other people.
90. Is concerned with philosophical problems; e.g., religions, values, the meaning of life, etc.
91. Is power-oriented; values power in self and others.
92. Has social poise and presence; appears socially at ease.
93. a. *Behaves* in a masculine style and manner.
    b. *Behaves* in a feminine style and manner. (If subject is male, 93a applies; if subject is female, 93b is to be evaluated.) (The cultural or subcultural concept is to be applied as a criterion.)
94. Expresses hostile feelings directly.
95. Tends to proffer advice.
96. Values own independence and autonomy.
97. Is emotionally bland; has flattened affect.
98. Is verbally fluent; can express ideas well.
99. Is self-dramatizing; histrionic.
100. Does not vary roles; relates to everyone in the same way.

NOTE: Judges, after reading the entire case, are asked to describe the individual by sorting the 100 cards in eleven piles, from highly characteristic (high placement) to highly uncharacteristic of the person (low placement).

References

Adler, A. "Significance of early recollections." *International Journal of Individual Psychology*, 3 (1937), 283–287.

Adorno, T. W., Frenkel-Brunswick, E., Levinson, D. J., and Sanford, R. N. *The Authoritarian Personality*. New York: Harper & Row, 1950.

Allport, G. W. *Pattern and Growth in Personality*. New York: Holt, Rinehart, & Winston, 1961.

Andreason, N. J. C., Noyes, R., and Hartford, C. E. "Factors influencing adjustment of burn patients during hospitalization." *Psychosomatic Medicine*, 34 (1972), 517–523.

Antonosky, A. *Health, Stress and Coping*. San Francisco: Jossey-Bass, 1979.

Aries, P. *Western Attitudes Towards Death*. Baltimore, Md.: Johns Hopkins University Press, 1974.

Back, K. W., and Morris, J. D. "Perception of self and the study of whole lives." In E. Palmore, ed., *Normal Aging, II: Reports from the Duke Longitudinal Study, 1970–1973*. Durham, N.C.: Duke University Press, 1974, pp. 216–221.

Bakan, D. *The Duality of Human Existence*. Chicago: Rand McNally, 1966.

Becker, E. *The Denial of Death*. New York: The Free Press, 1973.

Beigler, J. S. "Anxiety as an aid in the prognostication of impending death." *Archives of Neurology and Psychiatry*, 77 (1957), 171–177.

Bender, L. *A Visual Motor Gestalt Test and Its Clinical Use*. New York: American Orthopsychiatric Association, Research Monograph No. 3, 1938.

Bettelheim, B. "Individual and mass behavior in extreme situations." *Journal of Abnormal and Social Psychology*, 38 (1943), 417–452.

————. *The Informed Heart*. Glencoe, Ill.: The Free Press, 1960.

Binswanger, L. "Dream and existence." In *Being-in-the-World*. New York: Harper & Row, 1968, pp. 222–248.

Birren, J. E., ed., *Handbook of Aging and the Individual*. Chicago: University of Chicago Press, 1959.

————. *The Psychology of Aging*. Englewood Cliffs, N.J.: Prentice-Hall, 1964.

Birren, J. E., Butler, R. N., Greenhouse, S. W., Sokoloff, L., and Yarrow, M. R., eds. *Human Aging: A Biological and Behavioral Study*. Washington, D.C.: U.S. Government Printing Office, 1963.

Block, E. *Das Prinzip Hoffnung*. Berlin: Aufbau-Verlag, 1953.

Block, J. *The Q-Sort Method in Personality Assessment and Psychiatric Research*. Springfield, Ill.: Charles C Thomas, 1961.

Blumberg, E. M., West, P. M., and Ellis, F. W. "A possible relationship between psychological factors and human cancer." *Psychosomatic Medicine*, 16 (1954), 277–286.

Bondy, C. "Problems of internment camps." *Journal of Abnormal and Social Psychology*, 38 (1943), 453–475.

Boss, M. *Psychoanalysis and Daseinanalysis*. New York: Basic Books, 1963.

Boyd, I., Yaeger, M., and McMillan, M. "Personality styles in the postoperative course." *Psychosomatic Medicine*, 35 (1973), 23–40.

References

Boylin, W., Gordon, S. K., and Nehrke, M. F. "Reminiscing and ego integrity in institution-alized elderly males." *The Gerontologist*, 16 (1976), 118–124.

Brim, O. G. "Selected theories of the male mid-life crisis: A comparative analysis." Paper presented at the 82nd Annual Meeting of the American Psychological Association, New Orleans, September 1974.

Brim, O. G., and Kagan, J., eds. *Constancy and Change in Human Development*. Cambridge, Mass.: Harvard University Press, 1980.

Buhler, C. "The general structure of the life cycle." In C. Buhler and F. Massarik, eds., *The Course of Human Life: A Study of Goals in a Humanistic Perspective*. New York: Springer, 1968, pp. 12–26.

Butler, R. N. "The life review: An interpretation of reminiscence in the aged." *Psychiatry*, 26 (1963), 63–76.

Byrne, D. *An Introduction to Personality*. Englewood Cliffs, N.J.: Prentice-Hall, 1974.

Cameron, P., Desai, K. G., Bahador, D., and Dremel, G. "Temporality across the lifespan." *International Journal of Aging and Human Development*, 8 (1977–78), 229–259.

Camus, A. *The Myth of Sisyphus*. New York: Alfred A. Knopf, 1955.

Cannon, W. B. " 'Voodoo' death." *American Anthropologist*, 44 (1942), 169–181.

Cantril, H. "The human design." *Journal of Individual Psychology*, 20 (1964), 129–136.

Carson, R., and Heine, R. "Similarity and success in therapeutic dyads: A re-evaluation." *Journal of Consulting Psychology*, 30 (1962), 458.

Cattell, R. B. *Handbook Supplement for Form C of the Sixteen Personality Factor Test*, 2nd ed. Champaign, Ill.: Institute for Personality and Ability Testing, 1962.

Choron, J. *Modern Man and Mortality*. New York: Macmillan, 1964.

Cobb, S. "Social support as a moderator of life stress." *Psychosomatic Medicine*, 38 (1976), 300–314.

Coehlo, G. V., Hamburg, D. A., and Adams, J. E., eds. *Coping and Adaptation*. New York: Basic Books, 1974.

Coffman, T. L. "Relocation and survival of institutionalized aged: A re-examination of the evidence." *The Gerontologist*, 21 (1981), 483–500.

Cohen, E. A. *Human Behavior in the Concentration Camp*. New York: W. W. Norton, 1953.

Cohen, F. "Psychological preparation, coping and recovery from surgery." Doctoral dissertation, University of California at Berkeley, 1975.

————. "Personality, stress and the development of physical illness." In G. C. Stone, F. Cohen, and N. E. Adler, eds. *Health Psychology*. San Francisco: Jossey-Bass, 1979, pp. 77-111.

Cohen, F., and Lazarus, R. C. "Coping with the stresses of illness." In G. C. Stone, F. Cohen, and N. E. Adler, eds. *Health Psychology*, San Francisco: Jossey-Bass, 1979, pp. 217–255.

Cohler, B., and Lieberman, M. A. "Ethnicity and personal adaptation." *International Journal of Group Tensions*, 7 (May 1978), 20–41.

Coleman, P. G. "Measuring reminiscence characteristics from conversations as adaptive features in old age." *International Journal of Aging and Human Development*, 5 (1974), 281–294.

Comfort, A. *Aging: The Biology of Senescence*. London: Routledge & Kegan Paul, 1964.

Cooley, C. H. *Human Nature and the Social Order*. New York: Charles Scribner's Sons, 1902.

Cumming, E., and Henry, W. E. *Growing Old: The Process of Disengagement*. New York: Basic Books, 1961.

Dana, R. H. "Clinical diagnosis and objective TAT scoring." *Journal of Abnormal and Social Psychology*, 50 (1955), 19–25.

Decoster, D. "Housing assignments for high ability students." *Journal of College Student Personnel*, (1966), 10–22.

Derogatis, L. R., and Abeloff, M. D. "Psychological coping mechanisms and survival time in metastic breast cancer." Abstract presented at a meeting of the American Society of Clinical Oncology, Washington, D.C., April 1978.

Dudley, D. L., Verhey, J. W., Masuda, M., Martin, C. J., and Holmes, J. H. "Long-term adjustment prognosis and death in irreversible diffuse obstructive pulmonary syndromes." *Psychosomatic Medicine,* 31 (1969), 310–325.

Edelhart, G. "Consistency of self-concept across various self-concept measures." Masters thesis, University of Chicago, 1965.

Ellenberger, H. F. "A clinical introduction to psychiatric phenomenology and existential analysis." In R. May, E. Angel, and H. F. Ellenberger, eds. *Existence.* New York: Basic Books, 1958, pp. 92–126.

Engel, G. L. "A life setting conducive to illness: The giving-up complex." *Annals of Internal Medicine,* 69 (1968), 293–300.

Engel, G. L., and Schmale, A. H. "Psychoanalytic theory of somatic disorder." *Journal of the American Psychoanalytic Association,* 15 (1967), 344–363.

Erikson, E. H. *Childhood and Society.* New York: W. W. Norton, 1950.

————. *Identity and the Life Cycle.* New York: International Universities Press, 1959.

————. *Insight and Responsibility.* New York: W. W. Norton, 1964.

Fallot, R. D. "The life story through reminiscence in later adulthood." Doctoral dissertation, Yale University, 1977.

Farber, M. L. *Theory of Suicide.* New York: Funk & Wagnalls, 1968.

Feifel, H. "Judgment of time in younger and older persons." *Journal of Gerontology,* 12 (1957), 71–74.

Feldman, K., and Newcomb, T. *The Impact of College on Students.* San Francisco: Jossey-Bass, 1965.

Ferrono, C. L. "Adult developmental psychology and the reconstruction of earliest memories." Masters thesis, University of Chicago, 1981.

Festinger, L. *A Theory of Cognitive Dissonance.* Stanford, Calif.: Stanford University Press, 1957.

Fleisher, M., and Kulare, R. "Compatibility and stability in home care groups." *Social Psychiatry,* 7 (1972), 11–17.

Frank, J. D. *Persuasion and Healing.* Baltimore, Md.: Johns Hopkins University Press, 1961.

————. "The role of hope in psychotherapy." *International Journal of Psychiatry,* 5 (1968), 383–395.

Frankl, V. E. *Man's Search for Meaning: An Introduction to Logotherapy.* New York: Washington Square Press, 1963.

French, T. M. *The Integration of Behavior.* Vol. 1: *Basic Postulates.* Chicago: University of Chicago Press, 1952.

Freud, S. *General Introduction to Psychoanalysis.* New York: Garden City Publishing Co., 1938.

Friedmann, E. A., and Orbach, H. "Adjustment to retirement." In S. Arieti, ed. *American Handbook of Psychiatry.* New York: Basic Books, 1974, pp. 609–45.

Fries, J. F., and Crapo, L. M. *Vitality and Aging: Implications of the Rectangular Curve.* San Francisco: W. H. Freeman, 1981.

Gaylin, W., ed. *The Meaning of Despair: Psychoanalytic Contributions to the Understanding of Depression.* New York: Jason Aronson, 1968.

Gendlin, E. *Experiencing and the Creation of Meaning.* Glencoe, Ill: The Free Press, 1962.

————. "A theory of personality change." In P. Worchel and D. Byrnes, eds. *Personality Change.* New York: John Wiley & Sons, 1964, pp. 100–148.

Giambra, L. M. "Daydreaming about the past: The time setting of spontaneous thought intrusions." *The Gerontologist,* 17 (1977a), 35–38.

————. "A factor analytic study of daydreaming, imagined processes and temperament: A replication on an adult male lifespan sample." *Journal of Gerontology,* 32 (1977b), 675–680.

Gilberstadt, H., and Sako, Y. "Intellectual and personality changes following open-heart surgery." *Archives of General Psychiatry,* 16 (1967), 210–214.

Goffman, E. *Asylums: Essays on the Social Situation of Mental Patients and Other Inmates.* Garden City, N.Y.: Doubleday, 1961.

References

Gore, S. "The effect of social support in moderating the health consequences of unemployment." *Journal of Health and Social Behavior,* 19 (1978), 157–165.

Gorney, J. "Experience and age: Patterns of reminiscence among the elderly." Doctoral dissertation, University of Chicago, 1968.

Gottschalk, L. A., Springer, K. H., and Gleser, G. C. "Experiments with a method of assessing the variations in intensity of certain psychological states occurring during the psychotherapeutic interview." In L. A. Gottschalk, ed., *Comparative Psycholinguistic Analysis of Two Psychotherapeutic Interventions.* New York: International Universities Press, 1961.

Greene, W. A., Jr., Young, L. E., and Swisher, S. N. "Psychological factors and reticuloendothelial disease: II. Observations on a group of women with lymphomas and leukemias." *Psychosomatic Medicine,* 18 (1956), 284–303.

Greenfield, N. S., Roessler, R. and Crosley, A. P. "Ego strength and length of recovery from infectious mononucleosis." *Journal of Nervous and Mental Disease,* 128 (1959), 125–128.

Grinker, R., and Spiegel, J. *Men Under Stress.* Philadelphia: Blakiston, 1945.

Guilford, J. P. *Personality.* New York: McGraw-Hill, 1959.

Gunderson, E. K. E. "Personality history characteristics of Antarctic volunteers." *Journal of Social Psychology,* 64 (1964), 325–332.

Guntrip, H. *Psychoanalytic Theory, Therapy and the Self.* New York: Basic Books, 1971.

Gutmann, D. "Parenthood: A key to the comparative study of the life cycle." In N. Datan and L. H. Ginsberg, eds. *Life Span Developmental Psychology,* New York: Academic Press, 1975, pp. 167–184.

————. "The cross-cultural perspective: Notes toward a comparative psychology of aging." In J. E. Birren and K. W. Schaie, eds. *Handbook of the Psychology of Aging.* New York: Van Nostrand Reinhold, 1977.

Haan, N. " '. . . Change and sameness . . .' reconsidered." *International Journal of Aging and Human Development,* 7 (1976), 59–66.

Haan, N., and Day, D. "A longitudinal study of change and sameness in personality development: Adolescence to later adulthood." *International Journal of Aging and Human Development,* 5 (1974), 11–40.

Haberland, H. W. "Psychological dimensions of hope in the aged: Relationship to adaptation, survival and institutionalization." Doctoral dissertation, University of Chicago, 1972.

Hall, E. T. *The Hidden Dimension.* Garden City, N.Y.: Doubleday, 1966.

Hamburg, B. A., and Killilea, M. "Relation of social support, stress, illness, and use of health services." In *Healthy People, The Surgeon General's Report on Health Promotion and Disease Prevention Background Papers.* Washington, D.C.: National Institutes of Health, 1979.

Hartmann, H. "Comments on the psychoanalytic theory of the ego." *The Psychoanalytic Study of the Child,* Vol. 5. New York: International Universities Press, 1950, pp. 74–96.

————. *Ego Psychology and the Problem of Adaptation.* New York: International Universities Press, 1958.

Havighurst, R. J., and Albrecht, R. *Older People.* New York: Longmans, Green, 1953.

Havighurst, R. J., and Glasser, R. "An exploratory study of reminiscence." *Journal of Gerontology,* 27 (1972), 245–253.

Heller, A. "The effects of social support: Prevention and treatment implications." In A. P. Goldstein and F. H. Kanfer, eds. *Maximizing Treatment Gains: Transference Enhancement and Psychotherapy.* New York: Academic Press, 1978.

Hicks, M., and Platt, M. "Marital happiness and stability: A review of the research in the sixties." *Journal of Marriage and the Family,* 32 (1970), 553–574.

Inglis, J. "A paired-associate learning test for use with elderly psychiatric patients." *Journal of Mental Science,* 105 (1959), 440–443.

Jackson, B. "Who goes to prison? Caste and careerism in crime." *Atlantic Monthly,* 1 (1966), 52–57.

Jacobs, S., and Ostfeld, A. "An epidemiological review of the mortality of bereavement." *Psychosomatic Medicine,* 39 (1977), 344–357.

Jacobson, E. *The Self and the Objective World*. New York: International Universities Press, 1964.

Jahoda, M. *Current Concepts of Positive Mental Health*. New York: Basic Books, 1958.

James, W. *Principles of Psychology*, Vol. 1. New York: Henry Holt, 1890.

————. *Psychology: The Briefer Course*. New York: Henry Holt, 1892.

Janis, I. *Psychological Stress*. New York: John Wiley & Sons, 1958.

Janis, I., Mahl, G., Kagan, J., and Holt, R. *Personality*. New York: Harcourt, Brace and World, 1969.

Jarvik, L. F., and Blum, J. E. "Cognitive decline as predictors of mortality in twin pairs: A twenty year longitudinal study." In E. Palmore and F. C. Jeffers, eds. *Prediction of Life Span*. Lexington, Mass.: Lexington Books, 1971.

Jarvik, L. L., and Falek, A. "Intellectual stability and survival in the aged." *Journal of Gerontology*, 18 (1963), 173–176.

Kahn, R. L., Pollack, M., and Goldfarb, A. I. "Factors related to individual differences in mental status of institutionalized aged." In P. H. Hock and J. Zubin, eds. *Psychopathology of Aging*. New York: Grune & Stratton, 1961, pp. 104–113.

Kaplan, B. H., Cassel, J. C., and Gore, S. "Social support and health." *Medical Care*, 15 (1977), 47–58.

Kastenbaum, R. "On the meaning of time in later life." *Journal of Genetic Psychology*, 109 (1966), 9–25.

Kilpatrick, D. G., Miller, W. C., Allain, A. N., Higgins, M. B., and Lee, W. H., Jr. "The use of psychological test data to predict open heart surgery outcomes: A prospective study." *Psychosomatic Medicine*, 37 (1975), 62–73.

Kleemeier, R. W. "Intellectual changes in the senium, or death and the I.Q." Presidential address to Division 20 of the American Psychological Association. New York, September 1961a.

————. "The use and meaning of time in special settings." In R. W. Kleemeier, ed. *Aging and Leisure*. New York: Oxford University Press, 1961b.

Klopfer, B. "Psychological variables in human cancer." *Journal of Projective Techniques*, 21 (1957), 331–340.

Kobassa, S. C., Maddi, S. R., and Kahn, S. "Hardiness and health: a prospective study." *Journal of Personality and Social Psychology*, 42 (1982), 168–277.

Kohut, H. *The Restoration of the Self*. New York: International Universities Press, 1977.

————. *The Psychology of the Self*. New York: International Universities Press, 1978.

Kübler-Ross, E. *On Death and Dying*. New York: Macmillan, 1969.

Lawton, M. P. *Environment and Aging*. Monterey, Calif.: Brooks/Cole, 1980a.

————. "Environmental change: The older person as initiator and responder." In N. Datan and N. Lohman, eds. *Transitions of Aging*. New York: Academic Press, 1980b, pp. 171–193.

Lazarus, R. S. *Psychological Stress and the Coping Process*. New York: McGraw-Hill, 1966.

Leary, T. *Interpersonal Diagnosis of Personality*. New York: Ronald Press, 1957.

Lecky, P. *Self Consistency: A Theory of Personality*. New York: Island Press, 1945.

LeShan, L. "A basic psychological orientation apparently associated with malignant disease." *Psychiatric Quarterly*, 35 (1961), 314–330.

Levinson, D. J., Darrow, C. M., Klein, E. B., Levinson, M. H., and McKee, B. "The psychosocial development of man in early adulthood and the mid-life transition." In D. F. Ricks, A. Thomas, and M. Roff, eds. *Life History Research in Psychopathology*, Vol. 3. Minneapolis: University of Minnesota Press, 1974, pp. 243–258.

Lewin, K. *Field Theory and Social Science*. New York: Harper & Row, 1951.

Lichtenberg, J. P. "A definition and analysis of depression." *Archives of Neurology and Psychiatry*, 77 (1957), 519–527.

Lieberman, M. A. "Relationship of mortality rates to entrance to a home for the aged." *Geriatrics*, 16 (1961), 515–519.

————. "Intra-individual variability and age." Paper presented at a meeting of the American Psychological Association, Washington, D.C., August 1962.

————. "Social and psychological determinants of adaptation." *International Journal of Aging and Human Development*, 9 (1981).

424

References

————. "The effects of social supports on responses to stress." In L. Goldberger and S. Breznitz, eds. *Handbook of Stress*. New York: Free Press, 1982.

Lieberman, M. A., and Cohler, B. "Final Report: Constructing Personality Measures for Older People." University of Chicago (Photocopied), 1975.

Lieberman, M. A., and Lakin, M. "On becoming an institutionalized person." In R. H Williams, C. Tibbitts, and W. Donahue, eds. *Process of Aging*. Vol. 1: *Social and Psychological Perspectives*. New York: Atherton Press, 1963, pp. 475–503.

Lin, N. R., Simeone, S., Ensel, W. M., and Kuo, W. "Social support, stressful life events and illness: A model and an empirical test." *Journal of Health and Social Behavior*, 20 (1979), 108–119.

Lothrup, W. W. "The relationship between Bender-Gestalt Test scores and medical success with duodenal ulcer patients." *Psychosomatic Medicine*, 20 (1958), 30–32.

Lowenthal, M. F., and Robinson, B. "Social networks and isolation." In R. H. Binstock and E. Shanas, eds. *Handbook of Aging and the Social Sciences*. New York: Van Nostrand Reinhold, 1976, pp. 432–456.

Lowenthal, M. F., Thurnher, M., and Chiriboga, D. *Four Stages of Life: A Psychosocial Study of Women and Men Facing Transition*. San Francisco: Jossey-Bass, 1975.

McClelland, D. C. *Personality*. New York: Holt, Rinehart & Winston, 1951.

McMahon, A. W., and Rhudick, P. J. "Reminiscing in the aged: An adaptational response." In S. Levin and R. J. Kahana, eds., *Psychodynamic Studies on Aging: Creativity, Reminiscing and Dying*. New York: International Universities Press, 1967, pp. 64–78.

Maddi, S. *Personality Theories: A Comparative Analysis*. Homewood, Ill.: Dorsey Press, 1968.

Maddox, G. L. "Disengagement theory: A critical review." *The Gerontologist*, 4 (1964), 80–82.

Marcel, G. *Homo Viator: Introduction to a Metaphysic of Hope*. New York: Harper & Bros., 1962.

Martin, D. "Institutionalization." *Lancet*, 269 (1955), 1188–90.

Mason, R. C., Clark, G., Reeves, R. B., and Wagner, B. "Acceptance and healing." *Journal of Religion and Health*, 8 (1969), 123–142.

May, R. "Contributions of existential psychotherapy." In R. May, E. Angel, and H. F. Ellenberger, eds. *Existence*. New York: Basic Books, 1958, pp. 37–91.

Mead, G. H. *Mind, Self and Society*. Chicago: University of Chicago Press, 1934.

Mechanic, D. "Discussion of research programs on relations between stressful life events and episodes of physical illness." In B. S. Dohrenwend and B. P. Dohrenwend eds. *Stressful Life Events: Their Nature and Effects*. New York: John Wiley, 1974, pp. 87–97.

Melges, F. T., and Bowlby, J. "Types of hopelessness in psychopathological processes." *Archives of General Psychiatry*, 20 (1969), 690–699.

Menninger, K. "The academic lecture: Hope." *American Journal of Psychiatry*, 116 (1959), 481–491.

Menninger, K., and Menninger, J. L. *Love Against Hate*. New York; Harcourt, Brace, 1942.

Merleau-Ponty, M. *Phenomenology of Perception*. London: Routledge & Kegan Paul, 1962 [1945].

————. *The Structure of Behavior*. Boston: Beacon Press, 1963 [1943].

Minkowski, E. *Le temps vecu*. Paris: d'Artrey, 1933.

Mischel, W. "Continuity and change in personality." *American Psychologist*, 24 (1969), 1012–1018.

————. *Introduction to Personality*. 2nd ed. New York: Holt, Rinehart & Winston, 1976.

Modell, H. H. "Changes in human figure drawings by patients who recover from regressed states." *American Journal of Orthopsychiatry*, 21 (1951), 584–596.

Moltmann, J. *Religion, Revolution, and the Future*. New York: Charles Scribner's Sons, 1969.

Montgomery, J. E. "Living arrangements and housing of the rural aged in a central Pennsylvania community." In *Patterns of Living and Housing of Middle Aged and Older Persons*. Public Health Service Publication No. 1496. Washington, D.C.: U.S. Government Printing Office, 1965, pp. 83–96.

Moos, R. *Evaluating Treatment Environments*. New York: John Wiley & Sons, 1974.

Moss, G. E. *Illness, Immunity and Social Interaction*. New York: John Wiley, 1973.

References

Moss, H. A., and Sussman, E. J. "Longitudinal study of personality development." In O. J. Brim and J. Kagan, eds. *Constancy and Change in Human Development*. Cambridge: Harvard University Press, 1980, pp. 530–591.

Mowrer, O. H. *Learning theory and behavior*. New York: John Wiley & Sons, 1960.

Munnichs, J. M. "Old age and finitude: A contribution to psychogerontology." *Bibliotheca Vita Humana*, No. 4 (1966).

Murray, H. A. *Explorations in Personality*. New York: Oxford University Press, 1938.

Nardini, J. "Survival factors in American prisoners of war of the Japanese." *American Journal of Psychiatry*, 109 (1952), 241–248.

Neugarten, B. L. "Personality and aging." In J. E. Birren and K. W. Schaie, eds. *Handbook of the Psychology of Aging*. New York: Van Nostrand Reinhold, 1979, pp. 626–649.

Neugarten, B. L., and Datan, N. "The middle years." In S. Arieti, ed. *American Handbook of Psychiatry*. New York: Basic Books, 1974, 592–608.

Neugarten, B. L., and Havighurst, R. J. "Disengagement reconsidered in a cross-national context." In R. J. Havighurst, M. A. Munnichs, B. L. Neugarten, and H. Tomae, eds. *Adjustment to Retirement*. 2nd ed. The Hague, Netherlands: Van Gorkum, 1969, pp. 138–146.

Neugarten, B. L., Havighurst, R. J., and Tobin, S. S. "The measurement of life satisfaction." *Journal of Gerontology*, 16 (1961), 134–143.

————. "Personality and patterns of aging." In B. L. Neugarten, ed. *Middle Age and Aging*. Chicago: University of Chicago Press, 1968, pp. 173–177.

Neugarten, B. L., Moore, J. W., and Lowe, J. C. "Age norms, age constraints and adult socialization." *American Journal of Sociology*, 70 (1965), 710–717.

Obrist, W. D., Henry, C. E., and Justiss, W. A. "Longitudinal study of EEG in old age." Paper presented at the Fifth International Congress of Electroencephelography and Clinical Neurology, Rome, Italy, September 1961.

Oliveira, O. H. "Understanding old people: Patterns of reminiscing in elderly people and their relationship to life satisfaction." Unpublished manuscript, University of Tennessee, 1977.

Osgood, C. E., and Tannenbaum, P. H. *The Measurement of Meaning*. Urbana: University of Illinois Press, 1958.

Pancheri, P., Bellaterra, M., Matteoli, S., Cristofaris, M., Polizzi, C., and Puletti., N. "Infant as a stress agent." *Journal of Human Stress*, 4 (1978), 16–22, 41–42.

Parkes, C. M. *Bereavement*. New York: International Universities Press, 1972.

Pascal, G. R., and Suttell, B. J. *The Bender-Gestalt Test: Quantification and Validity for Adults*. New York: Grune & Stratton, 1951.

Pascal, G. R., and Thoroughman, J. C. "Relation between Bender-Gestalt test scores and responses of patients with intractable duodenal ulcer to surgery." *Psychosomatic Medicine*, 26 (1964), 625–627.

Pincus, M. A. "Toward a conceptual framework for studying institutional environments in homes for the aged." Doctoral dissertation, University of Wisconsin, 1968.

Pinneau, R. S. "Effects of social support on occupational stress and strain." Paper presented at a meeting of the American Psychological Association, Washington, D.C., Sept., 1976.

Postema, L. J. "Reminiscing, time orientation, and self-concept in aged men." Unpublished manuscript. East Lansing: Michigan State University, 1970.

Reichard, S., Livson, F., and Petersen, P. G. *Aging and Personality*. New York: John Wiley & Sons, 1962.

Reitman, F., and Robertson, J. P. "Reitman's pin man test: A means of disclosing impaired conceptual thinking." *Journal of Nervous and Mental Disease*, 112 (1950), 498–510.

Revere, V. F. "The remembered past: Its reconstruction at different life stages." Doctoral dissertation, University of Chicago, 1971.

Richter, C. P. "On the phenomenon of sudden death in animals and man." *Psychosomatic Medicine*, 19 (1957), 191–198.

426

References

Riegel, K. F., and Riegel, R. M. "Development, drop and death." *Developmental Psychology*, 6 (1972), 306–319.

Riezler, K. *Man: Mutable and Immutable*. Chicago: Henry Regnery Co., 1950.

Riley, M. W., and Foner, A. *Aging and Society*. Vol. I: *An Inventory of Research Findings*. New York: Russell Sage Foundation, 1968.

Robinson, J., Rusk, G., and Head, K. *Measures of Political Attitudes*. Ann Arbor: Survey Research Center, University of Michigan, 1968.

Rogers, C. *Client Centered Therapy*. Boston: Houghton Mifflin, 1951.

Rogers, C., and Dymond, R., eds. *Psychotherapy and Personality Change*. Chicago: University of Chicago Press, 1954.

Romaniuk, M. "Reminiscence and the elderly: An exploration of its content, function, press and product." Doctoral dissertation, University of Wisconsin at Madison, 1978.

Rosen, J., and Neugarten, B. L. "Ego functions in the middle and later years: a thematic apperceptive test study of normal adults." *Journal of Gerontology*, 15 (1960), 62–67.

Rosenberg, M. *Conceiving the Self*. New York: Basic Books, 1979.

Rosner, A. "Stress and the maintenance of self-concept in the aged." Doctoral dissertation, University of Chicago, 1968.

Rotter, J. B. "Generalized expectancies for internal versus external control of reinforcement." *Psychological Monographs*, 80 (1966), 1–28.

Rowland, K. F. "Environmental events predicting death for the elderly." *Psychological Bulletin*, 84 (1977), 349–372.

Sacher, G. A. "Life table modifications and life prolongation." In C. E. Finch and L. Hayflick, eds. *Handbook of the Biology of Aging*. New York: Van Nostrand Reinhold, 1977, pp. 582–638.

———. "On longevity regarded as an organized behavior: The role of brain structure." In R. Kastenbaum, ed. *Contributions to the Psychobiology of Aging*. New York: Springer, 1965, pp. 99–110.

Schachtel, E. *Metamorphosis*. New York: Basic Books, 1959.

———. "On memory and childhood amnesia." *Psychiatry*, 10 (1947), 1–26.

Schmale, A. H. "Relationship of separation and depression to disease." *Psychosomatic Medicine*, 20 (1958), 259–277.

———. "Giving up as a final pathway to changes in health." *Advances in Psychosomatic Medicine*, 8 (1972), 18–38.

Schmale, A. H., and Engel, G. L. "The giving up–given up complex illustrated on film." *Archives of General Psychiatry*, 17 (1967), 135–145.

Shanas, E. *Family Relationships of Older People*. Health Information Foundation, Research Series No. 20. Chicago: National Opinion Research Center, University of Chicago, 1961.

———. *The Health of Older People: A Social Survey*. Cambridge: Harvard University Press, 1962.

Siegler, I. C. "The psychology of adult development and aging," in E. W. Busse and G. Blazer, eds. *Handbook of Geriatric Psychiatry*. New York: Van Nostrand Reinhold, 1980, pp. 169–221.

Slaughter, D. T. "An exploration of ego energy in the very old." Masters thesis, University of Chicago, 1964.

Smith, H. *Condemned to Meaning*. New York: Harper & Row, 1965.

Snygg, D., and Combs, A. W. *Individual Behavior: A New Frame of Reference for Psychology*. New York: Harper Bros., 1949.

Soddy, K. *Men in Middle Life*. Philadelphia: J. B. Lippincott, 1967.

Sokolowski, R. *The Formulation of Husserl's Concept of Constitutions*. The Hague, Netherlands: Martinus Nijhoff, 1964.

Sommer, R., and Osmond, H. "Symptoms of institutional care." *Social Problems*, 8 (1961), 254–262.

Srole, L. "Social integration and certain corollaries: An exploratory study." *American Sociological Review*, 21 (1956), 709–716.

Staug, E., ed. *Personality: Basic Aspects and Current Research*. Englewood Cliffs, N. J.: Prentice-Hall, 1980.

427

Stavraky, K. M. "Psychological factors in the outcome of human cancer." *Journal of Psychosomatic Research,* 12 (1968), 251–259.

Stern, G. *People in Context: Measuring Person-Environment Congruence in Education and Industry.* New York: John Wiley, 1970.

Stone, G. C., Cohen, F., and Adler, N. E., eds. *Health Psychology.* San Francisco: Jossey-Bass, 1979.

Stotland, E. *The Psychology of Hope.* San Francisco: Jossey-Bass, 1969.

Strassman, H. D., Thaler, M. B., and Schein, E. H. "A prisoner of war syndrome: Apathy as a reaction to severe stress." *American Journal of Psychiatry,* 112 (1956), 998–1003.

Straus, E. W. *Phenomenological Psychology.* London: Tavistock, 1966.

Sullivan, H. S. *The Interpersonal Theory of Psychiatry.* New York: W. W. Norton, 1953.

Swenson, C. "Empirical evaluation of human figure drawings." *Psychological Bulletin,* 54 (1957), 431–466.

Tas, J. "Psychical disorders among inmates of concentration camps and repatriates." *Psychiatric Quarterly,* 25 (1951), 679–690.

Thoroughman, J. C., Pascal, G. R., Jenkins, W. O., Crutcher, J. C., and Peoples, L. C. "Psychological factors predictive of surgical success in patients with intractable disodenal ulcer." *Psychosomatic Medicine,* 26 (1964), 618–624.

Tillich, P. "The right to hope." *The University of Chicago Magazine,* 58 (1965), 16–22.

Tobin, S. S., and Etigson, E. "Effect of stress on earliest memory." *Archives of General Psychiatry.* 19 (1968), 435–444.

Tobin, S. S., and Lieberman, M. A. *Last Home for the Aged.* San Francisco: Jossey-Bass, 1976.

Tobin, S. S., and Neugarten, B. L. "Life satisfaction and social interaction in the aging." *Journal of Gerontology,* 16 (1961), 344–346.

Townsend, P. *The Last Refuge: A Survey of Residential Institutions and Homes for the Aged in England and Wales.* London: Routledge & Kegan Paul, 1962.

Tuma, H. A., and Gustaad, J. "The effects of client and counselor personality characteristics on client learning in counseling." *Journal of Counseling Psychology,* 4 (1957), 136–141.

Vaillant, G. E. *Adaptation to Life.* Boston: Little, Brown, 1977.

Vaillant, G. E., and MacArthur, C. C. "Natural history of male psychological health: The adult life cycle from 18–50." *Seminars in Psychiatry,* 4 (1972), 415–427.

Verwoerdt, A., and Scherer, J. "Psychological reactions in fatal illness: Hope and the experience of time." Paper presented at the 18th annual meeting of the Gerontological Society, Los Angeles, California, November 1965.

Vischer, A. L. "Psychological problems in the aging personality." *Bulletin der Schweizerischen Akademie der Medizinischen Wissenschaften,* 2 (1946), 280–286.

Weiner, I. W. "Psychological factors related to results of subtotal gastractomy." *Psychosomatic Medicine,* 18 (1956), 486–491.

Weisskopf-Joelson, E. "Meaning as an integrating factor." In C. Buhler and F. Massarik, eds. *The Course of Human Life.* New York: Springer, 1968, pp. 359–383.

Wolf, S., and Ripley, H. A. "Reactions among allied prisoners to three years of imprisonment and torture by the Japanese." *American Journal of Psychiatry,* 104 (1947), 130–193.

Wolff, H. G. "What hope does for man." *Saturday Review,* 40 (1957), 42–45.

Wylie, R. *The Self-Concept.* Lincoln: University of Nebraska Press, 1961.

—————. *The Self-Concept,* Vol. I. Lincoln: University of Nebraska Press, 1974 (revision of 1961 ed.).

Zinberg, N. E., and Kaufman, I. "Cultural and personality factors associated with aging: An introduction." In N. E. Zinberg and I. Kaufman, eds. *Normal Psychology of the Aging Process.* New York: International Universities Press, 1963.

Index

Abandonment, 124, 164, 316

Acceptance, 267–68, 279; progress toward, 294–306

Achievement fostering, 100–108, 110–13; assessment of, 381–84

Activity levels, 96, 151; and aggression, 198; assessment of, 118, 369–70; and distance from death, 208; and narcissism, 198; as personality disposition index, 178–83, 197; see also Passivity; Role activity

Adams, J. E., 8

Adaptation: and age changes, 107; and aggressiveness, 178–95; and congruence, 92–93, 95–99, 114–16; and cultural influences, 233–34, 237; and current functioning, 142–44, 155–67; defining, 18–19; and dominance, 233–34, 237; and environmental demands, 92–119; and environmental discontinuity, 108–13; and hope, 314, 316, 325–32; and life review, 291–92, 294; life-stage perspective on, 16–18; and personality, 172–99; and physical capacity, 14, 142–55; predicting, 141–71, 337–43; and psychological correlates of impending death, 205–34; and reminiscence, 262, 271–72, 288, 291–92, 294; and resources, 141–45, 148–55; and self-validation needs, 353–54; and threat and loss management strategies, 123–40; see also Stress

Adler, A., 240

Adler, N. E., 167

Adolescence, 240, 290

Adult development, see Developmental issues

Affect: assessing changes in, 236–37, 356–67; and distance from death, 208, 214–27, 232, 236–37; and flight from the past, 269–71; and hopelessness, 313, 317; and reminiscence, 268–76, 285, 307; and resolution, 277–78, 285; and stress effects, 31–32, 37

Affiliation: and distance from death, 218; institutional fostering of, 100–108, 110–13, 392–94; as personality disposition index, 178–80, 182, 185, 194

Age changes: and cultural factors, 233–34, 237; and environmental contingencies, 116–18; measurement of, 119; and self-identity maintenance, 250–51; see also Aging

Agency, 218, 220, 232

Aggressiveness, 96–97, 340, 342; and adaptation, 178–95; assessing, 371–73; and distance from death, 218, as personality disposition index, 178–83; and selective survival, 346; survival function of, 190–95

Aging: defining successful, 342; and self-identity maintenance, 242; theory of, 229–34; see also Age changes

Alloplastic defense activities, 130, 173, 214

Anger, 124, 176–78

Anomie, 321

Antonosky, A., 142

429

Index

Ferrono, C. L., 306
Festinger, L. A., 115
Fight stance, 191, 193–95
Fleisher, M., 115
Flexibility, 15, 168
Flight or fight response, 191
Frankl, V. E., 166
Franklin, B., 256
Freud, S., 220, 240
Freudian psychology, 239
Friedmann, E. A., 196
Functioning abilities, *see* Current functioning
Future, 18, 255, 263, 276, 288; daydreams of, 282; resolution and attitudes toward, 279; *see also* Hope

Gaylin, W., 315
Gender, 196; and aggression, 371–73; and dominance as linked to adaptation, 194, 233–34, 237; and personality disposition, 197; and selective survival, 346
Gendlin, E., 288, 311
Genetic factors, 214
Giambra, L. M., 282
Gilberstadt, H., 196
Glaser, G. C., 316
Goffman, E., 241
Gorney, J., 287
Gottschalk, L. A., 316
Grinker, R., 165
Guilt, 273, 275, 313; assessing, 378–79
Gunderson, E. K. E., 116, 197
Guntrip, H., 240
Gustaad, J., 115
Gutmann, D., 194, 232–33, 346

Haan, N., 241
Hall, E. T., 99–100
Hallucinations, 157, 159
Hamburg, B. A., 147

Hamburg, D. A., 8
Hartmann, H., 240
Havighurst, R. J., 196
Healing, 196, 314
Health care, *see* Medical care
Health status, *see* Physical health
Heine, R., 115
Helplessness, 191–92; *see also* Dependency
Henry, C. E., 206
Henry, W. E., 204
Hicks, M., 115
Homeostatic model, 341–42
Hope, 18, 189, 191; and adaptation, 314, 316, 325–32; defined, 316–17; depression differentiated from total absence of, 312–16, 326–30; dimensions of, 317–20; disappointment implied by 332; and distance from death, 330–31; historical overview of concept of, 314–15; methods for studying, 320–25; as a psychological dimension, 312–15
Hopelessness, 313, 331–32; and disease progress, 191
Hospitalization, 117
Hyperactivity, 157, 159

Illness, 164; and hope, 191, 314; illness behavior distinguished from, 143–44; and psychological factors, 165; and psychological functioning in terminal life phase, 213, 228; and social supports, 147
Illness behavior, 143–44, 167
Impulse control, 15, 145; and coping ability, 13–14
Independence, 43–44; *see also* Dependency
Individual differences, 123–40, 174, 214–15
Individuation, 100–108, 110–13; assessing, 384–85
Information: absorption of, 131; role of, 129

433

Index

Loss, 67–69, 191, 228; anticipated, 82–83; and investment in the past, 262–63; relocation as, 85–86; measuring, 82–85, 88–90

Lowenthal, M. F., 196

MacArthur, C. C., 196
McMahon, A. W., 307
Maddi, S. R., 115, 196
Magical expectations, 226–27, 232, 319, 332
Maladaptation, see Adaptation
Management strategies, 339; individual differences in, 123–40; and symbolic meaning, 124
Marcel, Gabriel, 315
Marital happiness, 115
Mastery, 131, 133–36, 140, 161, 339
Mead, George Herbert, 238–39
Meaning, 317, 319–20
Mechanic, D., 166
Medical care: and adaptive capacity, 101–8
Melges, F. T., 315
Memories, see Reminiscence
Menninger, Karl, 312, 317, 331–32
Mental health, see Psychological functioning
Mental patients, 23–25, 35, 51–64, 108–13, 154–55, 182, 241
Mental Status Questionnaire, 54–55, 162, 167–68, 355–56
Middle age, 196; and cultural influences, 233–34, 237; death awareness in, 225–27, 230, 237; reminiscence in, 281–82, 306
Migration, 117, 175
Minkowski, E., 288
Misanthropy, 331
Mischel, W., 241
Mobilization: and aggressiveness linked to adaptation, 187, 190, 193–95; physiological mechanisms associated with, 344
Moos, H. A., 94, 101–2

Morale, see Well-being
Morris, J. D., 196
Moss, G. E., 196
Moss, H. A., 336
Moving, see Relocation
Mowrer, O. H., 332
Munnichs, J. M., 204, 229–30
Murray, H. A., 103
Murray TAT cards, 76–78, 89–90, 125, 168, 225–27, 237, 244
Myth-making, 14, 264, 339; in reminiscence, 279–80, 292–94, 305–6, 310–11; and self-identity maintenance, 348–50

Narcissism, 13, 97, 214; assessing, 370–71; as personality disposition index, 178–83, 197–98
Nardini, J., 190–91
Neugarten, B. L., 147, 170, 195–96
Neurological examination, 168
Neurotic pessimism, 331
Newcomb, T., 116
Nonintrapunitiveness, 178–80
Nonreflectiveness, 197
Normative control, 118
Norm structure, institutional, 95–97
Nursing homes, 36

Obrist, W. D., 206
Oliveira, O. H., 307
Optimism, 124; and distance from death, 208, 235; measuring, 235; and postsurgical healing speed, 196
Oral passivity, 194
Orbach, H., 196
Ownership of life, 267

Paired Word Learning Test, 359
Pascal, G. R., 235

435

Index

Index

Unconscious material, 272
Unfriendliness, 197
University of Chicago, 335
Unresolved conflict, 264, 266–67, 272–76

Valliant, G. E., 166, 196
Visual hallucinations, 157, 159
"Voodoo" death, 190–91

Waiting lists, 36
Warmth, 100–108, 110–13; assessing, 387–91

Well-being, 164, 341–42; and adaptive capacity, 149, 151, 159–60; and aggressiveness linked to adaptation, 189; measures of, 157
Widowhood, 9–10
Wilcoxon matched-pair signed-ranks test, 218, 222, 235, 237
Withdrawal, 60, 176–77; and distance from death, 214, 218, 231; and hopelessness, 316
Wolf, S., 115
Working through, 131–32, 187
Wylie, R., 243–44

Zinberg, N. E., 246